Murder and Violence i...
America...

The *Bulletin of Latin American Research* Book Series

BLAR/SLAS book series editors:

Jasmine Gideon
Geoffrey Kantaris
Tony Kapcia
Lucy Taylor
Matthew Brown
Ann Varley

The *Bulletin of Latin American Research* publishes original research of current interest on Latin America, the Caribbean, inter-American relations and the Latin American Diaspora from all academic disciplines within the social sciences, history and cultural studies. The BLAR/SLAS book series was launched in 2008 with the aim of publishing research monographs and edited collections that compliment the wide scope of the Bulletin itself. It is published and distributed in association with Wiley-Blackwell. We aim to make the series the home of some of the most exciting, innovatory work currently being undertaken on Latin America and we welcome outlines or manuscripts of interdisciplinary, single-authored, jointly-authored or edited volumes. If you would like to discuss a possible submission to the series, please contact the editors at blar@liverpool.ac.uk

Murder and Violence in Modern Latin America

EDITED BY
ERIC A. JOHNSON, RICARDO D. SALVATORE
AND PIETER SPIERENBURG

This edition first published 2013
Editorial material and organisation © 2013 Society for Latin American Studies, text
© The Authors

Registered Office
John Wiley & Sons Ltd, The Atrium, Southern Gate, Chichester, West Sussex, PO19 8SQ, UK

Editorial Offices
350 Main Street, Malden, MA 02148-5020, USA
9600 Garsington Road, Oxford, OX4 2DQ, UK
The Atrium, Southern Gate, Chichester, West Sussex, PO19 8SQ, UK

For details of our global editorial offices, for customer services, and for information about how to apply for permission to reuse the copyright material in this book please see our website at www.wiley.com/wiley-blackwell.

The right of Eric A. Johnson, Ricardo D. Salvatore and Pieter Spierenburg to be identified as the authors of the editorial material in this work has been asserted in accordance with the UK Copyright, Designs and Patents Act 1988.

Library of Congress Cataloging-in-Publication Data
Murder and Violence in Modern Latin America / edited by Eric A. Johnson, Ricardo Salvatore, Pieter Spierenburg.
     p. cm. – (The Bulletin of Latin American Research book series)
  Includes bibliographical references and index.
  ISBN 978-1-118-65735-5 (pbk.)
1. Violent crimes – Latin America – History. 2. Murder – Latin America – History. 3. Violence – Latin America – History. I. Johnson, Eric A. (Eric Arthur), 1948- II. Salvatore, Ricardo Donato. III. Spierenburg, Petrus Cornelis.
  HV6810.5.M87 2013
  303.6098 – dc23

2013037266

A catalogue record for this book is available from the British Library.

This book is published in the following electronic formats: Wiley Online Library 978-1-118-65735-5

Set in 10 on 13pt and Palatino
by Laserwords Private Limited, Chennai, India
Printed and bound in the United Kingdom by Page Brothers, Norwich

Contents

Acknowledgements

Many people and institutions have made the publication of this book possible. Among those deserving special thanks are the main financial sponsors of this project: Central Michigan University, the Erasmus University Rotterdam and the Dutch Organization for Scientific Research (NWO). Central Michigan University and Erasmus University Rotterdam are also to be thanked for hosting a number of academic conferences directly related to this book project. Also we would like to thank the German academic journal *Historical Social Research/Historische Sozialforschung* and the Center for Historical Social Research at the University of Cologne for publishing a special issue devoted to aspects of our overall project on murder and violence in Latin American history dealing with an earlier time period than the present book. This special focus issue; of the journal is entitled 'Murder and Mass Murder in Pre-Modern Latin America' (*Historical Social Research/Historische Sozialforschung* **37**(3), 2012). It includes important articles by Wolfgang Gabbert, Caroline Dodds Pennock and Martha Few, as well as by the editors of the present book.

The editors also wish to thank various students and colleagues who were especially helpful in hosting the academic conferences and in helping make this book possible in a number of ways. Among these people are Amy Cusumano, Jennifer Bannister, Mike Rose and Professor Thomas Benjamin at Central Michigan University, and Mariëlle Duijndam and Marlies Gromicho at Erasmus University Rotterdam.

The editors are grateful to Professor Tony Kapcia of the University of Nottingham who has been enormously helpful in all stages of the publication of this book, including editing. We also wish to thank Sandra Fardon Fox of Wiley, the publishers, for overseeing the publication process, as well as the copy-editor, Sarah Price.

Finally, we wish to thank the contributors of the original essays in this book. It is their work and their patience that ultimately has done the most to make this book possible.

Introduction: Murder and Violence in Modern Latin America

ERIC A. JOHNSON

Central Michigan University, USA

RICARDO D. SALVATORE

Universidad Torcuato Di Tella, Argentina

PIETER SPIERENBURG

Erasmus Universiteit Rotterdam, the Netherlands

Violence and Latin America are no strangers to each other. That is just as true for the present as it was for the past. The very word 'Latin', referring to the Spanish and Portuguese languages spoken in that part of the world, reminds us of the bloody conquest that radically transformed the societies previously established on the continent. Many of those societies have been extremely violent in their turn. Yet, there have also been periods of relative tranquility in the history of the various regions that make up Latin America. For many, it is easy to look at this legacy of violence from a distance and express moral indignation. But understanding the magnitude, nature and expressions of violence in Latin American history is a much more difficult undertaking.

This book is the first to examine modern Latin American violence in a comprehensive and historical manner over the past two centuries. It does not attempt to cover every corner of the continent, but it does bring together the expertise of a number of renowned scholars, who focus on topics of often pressing and fascinating interest. The combined efforts of these prominent scholars provide the reader with a historical overview of what we know at this moment. That overview ranges from revolutionary to gang violence, from individual homicides to mass slaughter, from domestic settings to the state crime of 'disappearance', from dark alleys to the shining path, from Argentina to Mexico. It examines bloodshed by elites and peasants, by civilians and the military, politically motivated or for personal reasons, against men and women. Hence, this volume is a first step in extending to Latin America the long-term study of the incidence and patterns of violence on which historians and social scientists have been working in European societies for the past few decades.

Certainly more is now known about the long-term history and trajectory of violence in Europe, and also in North America, than in Latin America. Historians of Europe have traced back the story of murder and aggression to the Middle Ages. They have done so in many countries, with the exception of those in Eastern Europe. For one thing, they have calculated so-called homicide rates – estimates of the annual number of killings per 100,000 inhabitants of a town or region. These rates are relatively reliable markers indicating the level of serious violence among the population in the place and at the time concerned. Their calculation is based on the work of many scholars, each of them performing laborious research in local archives. As a result of this effort, we now have sufficient data to estimate aggregated homicide rates from the Middle Ages onward for countries such as England or Italy and regions such as Scandinavia. Thus, we are fairly certain of the long-term development of the incidence of homicide over some seven centuries. Perhaps surprising to some readers, this has been one of decline. Whereas rates of several dozen or more per 100,000 were common in the Middle Ages, they stood around one or fewer per 100,000 by the mid-twentieth century in many European countries. Prior to the twentieth century, the average of all estimates declined steadily over time with each successive century having a lower average than the preceding one. In the very last few decades since about 1970, however, European homicide rates have risen somewhat (and exploded in the countries of the former Soviet Union), indicating that even in Europe matters are not totally straightforward.

These homicide rates refer to what historians call interpersonal violence: altercations between two individuals, between two small groups or between an individual and a small group. When one group of attackers gets too large, we usually classify the event as collective or mass violence, about which we say a few things later. There are some more features of this interpersonal violence that we can outline fairly confidently in quantitative terms. Whenever and wherever homicide rates are very high, male-on-male fighting largely accounts for this. That is true for temporary upsurges. Homicide rates went up in Amsterdam, for example, during some two or three decades at the turn of the seventeenth and eighteenth centuries – a period that coincided with the heyday of knife fighting among men in the city. Even more important, this contribution of male-on-male fighting to the homicide rates tells us something about the long-term decline. It means that fighting among men was very common in the Middle Ages and that the subsequent drop in the incidence of homicide was due in large part to a drastic reduction of this particular type of violence. There was a reduction both in the sheer number of altercations among men and in the seriousness of these altercations. After 1800, in various European countries, men were more likely to fight with their fists than with knives, which made a lethal outcome less likely.

But the long-term decline of homicide in Europe was not due solely to the reduction of fights among men. Cases involving women, as victims, killers or both, also contributed to this decline. In order to show this, we must introduce another factor: the degree of intimacy. Perpetrator and victim in an act of violence may be either total strangers or mere acquaintances of each other. As a third possibility they can have an intimate relationship: spouse or (ex-)lover, sibling, parent or child. Although male-on-male murder includes cases in which, for example, two brothers confronted each other, such cases are not frequent. Most male-on-male violence involves acquaintances or strangers. By contrast, violence involving women is more likely among intimates, the incidence of which we know by approximation. A very rough estimate would be an average of two homicides of intimates per 100,000 total population in Europe during the Middle Ages, and 0.5 after 1800. Thus, cases in which killer and victim were intimates, many of them involving women, also contributed to the decline in homicide but much more modestly. In fact, as a result of the enormous overall decline, the proportion of intimates as victims in the entire murder rate rose significantly over time. Today it is usually between one third and one half. Note that all this refers only to homicide; domestic violence without a fatal outcome is less easy to detect, in the past and even today.

The prevailing nature and manner of the killing of intimates also changed over time, in particular in the case of the murder of spouses. In the sixteenth and seventeenth centuries, most spousal murders were related to the hierarchical structure of the family. A man who had killed his wife (an unlawful act) would claim that he had given her punishment (which was socially acceptable at the time) but that this regrettably got out of hand. Conversely, when a woman had killed her husband, this was in many cases the ultimate remedy after suffering long-time abuse, which the husband may have considered punishment but which had become unbearable to the wife. In England, for example, the murder of a husband was called 'petty treason', meaning that the wife had killed her 'little king'. This type of spousal murder became less frequent in Europe during the eighteenth century. In modern times most spousal murders have more of an egalitarian aspect to them, often having to do with tensions in the couple's affective relationship.

However, most qualitative shifts from one type of killing to another took place within the bounds of male-on-male violence. In medieval Europe many murders were acts of revenge, because a man's father had been killed, because his sister had been raped or for other reasons. As a rule, the victim's relatives considered this an affront against the whole family and held the perpetrator and his whole family responsible. In its turn, revenge often induced counter-revenge. When such a sequence led to a cycle of violence between two families, or sometimes between two parties that were not families, we speak of a feud or vendetta. Feuds were extremely common throughout the Middle Ages well into the sixteenth century. Moreover, feuding was not bound to a code of fair fighting. Many times, revenge pitted several powerful men against only one elderly man or, alternatively, an armed group ambushing a smaller group that had been taken by surprise. The bodies of slain enemies were ritually maimed and their genitals fed to the dogs.

All this changed during the early modern period. Feuding became uncommon, except in peripheral regions of Europe. Simultaneously, a code of fair fighting developed. That did not mean that treachery and unequal fights were now things of the past, but many men prided themselves in fighting only one against one. For the upper classes, especially aristocrats and military officers, this meant duelling, with the sword and later the pistol as weapons. The formal or official duel was a highly stylised form of combat bound by strict rules. Written codes described when and how to challenge opponents and how one should behave before, during and after the duel. Upper-class men considered this the only way of 'civilised' fighting and they looked down on all forms of violence practised in socially lower strata. Nevertheless lower-class men practised their own form of duelling, which we may call the popular variant. The popular duel, usually a knife fight of one against one, equally had its rules, although these were not written down. It should be added that both formal and popular duels were seldom fought until one of the participants died. When they turned lethal, it was obviously the final outcome that determined killer from victim. That is true for many violent conflicts even today.

In describing both the vendetta and the duel, European historians have paid a lot of attention to the subject of honour. Traditional male honour obliged a man to exhibit courage and a readiness to attack. He could undo a breach of his honour only by violence. This meant attacking the man who had insulted him or who had harmed or dishonoured a woman or a man dependent on him. This traditional notion of male honour continued to prevail in Europe from the Middle Ages throughout the early modern period. In the Middle Ages, however, almost all male violence, except murder during a robbery and some very devious killings, counted as honourable. Avengers upheld the honour of the whole family. In the early modern period, honour became increasingly tied to the principle of a fair fight of one against one. Consequently, honour became more of an individual notion. This was true for men of all social classes, but once again, upper-class duellists considered only their behaviour honourable. They continued to practise the formal duel until the Second World War, but it was increasingly fought 'at first blood', which made fatalities even more rare than previously. At the same time, the notion spread that a man could be both honourable and non-violent. This notion first affected elite groups, but in the twentieth century it became common even among the majority of the lower classes. In recent decades, however, related to the slight upsurge in homicides, traditional male honour appears to have been revived to some extent in Europe.

The subject of honour is associated with, but yet distinct from, that of ritual. Some historians believe that ritual always serves to mitigate violence, making it more benign as it were. That is certainly true for the rituals of duelling. However, some rituals serve precisely to degrade the victim, simultaneously hurting or killing the person attacked and dishonouring him or her, even if dead, in the eyes of others. Think of the feeding of a victim's genitals to the dogs, previously mentioned. In the case of non-fatal violence we can think of such acts as attacking a man while he is urinating or stabbing a woman's buttocks. A typically benign ritual, on the other hand, had a group of men drinking together in order to make peace after a violent conflict. Ritual violence always conveys a message and it needs a public that understands that message. In Europe ritual violence was more characteristic of the Middle Ages and the early modern period, whereas instrumental acts of violence such as robberies, were more characteristic of the modern period.

The subject of ritual conveniently takes us from interpersonal to collective and mass violence. In the European past, ritual was a common element in both. The religious riots in sixteenth-century France are a case in point. The word massacre, to denote mass killing, dates from this period of unrest and it originally meant a butcher's table. Religious opponents indeed butchered each other. The slaughter of religious and political enemies was performed on squares and marketplaces and recounted in published pamphlets. Here too, ritual violence conveyed a message and that message needed a public. Such ritual elements and, even more clearly, the publicity were completely absent from the Nazi gas chambers of the mid-twentieth century. Although many people saw the victims of the Holocaust being arrested and deported, their murder was most often concealed from public view and performed without ceremony.

Whereas the evidence appears to support the idea of a long-term reduction of ritual and public elements in mass killing in Europe, it is much harder to estimate variations in the incidence of collective violence over the centuries. Contemporary counts are often unreliable; even if they are reliable, mass violence, unlike interpersonal violence, never occurs on a year-to-year basis, nor is it always clear what the reference population should be. Many scholars have maintained that the Holocaust and other acts of genocide committed in the twentieth century were unprecedented and that, consequently, mass killing belongs to modern times more than to the distant past. We believe, however, that this is far from certain. Consider an episode of nearly 700 years ago in which the victims were also Jews. It happened during the devastating plague of the Black Death (1346–1350), which induced those who had not died yet to look for scapegoats. In various parts of Europe, Jews were accused of having caused the disease by poisoning the wells, and murdered and 'executed' en masse. This early slaughter of Jews in European history may be comparable in duration and geographic scope to the Holocaust. We will probably never know the exact number of victims, but it may well be that, related to the population of Europe at the time, the proportion equalled or even exceeded that of Holocaust victims.

Whereas the Holocaust had been carefully planned by the leadership of the German state, the slaughter during the Black Death took place in the absence of a state system in Europe. Violence is also related to the development of the state in Latin America, in several ways. In the past, states have both fostered and contained violence. As many scholars maintain, the long-term decline of homicide in Europe owed much to the pacification brought about by the gradual development of a stable state system in that part of the world. This pacification was only internal and it sometimes broke down during periods of revolution or (civil) war. During these tumultuous times, the incidence of homicide and mass killing increased. Yet there were also trends of decreasing state violence in ordinary times. These include a decline in executions, culminating in the abolition of the death penalty in many European countries and increasing restrictions on police violence. Violence between different countries, on the other hand, has not declined over time. The potential for destruction during wars has increased enormously in modern times, but this potential is not always actually employed. In Europe mass destruction and killing in war were concentrated in the first half of the twentieth century. Since then, with the exception of the break-up of Yugoslavia, war and mass killing have been absent from Europe.

What does all this mean for the history of Latin America? Obviously, this continent did not have its own 'Middle Ages'. Perhaps some of its pre-colonial native societies went through a phase that resembled the European Middle Ages, but we know relatively little about it. At the moment when the Spanish and Portuguese arrived in that part of the world, peoples such as the Aztecs and Incas already boasted complex state societies. The European conquest of the Americas must be considered at least in part as a case of interstate violence, in which the conquerors were helped much by the micro-organisms that they carried on them, unfamiliar to the natives. But the Conquest also involved direct and indirect murder and, as Ricardo D. Salvatore makes clear in his concluding chapter, the relative pacification that existed during the colonial period remained tainted by racism, slavery and extortion. After independence, state-building had once more to start anew.

This volume deals with many of the themes that are also important in the history of violence in Europe. In this way, it presents a first attempt at a comprehensive study of violence in Latin American history. For this continent, we are not yet able to construct a graph of homicide rates over several centuries, as has been constructed for much of Europe. However, a time series for Mexico since the beginning of the twentieth century and some more recent figures for Central America are presented in this book. As in Europe, traditional male honour was certainly involved in a number of these homicides. Honour and *machismo* have been widespread in Latin America in the past, and are still to some extent even today. If we do not know this from history, it is plain already to all readers of Gabriel García Márquez's novels. In its turn, male authority plays a role in violence against women and intimates, a theme represented in this book, covering two centuries.

This volume also discusses various aspects of collective and state violence, again touching on themes that are important in European history. It appears, for example, that the story of the disappeared in Argentina has parallels with the Holocaust. In both cases a public arrest was followed by a number of hidden steps that ended with murder. Neither was the killing of *senderistas* in the prisons of democratic Peru a public event. Collective violence with a public and ritual character, on the other hand, appears to have been more prominent in Latin America and it continued to be frequent until a much later period than in Europe. The ritual slaughter of *La Violencia* in Colombia in the 1950s was perhaps its most fateful expression. It can be maintained that until today both internal state violence and homicide have remained at a high level in Latin America when compared with Europe.

While a complementary but brief set of articles is available for colonial Latin America (Dodds Pennock, 2012; Few, 2012; Gabbert, 2012; Johnson, Salvatore and Spierenburg, 2012), it would be even more interesting to extend the long-term study of violence to yet other continents. Is such a long-term study possible in Africa, for example, whose history can be divided likewise in a pre-colonial, colonial and independence period? And what about China, whose known history covers a time span longer than that of any other nation today? Pre-twentieth-century China used to have a reputation as a relatively peaceful country but recent scholarship, focussing on such subjects as banditry and conflicts over property rights, challenges that view. A comparison with Africa and Asia would put violence in Latin American history within an even broader context.

The Contributors and Individual Chapters

When viewed from the perspective of Latin-American history, the contributions to this volume all enhance our understanding of interpersonal and political violence in a variety of historical and social contexts. Three of the chapters deal with the political violence between states and armed guerrillas in the 1970s and 1980s, in what appears to be a typically Cold-War context. In Argentina the military dictatorship that ruled the country between 1976 and 1982 confronted and exterminated armed guerrillas, the most important being *Montoneros* and the Ejército Revolucionario del Pueblo, extending its repression to the civilian population that the military considered sympathisers or accomplices of the guerrillas. In Guatemala a fierce military dictator, General Efraín Ríos Montt, claiming to fight a counter-insurgency war, unleashed a brutal and deadly extermination campaign against indigenous people, most of them peasants. In Peru a Maoist-oriented, guerrilla organisation emerged in 1980 to carry its message of terror to rural and urban populations. In 1986, the Alan García administration and its military establishment decided to put a dramatic end to this guerrilla group by killing most of its combatants detained in three Peruvian prisons. The chapters by Carlos Figueroa Ibarra, Emilio Crenzel and Carlos Aguirre analyse these episodes in order to understand the 'legacies of violence' left by these processes, presented by one side as 'counter-insurgency' campaigns and by the other as 'revolutionary' wars.

These instances of extreme political violence, most notably that of the concentration camps in Argentina during the military regime, can be interpreted as 'de-civilising reversals' (on the notion of civilising and de-civilising processes in the Latin American context, see the conclusion by Ricardo D. Salvatore). During these reversals the need to find a radical solution for pressing socio-political problems led to the erosion of restraints against the use of open, terror-inducing violence. In all these cases, the political actors appeared to operate from a logic of terror and extermination. These were cases of an either–or situation in which large abstractions such as 'socialism', 'Western civilisation' or 'imperialism' seemed to be at stake, so that the combatants on each side employed a maximum of violence in order to produce radical political effects.

Because the doctrine of national security was invoked by most of the repressive regimes that tried to get rid of revolutionary guerrillas and because the armed groups that apparently fought for a transition to socialism seemed to replicate strategies and tactics from revolutionary movements elsewhere, we can view these events against the background of the Cold War. Throughout Latin America, the Cuban Revolution had inspired revolutionary groups who claimed to represent oppressed peoples and wished to lead the way towards a socialist society. Yet, the timing of these revolutionary insurgencies varied by region. In 1980, when most other countries were on the road to democratisation again, the Shining Path launched an all-out war against capitalism, imperialism and the government in Peru. The ethnic genocide committed by General Rios Montt in Guatemala was also late in the chronology of Latin American revolutions. The assault against Mayan communities claimed more than 200,000 lives in the course of over 25 years. In the case of Argentina, armed struggle came to prevail over mass politics after the 1970 assassination of General Aramburu, an event that marked the adoption of guerrilla warfare by the new Peronist group, the Montoneros. Whether early or late, these violent revolutionary processes were met with equally violent and dramatic responses from the state in ways that violated elementary human rights.

Other contributions examine political violence nationwide in the twentieth century. Alan Knight discusses political violence during and after the Mexican Revolution, while Cristina Rojas and Daniel Tubb do the same for Colombia after the assassination of J. E. Gaitán in 1948, a process that historians have dubbed *La Violencia*. Comparing the Mexican and Colombian cases is instructive. As Knight reminds us, most of the violence during the Mexican revolution was instrumental and hence proportionate, neither expressive nor excessive. Admittedly, seven revolutionary years resulted in more than 1.5 million casualties, but most of this violence was the direct or indirect product of a civil war in which each group had clear political objectives. In Colombia the violence unleashed after 1948 was utterly excessive and expressive. The number of bodily mutilations was unprecedented and the aggressors used the bodies of victims to send messages to political opponents. Although civil war pitted conservatives against liberals, *La Violencia* unleashed all sorts of private vendettas between families, landowners, and political bosses.

In both cases a period of heightened violence was followed by a period of pacification. In Mexico, the centralisation of politics around the presidency, the growing influence of the Partido Revolucionario Institucional (PRI) and the control of local or regional situations through political patronage resulted in a long-term decline of violence, both by the military and by civilians without political motives. In the 1920s, Mexico started on a transition towards political stability, resulting in less social anxiety, greater opportunities for economic advancement and a reconstitution of peaceful sociability. In the 1930s and 1940s, newspapers criticised the impunity of the crimes of the powerful, the absence of a judiciary response to scandalous crimes and high levels of corruption and inefficiency in the Mexican police. These voices point at a certain success in the pacification that followed the revolutionary period. Colombia, by contrast, continued to be a fragmented national polity, divided by region, political affinity and ideology. After short periods of pacification, spurts of violence reappeared. Although there was a slow but persistent economic growth, political leaders failed to arrive at a solution for the problem of governance. As a result, attempts at pacifying social interaction proved short-lived and deceptive.

The chapters by Víctor Uribe-Urán and Orlando Pérez deal with a new type of violence and a new awareness of an old type, respectively. Uribe-Urán tackles the difficult problem of domestic violence or intimate-partner violence, showing to what extent this old problem had remained almost unchanged since colonial times, because of the legal prerogatives granted to male heads of households. Presently, however, under the influence of globalisation and the transnational women's movement, Latin American states are trying to solve this old problem. International organisations are forcing governments of the region to treat intimate-partner violence as a major public health issue and as a violation of human rights. Pérez's chapter analyses the recent transnational spread of youth gangs in Central America. Although this type of criminal organisation was not absent in the past, it is only recently, as a result of the United States' deportation of gang members to their native countries, that the number of *maras* and the sophistication of their operations have reached high levels. The spread of gang violence across Central America is one more indication that the process of globalisation can have ominous side-effects. These include not only youth gangs but also the upsurge of 'narco-violence' in Mexico, Colombia and Brazil. The recent wave of assassinations of women in Ciudad Juárez and Sinaloa reveals another disturbing dimension of this heightened cycle of violence.

Ordinary homicide and its judicial treatment are the subject of two chapters in this book. Ricardo D. Salvatore deals with the intriguing question of how it was possible to augment the punishment of violent crimes within a system of justice and a criminal code with rigid limits to sentences. The existence of an 'inflation' of penalties in modern Argentina (c.1880–1940) reveals the importance of penal justice in 'processing' violence within society and the influence of public opinion in the making of criminal sentences. Between 1900 and 1940, Argentina was a country where violent crime was largely under control by a state that had obtained a significant monopoly of force. Pablo Piccato's chapter deals with homicide in modern Mexico. He demonstrates a process of gradual attenuation of homicidal violence across Mexico between the 1940s and the late 1990s. During that period the press focussed upon common crime, particularly murder, commenting on the social and political realities of life in Mexico. Ordinary people wrote to the president to demand justice in unsolved murder cases, while journalists criticised police corruption, the impunity of the powerful and the inefficiency of police investigations. During this significant expansion of the public sphere in Mexico, interpersonal violence became a central issue of the national debate over governance and individual and social rights.

The concluding chapter in this book, written by Ricardo D. Salvatore, places the history of Latin American violence in context. Additionally, Salvatore examines how this particular context might relate or not relate to the seminal and controversial theory of a 'civilising process' written, some might think a bit oddly, during the Third Reich by Norbert Elias, a social theorist of German-Jewish background. Elias's views on the evolution of manners, morals and 'civilisation' have been influential in the construction of recent European histories of violence, but are heretofore relatively unknown in Latin America.

1

War, Violence and Homicide in Modern Mexico

ALAN KNIGHT

Oxford University, UK

When it comes to considering war, violence and homicide, Mexico seems a good place to start. The notion of Mexico as a violent place is common, and has been widely retailed by both Mexicans and foreigners. 'To be a gringo in Mexico, that is indeed euthanasia', declared Ambrose Bierce (prophetically, as it turned out) (Downing, [1940] 1996: 243, 251–252, 251) and British diplomats *en route* to Mexican postings in the 1920s were told, by their supposedly well-informed London friends, that they would very likely finish up as a human sacrifice, or a cannibal's dinner (Osbaldeston-Mitford, 1945: 5). Mexicans themselves have contributed to this image, pointing to the Día de los Muertos, the *torero* complex (as well as related *macho* characteristics), and its counterpart – stoic fatalism in the face of death (a characteristic often attributed to Indians) (Ramos, 1938; Knight, 2008: 7–8). At the time of the Revolution, the radical painters Siqueiros and Rivera regaled impressionable European women with stories of Mexican violence, bloodshed and contemporary cannibalism (Siqueiros, 1977: 114, 147–148). Scholars, too, have mined the same seam, attributing supposedly enduring cultural traits – violence, *machismo*, corporatism, corruption – to the *damnosa haereditas* of Aztec and Spanish imperialism (Riding, 1985: 346–7; Wiarda, 2001). Thus, just as the president embodies a modern *tlatoani* (emperor), so the state's resort to violence (such as in 1968) re-enacts the bloody rites that characterised Aztec Tenochtitlan (Krauze, 1997: 721–722, citing Octavio Paz). And, it is true, there is just enough (fairly) hard evidence to justify this emphasis on violence: Mexico did suffer the most violent revolution in twentieth-century Latin America (as I discuss below); and it stands somewhat high in global league tables of homicide.

In order to evaluate this stereotype, I shall focus principally on twentieth-century Mexico; in doing so, I will try (i) to develop a rough typology of violence and homicide and (ii) to suggest possible explanations of how and why different forms of violence and homicide have increased or decreased (or have been seen to do so: reality and perception tend to diverge quite a bit).

Typologies of Violence

Violence is a common but protean phenomenon. That is to say, it comes in many forms so, unless we (mistakenly) think that it can be readily grasped and explained as a unitary category, it is useful – and perhaps essential – to break it down into subcategories. In this respect, 'violence' resembles other protean concepts – like, for example, 'identity', 'protest' or 'resistance'. Some subcategories, while they may be fuzzy at the edges, are fairly straightforward: I shall, for example, say something about (criminal) homicide, and a good deal about war (chiefly civil war) and its attendant mortality. Hence, these – essentially descriptive – subcategories are flagged in the title. However, typological analysis can go much further. For example, while still in 'descriptive' mode, are we concerned with violence against people, animals (Fletcher, 1997: 109–115; Darnton, 1999) and/or property? My discussion concerns only people (although I would include the deliberate destruction of animals and property – for example, livestock and crops – when it clearly prejudices people's well-being). Do we opt for a relatively narrow definition, which denotes actual violence against people, as in Keane (1996: 6) or what Žižek (2008: 1, 9–10) calls 'subjective violence', or should the perceived threat of violence also be included? Here, I prefer a broader – and, I think, realistic – approach: if people, on the basis of hard experience, entertain a lively fear of violence (a fear that is not based on mere paranoid fantasy and that, furthermore, affects their behaviour) then it seems historically sensible to include such well-grounded fears. However, we then enter on a slippery slope, whereby forms of 'violence' that do not involve actual violent events start to proliferate: thus, we get Žižek's (2008: 8–9) varieties of 'objective' or 'systemic' violence ('symbolic' and 'ideological', the latter including, for example, 'racism, incitement, [and] sexual discrimination'). Some forms of 'structural violence' seem to me worth including in our discussion: for example, government policies that actively promote hunger and even famine, which are directly comparable to physical repression and which therefore form part of a broad repertoire of 'democide' or 'death by government' (Rummel, 1994). However, I would not wish to roll so far down the slope that we enter, for example, the zone of 'verbal violence' – violence which is not directly prejudicial to physical well-being and may be little more than a loose metaphor (and sometimes a metaphor deployed in order to stifle legitimate debate). In other words, my analysis seeks to preserve the crucial link with physical violation; a link that may display some elasticity (hence, realistic threats, based on experience, should not be discounted), but that should not be stretched to breaking point.

These considerations are descriptive: they relate to what violence looks like, hence how wide we should cast the net in seeking to catch and analyse it. But causation is also crucial: what causes violence and, perhaps, what can be done to alleviate it, by addressing the causes? (Of course, the etiology may vary according to the categories in question). When it comes to causality one basic consideration is whether violence should be seen as largely epiphenomenal – a by-product of other processes – or whether it is in some sense an independent variable that occurs 'relatively autonomously' of particular circumstances, perhaps as a result of 'human nature', or the hard-wired character of groups of people (men, Mexicans, maniacs: there are various 'group' options and permutations). I address that point at the beginning of this chapter, opting for an 'epiphenomenal' approach, which stresses circumstances and context. There is, however, a related question, which crops up regularly in the literature: the distinction between what is sometimes called 'instrumental' violence (violence that is in some sense calculated and rational, directed at perceived goals) and 'expressive' violence, which wells up within individuals, responds to personal emotions, and does not obey some rational ulterior goal (Fletcher, 1997: 52; Sofsky, 2003: 18). This is a distinction that may in turn parallel that between violence initiated at a distance – for example, from a height of 20,000 feet – and violence committed in face-to-face confrontations in the heat of battle or in drunken brawls, or what in Mexico is attributed to *coraje* (Friedrich, 1977: 8, 11, 15; ; Elias, [1939, 1978] 1978: 236–237; Gutmann, 1996: 261–263). This seems to me a valid – if, again, rather fuzzy – distinction, which I address in the Mexican context.

The above are rather general considerations, which crop up in the general literature on violence and to which I will return *en route*. Finally, let me clarify the typology I have adopted, in order to make sense of the phenomenon in modern Mexico (with no presumption that the same typology works worldwide). First, I adopt a three-fold distinction between (i) political violence, (ii) mercenary or criminal violence, and (iii) interpersonal – especially familial – violence. There are significant overlaps, as I note below; but overlaps are common enough in social-scientific analysis and do not necessarily invalidate the typology, which assumes that these three forms of violence broadly differ both descriptively (in terms of what they look like) and etiologically (what causes them). Political violence occurs in the context of political struggle; it is therefore, by and large, epiphenomenal (a by-product of circumstances) and rational; and it is geared to certain political goals, broadly defined, such as the acquisition and retention of power, the overthrow of hated authorities, the advancement of class, ethnic or sectional collective interests. I further subdivide political violence into 'macro-political' and 'micro-political' and compare 'top-down' and 'bottom-up' variants (explanations will follow). Mercenary or criminal violence involves the pursuit of material advantage by means of force: often individual, sometimes 'collective' in a 'small-group' sense (e.g. bandit gangs or, recently, narco cartels). Finally, interpersonal violence primarily obeys neither political nor mercenary goals. It involves violent disputes within families, between neighbours, in cantinas; it arises in zones of 'sociability' and is usually 'expressive' rather than 'instrumental'; it often involves notions of status, honour and respect (Piccato, 2001: 77–102; Gat, 2006: 33).

Having thus set out my stall, I must now disappoint some prospective customers. Given limitations of both space and expertise, I will, in this chapter, focus on political violence (macro and micro). I will, in conclusion, venture some thoughts on the relationship between political and mercenary violence – in particular, the recent upsurge in 'narco-violence'. Interpersonal violence, though common enough in Mexico and certainly worthy of study, will receive no more than passing mention. This neglect reflects both my own lack of knowledge and also the relative dearth of comprehensive data covering the time period. In other words, one can venture – and substantiate – generalisations about political violence and, with greater difficulty, mercenary/criminal violence; but interpersonal violence, to my mind, defies such long-term generalisations. Furthermore, while the links between political and mercenary can be explored, interpersonal violence appears (to me) to be a more detached phenomenon, with its own autonomous dynamic. Homicide, however, the most serious form of interpersonal violence, is the subject of Pablo Piccato's contribution on Mexico to this volume.

Lastly, a word is needed about methodology, especially statistics. It is clearly desirable – especially when dealing with an emotive topic such as violence – to attempt some clear-headed calculation, rather than to rely simply on 'anecdotal' examples (though anecdotes too can be revealing, by way of illustrating kinds and contexts of violence). Statistical series are particularly important when it comes to trends over time or comparisons between violent episodes, such as wars and revolutions. However, at the risk of sounding rather Rumsfeldian, one could say that there are forms of violence we can measure, forms that we could measure if we had the data, and forms that pretty much defy measurement. Thus, deaths are easier to measure than other forms of violence; and deaths in battle offer a meaningful form of comparison (hence their popularity among students of 'deadly quarrels') (Wilkinson, 1980). Similarly, cross-national homicide series offer some firm basis for comparison. However, even battlefield deaths are problematic: estimates differ widely; some accounts jumble up dead and wounded (of course, in the past the wounded often ended up dead); while some speak more vaguely of 'losses'. When it comes to civilian casualties, the problems are even greater, especially if we include losses indirectly caused by the destruction of crops, livestock and livelihood. In extreme cases – such as the Mexican Revolution – demographic data become relevant, but they record outcomes (not always reliably, to be sure), rather than causes. Lastly, if we turn to 'lesser' forms of violence that do not involve homicide, the data are often deficient, especially as we go back in time: they depend on the vagaries of policing and reportage; and, of course, they embrace a wide and varied range of violent acts – bar-room brawls, criminal muggings, political assaults, gang warfare, rape, violence against women and children. Needless to say, the list grows even longer if – slithering down the slippery slope – we include state 'violence' in the form of incarceration; or 'verbal violence'; or Elias's roster of barbaric behaviour (spitting, pissing and farting in public) (Keane, 1996: 22; Elias, [1939, 1978] 1978: 134–160). In short, the focus of this chapter is principally political violence, with the incidence of death used as the key index; and the statistical evidence is limited to those data – unfortunately few – that seem to be both exemplary and reasonably reliable.

The Longue Durée (800–1910)

First, I consider broad-brush attributions of Mexican violence and *thanatos* (Krauze, 1987), premised on some ancient cultural inheritance, to be useless, even counterproductive. The most damning evidence against such attributions is the sheer variability of violence throughout Mexican history. The Postclassic period (*c*.800–1520), especially the Late Postclassic (*c*.1300–1520), was certainly a violent era, characterised by endemic warfare, empire-building, rebellion, and extensive human sacrifice (Knight, 2002a: 118ff). At the dedication of the *templo mayor* of Tenochtitlan in 1487, thousands of prisoners were allegedly sacrificed; even allowing for the unreliability of historical computations in general and Spanish hyperbole in particular, this was a hefty hecatomb, comparable to few in the history of human sacrifice (Davies, 1977: 167). Whether such slaughter was prompted by population growth and protein deficiency, by grand cosmic preoccupations, or by the harsh logic of Aztec imperialism, it was done on a huge scale (Knight, 2002a: 152–163). However, following the fall of the Aztec empire, human sacrifice ceased and warfare diminished (so too did the population, of course: the question of relative casualties crops up here, as elsewhere).[1] While the Conquest was a bloody process, the society that had emerged in New Spain

---

1   This seems to me a crucial question. Like other social statistics (e.g. traffic accidents), homicide and mass murder can be calibrated in absolute or relative terms. There are good grounds for preferring relative figures, which reflect the chances of an individual becoming a victim. Thus, c.2000, about the same number of people were murdered in Mexico and the United States every year; but since the US population is nearly three times the Mexican, the murder rate is only about one-third. Similar considerations apply to wartime casualties. However, such relative calculations usually take the nation-state as the unit (understandably

by the seventeenth century was one in which warfare was rare, and largely confined to the outer extremities of the kingdom (Yucatán, Chiapas, New Mexico). While village riots and protest were common enough, they followed a regular, recognised pattern and did not lead to much bloodshed (Taylor, 1979). Above all, church and state seem to have enjoyed a genuine measure of legitimacy (Taylor, 1996); hence New Spain had no standing army until the later eighteenth century and even the notorious Inquisition was, in fact, quite limited in its scope and severity (Alberro, 1988: 168–169, 195). Compared to the Europe of the Thirty Years War, Mexico was a haven of peace and security.

If, therefore, Mexico lived with an Aztec legacy – if, for example, the viceroy was a *neo-tlatoani* – that legacy was strangely dormant for the best part of two centuries. Just such an argument was made by the celebrated criminologist Julio Guerrero , following the Juquila Indian revolt of 1896, an 'atavistic' phenomenon, produced by those 'sentiments of bloody ferocity' that, he claimed, 'had lain dormant for three centuries [. . .] during the colonial epoch, but which were never extirpated' (Guerrero, [1901] 1996: 190, 194). In the late colonial period, it is true, social and political tensions grew; the colonial military presence increased; and there is evidence of greater state repression (we could say, tentatively, that Mexico shifted along the Gramscian continuum from ideological hegemony to outright coercion) (Knight, 2007a). The imperial crisis of 1808, followed by the Hidalgo insurrection of 1810, pitched New Spain into a decade of rebellion and repression, unprecedented in its scope and severity (Van Young, 2001). The colonial – especially the

---

so in the case of wars fought by nation-states), although homicide rates are sometimes broken down by state/province or city. The question of the unit of analysis therefore arises. Wartime losses, for example, could be similarly broken down by community (think of all those war memorials in France) or even by family (the 'Private Ryan' calculation). The Mexican Revolution had a disproportionate effect on some states (such as Morelos, which lost 40 percent of its pre-1910 population (Womack, 1970: 370). The Cristero revolt of the 1920s was even more heavily concentrated in the centre-west (Jalisco, Michoacán, and parts of Guanajuato, Zacatecas and Colima). Contemporary narco-violence is also skewed towards certain cities and states (Tijuana, Juárez, Nuevo Laredo, the state of Sinaloa). When 45 campesinos were massacred at Acteal, Chiapas, in 1997 the national-statistical significance was minimal; but, given the population of Acteal, the local impact was profound. Whether we stick to aggregate national estimates or attempt sub-national breakdowns (whether by region, city, sector, class, gender, or age-group) depends a good deal on the question(s) we are asking: are we probing the causes, the impact, or the character of violence? At the very least, we should not automatically assume that the national unit is the right one for all analyses.

Habsburg – tradition of limited, local protest gave way to mass insurrection and bloody counter-insurgency campaigns, in which Agustín Iturbide, soon to be Mexico's first and penultimate emperor, distinguished himself by his sanguinary repression (Archer, 2003: 32–33).

Finally, by way of preamble to the twentieth century, Mexico's nineteenth-century experience was similarly chequered. For a generation after independence (1821–c.1854) government was unstable, both politically and financially; revolts and cuartelazos came thick and fast, evidence of the infant republic's tenuous legitimacy and shaky fiscal base (Tenenbaum, 1986) but the resulting death toll was probably quite low. The liberal-conservative civil war of 1832 is considered 'the greatest convulsion of violence' between independence (1821) and the Revolution of Ayutla (1854) and during the biggest battle, that of Gallinero, the defeated liberals lost 'at least a thousand killed' (Anna, 1998: 246, 252). Furthermore, the recurrent popular rebellions of the period have been plausibly seen as signs of pro-active popular mobilisation against the state and/or the landed class (Coatsworth, 1988: 55). In other words, early nineteenth-century violence had a somewhat demotic, popular, even 'progressive' quality (Tutino, 1988).

In terms of mortality, foreign aggression – chiefly the Mexican–American War of 1846–1848 – had a more severe impact than domestic conflict prior to 1858. Historians of the Mexican–American War seem to have great difficulty coming up with casualty figures, at least on the Mexican side. Regarding two salient battles – Buena Vista and Cerro Gordo (February and April 1847) – Weems states that the Mexican forces (of some 17,000) lost 2,000 'dead, wounded and captured' in the first, and up to half of their 10–12,000 man army in the second, but then adds, rather cryptically, 'the human cost was never calculated' (Weems, 1974: 311, 367). Bauer, ([1974] 1992: 209, 217), concurs that 'no reliable figures' of Mexican losses are available. A recent overview (Henderson, 2007: 179) cites figures of Mexican losses between 25,000 and 50,000. Hamnett (1999: 155) notes that, at 14 percent of combatants, American losses were the heaviest of any war that the United States has fought. In 1858, however, a more severe civil war began (the Three Years War): more severe in terms of its geographical scope, its socio-political polarisation, and its cost in blood and treasure. Furthermore, once the liberals had won (1861), the Three Years War swiftly mutated into the War of the French Intervention, which combined elements of a Mexican civil war (roughly, liberals vs. conservatives), with a foreign invasion and a war of national liberation. Again, the costs in both blood and treasure were heavy.

With the defeat of Maximilian and his French backers, and the emergence of Porfirio Díaz as the dominant liberal victor, Mexico again embarked on a period of relative peace and stability (the Porfiriato, 1876–1911). Díaz ruled, along with his ageing cronies; political stability underwrote economic growth; and armed challenges to his regime were increasingly few and futile. As an authoritarian regime premised on the positivistic principles of 'order and progress', the Díaz regime had no qualms about repressing dissent: whether that of political opponents (Garner, 2001: 85–86), dissident workers (Anderson, 1976: 111, 167–169), remote highland communities like Tomóchic (Vanderwood, 1998), or recalcitrant Indians (as in the time of the colony, the biggest popular-ethnic challenge came from the extremities of the country: the Yaquis of Sonora and the Maya of Yucatán and Quintana Roo) (Reed, 1964; Hu-Dehart, 1984). Violence tended to be top-down, especially as the regime consolidated itself after 1890, and as it capitalised on new technologies of control: railways, troop-trains, the telegraph and the machine-gun (Gat, 2006: 530–1). In some respects the Porfirian regime acquired the mentality and *modus operandi* of a colonial government. Very few, either in government or opposition, anticipated that this formidable regime, favoured by the foreign powers, would itself fall prey to armed insurrection and collective violence after 1910.

This brisk overview confirms that, prior to the twentieth century, Mexico experienced marked swings in the scale and severity of violence, and these depended on shifting social, economic and political factors that overrode any cultural legacy; and foreign dominion or invasion were crucial in four major bouts of deadly warfare: the conquest, the independence struggle, the Mexican–American War, and the French intervention. To clarify: even if such a legacy existed, which I doubt, and even if it created some kind of latent propensity to violence, the fact remains that latent violence became manifest only at certain times. Hence, it is the more proximate causes that turned latent propensity into manifest behaviour that really matter; in explanatory terms the latent propensity is largely irrelevant; note, for example, the racist rationalisation of Julio Guerrero ([1901] 1996). I shall develop this argument in the context of the twentieth century as I proceed.

Hard-Wired Violence?

There is, however, an additional set of explanations of violence that are (allegedly) even more deeply rooted and pervasive, since they apply not just to Mexicans, or descendants of the Aztecs, but to the entire human race, descendants of the handful of migrants who trekked out of Africa some 50,000 years ago (Wade, 2007). Here, the nub of the argument is sounder; but its relevance is very limited. Evolutionary biologists seem to concur that violence has been a constant feature of human society and that some aspects of human behaviour are pervasive and deeply rooted. These 'universals' include violence (as well as many behaviours that we might welcome rather than regret, such as the proscription of some forms of violence; but this is not a normative question) (Pinker, 2002: 56–57, 435–439, following Donald E. Brown). Sofsky includes evolutionary explanations of violence among his 'errors and illusions', adding, quite bizarrely, that such explanations are 'among the most comfortable hypotheses' concerning violence (Sofsky, 2003: 16). Quite the reverse, I would have thought. The hunter-and-gatherer societies that were the norm for most of human prehistory were well acquainted with violence and mortality rates appear to have been relatively high. Inter-band conflict was recurrent and chiefly involved younger men (Keeley, 1996; Gat, 2006: Ch. 2). The transition to chiefdoms and states did not eliminate such behaviour, but channelled it through new systems of authority, eventually making it more organised and hierarchical. Even the Mesoamerican Classic period was familiar with warfare and human sacrifice; contrary to some older accounts, the Classic Maya were far from being pacifist flower children (Farriss, 1984: 140; Schele and Frieden, 1990: 130–131, 145–146). When it came to war, empire-building and human sacrifice, the Aztecs were notable not for what they did, but the scale on which they did it.

Of course, the argument that interpersonal violence is ancient, ubiquitous and perhaps genetically influenced is not a normative justification for such conduct (any more than evidence of human promiscuity is an argument for cuckolding your spouse whenever the chance arises). It is an argument for recognising that violence is a feature of human society that cannot be attributed simply to the rise of the state, of social classes, or of 'civilisation and its discontents'; in fact, these historical institutions have served, in many cases, to limit interpersonal violence, especially in the last several centuries.[2]

There are two riders to this argument to be borne in mind. First, interpersonal violence has usually involved young men to a disproportionate degree (Cronin, 1991: 331–332; Ehrlich, 2000: 206; Gat, 2006; 76–86); and this cannot simply be explained away by the logic of, say, state-building, warfare, and military conscription. Young men may enjoy certain physical advantages (albeit less so in an age of mechanised warfare); but they also seem more disposed to interpersonal violence that goes beyond top-down mobilisation and inter-state (or inter-band) warfare and that is therefore

---

2 Elias's arguments have, I think, some validity; at the very least, he identified an important problem (the diminution and deprecation of overtly violent modes of behaviour, such as bear-baiting and public executions). However, his thesis relates primarily to Europe (even in European colonies, such as Mexico, the civilising influence of courtly manners is much less plausible); and, as he was fully aware, the 'civilising process' did not 'follow a straight line' and could involve halts and reverses (Elias, [1934, 1978] (1994): 186–167). For the purpose of this chapter, Elias can offer some useful insights, but his thesis is of limited relevance.

more obviously voluntary: for example, youth gangs, insurgent movements and criminal organisations. It is not surprising that the Mexican Revolution drew disproportionately on young – and often unmarried – men; or that post-revolutionary *pistoleros*, agrarian *luchadores* and later 'narco' thugs were often young men (and, given the nature of their trade, many did not make it into middle-age, hence the demand for new recruits remained brisk) (Knight, 1986b: 189; Friedrich, 1987). The explanatory power of this generalisation is quite limited: since the cohort in question does not vary much over time, it is hard to explain an increase in violence in terms of an increase in this particular cohort. However, social trends that affect this cohort may be relevant; so, high male youth unemployment (e.g. Mexico in the 1980s) or a rapid rate of demographic increase that boosts the youth population may be significant. Conversely, the 'greying' of a population may tend to depress rates of violent crime. Compared to the historico-culturalist thesis (the Aztec legacy, and so on) that I first mentioned, dismissively, the evolutionary–biological argument is more soundly based; but it can acquire some (limited) explanatory power only when it is combined with social, economic and political factors.

The second, related rider concerns sociopathology or psychopathology, the terms being interchangeable (Morrall, 2000: 38–39). Here we enter a psychological field where – for me and perhaps for others in this book – expertise is lacking and caution is at a premium. If we approach the topic from a historical perspective, it is clear that some human violence is the work of sociopaths who lack restraint or who positively enjoy that sort of work: in the Mexican Revolution, we encounter the likes of Rodolfo Fierro (a prominent 'sidekick' of Pancho Villa) (Katz, 1998: 221, 269–270, 328, 457), the notorious Michoacán bandit/rebel José Inés Chávez García (González, 1972: 129–132; Ochoa Serrano and Pérez Martínez, 1994: 83), or Pancracio in Azuela's *Los de abajo* (a fictional characer, it is true, but one who was based on a real person, described by Azuela as 'fearsome, rancorous, vengeful and cruel, entirely lacking in moral sensibilty': Azuela, 1974: 133). Top-down state violence can serve as a magnet to such sociopaths: they get paid and promoted for doing what they like to do – or certainly have few qualms about doing. Whether they were born sociopaths or had sociopathology thrust upon them (by upbringing, hard experience, or official training: for example, in formal military outfits or informal paramilitary gangs) (Santos, 1984; Friedrich, 1987; Browning, 2001), they distinguish themselves by their readiness to engage in interpersonal violence, violence that is often extreme and sometimes sexual (Ochoa Serrano and Pérez Martínez, 1994: 23). To the extent that sociopathology is, like schizophrenia (Horrobin, 2001), a condition influenced by genetic make-up, the conclusion must be that it is in some measure unavoidable, given the 'right' (that is, the wrong) historical circumstances: an armed revolution, an invasion, a dirty war, a repressive counter-insurgency campaign, especially when these are directed against some demonstrably different, hence readily demonised, 'others', such as Jews, 'geeks', leftist subversives, and the like (Keen, 1991; Browning, 2001: 73, 152, 159–160). If those in power promote these kinds of activities, they must expect sociopathological behaviour to ensue; in fact, of course, they often allow or encourage it (hence we get Abu Ghraib). The sociopathological factor may also help explain why, in some historical cases, expressive violence seems to trump instrumental violence (as I mention below): that is to say, people engage in violence that seems wholly disproportionate to the political or economic goals they are ostensibly pursuing.

Evolutionary psychology thus affords some relevant insights, whose explanatory 'value-added' is, in my view, rather greater than the generally worthless 'explanations' couched in terms of historico-cultural determinism. It makes more sense to see Rodolfo Fierro or José Inés Chávez as sociopaths rather than as descendants of the sanguinary Aztecs; or to note the fact – obvious enough, it is true – that the armed revolution was disproportionately the work of young men; or to observe the way that narco-violence offers a route to rapid – if precarious – power, prestige, and prosperity for young men from the *barrio* (Poppa, 1998: 140–150).

Whatever the value of these competing explanations, they all suffer from the fundamental fault of being too general to explain the historical incidence and severity of violence in a particular country such as Mexico. Neither the *Pax Hispánica* nor the *Pax Porfiriana* can be attributed to a random mutation that made Mexicans more peaceable; nor was either 1810 or 1910 the work of a new generation of sociopaths. The 'generation of the volcano', as the cohort of the Revolution were known in western Michoacán (González, 1972: 133), derived their volcanic character from the historical predicament in which they found themselves; and that predicament was the result of specific social, political and economic trends, to which we must now turn.

The Armed Revolution, 1910–1920

The sweeping historical preamble above made the obvious – and, I think, incontestable – point that levels of violence have varied markedly throughout some 500 years of Mexican history. The same is true of the twentieth century. The first decade was peaceful, there were scant rebellions, the Revolution of 1910 was not presaged by mounting febrile agitation; indeed, revolts attempted by the radical Partido Liberal Mexicano (PLM; Mexican Liberal Party) in 1906 and 1908 were easily put down. State violence was apparent – particularly the campaigns against the Yaqui and Maya Indians and the repression of workers at Cananea and Río Blanco, already mentioned – but the scale of the repression was quite limited (hence my sympathetic critique of Rummel, 1994).[3]

Of course, it is a feature of all violence, and perhaps particularly of top-down state violence, that, if it is sufficiently credible, the threat of violence will often obviate the need for its use, just as an efficient police and criminal justice system should, by making deterrence convincing, diminish crime and empty prisons.[4] As General Blanquet reported to President Díaz after the annihilation of Tomochic, such exemplary repression had 'a calming effect on the entire area. Victory helps to ensure peace in the country' (Vanderwood, 1998: 284). Thus, actual violence exists within a much broader penumbra of threatened and remembered violence, and it is a difficult, but vital, task to try to estimate the two. How well-learned are the lessons of repression? And, more generally, how powerful are the memories of violence and upheaval, which may serve to deter future protest (Stevenson and Seligson, 1996)? A similar question can be posed from the 'top-down' perspective: have the lessons of (violent) popular protest been learned by elites? Do they tread more carefully when it comes to fiscal demands, agrarian policy, political appointments, army recruitment, and so on? Again, there are swings throughout history, depending on the relative power of *los de arriba* and *los de abajo*: a recent popular insurrection may empower the 'plebs' and make elites cautious (this seems to have been true of the generation after Mexican independence and, again, in the post-revolutionary period, *c*.1910–*c*.1940); but a long phase of stability may make elites over-confident and complacent (as the Porfirian elite seems to have been on the eve of the Revolution). If we bear in mind the Gramscian continuum, we should ask whether state coercion is proportionate – that is, calibrated to deter subversion without

---

3   The two labour disputes (Cananea and Río Blanco) cost the lives of about 100 workers; and they provoked severe criticism, and perhaps delegitimisation, of the regime. A good many more Yaqui and Maya Indians were killed by the regime in the last decade of the Porfiriato, but that 'democide' – being more discreet, remote, incremental and, above all, directed against 'uncivilised' Indians – generated relatively less indignation and protest.

4   Keane notes how 'the modern state [...] places its subjects permanently under a cloud of threatened violence' (1996: 28). I see no reason why the 'modern' state should be thus differentiated from pre- or non-modern states (many of which, as Elias pointed out, were a great deal more violent in their domestic – e.g. judicial – proceedings). In fact, the modern/pre-modern distinction is, here as elsewhere, rather a red herring. The point to stress is that violence has an effect (whether we choose to call it a 'cloud' or, as I prefer, a 'penumbra') that goes beyond any particular act of violence, in respect of both time and space. Measuring the scope of the penumbra would seem to be an important, if difficult, historical task.

provoking greater opposition. Does the state rest complacently on its old laurels, confident that the absence of violent opposition is proof of popular legitimacy (a risky inference, as James Scott (1990) reminds us; and as the outbreak of the Mexican Revolution in 1910 seems to confirm)? For, by the 1900s, the stability of the regime was taken for granted, along with the folly of rebellion; hence it took a quixotic character such as Madero to chance his arm in 1910 when wiser voices were counselling caution (Knight, 1986a: 76–77). The Porfirian regime had weathered rebellions in the 1880s and 1890s and, by the 1900s, serious rebellion seemed to be off the agenda (Katz, 1980: 3). For that reason, Díaz was content to cut military spending, yet he took few steps to institutionalise his regime or to enhance its dwindlng popularity.

The sudden outbreak of revolution – or, we should say, of a series of rebellions that eventually coalesced into a fully-fledged social revolution (Knight, 1990: 175–202) – thus came as a surprise, rather like some other major revolutions. And it heralded a sudden shift from Porfirian stability to revolutionary violence, a violence that was not only extensive and costly, but also – as revolutionary violence usually is – demotic and popular, since it involved popular groups venting violence on elites, rather than the other way round (which is more usual). Hence, the sense of social bouleversement, of 'the world turned upside-down' (Hill, 1975; Knight, 1986a: 244–245). The one-way coercive traffic of the Porfiriato now became a two-way street, as insurgent peasants attacked *haciendas* and *mayordomos*, as crowds rioted in the streets, as local officials were run out of town or, occasionally, lynched, as army officers were summarily shot, and as the property of the well-to-do – the lush sugar plantations of Morelos, the sprawling cattle spreads of Chihuahua, the elegant town houses of Mexico City – were plundered and expropriated. Of course, there was a great deal of top-down repression too, especially during the year-and-a-half of the Huerta military dictatorship (1913–1914), when the government vastly increased the size of the federal army, vowing to impose peace 'cost what it may', and ran the whole gamut of early twentieth-century counter-insurgency measures (arbitrary executions, the *ley fuga* – ('shot-while-trying-to-escape'), razing villages, concentration camps, blockhouses, even a primitive form of defoliation) (Knight, 1986b: chap. 1). But Huerta failed; repression bred further resistance (for example, in Morelos and the Sierra Norte de Puebla) (Knight, 1986b: 55–6, 59–60); and the Revolution gathered strength, finally triumphing in the summer of 1914. That did not end the violence, however. Unable to achieve a governing consensus, the leaders of the Revolution fell out and fought a final 'war of the winners' among themselves (1914–1915); and for five more years the victors – roughly, the *carrancistas* – clung precariously to power amid continued rebellion, extensive banditry and urban disorder. Only gradually, during the 1920s, was the new revolutionary regime consolidated, the threat of further insurrection countered, and the incidence of violence curtailed (as I describe below).

If we review the decade of the Revolution, several key points stand out. First, as I have said, it represented a more demotic or democratic form of violence, in that it involved plebeian assaults on elite wealth and power, which left an indelible mark on the country. Although the *carrancistas* and – more successfully – their post-1920 successors (roughly, the Sonorans) rebuilt a functioning state, premised on a broadly capitalist economy, they had to take note of popular demands to a far greater extent than had the preceding Porfirian regime. Though the state was not conventionally democratic, it incorporated 'mass publics' (in the form of trade unions, peasant leagues and political parties); it distributed land, built schools, courted organised labour, recruited plebeian *políticos*, and developed an agglutinative ideology of nationalism and *indigenismo*. This was what made it a revolution, and the outcome was in great measure the result of popular mobilisation and violence. Furthermore, mobilisation and violence continued, albeit at a lower level, throughout the 1920s and 1930s.

Second, the Revolution was almost entirely a domestic civil war; foreign intervention occurred, but was not, in my view, crucial to the outcome; and the costs and casualties of foreign intervention were scant. The US occupation of Veracruz cost some 200 Mexican lives (and just nineteen American ones); the Pershing expedition of 1916–1917 was much less costly (Quirk, 1967: 103). In this respect the Revolution was radically different from the four preceding deadly conflicts mentioned: the Conquest, independence, the Mexican–American War and the French Intervention.

Third, although the killing was internecine and not international, the Revolution was still very deadly. Recent research by Robert McCaa (2003) suggests that the demographic cost of the Revolution (1910–1920) was about 2 million, of which some 10 percent was due to emigration and 25 percent to lost births (that is, births that did not happen because of the revolutionary condition of the country). Two-thirds of the population loss was therefore caused by excess deaths and, somewhat surprisingly, deaths-by-violence (roughly, 'battlefield deaths') accounted for more than deaths from disease, numerous though these were (Knight, 1986b: 419–423). 'Battlefield deaths' should be taken – broadly – to include deaths-by-violence that also occurred as a result of skirmishing, banditry, political assassinations, the *ley fuga* and counter-insurgency repression; 'conventional battlefield deaths' would, of course, be fewer. As a result, McCaa estimates, the excess deaths included 900,000 men, as against 400,000 women. In absolute terms, the Revolution thus constitutes a 'magnitude 6' event, in Richardson's scheme of 'deadly quarrels', and ranks 27th in his compendious list of such global events for the period 1820–1945 (Wilkinson, 1980: 12, 132–133).

•

Although McCaa's analysis plays down deaths from disease and deprivation (and, of course, disease exacerbated by deprivation, like the Spanish influenza epidemic of 1919), an important question remains, regarding the way we choose to categorise mortality of this kind. We can certainly distinguish, analytically at least, between deaths caused by direct violence (battles and bombardments) at one extreme and deaths occasioned by war-induced disruptions and shortages, for example, the Bengal famine of 1943 (Sen, 1991: 9–13), at the other. All are the products of war – absent the war, they probably would not have happened – but the causal connections are rather different; in the second cases there is, perhaps, less direct culpability and there is certainly less scope for individual sociopathic behaviour. Mexicans and Bengalis starved or sickened not necessarily because malign individuals willed such a consequence, but because of official neglect, incompetence or downright incapacity. In between these analytical extremes is a grey zone where matters are more opaque: as Stalin's campaign against the kulaks showed, hunger and destitution can be the fruits of deliberate policy, rather than unfortunate by-products of systemic failure. Similarly, Huerta and Juvencio Robles set out to crush the *zapatista* insurgents by any means possible, including the destruction of crops and livestock (Womack, 1970: 119–122, 138–142, 167–170). Hardship and increased mortality were, in this instance, direct and deliberate consequences of the war.

The classification we adopt therefore depends, I think, on the question(s) we are interested in (a common enough investigative conclusion). In terms of the demographic impact of the Revolution, it is the grand total that matters. But if we are trying to understand the nature of the Revolution, the kind of violence it provoked, and the memories it laid down, it makes a difference whether casualties resulted from fighting on the battlefield, from deliberate maltreatment of civilians or prisoners-of-war, or from the inevitable but indirect consequences of state failure and economic turmoil. The latter suggests a process that is impersonal, uncontrollable and beyond the power of any human agency (an image that crops up frequently in the literature and testimony of the Revolution: for example, in the novels of Azuela or many oral history accounts) (Warman, 1976: 104–105). The former, however, involves agency and therefore responsibility and culpability; thus, although the Mexican Revolution prompted no truth commission or human rights prosecutions, it would clearly be plausible – if anachronistic – to argue that Huerta and Robles, like Pinochet, would have been potentially liable to indictment. It is for this reason that, while Díaz still stirs mixed feelings in Mexico, and has been subject to recent 'revisonist' rehabilitation, Huerta is generally regarded as a dyed-in-the-wool villain (Benjamin, 2000: 60–61; Garner, 2001: 2–3).

As a historian, I think it would be very difficult to offer a precise breakdown of the 1–1.5 million deaths that can be directly attributed to the Revolution (whether as 'battlefield dead', broadly defined, civilian casualties, or victims of war-induced disease and destitution). It is, however, quite feasible to chart the course and characteristics of revolutionary violence as it unfolded during the revolutionary decade. If we unpack the military history of the Revolution (1910–1920), we see five distinct phases:

(i) An initial period of limited warfare between the forces of Madero and Díaz (November 1910–May 1911), leading to a hasty armistice in the early summer of 1911.
(ii) Diverse ('left' and 'right') rebellious challenges to the weak Madero government, from the autumn of 1911 until February 1913.
(iii) A renewed, more serious and prolonged war between a re-assembled revolutionary coalition and the counter-revolutionary Huerta regime in 1913–1914.
(iv) The 'war of the winners', a fratricidal battle for control of the Revolution in 1914–1915.
(v) The long struggle of the Carranza government (1915–1920) to survive in the face of multiple violent challenges – challenges that could weary and weaken the government without actually ousting it.

The associated mortality varied according to the nature of the conflict. In phase (i) the forces involved were relatively small, casualties were low, and there was only one pitched battle for control of a significant town (Ciudad Juárez). Phase (ii) involved both conventional battles (the federal army against the *orozquistas* at Bachimba and Rellano) and decentralised guerrilla warfare, coupled with counter-insurgency in Morelos and several lesser theatres; although figures would be very hard to come by, we can safely assume that phase (ii), being more protracted, was more lethal than phase (i). Phase (iii) represented a significant step change, as the re-assembled revolutionary coalition created large conventional armies (notably Pancho Villa's Division of the North), which over a year and a half battered the – greatly expanded – federal army into submission; battles such as Torreón (April 1914) and Zacatecas (June 1914) involved sizeable forces and heavy casualties (Katz, 1998: 353), over and above the continued toll taken by guerrilla and counter-insurgency campaigns, notably in Morelos and the states around the Valley of Mexico. By phase (iii), furthermore, the economy had begun to feel the effects of the Revolution; currency, credit and infrastructure suffered; and living standards tumbled, thus favouring the spread of disease, notably typhus. Phase (iv) also witnessed costly conventional battles, made all the more costly by Villa's headstrong military tactics; it was during this short-lived but violent period (roughly, the spring and summer of 1915) that Mexican revolutionary warfare most resembled the battles of the First World War, with conventional armies deploying artillery, machine-guns, barbed wire and trench systems, which took a heavy toll, especially of attacking forces (thus, the state of military technology had major implications for casualty rates) (Knight, 1986b: 322–8; Gat, 2006: 532). Finally, phase (v) was the longest; it pitted a fragile government and a large, rather corrupt and heavily politicised ('revolutionary') army against a host of lesser forces – bandits, bushwhackers, residual popular guerrillas, and counter-revolutionary militias (notably in the 'states-rights', 'anti-revolutionary' south) (Knight, 1986b: 375–391). During this final phase, the economy reached its nadir, and disease and destitution peaked; fighting was widespread, but messy, decentralised, and – if a rather normative term can be used – distinctly inglorious; it was, we might say, a war of positions, as groups both within and against the regime staked out claims to power, especially at the local level. When Obregón – the Napoleon of the Revolution – seized power in 1920 he set about negotiating deals right and left, creating a patchwork of political fiefs under the loose aegis of the central government; this pragmatic approach – coupled with the culling of dissidents and the disciplining of the army – provided a basis for gradual pacification during the 1920s.

If we stand back and review the armed revolution that I have just described, we can see that in quantitative terms it dominates the story of Mexican violence in the twentieth century, just as the two world wars dominate the European story (Wilkinson, 1980). Apart from the Conquest, the 1910 Revolution was the only 'event' to reverse Mexico's demographic growth, with the data on the War of Independence, 1810–1821, too ambiguous (Van Young, 2001: 85–86). The Revolution alone makes Mexico a very violent country by the standards of twentieth-century Latin America. (So, to that extent, Siqueiros and Rivera had a point.) The Cuban and Bolivian revolutions cannot compare in scale; the closest comparators (in respect of lives lost in civil conflict, relative to population) would be Colombia, Guatemala and El Salvador. The Colombian *Violencia* (1948–1955) involved a Liberal–Conservative civil war that ended in stalemate (some have called it a social revolution *manqué*, but the stress should be on the qualifier *manqué*). The Central American conflicts – El Salvador in 1932 (Anderson, 1971:, 134–136) and again in the 1980s, and Guatemala in the 1980s – were civil wars in which the Right won and, in doing so, killed vastly more people than the Left (i.e. the death toll came from repression rather than revolution: this was 'death by government', in Rummel's phrase). In other words, the Mexican Revolution is unique in terms of being a prolonged and bloody but successful social revolution, which achieved substantial – and in some senses 'progressive' – socio-political change. Of course, opinions about this outcome, being premised on different normative preferences, will vary (and have varied): some – conservatives and Catholics – condemn the Revolution and all its works; hence for them the sacrifice was in vain. Some might applaud the outcome but consider the cost too high; and some might argue that, as Lenin rather callously put it, 'you can't make an omelette without breaking eggs' (Siqueiros, 1977: 108; Keane, 1996: 8). Of course, such an *ex post facto* cost–benefit analysis is rather unreal, because the participants were not granted straightforward options and could not foresee the outcome, or debate the merits, of dynamic processes in which they were immersed.

These Latin American comparisons suggest a couple of additional points that may be worth making, even if they are somewhat 'impressionistic' and (like many things in history) incapable of statistical demonstration. They concern the way that the fighting was conducted. Any war, be it civil or international, raises the question of proportionality: what degree of force is justified in the circumstances? (Walzer, [1977] 1992) Clearly, answers will vary (consider poison gas, the bombing of civilians, the taking of hostages, and so on). But at different times and places there have been loose consensuses – regarding, for example, the conduct of medieval sieges or the treatment of prisoners-of-war (Gillingham, [1982] 2005a: 123, 153–154). Although the Mexican Revolution began with a clear commitment to humanitarian practice (Ross, 1995: 116), these initial good intentions were soon overtaken by events. Thus, no codified set of rules prevailed, but some loose assumptions and practices can be identified.

First, the experience of revolution and counter-revolution tended over time to harden hearts and promote a kind of ruthless *Realpolitik*. Madero, the first revolutionary leader and president, was a genuine idealist and humanitarian: his agreement with the Díaz government in May 1911 was, in part, prompted by humanitarian concerns; and his treacherous overthrow was facilitated by his naively benign view of those around him. But his overthrow and murder in February 1913 induced a more hawkish response on the part of the next generation of revolutionary leaders – Carranza, Villa, Obregón, and Calles (Knight, 1986b: 13, 102, 104; Katz, 1998: 218–19). There would be no more negotiation; the Huerta regime (and with it the federal army) would be destroyed; the revolutionaries would not share power. 'A Revolution which compromises is a lost Revolution', as Carranza put it (and plenty of grassroots revolutionaries agreed); Mendoza Vargas, describing grassroots hostilities in the Huasteca, echoes this Realpolitik sentiment: 'there was no pardon, no truce, no yielding, not for anyone' (Mendoza Vargas, 1998: 50). This was no mere rhetoric: Carranza also revived an old *juarista* law mandating the death penalty for all supporters of the Huerta regime. Federal Army officers were regularly shot (Villa, it was said, lined them up in threes in order to save bullets), but the Federal rank-and-file, being largely reluctant conscripts, were allowed to join the ranks of the Revolution – or to melt away in the mounting chaos of the country (Knight, 1986b: 41, 117, 146; Brunk, 1995: 101–102; Katz, 1998: 220–221). There were no prisoner-of-war camps, hence no repeat of the horrors of Andersonville (the Confederate prisoner-of-war camp in Georgia where as many as 10,000 Union soldiers died); some defeated Federals found their way across the border and spent an unpleasant time at Fort Bliss, but they lived to tell the tale (*New York Times*, 23 January 1914: 2). When it came to atrocities perpetrated against civilians, it was Huerta's Federal Army that stood out, notably in Morelos, where General Juvencio Robles, faithfully enacting the president's will, burned, pillaged, slaughtered and 'reconcentrated', employing the kind of tactics that General Valeriano Weyler had used in Cuba twenty years earlier (Womack, 1970: 138). Similar forms of repression were used, if less systematically, elsewhere. Repression was justified (as far as one can tell) by a belief in the evil of the Revolution, which stood for disorder, rapine and social upheaval. Zapata, in particular, was denounced as a bloodthirsty bandit – the 'Attila of the South' – who threatened property and practised refined tortures on his victims (Womack, 1970: 100, 112–113, 422; Brunk, 2008). In 1914, as the Revolution spread and Huerta's fortunes declined, the inhabitants of Mexico City – the *chilangos* – tossed sleeplessly in their beds, expecting an imminent massacre at the hands of Zapata's 'Indians' (the ethnic factor clearly counted, in subjective terms, though it seems likely that most *zapatistas* were not 'Indians' according to usual criteria) (Womack, 1970: 70–71, 187–188; Brunk, 1995: 135). In fact, when Huerta fled and the Zapatistas entered the capital, they did so diffidently and largely peaceably (the *villistas*, who soon followed them, proved rather rougher), but the exaggerated fears of the *chilangos* were never confirmed and, with the brief exception of the 'ten tragic days' in February 1913 (when, following a military coup against the Madero government, military golpistas – not insurgent Indians – subjected downtown Mexico City to intense fighting) the capital experienced very little violence in the course of the Revolution (we could compare with the experience of Paris in 1789, or La Paz in 1952).

Villismo, the great popular movement of the north, also provoked greatly exaggerated fears on the part of middle- and upper-class townspeople. During 1913–1914, however, as Villa's star ascended, they came to see him as a force for order and stability, as did the Catholic Church and foreign businessmen, at least until mid-1915. Thus, in the course of the Revolution, scare stories were confected and diffused – about raped nuns, abducted young women, tortured prisoners and the like (Kelley, 1916). Most were apocryphal. Huerta's Federal Army committed many more atrocities against civilians than did the revolutionaries, which is hardly surprising, because the revolutionaries enjoyed majority support, especially in central and northern Mexico (when revolutionary carpet-baggers headed south in 1914–1915 the story was somewhat different). Hence, while Huerta's enemies were legion, the enemies of the Revolution were few and getting fewer as the well-to-do fled the theatres of war to find safe havens in Mexico City, Havana, San Antonio and Paris. Like other wars and insurgencies, therefore, the Revolution prompted caricatured images and hypertrophied fears; although there was no one 'Big Fear' (as in France) (Lefebvre, [1932] 1973), there were many lesser panics, most of them exaggerated, some of them entirely groundless.

For, in fact, the level of violence in the Mexican Revolution was, I would argue, quite proportionate. That is to say, violence served particular ends, hence was largely instrumental and 'rational'. Killing had a businesslike quality: 'it became fixed in my mind', a revolutionary veteran recalled of his youth, 'that, sometimes, in order to save life, it is necessary to kill' (Mendoza Vargas, 1998: 56). There were, as I have mentioned, some nasty customers who seem to have relished the violence; and, no doubt, many more who became inured to it, as a matter of ineluctable experience (and this, I will argue, had consequences for the future). But there is rather little evidence of wanton atrocities or 'symbolic', 'expressive' violence, of the kind which, for example, the Colombian *Violencia* produced or which the military in Guatemala or Argentina perpetrated in their respective dirty wars (see the chapters by Rojas and Tubb, Figueroa Ibarra and Crenzel in this volume; also: Bergquist and Penaranda, 1992; Fagen, 1992). True, Huerta's Federal Army ravaged Morelos (and some other places); but these were standard counter-revolutionary tactics, aggravated, no doubt, by a measure of racism. But, as far as I know, we do not find Mexico's contending forces engaging in mass atrocities, gang rape or refined torture. If true, this – again – has nothing to do with national character or long-term historico-cultural determinism. I would not wish to substitute a 'nice civilised Mexican' stereotype for the old 'nasty barbaric' one. The answer more likely lies in the nature of the conflict. The Mexican Revolution was a major war, in which each side sought military victory. Victory might require counter-insurgency repression, but it did not involve a dirty war against shadowy civilian opponents (like Argentina's Montoneros, for example); the opponents were all too apparent on the battlefield. There were, as I have said, no prisoner-of-war camps, hence, while there were plenty of summary executions (and probably quite a few implementations of the *ley fuga*), there was no protracted imprisonment. Indeed, imprisonment would have been impractical: Mexico lacked the facilities; armies were often on the move, and did not want to be burdened by cabooses loaded with hungry prisoners.[5] Nor was there much by way of prisoner interrogation. Sergeant Isunza's resort to clipping the ears of prisoners was, therefore, a gruesome but logical response to these circumstances.

---

5   This refusal to take and hold prisoners is, of course, a very old phenomenon (to put it differently, organised prisoner-of-war camps are relatively new in history);

Finally, there was a measure of mutual respect, especially during the 'war of the winners', which pitted revolutionary against revolutionary. It is often assumed that civil wars are especially brutal and vindictive. Some – such as the Spanish Civil War – probably are; but so are some international conflicts – the Russian front and the Pacific theatre of the Second World War, for example. The degree of brutality thus varies across all wars. During the Mexican Revolution there was high mortality, but combatants treated other combatants with some respect (perhaps there are parallels to be found on the Western Front in 1914–1918). The 'sunrise greeting against the adobe wall' – that is, the early morning firing squad – was conducted according to certain unwritten rules, whereby the victims displayed nonchalant bravado, the executioners a measure of minimal courtesy. Thus, the old rebel 'Cheche' Campos, led out to be shot, 'refused with contempt to plead or whimper', declined a blindfold, and requested 'that you pour me three fingers and play me El Abandonado' – that is, a large shot of *sotol* (a northern-Mexican distilled liquor) and and a rendition of his favourite *corrido* (popular ballad) (O' Hea, 1966: 60). General Pantoja begged the firing squad to shoot straight and avoid damaging his beloved silver-encrusted sombrero (Siqueiros, 1977: 156). An anonymous captain appealed to the commanding general to witness his execution, not because he wished to beg for pardon, but because he wanted him 'to see how the men of Sonora know how to die' (Mendoza Vargas, 1998: 90–1). Even an anonymous deserter rose to the occasion, urging the firing squad: 'shoot, my comrades / bravely shoot / two in the head / and three in the heart' (Ochoa Serrano and Pérez Martínez, 1994: 228). The firing squad was thus a kind of performative ritual, in which both victim and executioners followed a rough script embodying honour and a sort of crude chivalry. No doubt there were many exceptions (about which we hear little); but the script mattered and helped mitigate some of the worst excesses of wartime killing.

Macro-Political Violence (after 1920)

After 1920 the fledgling revolutionary state consolidated, quelled several military rebellions (1923, 1927 and 1929), fought a bitter counter-insurgency campaign against Catholic rebels in central-western Mexico (the Cristero rebellion, 1926–1929) and, above all, survived. Its survival depended in part on its incorporation and mobilisation of mass organisations – labour unions, peasant leagues and political parties – which gave it a social base that

---

pre-industrial wars might involve capturing slaves, wives or sacrificial victims; but, frequently, defeat meant death, not prolonged incarceration.

the Porfirian old regime had lacked. Any analysis of the regime must run the length of the Gramscian continuum, noting the extremes of repression and ideological engagement, as well as the crucial intermediate practices of patronage and corruption. For the purposes of this chapter, it is the violent end of the continuum that matters most, violence being the explanandum of the book; but, as I would stress throughout, violence can only be understood in context, as a 'by-product' of particular circumstances (Tilly, Tilly and Tilly, 1975: 243), and as one strategy within a much wider 'repertoire' that circumstances permit or encourage (Tarrow, 1994: 6, 31–47). To understand the incidence of violence, therefore, we must pay some attention to the entire repertoire. And, since violence itself comes in many shapes and sizes, and obeys many rationales, the task is a daunting one – more so, I would suggest, for the post-revolutionary period than for the armed revolution that I have just summarised. The armed revolution lasted a decade; the post-revolutionary period (depending on one's definition) ranges from 20 to 40 to 80 years.[6] Also, the violence of the armed revolution served grand military goals: winning the war, seizing and retaining power. After 1920, the war had been won and the revolutionaries were in power (and we know, with hindsight, that they would not be ousted. They probably reached that conclusion themselves by the late 1920s or early 1930s). Political violence now served a range of lesser goals, which tends to make analysis more complicated.

I shall try to make some sense of this protean phenomenon by addressing primarily (i) political violence (both macro and micro) and, more briefly, (ii) mercenary violence (as I explained at the outset, social, or familial violence is largely ignored). Compared with what has gone before in this discussion, (i) is a logical (but evolving) continuation, while (ii) and (iii) are relatively new – not because mercenary and interpersonal/familial violence were unknown during 1910–1920, but because they were dwarfed by the hecatomb of the armed revolution, hence lacked salience. However, as (i) declined, so (ii) and (iii) became relatively more important; although, I suspect, it is impossible to quantify this weighting with any precision.

By 'macro' political violence I mean violence that is collective, organised and directed towards macro-political goals (the capture of state power, the transformation of the state or national 'project'). Of course, there is a sense in which, just as 'all politics is local' (Tip O'Neill), so all – or a great deal

---

6 I would favour the shorter period, thus restricting the post-revolutionary period to 1920–1940. Some would stretch it to 1968; some to the 1980s (José López Portillo, 1976–1982, being, in his own words, the 'last president of the Revolution').

of – political violence is local, in that it takes place at a particular site, is often associated with local feuds and rancours, and reflects local ways-of-doing-things. Thus, violence in Mexico City is not quite the same as violence in the hot country of Guerrero. (Given Mexico's celebrated diversity, such local variations are probably more marked than they are, perhaps, in England or Japan or Denmark). Therefore macro-political violence is refracted through local lenses.[7] Nevertheless, among the several ways that one can approach the teeming universe of 'violence', the macro/micro distinction offers one useful point of entry.

The 'war of the winners' determined who would rule Mexico after 1915; Obregón's ouster of Carranza in 1920 (the last successful military uprising) changed some of the personnel and policies of the regime, but not its basic format. Subsequent rebellions similarly challenged personnel and perhaps policies; they were triggered by presidential succession crises (in 1923, 1927 and 1929); but none succeeded. The regime survived and strengthened not because it was able to assert a monopoly of legitimate violence (that Weberian goal has eluded all Mexican administrations), but because it could assemble a preponderant winning coalition – narrowly in 1923, more convincingly in 1927 and thereafter. This meant it could mobilise enough of the army – its own 'revolutionary' army – and of paramilitary allies (armed workers and peasants, especially the latter) to achieve victory. To do so it had both to professionalise and to reward the military (a somewhat contradictory process, in that rewarding involved lavish bribery of 'professional' officers), while at the same time forging paramilitary alliances on the basis of government patronage and social reform (land reform in particular).[8] The campaigns of 1923, 1927 and 1929, like the preceding War of the Winners, pitted revolutionaries against revolutionaries, and tended to be fought in the same spirit; they were ruthlessly instrumental, but coloured by a certain bluff camaraderie. We see this, for example, in the execution, following a lightning court-martial, of General Barrios in 1927; or, even better, General Estrada's chivalrous treatment of the captured and wounded General Lázaro Cárdenas (Dulles, 1961: 242; Downing, [1940] 1996: 3–4).

Meanwhile, successive government victories made it clear – to all but the most obtuse or quixotic – that the regime was here to stay and that ambitious

---

7   As Richard Cobb put it, 'the verb *terroriser* conjugates quite differently from one Department [of France] to another' (Cobb, 1972: xvi–xvii).

8   This could be seen as a shift from decentralised, popular collective action, perhaps of a 'reactive' kind, to more 'proactive' forms of mobilisation, involving mass organisations, and conducted under the aegis of the state. The reactive/proactive dichotomy comes from Tilly, Tilly and Tilly (1975: 48–55, 243).

generals should work within, not against, the regime. That meant, first, that they should not flirt with rebellion (the mistake made by De la Huerta, Serrano, Gómez, Escobar and others) and that, second, they should channel their ambitions through the federal government (like Cárdenas) and not through semi-independent power blocs in the provinces (like Tejeda) (Ginzburg, 1997). By the 1930s these lessons had been largely learned and subsequent revolts – like that of Cedillo in 1939 – proved to be damp squibs. At the macro-political level, therefore, the ageing revolutionary elite – sometimes called the 'revolutionary family' – which controlled the state enjoyed a secure tenure of power and had devised a set of rules of the game that circulated jobs and spoils, while maintaining a measure of clientelist – and perhaps ideological – support. The nascent official party, the Partido Nacional Revolucionario (PNR) (1929), the product, perhaps, of a quintessential 'elite pact', was both proof and further guarantee of this macro-political stability (Knight, 1992). One important consequence was a marked diminution of macro-political violence. In 1923, De la Huerta raised over half the army in revolt and nearly toppled the government. In 1927, in contrast, the revolt barely got off the ground and in 1929 it mobilised only a fraction of the military. A swathe of ambitious generals was thus removed – sometimes with ruthless efficiency – and the survivors adapted to the rules of the game. Calles, for example, emulating Díaz, was quite prepared to issue 'mátenlos en caliente' ('kill them on the spot') orders (Dulles, 1961: 350) .Those rules now became less violent. When Calles was himself ousted by Cárdenas in 1936, he fully expected to be stood up against a wall and shot (after all, he had done as much to plenty of previous dissidents), but instead he was bundled aboard a plane, destined for a comfortable period of exile in San Diego, California; and he returned to stand shoulder-to-shoulder with a clutch of ex-presidents on the balcony of the national palace in 1942. This retreat from violence may have been accelerated by President Cárdenas (1934–1940), who was rightly renowned for being more magnanimous and less sanguinary than some of his predecessors; but the basic reason was structural rather than individual. Members of the Mexican political elite no longer needed to kill each other; force – at the macro-political level – had receded into the background; more peaceful and decorous ways of controlling and punishing dissidents had been devised. As the *New York Times* correspondent noted in 1939: 'sordid killing as a means of enforcing the official will has disappeared' (Kluckhohn, 1939: 3).[9] Cedillo returned to the old revolutionary warpath

---

9   Since Kluckhohn had been expelled from Mexico by the government for his reportage following the oil expropriation of 1938, he was not exactly an apologist for the regime.

in 1939, but his swift annihilation confirmed the folly of rebellion and the wisdom of compliance. The lesson was not lost on Almazán who, having contested and lost the presidential election of 1940, decided that discretion was the better part of valour and that, grudgingly, he should accept defeat.

However, the post-revolutionary period did witness a form of macro-political conflict, which, though quite different in character and significance, had somewhat similar consequences: a strengthening of the revolutionary state and a diminution of macro-political violence (including both the actuality and the threat of such violence). For reasons which lie beyond the scope of this chapter, the Revolution had provoked a severe recrudescence of church–state conflict. The state now sought to go beyond the liberal anti-clericalism of the nineteenth century (which had disestablished the church and confiscated its vast material possessions) and set out to dominate the church, even – as some jacobin *enragés* hoped – to eliminate the irrational beliefs and superstitious practices of Catholicism altogether. The result was a battle for hearts and minds, all the more intense in that the new mass organisations of the state – schools, parties, *sindicatos* and *ejidos* (agrarian reform communities) – now confronted the church's rival mass organisations (again, schools, as well as youth organisations, workers', women's, parents' and student associations). After several years of politico-cultural skirmishing, following the promulgation of the anticlerical 1917 Constitution, the conflict turned violent with the Cristero rebellion of 1926–1929 (Meyer, 1976). This, too, was a form of macro-political violence: it involved the two most powerful national institutions in the country, church and state, as well as two sharply contrasting ideologies and 'national projects'; and, while the fighting was largely limited to the centre-west of the country, the consequences were severe. Though pitched battles occurred – and the Cristeros won a few – the conflict took the form of regular army counter-insurgency campaigns against a mobile enemy, familiar with the territory and enjoying widespread popular support. The army – itself the product of a popular revolution a decade earlier – now acquired many of the characteristics of the old Porfirian force: it was riddled with graft, relied on conscription, suffered serious desertions, and practised heavy-handed repression against its elusive opponents and those who supported them. Casualties were heavy and material destruction – of farms, livestock, crops and infrastructure – was severe (Meyer, 1976: 178). Furthermore, this kind of macro-political conflict was ideologically charged and could not be mitigated by sentiments of revolutionary camaraderie. Revolutionary and Cristero commanders were bitter enemies. The Cristeros firebombed trains, the Federals resorted to mass lynchings and torture; the result has been described as 'mutual bloodletting of unspeakable ferocity' (Gledhill, 1990: 91; Meyer, 1976). Popular ballads confirm that loyalties ran deep – hardly surprising, when the state claimed that the church, allied to 'Reaction', was obstructing the redemptive work of the Revolution, and the church excommunicated the agents of the state and instituted a boycott of church services. This was a conflict over hearts, minds and souls, not just jobs, perks and pesos.[10] Thus, it tended to be more violent and less susceptible to compromise. In the end, compromise came about, not least thanks to the insistent pressure of Rome and the persuasive diplomacy of Washington. An agreement was reached in 1929: many rank-and-file Cristeros were dismayed at what they saw as betrayal, and some were swiftly hunted down and eliminated.

The battle for hearts and minds was not in fact won, but church and state established a wary *modus vivendi*, which slowly matured with time. The *Cristiada*, the most violent conflict of the 1920s – a kind of mini-revolution, with the old roles reversed – thus came to an acrimonious end. For all its faults, the Federal Army had prevailed (it had certainly not been defeated); and the Cristeros and their supporters concluded that they would have to build the kingdom of Christ on earth by other, more peaceful means. Catholic political mobilisation continued apace during the 1930s, by means of Acción Católica (Catholic Action), the more militant Unión Nacional Sinarquista (Sinarquista National Union), and the quasi-Christian Democratic Partido Acción Nacional (National Action Party) (1939). Again, this shift had some of the characteristics of Tilly's transformation of 'reactive' into 'proactive' protest; to put it simply, militant Catholics realised that they could neither subvert nor entirely shun the state. Low-level violence continued, notably with Catholic attacks on 'socialist' schools,[11] and sporadic leftist/anticlerical reprisals. But this skirmishing did not threaten the state and it could not remotely compare with the Catholic/anti-clerical violence that, in the same years, was unleashed by the Spanish Civil War (Knight, 2007b). Church–state conflict remained on the political agenda, but it was no longer an issue that provoked macro-political violence. Thus, by the 1930s, two major sources of such violence – dissident revolutionaries and radical Catholics – had been neutralised, making Mexican politics a somewhat more peaceable and less bloody business at the national level.

---

10   'Yo fui revolucionario / pelié por mi religión / no fui un estrafalario / lo hice de corazón' ('I was a revolutionary, I fought for my religion, I was no mere deadbeat, I did it for conviction') (Ochoa Serrano and Pérez Martínez, 1994: 275).

11   Raby (1974: 181–197), who concludes that 100 schoolteachers were killed by Catholic militants in the 1930s; some appear to have been sadistically killed (for example, p. 183, on the murder of a schoolmistress at Etzatlán, Jalisco).

Micro-Political Violence (after 1920)

For this reason, many broadbrush analyses of Mexico tend to assume that violence as a whole had been decisively curtailed. But such a view is misconceived, and places too great an emphasis on the national picture. If we turn to the localities, to what I am loosely terming micro-political violence, a different picture emerges. Here, political violence continued briskly; indeed, it could be argued that pacification at the top – the church–state *arreglos* and the 'elite pact' of 1929 – displaced and/or concealed the endemic violence that afflicted local communities.

By 'micro-political' I mean violence that is collective and geared to some (limited, often local) socio-political purpose: most clearly, it involves outright political conflict over elections, candidacies, political jurisdiction and the pursuit of office. More broadly – and here I am stretching the qualifier 'political' – it includes the collective struggles of workers and peasants (and their opponents: bosses and landlords, as well as other workers and peasants). One strong justification for retaining 'political' as a catch-all label is that, in twentieth-century Mexico, such conflicts were inevitably political in the sense of involving state actors – actors whose sphere of operations had greatly expanded with the state's assumption of new regulatory and redistributionist powers following the Revolution (notably in the fields of land and labour reform). In other words, the Mexican state was not a neutral 'nightwatchman' state; but then it had never been.[12] Micro-political and macro-political violence thus shared many features: both, as I have said, involved collective goals and organisation (hence were different from what I categorise as mercenary/economic and familial/interpersonal violence); the difference lay in the scale and the stakes. During the 1910s – as the armed revolution raged – macro-political violence occurred on a massive scale (including deadly conventional warfare), and its outcome mattered profoundly. During the 1920s, as I have shown, such violence declined and with it the political death toll (though I can offer no hard-and-fast figures). In addition, the stakes diminished: after 1920 or, at the latest, 1924 it became increasingly clear that the revolutionary regime was there to stay, and that armed challenges, whether from disaffected army officers or intransigent Catholics, were bound to fail. Regime change was not a realistic option; micro-political violence focussed on narrower (though still important) issues, such as unionisation, labour contracts, land reform, and the unending quest for political office (that 'perpetual and restless desire of power[...] that ceaseth only in death', as

---

12   We should note that the state grew chiefly in terms of its regulatory powers rather than of its spending or payroll, at least until the 1970s (Knight, 2002b: 244–5).

Hobbes put it ([1651] 1998: 66). Such violence was therefore 'micro' by virtue of being less prevalent and portentous than what had gone before. But it remained significant (especially if we bear in mind the 'penumbra' effect), and it can reasonably be seen as the continuation of the armed revolution, albeit at a lesser tempo. It involved the same struggles – struggles over the distribution of political power and material resources – but these issues were now mediated through the emergent revolutionary state. The latter had become an established fixture and it set – at least some of – the rules of the game; but it was far from being a model Weberian state exercising a monopoly of legitimate political violence: indeed, it allowed, even encouraged, a fair amount of particularist or patrimonial violence, perpetrated by local militias (notably the ubiquitous *defensas sociales*), by political hired guns (*pistoleros*), and by union thugs.[13] Sometimes the state would intervene to curtail the more egregious or embarrassing manifestations of this phenomenon (i.e. it would make a show of asserting its supposed Weberian monopoly); but too often it was either incapable or unwilling: unwilling, because the perpetrators of violence were useful allies whom the state needed. Indeed, the armed revolution had created a generation schooled in violence, possessed of arms, and ready to use them for collective gain (Knight, 1997: 120–1). Meanwhile, the judicial system was both lax in respect of punishment and disposed to collude with the dominant executive branch. As a result, the threat of arrest, conviction, or punishment was weak and violence remained remarkably unpunished.

Three aspects of this 'revolutionary legacy' may be identified, by way of explaining its scope and longevity. First, and most importantly, the final triumph of the Revolution – whether we date it to 1920, 1924 or even 1929 – did not bring the consummation of revolutionary goals (that is, the goals for which the revolutionaries had fought). Land reform came gradually; labour reform was subject to recurrent vicissitudes; and the battle for political office, both collective and individual, was relentless and unending. Hence there was plenty to fight about: the triumph of the Revolution determined the context of the fight, and the broad rules of the fight-game; but it remained to be seen who would win.

Second, the revolution put weapons in people's hands and, despite recurrent attempts to retrieve them, the state could never 'depistolise' society

---

13 *Defensas sociales* were local defence forces – vigilantes or paramilitaries, we might call them – who were set up to protect communities from predation in the later years of the Revolution; they continued to exist through the 1920s and 1930s, often serving as the armed wing of agrarian movements; and they supplied a generation of local – sometimes regional – political strongmen (Knight, 1997: 114).

(nor, as I said, did it necessarily want to). The weaponry required for micro-political violence was not necessarily sophisticated: ruthless political bosses such as Gonzalo N. Santos (1984) boasted of their firepower (indeed, there seems to have been something of a cult of gunplay); but a few Maussers – and even the dependable machete of the hot country – could prove useful. The Federal Army now had a monopoly of heavy weaponry (artillery, troops trains, and, increasingly, airplanes), hence in part its 'macro-political' invulnerability, but for the kind of 'micro' skirmishing that typified the post-1924 period, simple, cheap and accessible weaponry was sufficient, since this was not an epic struggle between conventional armies, but rather a sordid saga of assassinations, ambushes, street fights and *barrio* brawls.

Third, the protagonists of micro-political violence were usually men – to begin with, young men – who had been inured to violence during the years of armed conflict, if not before. Paul Friedrich's 'Princes of Naranja' (1987) are classic exemplars. Often, they were related, literally or fictively; and they had forged close bonds during the years of revolutionary warfare (we might hazard comparisons with those First World War veterans who made up the Italian *arditi*, the German Freikorps, and the British Black and Tans). Not only did revolutionary veterans possess arms and para-military knowhow; they had also crossed the psychological threshold that divided pacific from violent behaviour. They did not flinch from ambushes, assassinations, intimidation and, occasionally, torture, all of which became features of the *política cochina* ('dirty politics') of the 1920s and after. These were hard men, reared in a hard school. Some experts-in-violence may well have had psychopathic tendencies – revealed or stimulated by the armed revolution; but it seems unlikely that they were a majority, or that the pervasive micro-political violence of the 1920s, 1930s and after was primarily the product of induced psychopathology. Rather, it was a rational and ruthlessly instrumental way of conducting politics.

This can be seen if we cursorily review the main micro-political conflicts of the time. Class antagonisms, which had helped fuel the armed revolution, continued into the 1920s and beyond. Peasants sought land – as the revolutionary Constitution encouraged them to do – and landlords resisted. While the state laid down legal procedures for land reform (Simpson, 1937: Ch. 6), the process also involved intense political lobbying and both the threat and actuality of violence. *Agraristas* slew landlords (like the luckless Rosalie Evans) and landlords murdered *agraristas* (like the *michoacano* martyr Primo Tapia) (Friedrich, 1977; Henderson, 1998). Although the former had numbers on their side, the landed class could recruit specialists-in-violence (often called *guardias blancas*, 'white guards') and could count on the support of peasant 'trusties' who allied with the *hacienda* against the agrarian threat.[14] The conflicts that ensued through the 1920s and 1930s had little of the redeeming chivalry that, as I noted, characterised (some) revolutionary warfare in the 1910s. Rather, they resembled ruthless dog-eat-dog Darwinian struggles, conducted by small groups striving for control of particular localities. Intimidation, espionage, assassination and torture were inescapable features of these struggles, as they were of comparable socio-political confrontations – in post-1918 Italy, for example, or the Southern Cone in the 1960s and 1970s. Not until the sweeping *reparto* of the 1930s was this tense stand-off partly resolved, in favour of the *agraristas*; but even then pockets of agrarian conflict remained and, indeed, new conflicts broke out, especially where commercial cashcrop production flourised, pushing up land values in hitherto marginal zones (Knight, 1999: 114–115). And even when *ejidos* were set up, the factional battle for control – of land, resources, and political office – continued, punctuated by skirmishes and schisms (Friedrich, 1977; Simpson, 1937).

A roughly comparable form of class polarisation occurred in some industrial sectors. Following the Revolution, unionisation rapidly increased, and the revolutionary state took a close interest in both fomenting and controlling the infant labour unions. While control sometimes involved outright repression, the state needed its political alliance with organised labour and wanted to boost industrial production; the stick therefore had to be complemented by the carrot; and the carrot involved both material benefits (better pay and conditions) and organisational concessions (the right to unionise and, in particular, to declare a closed shop). As in the rural sector, labour violence took the form both of workers battling bosses and of workers battling fellow-workers in order to secure local dominance. My impression is that the latter pattern was particularly pronounced in the labour sector, for example in the notoriously violent textile towns of Atlixco and Orizaba (Consul Burt to State Department, 3 Feb. 1938, US State Dept Records, Internal Affairs of Mexico, 812.504/1703; Bortz, 2008: 170–173). Here, rival unions contested for power, resorting to assassinations and street battles. Although the contest took on some ideological coloration, it was primarily a battle for power and perks. Politicians took advantage of such circumstances to strike advantageous bargains; those – like President Cárdenas himself – who tried to mediate and pacify found the task intractable (Ashby, 1967: 106–116). Violence also characterised mining towns and oil camps (Siqueiros, 1977: 248). The 'Leviathan' state was not as powerful as sometimes imagined; or, to put it differently, the dynamics of local conflict often defied the state's desire

---

14   A notorious case is described in Santoyo (1995). There are evident parallels here with the birth of the Mafia in nineteenth-century Sicily: see Blok ([1974] 1988).

or capacity to enforce order. Micro-political disorder was, perhaps, the price paid for macro-political stability. Thus, even within the single dimension of political violence, trends were neither uniform nor unilinear.

Though similar, agrarian and industrial violence differed in important respects. Agrarian reform eliminated a good many landlords and converted *haciendas* into *ejidos*; schematically, what began a class struggle (landlords vs. peasants) then gave way to intra-peasant factional squabbles, often confined to the narrow radius of the *ejido*. Like other post-reform peasantries, that of Mexico thus tended to become somewhat fragmented, introverted and factionalised, ripe for political manipulation – as in post-1952 Bolivia (Knight, 2003: 75–76). Save for a few major examples, such as oil and railways, the means of industrial production remained in private hands; and even when major nationalisations occurred (in the oil and railway sectors) the workers had to deal with a powerful state bureaucracy, such as PEMEX. Syndical class struggles therefore continued through the 1940s down to the 1970s – for example, with the miners, the railwaymen, the electricians and auto-workers. But in order to prosecute these struggles, the workers needed to acquire a measure of organisational autonomy of the state and its allied labour *centrales* (in the 1920s the Confederación Regional Obrera Mexicana [CROM], in the 1930s and after the Confederación de Trabajadores de México [CTM]). Mexican labour history therefore witnessed recurrent insurgencies as independent unions formed and fought for recognition. Necessarily, they fought on two fronts: against their employers (private or, in the case of oil and railways, the state) and against rival workingclass organisations, notably the *'charro'* ('yellow') unions promoted by the bosses and/or by the state. The ensuing violence therefore included both repression from above (such as the breaking of the railway unions in 1948 and again in 1958) and conflict at the grassroots (Middlebrook, 1995).

Although violence therefore played an important and enduring role in labour and agrarian micro-politics, the scale of such violence is hard to calibrate. Clearly, it was on nothing like the scale of the armed revolution. Nor – especially if we control for population – did it compare to the repression of working-class organisations evident in, say, Argentina and Chile in the 1970s. Mexico's reputation for stable civilian government, though exaggerated by many, was not wholly unfounded. Indeed, Mexican *políticos* prided themselves (I suspect) on managing their business with adroit discretion. Massacres were not good for business; they were an admission of (partial) failure; they also controverted the rather folksy, familial ideology of the Mexican Revolution. The Guatemalan military might engage in ethnocide, and the praetorian regimes of the Southern Cone might shout their national security doctrine from the rooftops, but the regime of the PRI preferred low-key, limited repression, offset by occasional concessions and a great deal of populist, inclusionary rhetoric. This combination of practice and ideology (and I would place more emphasis on the practice, the rules of the governing game, than on the populist and patriotic ideology) inhibited extreme and exemplary violence. *Caciques* and governors who overstepped the mark risked being ousted. By the same token, high-profile big-city violence – such as the killing of student demonstrators in Mexico City in 1968 and 1971 – was a shock to the system, while suitably remote, rural repression could be more easily overlooked, especially in an age when the media were reluctant to snoop in dark corners. No doubt the social and ethnic make-up of the victims also mattered: official *indigenismo* notwithstanding, it was easier to repress 'Indian' campesinos in Guerrero than white/*mestizo* students in Mexico City (Castellanos, 2007).

A good deal of Mexican micro-political violence thus arose in the context of agrarian and labour struggles. As I stressed, these were inevitably 'political', since the state had an interest not only in public order (as any would-be 'Weberian' state should), but also in material distribution, clientelism and rent-seeking (alias corruption). In addition, 'normal' Mexican politics embodied a quantum of violence. No doubt that is true of politics in many countries; the problem is to compare the scale, character and impact of political violence. Ostensibly, Mexico was a stable civilian polity, where, especially during the heyday of the *Pax PRIísta* (1952–1976), presidents came and went with clockwork precision, military revolts were a thing of the past, and political stability underwrote sustained, low-inflation economic growth. No major Latin American country could claim a comparable record. But there remained a worm in the apple, even if the apple looked appealingly rosy and the worm was small and well concealed in the core. Long after presidents ceased to be slaughtered, lower-level *políticos* paid the price for their involvement in what remained a somewhat dangerous game. In the 1930s shootouts were common, while even at the height of the *Pax PRIísta*, political assassinations continued (Knight, 1999: 111). Lower in the hierarchy and out in the provinces, micro-political violence was even more pronounced: it arose from factional divisions within the PRI, opposition challenges, and battles for jurisdiction between rival communities (Gillingham, 2005b).

We can conclude that the Mexican political system, for all its macro-political civilian stability, allowed – and in some measure even encouraged – a measure of micro-political violence, some of it class-inflected, some of it the product of the Hobbesian struggle for power. The system could not, or would not, eliminate this endemic violence that, though at the outset a legacy of the armed revolution, was clearly no mere declining vestige of the past. Violence responded to concrete interests (both class and political) and it was regularly used by contenders for power, including the top echelons of the PRI. But violence was used discreetly and evasively. Politicians did not (usually) boast of their violent accomplishments; they preferred to dissimulate, relying on the fact that, whatever naive foreigners might think, Mexicans were well aware of what went on and adjusted their political behaviour accordingly. Again, given the 'penumbra effect', a modicum of didactic violence could have disproportionate effect. The result was a 'schizoid', but stable, 'political culture' (Knight, 1996).

Mercenary Violence

Alongside the political violence I have discussed there coursed two rather different rivers of violence, one 'mercenary' or 'criminal', the other 'interpersonal' (perhaps also 'expressive'). The first involved violence perpetrated for the purpose of criminal gain: robbery, muggings, and organised (mafioso) crime, often associated with drugs. The second included family violence, especially violence against women, as well as interpersonal fights arising from what we might euphemistically call situations of sociability (thus, barroom brawls, drunken confrontations, squabbles between neighbours). It is important to note that these are sometimes hard to distinguish from the micropolitical violence already discussed. The weaponry was similar; drink (whose association with violence is pervasive) (Friedrich, 1977: 42, 48, 67, 127, 156; Romanucci-Ross, 1986: 136–138; Flanet, [1977] 1989: 137, 141–142, 179–180; Browning, 2001: 69, 82–83, 85, 93) figures prominently in all three categories; and 'political' motives can mingle with the mercenary and the interpersonal. Thus, organised crime, though geared to making money, cannot remain apolitical (any more than trade unions or peasant organisations can). Politicians are often paid off and sometimes bumped off.[15] In respect of interpersonal violence, it seems unlikely that domestic violence (e.g. wife-beating) is much influenced by partisan poltics, but there are plenty of instances where, for example, *cantina* fights, fuelled by alcohol, carry a political charge.[16] In such

---

15   There is, of course, a much broader argument – advanced, not least, by St Augustine – that political authority may serve highly mercenary ends, hence states may resemble robber bands or, we might say today, political mafias. In that case, the political/mercenary distinction partly collapses. However, even if the distinction becomes blurred in respect of ends (politicians and criminals are all on the make), their means – their modi operandi – clearly differ; politicians profit from power, criminals from crime; and, if the politicians are adroit, their power appears legitimate and their profiteering is not regarded as crime.

16   For example, during the contentious 1940 presidential election campaign, a pistolero shot dead a soldier in the Hotel Toluca for shouting 'Viva Almazán' ('Long live Almazán' – the opposition candidate) and a similar fate befell a drunk chauffeur (possibly a pistolero too), who was gunned down by the Chief of Police of Tenango for expressing similar sentiments (Knight, 1997: 119).

cases, it is difficult to know in what measure the fight should be blamed on (i) drink, (ii) personal animosity, and/or (iii) political antagonism.

However, while all these forms of violence (political, mercenary and interpersonal) may to some extent obey common causes – the prevalence of guns and *armas blancas*, the effects of drink, the weakness of the police and judicial systems – they are also different, and not simply in some rarefied analytical fashion. Being different, they cannot be subsumed under a grand, catch-all explanation (such as the 'Aztec legacy'), nor should we assume that these forms of violence all rise and fall together. For example, if we compare cycles of political and mercenary violence over time they reveal both convergences and divergences. Political disorder in the nineteenth century appears to have fostered related mercenary violence, such as brigandage and highway robbery (hence the celebrated bandits of Río Frío and the *plateados* of Morelos) (Frazer, 2006: 50, 55, 118–119, 123–130). The *Pax Porfiriana* (1876–1911) also appears to have borne down on both: rebellions declined in number and significance, while Porfirian public order was celebrated – and probably exaggerated – by both Mexican and foreign observers (Vanderwood, 1981). The Revolution re-ignited a cycle of violent political upheaval and, slightly later, mercenary crime also increased dramatically, stimulated by unemployment, hardship and the collapse of the state. Even after the last major battles of the Revolution had been won and lost in 1915, the cycle of mercenary crime – including banditry in the Bajío and Michoacan, and muggings in Mexico City – continued vigorously (Knight, 1986b: 392–406; Piccato, 2001: 26, 176–180). Thereafter, following a significant time-lag, violent crime in Mexico City began to decline once again (see Piccato in this volume) (Romanucci-Ross, 1986: 133–134; Piccato, 2001: 53–54). This Porfirian/revolutionary pattern tends to suggest a causal link between socio-political upheaval and (consequent) crime, crime being the dependent variable.

But crime, both violent and non-violent, clearly responds to a range of other causes that are not intimately connected to socio-political cycles. Border crime – smuggling and its associated violence – has historically derived from US demand (for drugs, drink and prostitution), hence it obeyed its own regional dynamic, divorced from trends in the capital (Astorga, 2003). More recently, the drugs boom of the 1980s and after has fuelled contraband and violence. Again, the chief cause has been burgeoning US demand and the capacity of Mexican cartels to meet that demand. However narco-violence is not a simple reflex of economic activity. First, crime and violence appear to have increased throughout Mexico in the 1980s and early 1990s, as a result of successive economic crises and ensuing unemployment and hardship (the fit between crime and negative economic performance looks quite convincing). However, in recent years (roughly, post-1995) the economy has recovered and crime figures have declined. Narco-violence, however, has increased sharply, to the point where about 700 deaths are being recorded per month and there is grim talk of the 'Colombianisation' of Mexico. Thus, narco-violence appears to follow its own trajectory, which I would explain in terms of the cartels' ruthless battle for territorial control (e.g. of border ports such as Nuevo Laredo) and of the relative absence of state oversight. For, once upon a time, the state – in the hands of the monopolistic PRI – exercised effective control over the narco interests, which were smaller, poorer, and dependent on the favour and collusion of a strong, centralised, corrupt state. The narco interests were 'cash cows' to be protected, domesticated and milked (Pimentel, 2003: 40). Since the 1980s, the decline of the PRI and the onset of democratic *alternancia* have eroded this control, at a time when, thanks to prodigious US demand, the cartels have become richer, more heavily armed, and more ambitious in their quest for power and profit. The cartels can now buy up políticos of different stripe and, at the same time, outgun the police. Indeed, they can, after the manner of Hobsbawm's famous 'social bandits', garner a good deal of popularity, on the grounds of being generous, brave, resourceful and patriotic (after all, they make their money from the gringos and they cock a snook at unpopular authorities on both sides of the border) (Edberg, 2001).

The collapse of Leviathan really has created a kind of Hobbesian state of nature, especially in zones along the border and in the narco-production regions of the interior (such as Sinaloa). Furthermore, contemporary narco-violence is notably extreme and exemplary. Victims are tortured and killed in barbaric fashion, often in order to make a point. Whether such extreme violence is instrumental and proportionate (that is, calculated to achieve maximum results by way of intimidation) or gratuitously expressive (the work of psychopaths and/or hardened ex-policemen who enjoy their work) it is hard to say.[17] But the result is a form of violence that goes beyond the old norms of revolutionary times and displays elements of 'Colombianisation'. The recent administration of President Calderón has responded with extensive military deployments; however, it seems unlikely that these will be any more successful than previous military-style solutions to the narco business; and the policy of militarisation carries risks of both tainting the army, while extending the violence.[18]

---

17 The recent increase in extreme narco-violence has been attributed in part to the activities of the Zetas, ex-Mexican military, now prominent in the Gulf cartel: see Blanco (2005).

18 Violence is extended in several ways: the army combats the narco interests; the narcos battle each other in order to survive and prosper amid the upheaval; the removal of narco bosses prompts violent internal battles for power; and, in accordance with the so-called 'cockroach effect', narco interests that are run out

Conclusions

This brief excursion into mercenary violence helps illustrate a key point of my argument. There are different forms of violence (I have identified three, but I do not presume that this trinitarian typology is the only or even the best on offer; it is one that seems to me to fit the history I know). These forms obey different causes and rationales. Hence, while they necessarily interact – revolutionary violence, for example, tended to encourage mercenary violence, not least by generalising weaponry and expertise – they also follow contrasting rhythms. Blanket explanations of violence, based on some supposed historico-culturalist legacy, are therefore useless. (These are to be distinguished, of course, from much shorter causal chains, such as the 'legacy' of the armed revolution). We could also speak of contrasting violent syndromes: the 'affective' concern for honour and respect, which permeates a good deal of interpersonal violence (Piccato, 2001), is less apparent where 'mercenary' crime, instrumentally geared to the profit motive, is concerned; while the relative camaraderie of conventional revolutionary warfare, especially in 1914–1915, contrasts with the atrocities of the *Cristiada*, the vicious quality of some 'micro-political' repression (e.g. the death of Primo Tapia), and, of course, the extreme, perhaps psychopathic, violence of current narco turf wars. Statistically, however, it was the Revolution that had by far the biggest impact: nearly as many died at the battle of Zacatecas in June 1914 as die annually in recorded homicides today; and the population in 1914 was about 15 percent of what it is now. Today's homicide rate is high by world standards, but, despite recent narco killings (which may add as much as 50 percent to the pre-2006 total), it is lower than it was earlier in the twentieth-century. Mexico may not be a model of Eliasian progress from barbarism to civilisation, but, despite current moral panics, it is actually a less violent place now than it was 100 years ago.

As for the Revolution itself, two concluding points might be made: first, contrary to what some revisionist historians suggest, it was far from being a 'tale of sound and fury, signifying nothing' (to cite Shakespeare's *Macbeth*); on the contrary, it signified substantial changes in Mexican politics and society. Violence, to repeat the old cliché, was the midwife of change. We may dislike the change (nostalgia for the Porfirian old regime has become quite fashionable in recent years), but it is hard to deny that change occurred, that violence

---

of one corner of the country scuttle elsewhere, hence once relatively peaceful cities (like Monterrey) begin to experience narco-related violence.

produced results, including – an important qualification – results that some-times corresponded to purposive socio-political goals.[19] Political violence, both macro and micro, was therefore instrumental and rational. More recently, too, the stability – the ostensible macro-political peacefulness – of the PRI regime co-existed with, and arguably depended in part upon, continued, low-level, micro-political violence; such violence was again instrumental and rational, in that it served purposive socio-political goals, albeit goals that were now less progressive, 'bottom-up' and system-changing than conservative, 'top-down' and system-maintaining.

Furthermore (the second point), Mexicans have been well aware of their violent past, and of the relative benefits of peace (Stevenson and Seligson, 1996); hence they have been leery of further revolutionary appeals, suspicious of neighbouring insurgencies (e.g. in Central America), and often unsympa-thetic to confrontational politics.[20] Far from leaving a legacy of endemic violence – a nation of potential Pancho Villas eager to *ir a la bola* – the Revo-lution has, over the long term, made Mexicans cautious of violent political solutions. It has cast a long shadow.

Finally, although historians should strenuously resist the lure of policy prescriptions (Knight, 2006), there is one practical conclusion that perhaps follows. Today, many lament, with good reason, the weakness of the 'rule of law' in Mexico. But we should regard violent – and other – deviations from Weberian norms not as some irrational pathology nor, as I have stressed, as some ineluctable *damnosa haereditas* of the distant past, but, more often than not, as rational and instrumental responses to circumstances or, if you prefer, to a system of structured incentives. Violence often occurred because it worked. As such, of course, these deviations may be somewhat more amenable to correction than if they were hardwired in Mexican genetic make-up or mysteriously inscribed, like Aztec hieroglyphs, on Mexico's immutable national psyche.

---

19   A good many consequences of the revolution – e.g. population loss – were unin-tended, hence did not correspond to any purposive plans; however, others – such as land reform – were intentional. Whether we agree with those plans is not impor-tant; the point is that they were furthered by – rational, instrumental – violence.

20   As I noted above, recent Mexican politics, including presidential elections, have been influenced by the 'fear' factor, which favoured Zedillo and the PRI in 1994, Calderón and the PAN in 2006.

2

Physical Violence Against Wives and the Law in the Spanish American World, 1820s–2000s

VICTOR M. URIBE-URÁN

Florida International University, USA

Violence against women is a manifestation of historically unequal power relations between men and women, which have led to domination over and discrimination against women by men and to the prevention of the full advancement of women [. . .]. (United Nations, 1993)

Worldwide, an estimated one in five women will be a victim of rape or attempted rape in her lifetime. One in three will have been beaten, coerced into sex or otherwise abused, usually by a family member or an acquaintance. More often than not, the perpetrators go unpunished. Each year, hundreds of thousands of women and children are trafficked and enslaved, millions more are subjected to harmful practices. Violence kills and disables as many women between the ages of 15 and 44 as cancer. And its toll on women's health surpasses that of traffic accidents and malaria combined. (UNFPA–United Nations Population Fund, 2005)

This chapter provides a long-term historical and comparative approach to heterosexual physical aggression against women by intimate partners, especially husbands, in representative areas of Spanish America (Mexico, Guatemala, Costa Rica, Colombia, Venezuela, Peru, Argentina, and Puerto Rico). The chapter tries to assess the reasons behind this aggression and the legal responses to the problem. As the sources cited make clear, abundant historical research has focussed on domestic violence in specific regions and periods, as well as on its legal ramifications. I should mention in particular an ambitious interdisciplinary long-term approach to state/gender relations in Latin America (Dore and Molyneux, 2000). Furthermore, there is the long-term perspective on women, property rights and the law (León de Leal and Deere, 2001); a comprehensive overview of gender and society, politics, the economy and demography in Latin America since the 1970s (Chant and Craske, 2003); and a review of the historiography ('Gender and Sexuality in Latin America', 2001).

To date, however, there has been no study addressing the overall evolution of the phenomenon in Spanish America from a long-term and comparative perspective; this chapter is a preliminary effort to fill the gap. At the same time, it is an attempt to assess to what extent domestic violence has declined over 200 years, as the influential work of sociologist Norbert Elias predicted that all forms of violence would, in response to 'civilising processes' (Elias, [1934, 1978] 1994).

According to a comprehensive definition developed recently by the United Nations (UN) World Health Organisation, heterosexual 'intimate-partner violence' includes not only acts of physical aggression (slapping, hitting, kicking, beating, punching and more severe assaults) but also psychological abuse (intimidation, constant belittling and humiliation), forced intercourse and other forms of sexual coercion, and a series of controlling behaviours, such as isolating a woman from family and friends, monitoring her movements or restricting her access to information and assistance (Heise and García-Moreno, 2002: 89). The historical evidence typically available (police and criminal justice records, divorce records, newspaper chronicles, congressional debates, legislation) is more ample for physical aggression than for other modalities of domestic violence. Due to the evidentiary and related limitations, this chapter focuses mainly on physical aggression by spouses against women in the Hispanic American world, with passing references to abuse by lovers, and sexual and psychological abuse.

Today, the United Nations Population Fund considers gender-based violence 'perhaps the most widespread and socially tolerated of human rights violations' (UNFPA, 2005: 65–73) In addition, as the UN contends, intimate-partner violence represents a serious public health problem at the world level. This, together with evidence concerning historical trends in the United States and Europe, leads us to believe that, instead of diminishing with the progress of civilisation the problem has either increased or at best remained constant through time (Ramírez-Rodríguez, 2006: 318). However, quantifying the increase or decrease over time in the magnitude of the various modalities of intimate-partner violence is difficult. So is quantifying its relative variation across different countries of Spanish America. Only in the last few decades have some countries begun gathering systematic statistical information about these behaviours and crime in general. Information for earlier periods is fragmentary.

Interpersonal violence has been the subject of more systematic historical inquiry in the United States and Europe; not so in Latin America. Randolph Roth (2009) found that peacetime murder rates in the British American colonies ranged from 100 to 500 annually per 100,000 adults. The murder rate in the United States today is ten to 50 times lower, a product of long-lasting political stability and increasing solidarity among subjects. In a recent book summarising the available scholarship on the long-term evolution of murder in Europe from medieval to recent times, Pieter Spierenburg (2008) concludes that in the 'Old Continent' murder and other forms of interpersonal violence have decreased considerably over time. A chart concerning homicides in Europe from the 1450s to the 2000s indicates a decline from 35 to less than five per 100,000 inhabitants annually. This was in part a result of Norbert Elias's 'civilising process'. The monopolisation of force by the state, the reduction of inter-state conflicts, stronger social integration, and increased individual self-restraint were factors influencing such a process.

However, domestic homicides seem to have followed a different trend. The dramatic decline in the homicide rate in the United States did not take place in the case of homicides involving lovers, spouses and other relatives. Roth (2009: 108) found that, from the seventeenth to the nineteenth centuries, family and intimate homicide rates varied very little. Apparently, these rates responded to distinct forces from those driving homicides among unrelated adults. Contrary to the decline of murder rates, in Europe also domestic violence seems to have actually increased considerably. The percentage of intimate homicides rose from 5 to 10 percent of all murders in the seventeenth century to 30 to 50 percent of all murders in the nineteenth and twentieth centuries (Spierenburg, 2008: 133–134) – note, however, that this is a *relative* increase (see the introductory chapter to this volume). Norbert Elias's model did not address domestic violence, only forms of male public violence in wars, and male interpersonal violence associated with processes of state-formation. The increasing proportion of domestic aggressions has been attributed to factors such as the reluctance of the state to interfere with 'private conflicts', social tolerance, prevailing honour codes and legal discourses – for Elias's lack of attention to gender violence, see Fletcher (1997: 49–50); for reasons behind the increasing rate of domestic violence in Spain, see De la Pascua (2002: 86), and Spierenburg (2008: 135). Legal discourses, in particular those found in criminal and civil codes concerning the understanding of the 'appropriate correction' to which husbands were entitled and the general treatment of domestic disputes, are particularly emphasised in this work.

In the Spanish American world, from the early nineteenth century all the way through to the present, women have been regular victims of physical, psychological, and sexual abuse by their intimate partners. In the past, and today, such abuse has involved disputes over autonomy, obedience, deference, sex, money, domestic chores, children, relatives, and drinking. In general, it could be said that domestic violence was related to clashes over the understanding of reciprocal marital rights and duties. The triggering factors have typically included alleged disobedience on the part of women, their response to verbal attacks by partners, failure to prepare and serve meals correctly or on time, alleged neglect of household or child care duties, impertinent questions about money or relations with other women, unjustified absence from the domestic space, refusal to have sexual intercourse, or suspected infidelity (Stern, 1995; Heise and García-Moreno, 2001: 95). These tensions have operated in a sexist and patriarchal social and cultural context in which men concentrate power, status and authority in both public and private spaces, deriving from their power sexual, economic, social, political and cultural benefits.

To understand the long-term evolution of domestic violence, this chapter focuses on representative countries in North, Central and South America, and the Caribbean, for which valuable evidence is available. It addresses in particular periods of economic, social, political, and formal legal change in which substantial transformations in gender relations and practices did not always occur. First, it examines the early post-colonial decades, a time of possible transition in the regulation of patriarchy (understood as the socially constructed and sanctioned authority and power of senior males over family and, more specifically, the power over female sexuality, mobility, labour, property, and general comportment) – for meanings and uses of patriarchy with regard to gender inequalities and hierarchies and an operational definition for historical research purposes, see Stern (1995: 21). This was a time when most of the new nations in Latin America were forged, as well as some modern state institutions, including civil and criminal codes containing family-related provisions. Subsequently, it looks broadly at the third quarter of the nineteenth century, in particular the 1850s to 1880s, to see to what extent the advent of a secularising and progressive liberal ideology may have been a watershed in matters of policy and conduct relating to domestic abuse. Third, the chapter examines another period of general change, the 'long' early twentieth century, approximately the 1890s to 1940s, when modernisation derived from a rapid process of export growth is alleged to have caused major material, social, cultural and institutional transformations. These changes included another wave of legal reforms and codifications leading to modernised forms of patriarchy. To conclude, it examines the decades from the 1980s to the present, a time of progressive legal change, both nationally and internationally, that coincided with the availability of national and international polls, well-developed medical surveys and measurement instruments, and regular country-wide official statistics. These innovations, in some cases, may yield more accurate information about various trends, including the intensity and general rate of intimate-partner violence across the region.

In the final section we discuss the internationalisation of concern over, and policies regarding, domestic abuse, through the intervention of the UN and its different organisms and similar international and global entities, such as the Pan-American Health Organisation, the World Bank, and the Interamerican

Development Bank. This transition to a world forum marks a significant change from the mostly private and national treatment given previously to patriarchal power and domestic abuse in each country. In the historical process under examination we seem to be witnessing the exit of patriarchy and family violence from the privacy of the home (where it was tolerated): first, to each country's public sphere, where it was ineffectually forbidden and chastised; and, then, to the international sphere, where pressure has been building to reduce it, as a global human rights and public health concern. Today, intimate-partner violence is no longer a merely private issue but is a public and truly international concern – a positive development, even if the problem is far from over in Latin America.

Liberal Patriarchy: Increasingly Secular Polities without Domestic Peace

In the three decades after independence, and through part of the second half of the nineteenth century, some preliminary evidence is available to discuss the evolution of intimate-partner violence and legal responses to it in countries such as Bolivia, Colombia, Mexico, Peru,Venezuela and the island of Puerto Rico (at the time still a Spanish possession). All of these societies had experienced significant demographic changes as a result of the wars of independence, internal migration, and natural population growth. Mexico City continued to be the largest urban centre in Spanish America, with a population of between 160,000 and 200,000 in 1850. Half of the city's inhabitants were descendants of Spaniards and the rest Indians, mixed race, and Afro descendants (Wasserman, 2000: 37; Almandoz Marte, 2002: 15). Lima had over 90,000 inhabitants in the mid-1850 s, of whom more than one-third were Indians, another third were whites, and the rest a mixture of blacks and *mestizos*. Buenos Aires also had a population of about 90,000, with whites representing just about one-third (Bethell, 1987: 338; Hunefeldt, 2000: 19; Almandoz Marte, 2002: 15, 231). Santafé de Bogotá and Caracas averaged 40,000 and 35,000 respectively; in both cities, non-whites represented a fair share of the population. At the time San Juan de Puerto Rico was a city of just over 13,000 people, most of whom were people of colour and female (Matos Rodríguez, 1999: 37). Even by the mid-nineteenth century, all of the countries and territories in question continued to be predominantly agrarian with livestock-based economies, plus some mining, internal trade and very limited industry (in particular textile mills) and, in at least some places, incipient railroads.

Although the available census data are defective, women seem to have outnumbered men slightly by the middle of the nineteenth century in places such as Mexico City. The rate of marriage at the time continued to be relatively low, with close to 50 percent of adult women marrying, and almost one-sixth (mostly Spanish women) remaining single. Consensual unions were widespread, however, especially among the lower classes. In addition, some women married rather late in life, although the average marriage age was twenty for women and 23 for men. By the time they were in their 40s, women had as many as five surviving children, despite high infant mortality rates (with almost one-third of children born then dying) (Arrom, 1985: 98–153). It is difficult to generalise across Spanish America. These are just approximations that may not hold true for other cities and regions. If anything characterised the Spanish American family during this and other moments of history, it was diversity. Intimate-partner violence, though, followed more or less the same patterns wherever it happened to be recorded.

Overall, the mostly qualitative information available leads to the conclusion that, in spite of the enactment of 'modern' civil and criminal codes, as well as the secularisation in the treatment of family relations and domestic disputes, there was more continuity than change in these areas, relative to colonial times. Domestic violence continued to be a common feature of everyday family life, was perceived as an entirely private matter, and elicited a mild response from justice officials. Husbands continued to exert *patria potestad* over their children or *potestad marital* over their wives. They proclaimed and enforced their right to reprehend disobedient wives, and mete out 'moderate' punishment (whatever this meant). They continued to justify this by citing insolence, attacks against their honour, alleged infidelity, or simply uncontrollable passion or confusion, all regarded as extenuating circumstances under the law.

There is historical evidence that, during the 1830s, in parts of Northern Mexico such as Laredo and Matamoros, some Catholic clergymen were in favour of separating married couples in cases of pervasive domestic violence. When some of these regions, including Texas, were incorporated into the United States in the late 1840s, women seem to have found it much easier to have violent husbands prosecuted and even punished (Valerio Jiménez, 2009: 16, 25). A rich study relies on more than 500 judicial cases from the 1850s to the 1890s, including 292 incidents of divorce. The majority of cases involved the middle classes, a minority the wealthy, and an intermediate figure, about one-quarter, the poor (García Peña, 2006: 78–80). Abusive husbands were the main reason that wives sought divorce during these four decades; for the entire century, this complaint accounted for about two-thirds of petitions. Husbands alleged abuses by their wives in less than 10 percent of the cases (García Peña, 2006: 88–89).

Semantic and rhetorical debates persisted in Mexico in the second half of the nineteenth century over what constituted abuse and what was acceptable 'correction' of insubordinate wives (García Peña, 2006: 94). Husbands continued to batter their wives and claim the authority to reprehend their insolent, disobedient, and irresponsible behaviour.[1] An important change in most regions of Mexico during the 1850s was the secularisation of divorce proceedings; instead of ecclesiastical tribunals, civil judges were charged with hearing divorce cases. In the portions of Mexico annexed by the United States in the late 1840s, women experienced this change a decade earlier, when US civil officials (rather than the Catholic Church) began hearing divorce cases and resolving domestic disputes (Valerio Jiménez, 2009: 10–33). By the mid-century, therefore, the mores and beliefs of Catholic priests ceased to be the driving force in resolving battery and domestic disputes; secular magistrates decided on such cases.

In the 1870s, divorce petitions in Mexico soared suddenly; divorce suits rose from an average of 60 annually to almost twice that number, a total of 104. Although this could be a function of patchy and irregular records, the increase has been attributed to the enactment of legal reforms, including the 23 July 1859 law of civil marriage and the new pro-divorce Civil Code introduced in 1866, under Emperor Maximilian. In 1871, after Maximilian had been deposed, a new code prohibited civil divorce, forcing spouses once more into conciliation (García Peña, 2006: 109). However, although it did not necessarily bring greater equality for women, liberalism did increase the 'criminalisation of domestic violence'. In places like the rural *pueblo* of Namiquipa, Chihuahua, men accused of domestic violence were put in jail and many were reprimanded by judges and sentenced to between eight and 30 days in the local jail. Not a few were recidivists who continued to assert their right to 'correct' their wives. Judicial authorities also continued to favour women who showed 'subordination to domestic patriarchy' (Alonso, 1995: 41).

In Colombia, liberal developments in the treatment of domestic conflicts may have been related to the Criminal Code of 1837, the first comprehensive post-colonial statute on crime. Modelled on the 1810 French Code and the Spanish Code of 1822, this was not just a liberal statute but contained utilitarian and natural law-based doctrines. It included provisions for 'threats against domestic authority', as well as the criminalisation of misconduct against fathers by their offspring and wives. The Code also contained penalties for men who mistreated their wives, abandoned them, or engaged in dissolute behaviour (*conducta relajada*) (Peñas Felizzola, 2006: 73–75; Villegas del Castillo, 2006: 76).

---

1   The same study alludes to over 30 ecclesiastical requests for the annulment of Catholic marriages, yet it does not touch on intimate-partner violence, this being an unacceptable cause for annulment (García Peña, 2006: 121–123).

As could be expected from historical patterns, more women than men denounced spousal violence in judicial courts and tribunals in the republican era. In their complaints, men typically accused their wives of insolence, sexual liaisons with other men (*amancebamiento*), or concubinage. Republican judges frequently settled cases of battery, psychological and verbal abuse by admonishing couples to mend their ways in order to preserve (and fit the ideal of) a truly Catholic union. If domestic disputes caused *escándalo público* and judicial admonishments did not suffice, man and wife could, according to Article 472 of the Colombian Penal Code, be detained separately in a *casa de reclusión* at the discretion of the judge for no more than one year (Colombia, Congreso de la República, 1837; Villegas del Castillo, 2006: 75–77). Several women subjected to this procedure reported being mistreated from early on in their marriages; they turned for help to neighbours, friends and relatives before reporting the situation to the authorities, normally several different ones. First, they appealed to local mayors, then talked to priests and the ecclesiastical authorities, and finally resorted to criminal courts. Some of the most recent works on this topic, while otherwise informative and useful, do not elabourate statistically on the situation (Villegas del Castillo, 2006).

During the height of a liberal revolution, in the mid-1850s, Colombia passed laws instituting civil marriage and divorce. As a result of the Church's and the Conservative Party's opposition, however, civil divorce was again outlawed three years later; two decades thereafter, civil marriage was restricted to non-Catholics. Except for short interludes, therefore, during the second half of the nineteenth century Colombian women who sought redress from abusive husbands had no better chance of controlling male patriarchs than their colonial predecessors (León de Leal and Rodríguez Sáenz, 2005: 41). Whereas civil legislation, for instance, stated that husbands were obliged to 'protect' their wives, it also ruled that women were, in turn, obliged to 'obey' their husbands (Article 176). The Civil Code of 1873 also gave husbands *potestad marital*, understood as a series of rights over wives and their property. They included the right to administer common patrimony and even the wife's property; the right to determine the couple's place of residence, and be followed by the wife whenever this changed; and the right to authorise wives to sign contracts or appear in court, save in criminal cases against them or in lawsuits filed by them against their husbands (Articles 178, 180, 181, 182), logically including petitions for divorce or criminal accusations. Civil legislation considered domestic violence valid grounds for divorce, but only in cases where the life of the spouse was endangered or 'domestic peace and quiet' became impossible (Article 154, no. 5). In 'urgent cases', once divorce proceedings began, judges could order women to be 'deposited' in the homes of their parents or close relatives as a protective measure (Article 157, no. 2) (*Código Penal de los Estados Unidos de Colombia*, 1873).

Criminal legislation clearly favoured men; it failed to consider domestic violence as a serious offence. According to the Criminal Ccode of 1873, still in force during the period under consideration, men who battered or killed their wives as a result of an 'involuntary lapse of reason' (Article 87), or during 'absolutely involuntary inebriation' (Article 88), were excused of any responsibility for their actions. Although committing a crime against a woman was an aggravating circumstance (Article 100, no. 9), several extenuating circumstances brought lighter penalties for crimes of domestic violence. These circumstances included crimes committed 'for love' (*por amor*) under momentary provocation or agitation, or as a result of the 'sudden influence of passion' (Article 101, no. 2). 'Simple homicide', the least severe form of homicide and punishable by four to six years in prison, included murders committed under the effect of 'sudden passions' or in order to defend one's 'honour' (Article 461). Another extenuating circumstance was the element of 'surprise', which included finding one's 'legitimate wife' in bed or performing 'preparatory' acts with another man (Article 466, no. 6). In this case, the punishment was reduced to between six months and two years in prison (Article 467). The same leniency was shown to men who, under similar circumstances, battered, but did not kill, their wives (Article 500) (*Código Penal de los Estados Unidos de Colombia*, 1873).

In early republican Venezuela, married women could file suits against their husbands in criminal courts, without the marital authorisation required in colonial times. Although there is no reliable statistical information about this matter, wives seem to have understood and made use of their newly granted citizenship rights. They were ready to accuse men and petition for divorce, not only in cases of regular physical abuse but also in instances of affronts to their dignity and honour, including, for example, the use of foul language (Díaz, 2004: 154–156). The law, however, sanctioned the submission of wives to their husbands, depriving them of a real juridical identity. Even the liberal Civil Code of 1873 did this, although it introduced the complete secularisation of marriage. This brought about some modification of the divorce laws: a husband's adultery now became valid ground for divorce, as long as he and his concubine lived in his house or a 'publicly known place', thereby causing insult to the wife. Physical abuse continued to be a valid cause for divorce, but only when it was 'extreme'. Still, in a sample of divorce cases from 1875 to1880, the largest group (almost 60 percent) cited physical abuse or abandonment by husbands (Díaz, 2004: 197–205, 297).

Research in Peru has found that between 4 and 6 percent of all nineteenth-century couples in Lima and other cities were involved in divorce suits, some of which were caused by intimate-partner violence. Unlike in Mexico or Venezuela, post-independence Peru did not experience a liberal transfer of jurisdiction over divorce cases, from the Catholic Church to civil authorities.

Until 1918, the clergy continued to play a leading role in mediating domestic disputes, even those arising from physical violence. Priests usually encouraged estranged spouses to reconcile (Hunefeldt, 2000: 148); some studies report increased state intervention in marital conflicts after independence. The police, however, took limited action in cases of battery. Some men excused themselves by claiming that they were 'defending their honour' against their wives' infidelity (Christiansen, 2004: 48, 66, 69–70). In Peru, on the question of domestic violence, there appears to have been more continuity than change, with regard to the colonial period.

Continuity also seems to have been the norm in neighboring Bolivia, where *de facto* social and gender hierarchies favouring domestic violence prevailed. The solemn proclamation of new civil and criminal codes in 1831 and 1832, and the legal establishment of a secularised society with formal equality, did nothing to reduce domestic violence. The Bolivian Civil Code, for instance, granted husbands the authority to use 'moderate domestic punishments' against disobedient wives who refused to change their behaviour. This provision was broad enough to legitimate intimate-partner violence of a 'benevolent' kind (Barragán, 2005: 66–86).

Records from northern and interior Puerto Rico, including the coffee-producing region of Ponce, show domestic violence to have been an ordinary fact of daily life in approximately the last three decades of Spanish rule (1860–1895). Intimate-partner violence was treated as a negligible misdemeanour, handled, not by criminal or ecclesiastical courts, but rather by justices of the peace, laymen who settled minor local conflicts. Despite the fact that most divorce petitions by women of all social groups were based on domestic violence, divorce itself (based on any grounds) 'was virtually impossible to obtain' until the late 1880 s. This meant that even those women who suffered 'brutal beatings, lashings with horsewhips, and knife wounds' had 'no chance of actually being formally released from their abusive marriages' (Suárez Findlay, 1999: 113–114). Once a divorce petition was accepted, the woman was placed on *depósito*, under the care of a 'respectable family'. Husbands were required to pay for their room and board and prohibited from harassing or visiting them during the proceedings. The handful of divorce cases actually filed at the time made all of these provisions meaningless in practical terms. Ultimately, gender hierarchies in that territory empowered husbands to repress their wives. The island's first modern criminal code, issued in Spain in 1822, allowed husbands to punish disobedient wives. In cases of injuries, marriage acted as an extenuating circumstance; in 1870, a new Spanish penal code, imbued with liberal and humanitarian ideals, made marriage an aggravating circumstance instead, under the logic that civil legislation imposed on husbands the duty to protect their spouses. At the same time, however, the 1870 code condoned domestic violence when it resulted from the husband's jealousy, the wife's disobedience, from 'irresistible impulses' or from 'passionate states of mind'. This gave aggressors a justification for their actions and, in practical terms, was tantamount to eliminating any possible aggravation of their crimes (Cubano Iguina, 2002: 129–145; Cubano Iguina, 2004: 543–544; Cubano Iguina, 2006). The Spanish Civil Code of 1889 finally granted the possibility of civil matrimony, and also divorce from civil marriages, although religious marriages remained indissoluble. Therefore, almost until the end of Spanish rule in 1898, Puerto Rican women had little official protection from domestic violence; for the entire island, only 26 divorce cases reached advanced proceedings between 1840 and 1898, with domestic violence accounting for most of them (Suárez Findlay, 1999: 113–114); 22 of these were filed by women, but, because of the resistance of church officials, only three of them were ever decided, As will be seen later, the US occupation brought reforms in family law that made it easier to break the bonds of abusive marriages.

The enactment of republican constitutions, modern civil and criminal codes, and some pro-divorce and secularising legislation, does not seem to have had any significant effect on the way in which civil and ecclesiastical authorities approached the problem of intimate-partner violence. Battered women continued to face major difficulties when seeking redress, not only because of the persistence of deeply entrenched cultural values and social practices, but also because the law left husbands with various avenues to justify their conduct. Even when physical, psychological or sexual harm resulted, for one of the parties, the authorities continued to perceive family relations as a fundamentally private matter.

Modernised Patriarchy: The Long Early Twentieth Century

In the last quarter of the nineteenth century, many Latin American nations experienced major economic and social transformations, as a result of the boom in the export of agrarian and mining products. Industrialisation, led by export growth, also entered the scene, mostly represented by food-processing plants, breweries, textile mills and railroad expansion. Economic progress accompanied the growth of cities and population in general, a growth sometimes driven by internal migration or massive foreign immigration. The Mexican population as a whole grew from around 8 million inhabitants in the 1850s to 15 million in the 1910s; the population of Mexico City doubled between 1869 and 1910, jumping from 230,000 to 470,000 inhabitants, many of whom were internal migrants (McCaa, 2000; Wasserman, 2000: 198). The population of Colombia grew more slowly, partly as a result of civil war, increasing by just over 1 percent per year between 1870 and 1930; even so,Bogotá grew from around 41,000 inhabitants in 1870 to 121,000 in 1912

(Salvucci, 2006: 278). Population growth also occurred in Peru, which by 1910 was a country of 4 million; Lima was by then a city of 170,000, compared to 100,000 in the 1870 s. At this point in the nineteenth century, the Argentine population was about 1.8 million, only one-third of whom lived in cities such as Buenos Aires, then a place of about 182,000. The influx of immigrants was massive in the following four decades, however, and by 1914 the entire country totalled 7.8 million inhabitants, with close to 1.6 million living in Buenos Aires. Puerto Rico, to take one final example, saw its population increase from about 500,000 to more than 1.1 million over the same period, with San Juan growing from a city of around 18,000 to more than 48,000 by 1910 (Lahmeyer, n.d.: 83–84). Material progress and demographic growth, as might be expected, brought about changes in the composition and dynamics of households, but, unfortunately, these changes did not include a reduction in the incidence of domestic violence.

Judging by information for Lima, infant mortality continued to be high (around 23 percent), and both life expectancy and fertility (2.1 children) were rather low in the late nineteenth and early twentieth centuries. Low fertility, one might add, applied to both formal and informal unions; one-third of couples did not have any children at all. Informal unions were numerous and were the source of around 20 percent of all children born at the time, while one-third of legitimate children were the offspring of couples who had migrated from elsewhere in Peru and then married in the capital. Although not as impressive as in Argentina, foreign immigration was significant enough to account for about one-seventh of marriages in Lima; it was also one of the causes, along with self-reporting, for the relative increase of whites and the steady growth in the mestizo population, which jumped from 44 percent in 1812 to 82 percent in 1920. The percentage of the indigenous population seems to have fluctuated, but there was an apparent decrease in the number of blacks. During the nineteenth century, a large number of the city's households, mestizo or otherwise, lived in overcrowded neighbourhoods and on the outskirts of the city. To supplement the meagre household income, numerous women worked as low-paid seamstresses, domestics, laundresses and cooks. Most men worked in agriculture, although a minority were active in small industries, the guano export sector or related trades such as the railroads (Hunefeldt, 2000: 20–30). Another proportion worked in the service sector, particularly taverns that sold corn beer (*chicha*) and sugar cane-based alcohol. As was the case elsewhere, liquor consumption was significant and led to an increase in violence (Hunefeldt, 2000: 43). In Peru and elsewhere, a fair share of such violence targetted female partners.

In Mexico, as a detailed local study demonstrates, women continued to experience a high incidence of domestic abuse and other forms of violence during the period 1880–1910. On the eve of the Mexican Revolution, in the rural peasant district of Tenango, in central Mexico, women rarely committed any violent crimes against men and were responsible for just a handful of other types of criminal conduct (such as theft or adultery). At the same time, they were the regular victims of various forms of violence at the hands of men, including both individual and collective rape, battery and deadly attacks. Of a sample of 138 cases of physical violence in the region over a 30-year period, 80 percent were committed by husbands or intimate partners of the victims. In three-quarters of all cases of aggression against female intimate- partners by formal or common-law husbands, men accused women of failing to prepare meals on time or serve them politely, leaving the house without permission, or disobeying their orders. Tenango's men also used violence when their intimate partners complained about their affairs with other women or their drinking. The most severe form of violence appears to have occurred when local women were accused of infidelity; suspected adulteresses were often killed, their corpses skewered with a stick (*empalar*), and left along a public road as a warning to other women of the consequences of such behaviour (González Montes and Iracheta Cenegorta, 1987: 111–141, 128–131).

It was not just in rural Mexico that domestic violence continued to haunt women. Recent research demonstrates the 'systemic and systematic' nature of such violence throughout the entire country. Unless it led to death, bloodshed or excessive publicity, the seriousness of violence against women was minimised by both the press and the judicial system (Buffington, 2005: 291, 315; Piccato, 2001: 105–107). Widespread, and neglected by authorities and the media, domestic violence against women was considerably under-reported; public opinion considered it a normal aspect of domestic life. As the problem remained confined within the private sphere, judicial activity failed to reflect its true magnitude (Piccato, 2001: 79, 108, 110). Though available statistics are defective, they indicate that the majority of cases were brought by women, rather than men: 80 percent of a sample of 113 cases of injuries and homicides committed between 1900 and 1930 (Piccato, 2001: 111; Speckman Guerra, 2006: 63). The women in these cases were battered for reasons that should by now seem familiar: not delivering meals appropriately, speaking disrespectfully, being suspected of infidelity, leaving the home without authorisation, and so on (Piccato, 2001: 77–131).

The criminal legislation in place at the time, the Code of 1871, afforded men several valid excuses or extenuating circumstances (Speckman Guerra, 2002). The main excuse was the defence of one's honour. For instance, husbands who found their wives committing adultery received one-sixth of the regular sentence for battery, and a shorter sentence for homicide. Battery received no punishment at all if it was performed in 'the exercise of the right to punish the victim, even if the correction is excessive'. (Piccato, 2001: 82; Rivera Reynaldos, 2006: 2–10). Detailed research on 'crimes of passion' in Guanajuato and Querétaro has found that consideration of men's honour and 'justifiable' jealousy and rage meant that spousal murder was punished rather lightly. Death sentences were usually commuted to jail terms, which were further reduced upon completion of one-quarter of the penalty (Rivera Reynaldos, 2006: 3–4). Punishment was also waived in cases of drunkenness, a relatively common circumstance among abusive husbands (Piccato, 2001: 85). While passion and rage were invoked as valid excuses to explain male violence against intimate partners, women who committed similar crimes were censured and, with a few notable exceptions, condemned (Speckman Guerra, 1998: 113–139; Rivera Reynaldos, 2006: 4–7; Macías González, 2009: 239). Women could not even press charges against adulterous husbands unless the adultery was committed in the couple's home, caused public scandal or involved a steady concubine (Piccato, 2001: 108). In other words, the material progress and the claim to 'modernity' of the Porfiriato was not accompanied by significant changes in the way that Mexican justice approached domestic violence.

Even after the enactment, by revolutionary leader Venustiano Carranza, of a 1914 decree legalising divorce, the pro-divorce provisions of the 1917 Constitution (February 1917), and the fairly egalitarian Law of Family Relations (9 April 1917), sexual double standards and patriarchal practices continued in Mexico. To be sure, the modernised *patria potestad* was now shared by husband and wife, women were given the right to administer their property and to enter into contracts without their husbands' permission, divorce by mutual consent became possible, adultery became illegal irrespective of gender, and, as long as it rendered marital life 'impossible', battery was also a gender-neutral cause for divorce (Article 76, no. vii). However, women still needed their husband's permission to work outside the home and were charged exclusively with the household duties (*asuntos domésticos*). Furthermore, whereas female adultery was 'always' a cause for divorce, male adultery was only a cause for divorce when it took place in the family home or was combined with concubinage, public scandal, insult or ill treatment of the wife, either by the husband or his lover (Article 77). Finally, divorced men were allowed to marry much sooner than divorced women, who had to wait 300 days after the dissolution of their first marriage (Article 140). Thus, not even the Mexican Revolution was able to put an end to patriarchal rule (McGee Deutsch, 1991: 266–271).

In Colombia, for the period under consideration, historical research on the issue of domestic violence is scarce. Judging by trends in Mexico and neighbouring countries, however, we can assume that such cases persisted. Colombian law continued to favour husbands over wives. The new conservative Criminal Code of 1890 made victimising women an aggravating circumstance for any crime (Law 19, art. 117, no. 10), yet the same code provided abusive husbands with a number of expedients to defend themselves when charged. For instance, those involuntarily 'deprived of their reason' at the time of the crime would not be responsible for their conduct (Article 29, no. 1). The code also stated that crimes committed 'on account of love', during momentary rage or as a result of 'passion' (Art. 118, no. 2), and those committed under 'involuntary inebriation' (Art. 118, no. 6), were to receive lighter sentences. Like the 1873 Criminal Code, the 1890 law also included killings committed to protect one's honour (Article 587, nos 1 and 2) or as a result of sudden outbursts of passion (Article 587, no. 6) in the lightest category of intentional homicide (*homicidio voluntario*), punishable by six to twelve years in prison (Article 600). Offenders who killed as a result of an 'excessive use of the prerogative to discipline' persons under their charge were subject to a reduced penalty of four to eight years in prison (Article 601); if the homicide was committed to avenge an insult or attack against one's honour, the punishment was a mere six months to one year (Article 604). The 1890 statute waived all punishment for husbands who killed wives or daughters found having sex or 'preparing for it' with men other than their legitimate husbands (Article 591, no. 9). The exemption from penal responsibility extended to killing the men surprised in these acts (*Código Penal de la República de Colombia*, ([1890] 1906). Lighter punishments were also applied to men who injured their spouses under circumstances like those just described (Art. 660). While the code did contain an article that prescribed a penalty up to 50 percent more severe for men who intentionally injured their wives (Article 652), circumstances that indicated excessive zeal in exercising the right to discipline reduced the punishment to just one-fifth of the standard (Article 665). By making use of these excuses and loopholes, men tried for domestic battery or murder under this rather benevolent legislation could hope to get off with a relatively light punishment (Bernate Ochoa, 2004: 535–558).

The same applied under the 1936 Criminal Code (Código Penal de Colombia, [1936] 1937), which contained many provisions similar to some of those just examined. While decreeing harsh punishment for homicides committed against one's spouse (Article 363, no. 1) and increasing the penalty for injuries caused to pregnant women who suffered premature birth or miscarriage, it justified related crimes: these included domestic violence and killings committed 'under the necessity of self-defence [. . .] against present or unlawful violence against the person [or] his honour' (Article 25, no. 2). The new Criminal Code also reduced the penalty for crimes committed 'during a state of anger or intense suffering due to grave and unlawful provocation' (Article 28) and attenuated the liability of offenders 'acting under the influence of excusable passion or emotion caused by intense pain or under the impulse of unjustly provoked anger', considering such criminals to be 'less dangerous'

(Article 38, no. 3). Contrary to prior legislation, it also imposed lighter punishment on those acting under 'voluntary drunkenness' (Article 38, no. 5).

Perhaps the greatest liberal innovation was that men who killed or injured 'spouses, daughters or sisters of (previously) chaste life, whom they surprised in unlawful sexual intercourse', or who were co-participants in such act, were not entirely excluded from criminal responsibility, as was the case in the late nineteenth century. Like those who acted 'in a state of anger or intense suffering caused by such offence', they received a lighter punishment (Article 382). The code did leave the door open for 'judicial pardon' in cases where attenuating circumstances (such as excusable passion, intense pain, unjustly provoked anger, voluntary drunkenness, and so on) indicated a 'lesser degree of dangerousness in the guilty party' (Article 382), one of several categories typical of the Positivist criminology inspiring the statute (*Colombian Penal Code*, 1967; Speckman Guerra, 2002: 93–114). Perpetrators of domestic violence were unlikely to have been deterred by this law, which continued to offer them favourable legal treatment.

It is not surprising to find similar trends in other Latin American countries, around the same period. In Ecuador, until 1903, divorce cases continued to be handled by ecclesiastical authorities, who followed the colonial tradition of seeking the repentance of the culprit, pardon by the victim and the reconciliation of spouses. Civil divorce was introduced in 1903 and lay courts were at last put in charge of hearing divorce cases. Even then, however, for battery to justify divorce it had to be constant, habitual and atrocious. Yet, 65 percent of a sample of 211 marital disputes between 1860 and 1920 were based on battery (*sevicia atroz*), which constituted sufficient grounds for divorce only if it was permanent. Starting in 1910, when divorce by mutual consent was introduced, some women could free themselves from abusive marriages as long as their husbands were in agreement. This seems to have occurred in only 17 percent of all cases (Moscoco, 1994: 214–219). In the meantime, women went on being battered (*estropeadas*), as well as verbally and psychologically abused (Moscoco, 1994; Montufar, 1992: 377–398).

In Argentina, the Civil Code of 1869 kept ecclesiastical authorities in charge of hearing divorce cases; this continued to be the case well into the 1950s. Couples who came before ecclesiastical judges, as a result of domestic violence or other causes, were urged to reconcile; if this failed, a temporary separation could be ordered. At this point, husbands, even those accused of battery or other abuse by their wives, could petition for the women to be placed on *depósito*, i.e. under the care and vigilance of relatives or other individuals or a special institution. *Depósitos*, understood as a means to preserve male honour and female virtue and faithfulness, took place in 'honest' houses of internment, such as religious institutions, hospitals or private homes. While on *depósito*, women were treated as true detainees or prisoners, to be corrected through religious instruction, spiritual exercises, moral training and work; their release could be delayed for days, months or even a year (Ruggiero, 1992: 253–270; Gayol, 2004: 475–498). In keeping with historical trends, available divorce data for 1927 indicate that a majority (64.2 percent) of cases (841) were filed by women. Of the few cases where divorce was ultimately awarded, the majority (72 percent) were based on the husband's ill treatment and abandonment of his wife (Lavrin, 1995: 242).

In contrast with civil legislation, the Penal Code promulgated in 1886 (Código Penal de la República Argentina, [1886] 1894), contained relatively liberal provisions, some of them gender-neutral. It considered crimes against spouses an aggravating circumstance (Article 84, no. 1), and prescribed the death penalty for cases that culminated in the victim's death (Article 94).

There were some exceptions. The responsibility of offenders was considered *leve* (light) if they suffered from a 'moral affliction' and were unable to understand the consequences of their actions (Article 17, no. 2). Such offenders were generally subject to arrest for up to two months (Article 20, no. 2). The penalty was also reduced for offenders who injured another party, spouses included, after being 'provoked' or 'offended', or when injuries resulted from anger (*irritación*) or rage (*furor*) (Article 83, no. 6; Article 97). Spouses who found their mates in 'flagrant adultery' were entirely exempted from any criminal responsibility if they injured or murdered either of the lovers (Article 81, no. 12). Husbands, however, were only guilty of adultery in cases when they had a permanent concubine (*manceba*) (Article 123) (*Código Penal de la República Argentina*, 1886). Until further research on domestic violence in Argentina around this time becomes available, a summary review of the legislation suggests that men still benefitted from lighter treatment in domestic violence cases.

Soon after the United States took control of Puerto Rico in the late 1890 s, free civil marriages were legalised there; the new colonial administration favoured full divorce, as a result, in part, to numerous women's petitions for protection from violent husbands. By 1902, the new Civil Code made adultery or 'cruel treatment' by either spouse, as well as habitual drunkenness or narcotics use, valid grounds for divorce (Suárez Findlay, 1999: 121–123). This brought about a steady rise in divorce petitions, to the point that, in the eleven years from 1900 to 1911, a single judicial district handled six times as many divorce cases as had been filed in the entire island from 1840 to 1900. The leading reasons for such petitions were financial and physical abandonment by husbands. Male adultery also started to occupy a prominent place, now that standards were equalised for both sexes and men lost their traditional prerogative to maintain numerous sexual partners. Battery, the dominant cause for divorce in the nineteenth century, continued to be cited in at least 15 percent of cases. In awarding Puerto Rican women (who filed the majority of divorce petitions) the 'right to terminate abusive, shameful, or unreliable marriages', colonialism thus had a somewhat 'civilising' impact on family life (Suárez Findlay, 1999: 124–130, 133).

Even though, because of space limitations, this chapter has not dealt with the case of Brazil, it is impossible to neglect the significance of events there during the period under consideration. Public sentiment against the law's tolerance of domestic violence, in particular the large number of legally acceptable wife-killings, reached a peak in the early twentieth century. The result was the beginning of a collective 'social hygiene' campaign, sparked by middle-class female writers who published angry pieces demanding change. In early 1925, a group of male professionals followed suit with an organisation, the Brazilian Council on Social Hygiene, with the goal of ending impunity and complacency for men accused of crimes of passion. 'In courtrooms, public lecture halls, legal journals, books, professional organisations, and the popular press', one study notes, they fought against the legal protections for wife-killers and managed to bring about the revision of the Penal Code (Besse, 1989: 654). Starting in 1940, criminal legislation ceased to accept emotion or passion as a justification for killing one's spouse (Amado, 1962; Besse, 1989: 654, 1996; Caulfield, 2000). Prior to this time, as was the case elsewhere in Latin America, Brazilian women had little protection against violent outbursts from their husbands.

The long early twentieth century (1880 s–1920s) witnessed some important changes in the regulation of patriarchy, marriage and domestic violence. In addition to the further secularisation of family relations, including the widening of civil marriage rights and full divorce in at least some countries of the region, gender-neutral language found its way into some criminal codes, most notably in Argentina (1886) and Puerto Rico (1902). These codes outlawed male adultery for the first time in each country's history. As in Brazil, a few decades later, these statutes also made it illegal for husbands to kill their wives. They did not bring an end to patriarchy, not only because patriarchal customs trumped formal legal changes but also because, under civil legislation, men continued to enjoy various legal powers over women. However, they did modernise it by providing women with some additional instruments to defend their rights and fight back. And fight they did.

Even though the period from the 1940s to the 1970s witnessed the rise of industrialisation in the bigger countries of Latin America, a period during which the participation of women in the labour market inceased considerably, the legal treatment of domestic violence did not experience any significant changes. It was not until the 1980s that truly dramatic transformations took place.

Global Concern over Patriarchy: The Long Late Twentieth Century

The last three decades were a period of further demographic change, growth, urbanisation, and political and economic transformation. It was also a time of considerable legal reform, perhaps the deepest to date, in matters of domestic abuse at both the national and international levels.

Latin American societies experienced watershed historical changes in this period. In the 1990s (in part as a result of the 'debt crisis' in the previous decade), most of the region's economies, to a greater or lesser extent, introduced wide-ranging trade reforms, deregulation of labour markets, and the large-scale privatisation of utilities, banks, energy, transportation and of a number of other formerly state-owned sectors. This led to the increasing 'globalisation' and deindustrialisation of economies throughout the subcontinent. Although debate continues about the social effects of these policies, poverty, drug trafficking, violence and social unrest seem to have increased accordingly (Chant and Craske, 2003: 1–18). From the 1990s until recently, however, political systems experienced an expansion of democratic government, intense feminist organising and a number of progressive constitutional and legal reforms. Some of these reforms touched on family relations, gender equality and women's rights. The most significant legal reforms took place in the international arena, in response to long-simmering pressures from feminist movements, among others. One could even argue that concerns over human rights and, later, public health led to a true globalisation of policies toward patriarchy.

The Latin American family changed, along with the other transformations taking place in the region's societies. The size of households declined as a result of family planning programmes, promoted by international agencies, leading to between 50 percent and 70 percent contraceptive use among the married adult population (in most of Latin America, except Cuba, abortion is either illegal or acceptable only in exceptional circumstances). Improvements in diet, living standards and the reduction of poliomyelitis and smallpox brought about a significant decline in infant mortality rates. Life expectancy also rose from 61 to 68 years between the 1970s and the 1990s. Even so, the overall pace of demographic growth slowed down (Chant and Craske, 2003: 71–97).

Household diversity continued to characterise Latin America, where contractually married and informal unions, nuclear and extended families, two-parent and single-parent households remain common. There was a pronounced trend, however, toward the decline of the patriarchal household and the growth in female-headed households. This has been attributed to migration patterns, socio-legal changes in marriage and divorce, and economic restructuring (Chant and Craske, 2003: 174–181). Concomitantly, higher female enrolment in secondary education created greater employment opportunities for women and growing participation in the national labour force. Yet gender inequality persists, in part because women who face more work at home and in their communities have less freedom for extra-domestic pursuits than their male counterparts, and because of needed improvements in maternal and child health (Chant and Craske, 2003: 98–127). Data on domestic violence afford some evidence of these problems.

Table 2.1 shows some comparative statistics on intimate partner violence in various Latin American and Caribbean nations in the late 1990s.

Source: Heise and García-Moreno, 2002: 90.

As can be observed from Table 2.1, domestic violence continued to be pervasive in several Spanish American nations during the 1990s, without seeming to have declined significantly, if at all, from the 1940s to the 1980s.

If we take Mexico first, we see that, in regional studies conducted in 1996 in Guadalajara and Monterrey (listed in Table 2.1), between 17 percent and 20 percent of the women in two large samples (650 and 1,064 women, respectively), all of whom were fifteen years of age or older, had experienced domestic violence at some time in their lives. The first national survey of domestic violence conducted in 2003 (Encuesta Nacional Sobre Violencia Contra las Mujeres (ENVIM)) indicated even higher proportions; it established that two out of every ten women of fifteen years of age or older who used various public health services had suffered violence at the hands of their intimate partners during the previous year, and four out of every ten had experienced some kind of violence at the hands of people close to them (INSP, 2003). In that same year, another national survey, the Encuesta Nacional de Dinámica en las Relaciones de los Hogares (ENDIREH), showed that 47 percent of all women surveyed had suffered emotional, economic, physical or sexual violence by their intimate partners. In that group, 9 percent suffered physical violence, 8 percent economic violence and 38 percent and 29 percent were afflicted by emotional and sexual violence, respectively (INEGI, 2003).

A 2006 comprehensive study of domestic violence in Mexico set a series of innovative trends that currently characterise the field of study in this area. The first thing worth highlighting is the fact that significant quantitative and qualitative scientific research on domestic abuse in Mexico now exists in a variety of fields, including anthropology, history, epidemiology, law, medicine, nursing, psychology and sociology (Ramírez Rodríguez, 2006: 315–327). At least some of this research originates in specialised academic groups, think tanks and organisations exclusively devoted to the theme in question. These groups are interested not only in the general phenomenon but also in specialised aspects, such as its impact on reproductive and mental

Table 2.1. Physical Assault on Women by Intimate Male Partners, Selected Population Base Studies, 1982–1999

Country coverage	Year of study	Sample: Study population[a]	Size	Age (years)	Proportion of women physically assaulted by partner (%): During the previous 12 months	In current relationship	Ever
Latin America and the Caribbean							
Antigua	1990	National	I	97	29–45			30[d]
Barbados	1990	National	I	264	20–45			30[c,e]
Bolivia	1998	Three districts	I	289	≥20	17[c]		
Chile	1993	Santiago province	II	1000	22–55		26/11[f]	
Chile	1997	Santiago	II	310	15–49	23		
Colombia	1995	National	II	6097	15–49		19	
Mexico	1996	Guadalajara	III	650	≥15			27
Mexico	1996	Monterrey	III	1064	≥15			17
Nicaragua	1995	León	III	360	15–49	27/20[f]		52/37[f]
Nicaragua	1997	Managua	III	378	15–49	33/28		69
Paraguay	1998	National	III	8507	15–49	12/8[f]		28/21[f]
Peru	1995–1996	National (except Chaco region)	III	5940	15–49	31		10
Peru	1997	Metro Lima (middle income and low income)	II	359	17–55			
Puerto Rico	1995–1996	National	III	4755	15–49			13[g]
Uruguay	1997	Two regions	II[h]	545	22–55	10[e]		

Source: Part of a larger table presented in Heise and Garcia-Moreno 2002, p. 90, and originally taken from the work by L. L. Heise, M. Ellsberg an M. Gottemoeller, 1999.

[a] Study population: I = all women; II = currently married/partnered women; III = ever-married/partnered women.

[b] In past 3 months.

[c] Sample group included women who had never been in a relationship and therefore were not at risk of partner violence.

[d] Although sample included all women, rate of abuse is shown for ever married/partnered women (number not given).

[e] Physical or sexual assault.

[f] Any physical abuse/sexual abuse only.

[g] Rate of partner abuse among ever-married/partnered women recalculated from author's data.

[h] Not random sampling techniques used.

health, its particular incidence during pregnancy, its connection with the consumption of drugs and alcohol, and its relation to children's weight and emotional development (Torres Falcón, 2004). Systematic research conducted over the past fifteen years at the local, regional and national levels, mostly in urban centres, has concluded that domestic battery is a major human right and public health problem in such cities as Cuernavaca, Durango, Guadalajara, Mexico City and Monterrey, in the states of Aguascalientes, Chiapas, Jalisco, Mexico, Morelos and Puebla, and, more generally, at the national level as well (Ramírez Rodríguez and Patiño Guerra, 1997: 5–16; Alvarado-Zaldívar, 1998: 481–486: González Montes, 1998: 17–54; Granados-Shiroma and Madrigal, 1998: 107–133; Miranda, Halpering, D., Limón, F., et al., 1998: 19–26). Its greatest impact is on women from lower socio-economic groups and it tends to be hidden among the dominant social strata. Due to the widespread and intense nature of the problem and its damaging impact, local and national surveys are now conducted about this issue on a more or less regular basis, such as the Asociación Mexicana Contra la Violencia Hacia las Mujeres (1995), the Instituto Nacional de Estadística Geografía e Informática (2001) and the Instituto Nacional de Salud Pública (2003 and 2006). Information and victim-assistance centres, as well as some specialised public facilities and non-governmental organisations (NGOs), are taking a professional approach to the problem, such as the Asociación Mexicana Contra la Violencia Hacia las Mujeres (ACC), Colima´s Centro de Apoyo a la Mujer (CAM), the Centro de Investigación y Capacitación de la Mujer (CICAM), the Comisión Nacional de la Mujer, which presides over the Programa Nacional Contra la Violencia Intrafamiliar (PRONAVI) (Valdez Santiago, 2004: 417–447). By early 2009, Amnesty International estimated that Mexico had around 60 shelters (still an insufficient number, but an improvement) to protect female victims of gender violence; some of these were administered by the government and others by private social groups (Amnesty International, 2009).

All of this would have been unthinkable just several decades ago. Domestic violence in Mexico is unquestionably a public phenomenon and a source of concern for ample sectors of society interested in protecting human rights and public health, including reproductive and mental health, Mexico perhaps being the Latin American country where the clearest understanding of the issue exists. In April 1996, the Mexico City government passed the Law of Attention to and Prevention of Intra-familial Violence, the country's first (Brena Sesma, 1996: 43–45; Pérez Contreras, 2000: 909–924). In December 1997, related reforms were introduced to the country's civil, civil procedural, criminal and criminal procedural codes.[2] In the early 2000s, Mexico issued an

---

2   An additional chapter on 'domestic violence' was added to Book I, Title VI of the Civil Code, which changed its name accordingly. The Code of Civil Procedure

official national statute (Official Mexican Norm, or ONM-190-SSA-1999) to orient health services in the prevention and treatment of domestic violence. The norm required health services to report cases to the judicial authorities (ONM-190-SSA-1999). Finally, as a culmination of 30 years of feminist struggle, in December 2006 the Mexican legislature passed a law to protect women from violence in general, the Ley General de Acceso a Una Vida Libre de Violencia, the first comprehensive legislation to combat gender violence in the country. The law created, among other things, a national system to prevent violence against Mexican women and girls and to assist and protect victims.

In sum, social and official attitudes toward domestic violence have changed considerably in Mexico. Similar trends can be observed in other countries of the region as well. The 1990s brought a series of anti-domestic violence laws to various parts of Latin America, and the start of the new century witnessed yet another wave of legal reform, this time integral laws concerning violence in general against women and girls. This chapter will argue below that, rather than being a coincidence, this was in great measure the result of not only local feminist movements but also developments in international law, through which patriarchy reached truly global dimensions. In the meantime, the chapter looks briefly at some other national examples, the cases of Nicaragua, Colombia and Puerto Rico, although others, such as Guatemala, have been addressed elsewhere (Menjivar, 2008: 109–136).

Until the mid-1990s, lack of data was an obstacle to public awareness of the seriousness of domestic violence in Nicaragua. At that time, scholars from a university in León teamed up with Swedish academics and a local NGO to gather vital new information. As Table 2.1 indicates, two regional studies and a national one, conducted in the mid-1990s, found a considerable incidence of domestic violence throughout Nicaragua, the country with the highest indices in the entire chart. In the northwestern region of León, 27 percent of the women in the sample had experienced physical abuse by an intimate partner in the twelve months preceding the study, with 20 percent reporting that the abuse was severe. In the same region, 52 percent of the respondents said that they had experienced such abuse at some point in their lives, with severe cases accounting for 37 percent in this category. In Managua, in the year before the study, 33 percent of women had experienced some form

---

was amended to facilitate procedures for cases of intra-familial violence and require family judges to consider as key evidence technical concepts from public and private institutions with expertise on the subject. The Criminal Code was amended with increased penalties and economic responsibilities for offenders found guilty of various family related crimes. See Mexico (1997).

of violence and 28 percent severe physical violence. The proportion that reported having been the target of violence at some point in their lives was a staggering 69 percent in Managua. In the country as a whole, in a large sample of more than 8,000 women, 12 percent of the respondents had experienced some kind of violence in the previous year and and 8 percent described this violence as severe. In this national sample, 28 percent of respondents had suffered general violence of any kind, whereas 21 percent experienced severe physical violence at the hands of intimate partners (Ellsberg et al., 1998). The various studies agreed on the seriousness of psychological injuries and the need for protective measures, including restraining orders, to safeguard women.

These findings were generally confirmed in a 1997 study of the costs of violence in Nicaragua and Chile, carried out by the Inter-American Development Bank. Of the women consulted for this study, 70 percent had experienced domestic violence at one point or another in their lives, and 33 percent had experienced it during the year prior to the study (Morrison and Orlando, 1997). Similar findings were reiterated in a 1999 report by the UN, indicating that 94 percent of battered Nicaraguan women were also psychologically mistreated and humiliated. Because of underreporting among rural and upper-class women, the majority of cases considered involved poor women from urban areas (PNUD, 1999).

Since at least 1990, positive steps to combat domestic violence have been taken by both the Nicaraguan state and civil society. In 1990, Nicaragua established an inter-institutional National Commission against Violence, charged with establishing a National Plan on Violence against Women. Two years later, a National Women's Network against Violence was formed, with the participation of 130 groups and hundreds of individual women. That same year, the Panamerican Health Organisation identified a number of groups providing services to women all over Nicaragua: sixteen organisations, providing services in 52 alternative women's centres, in 24 towns and cities through the country (Ellsberg, Lijestrand and Winkvist, 1997: 82–92). In 1993, Men's Groups Against Violence were also created, first in Managua and then in eight more municipalities (Castañeda, 2000). Along with the efforts of the local women's movement, their male allies and service providers, several of the studies listed above responded to growing pressures derived from a number of international meetings in which Nicaragua participated and conventions to which it became a signatory. The first one was the 1993 United Nations Conference on Human Rights in Vienna, whose plan of action contained sections on women's rights and led to the UN's adoption, five months later, of a Declaration on the Elimination of Violence Against Women; then came the 9 June 1994 Belém do Pará Inter-American Convention for the Prevention, Punishment and Eradication of all Forms of Violence Against

Women, ratified by Nicaragua in 1995; finally, there were the 1994 Cairo United Nations Conference on Population and Development and the 1995 Beijing Conference on Women, both of which referred to the urgency of reducing violence against women and children, a call that reinforced actions already taking shape in Nicaragua.

In this context of growing local and international activism, Nicaragua passed a series of acts of legislation: first, an amendment to the laws on rape (Law 150, 11 June 1992); a project modelled on similar efforts in Argentina, Brazil and Peru, to create Women's and Children's Police Stations (Comisarias de la Mujer y la Niñez); and, finally, Law 230 of 19 September 1996, concerning the prevention and punishment of domestic violence. The bill was drafted by a group of female lawyers and judges, and submitted to the legislature by the national Women's Network Against Violence (WNAV), with 40,000 supporting signatures. The 1992 law broadened the definition of rape and strengthened its penalties, although it contained two controversial provisions. First, rather than weakening them, as was intended, it actually strengthened the anti-sodomy provisions of the 1974 criminal code; and, second, it denied raped women the right to an abortion (Kampwirth, 1996: 67–86). The special police stations were created jointly by the police, the National Women's Institute and alternative women's health centres, with the goal of giving women access to treatment and prevention in spaces staffed by personnel sensitive to gender needs. As for the 1996 legislation, it was ultimately passed thanks to the lobbying efforts of the WNAV. It provided female victims of violence with mechanisms to seek protection and introduced psychological injuries as a significant component of the general definition of battery. Although the new law did not stiffen penalties, it did consider family ties between victims and culprits an aggravating circumstance, warranting the highest possible punishment prescribed by law (Ellsberg, Lijestrand and Winkvist, 1998).

Independent studies conducted in Colombia during the 1980s and 1990s revealed the widespread and grave nature of domestic violence in various parts of the country (Berenguer Visbal, 1986, 1993: 110–123; Casa de la Mujer, 1988). Starting in 1990, the country also began to develop a series of ambitious national demographic and health surveys (ENDS) that every five years quantitatively documented the seriousness of the situation. The 1995 survey, which included more than 11,000 female respondents aged from fifteen to 49, served as the basis for the information on Colombia in Table 2.1. It found that one in every three women in the sample had been verbally abused by their partners, and close to one in every five women had suffered physical violence at the hands of their current partner. The most common forms of violence were slapping (88 percent), kicking (27 percent) and pushing (24 percent); lashings and beatings with leather belts, clubs or machetes were

Table 2.2.   Evolution of Domestic Violence in Colombia Over a 15 Year Period, 1990–2005

	1990[a]	1995[b]	2000[c]	2001[d]	2003–2004[e]	2005[f]
Victims of psychological violence	27% to 32%	32% to 34%	30% to 33%	26%	12% to 17%	27% to 31%
Victims of physical violence	15% to 20%	17% to 21%	38% to 44%	13% to 27%	14% to 17%	38%
Victims of sexual violence	7% to 9%	4% to 10%	7% to 14%	N/A	N/A	7% to 12%

Sources:
[a] Asociación Probienestar de la Familia Colombiana (1990): Chapter 11;
[b] Ordoñez et al. (1995): Chapter XI;
[c] Asociación Probienestar de la Familia Colombiana (2000): Chapter 12;
[d] Klevens (2001);
[e] Duque and Montoya (2008);
[f] Asociación Probienestar de la Familia Colombiana (2005): Chapter 13.

also relatively common (13 percent). The main reasons reported for such situations were a husband's drunkenness (33 percent), jealousy (28 percent), bad temper (11 percent), reactions to the woman's defence of their children (5 percent), or allegations of the woman's infidelity (2.5 percent) (Asociación Probienestar de la Familia Colombiana, 1990: 151–170). Only 27 percent of the women brought such incidents to the attention of the authorities, a proportion that seems low but was in fact more than twice as high as had been the case in the first, 1990, survey. The women who did not go to the authorities gave reasons such as a belief that they could handle the situation on their own (31 percent), fear of retaliation by their husbands (21 percent) or a belief that their husbands would change (17 percent). Others were afraid of being left alone (5 percent) or were sure that the authorities would not take their needs seriously (5 percent) (Asociación Probienestar de la Familia Colombiana, 1990: 157). The results were more or less consistent with findings from prior and subsequent studies of a similarly high scientific reliability (Asociación Probienestar de la Familia Colombiana, 1990: 165–178, 2000: 105–119, 2005: 313–342; Klevens, 2001: 78–83; Duque and Montoya, 2008: 27–39) (Table 2.2).

Similar to Nicaragua, and also in response to international and local pressures, backed by qualitative and quantitative data available for the first time, Colombia passed special legislation to contain domestic violence. With Law 248 of 29 December 1995, the country became a signatory to the 1995 Inter-American (Belém do Pará) Convention to Prevent, Eradicate and Sanction Violence Against Women. Just seven months later, on 18 July 1995, the National Congress passed Law 294 to 'prevent, correct and sanction intra-familial violence'. Under this law, victims of domestic violence became immediately entitled to protective measures, including restraining orders, and also had the right to receive special state assistance. The law described domestic violence as a 'crime against family harmony and unity' and deprived offenders who violated restraining orders of the right to parole or equivalent benefits. It also required the Colombian Institute of Family Welfare (ICBF) to design public policies to prevent and eradicate domestic violence in the country (Articles. 5, 20, 22 and 26).

Further reforms were introduced by a new criminal code (Law 599), enacted on 24 July 2000. It contained a 'title' or section exclusively devoted to crimes against the family, with a separate chapter for the crime of intra-familial violence (Book 2, Title VI). The definition of this crime was fairly broad and included physical, psychological and sexual violence. Nevertheless, it was followed later that year by Law 575 of November, 2000, a controversial statute that allowed lay justices of the peace to handle domestic violence cases. Feminist organisations charged that this went against international human rights provisions. A previous law (882, on 2 June 2004) had already narrowed the ample definition of intra-familial violence embraced by the code to exclude sexual violence, perhaps because such crimes were included in a separate section in the code and punished more harshly. The list of aggravating circumstances, however, included cases in which the victims were female , and shortly afterwards (7 July) another law toughened the punishment for such crimes, increasing the minimum penalty by one-third and the maximum by 50 percent (Law 890).

More importantly, unlike in Nicaragua, but similar to the trend observed in Mexico, on 4 December 2008 Colombia passed a law (Law 1257) to 'raise awareness of, prevent and punish all forms of violence and discrimination against women'. The law's main goal was, more precisely, to 'guarantee all women a life free from violence, both in the public and private realms, and the exercise of all rights recognised in both internal and international law, affording them administrative and judicial procedures for their protection and assistance, and the implementation of the public policies needed to make such rights effective' (Article 1). Unquestionably, this was the result not only of local efforts by human rights and women's organisations and the Colombian Congress's female caucus, but also of international developments already mentioned, and further discussed at the end of this chapter (Federación Iberoamericana del Ombudsman, 2008). Despite the various reforms, however, Table 2.2 shows that intimate-partner violence has remained constant at best, clear evidence that legal reforms are not sufficient on their own if institutional and cultural changes do not keep pace with the law.

Puerto Rico provides a final brief example of changes in the area of intimate-partner violence. As Table 2.1 shows, a national study of more than 4,700 women, aged between fifteen and 49, conducted in 1995–1996, found that 13 percent had suffered intimate-partner violence at some point in their lives. Earlier in this chapter it was noted that progressive divorce legislation in the early twentieth century had provided women with the legal mechanisms to leave violent husbands. Therefore it should be no surprise to find Puerto Rico with one of the lowest percentages of women reporting domestic violence (Paraguay had the lowest). Puerto Rico was the first place in Latin America to pass a law to combat intra-familial violence. Law 54 of August 1989 identified psychological, physical and sexual modalities of intimate-partner violence and punished intimate partners who placed unjustifiable restrictions on a woman's freedom. For the first time, this legislation incorporated protective measures, such as restraining orders to afford immediate protection to women at risk. However, according to data from the Oficina de la Procuradora de las Mujeres, and based on statistics from the Puerto Rican police, between 1990 and 2006 the number of cases of domestic violence against women reported to the authorities increased from a low of 12,593 in 1995 to a high of 19,395 in 2005. Women were the victims in 89 percent of all cases brought to the attention of the police (Vega, 2009: 2). This suggests that, even in relatively progressive and protective legal environments, intimate-partner violence can be quite resilient and hard to contain, although increasing awareness and the availability of legal recourses are unquestionable signs of progress.

In conclusion, virtually every country in Latin America has continued to record alarming levels of domestic violence in recent decades. Detailed statistics now available in several countries, including Mexico, Colombia, Nicaragua, and Puerto Rico, document this situation more scientifically than ever before. Across the region, governments have instituted watershed legal reforms, including protective measures for battered females and a host of state and civil society mechanisms for victims to receive information and assistance. The concluding portion of this chapter examines the reasons behind these changes.

Conclusion

Intimate-partner violence has gained increasing recognition in contemporary societies, but this is a recent development. Since the 1980s and 1990s, the world community has begun framing these behaviours as discriminatory and a major human rights violation. In the last decade, the World Health Organisation also elevated physical, psychological and sexual violence against women to the category of a grave public health problem (Harvey, García-Moreno and Butchart, 2007: 1). As should have become evident early on in this chapter, this acknowledgement was long overdue. There is ample historical evidence that physically, psychologically and sexually damaging acts of aggression have characterised intimate relations in Spanish America for centuries, showing considerable resilience at different moments of the 'civilising process' in the region. This has been largely the result of permissive legal discourses sanctioning patriarchal domination and related honour codes.

Of course, bits and pieces of historical information about intimate-partner violence are variegated and hard to compare with one another over the long term, a challenge common to comprehensive works in comparative historical sociology (Skocpol, 1984; Tilly, 1985: 11–52; Hunt, 2004). The earliest information can be gleaned from a combination of individual criminal cases and patchy divorce data; the most recent comes from comprehensive local, regional and national surveys and quantitative studies, based on scientific polling and systematic new measurement methods developed since the late 1970s, and put to some use mostly in the 1990s. Quantitative techniques, such as the Conflict Tactics Scale, the Index of Spouse Abuse, the Danger Assessment Instrument, or the Severity of Violence Against Women Scales are rather new, and have not yet been widely used in Latin America (Strauss, 1979: 75–88; Hudson and Mcintosh, 1981: 873–885; Campbell, 1986: 36–51; Marshall, 1992: 103–121). When combined for the sake of obtaining a tentative aggregate historical picture, the diverse data available leaves little doubt that, over the last 200-odd years, domestic violence has been widespread and pervasive in Spanish America. Rather than declining, even during periods when more aggressive legal action began to be deployed against it, it appears to have remained a constant.

Rather than serving as a deterrent, corrective and punitive legal measures have been historically insufficient in stemming the problem of domestic violence. In fact, if anything, for a long time the law largely served as an incentive for battery. Legal changes have been piecemeal, few and far between, and relatively ineffective in the face of longstanding patriarchal structures. Starting in the middle to late nineteenth century (in some cases, the early twentieth century), the most notable reforms historically included, first, a series of laws that introduced civil marriage, made divorce more widely available, and charged local secular authorities (rather than the Catholic Church) with handling domestic conflicts. Although generally restricted to 'habitual', 'cruel', 'atrocious' or 'publicly scandalous' mistreatment, these laws set limits on wives' obligation to stay in abusive marriages and afforded women avenues to leave violent partners, an opportunity that they seemed to seize in some places, such as Puerto Rico. From early on, some provisions existed to shelter abused wives by putting them on *depósito*, although, as in late nineteenth-century Argentina, men could and did use this system to their advantage. Even the legal recourses resulting from liberal or modernised versions of patriarchy, however, which took domestic violence from the private into the public arena, in the hope that redress would be found there, were no match for such a longstanding, socially rooted and culturally entrenched practice inherent to patriarchy itself. Intimate-partner violence, viewed as part of 'sporadic' and 'moderate' correction under *potestad marital*, had been a natural component of married life from times immemorial, and the mandatory 'conciliation' of disputes served to prolong it. Liberal civil laws on marriage and divorce, as well as classical and positivist criminal codes, were full of loopholes and provided male batterers or wife killers with valid excuses (e.g. unjust provocation, justifiable passion and rage, defence of one's honour, flagrant adultery, inebriation) to avoid harsh sentences (or any prosecution at all). The campaigns against wife-killing in Mexico or Brazil make it clear that extreme gender violence remained extensive well into the mid-twentieth century. Efforts to contain 'femicide' in contemporary Chile or Colombia are another reminder that we are far from breaking away from this past (Escobedo, 2007; Rozo Lesmes, 2008).

Nevertheless, there has been a dramatic increase in the amount of attention paid to domestic violence on the part of legal, human rights and public health activists in virtually every nation of Latin America over the last three decades. It has been accompanied by the establishment of new gender-sensitive and women-focussed public institutions, protective policies, awareness campaigns, service guidelines and action plans (*rutas críticas*) (Montserrat Sagot, 2000). Puerto Rico was the first Latin American country to enact comprehensive laws against violence within the family, in 1989, followed by Argentina (1994), Bolivia (1995), Chile (1994), Colombia (1996), Costa Rica (1996), Ecuador (1995), El Salvador (1996), Guatemala (1996), Honduras (1997), Mexico (1996), Nicaragua (1996), Panama (1995), Peru (1993, 1997), Trinidad and Tobago (1991), and Venezuela (1998). The same trend was occurring in other parts of the world, including Europe – Austria (1996), Belgium (1997), Great Britain (1996), Ireland (1996), Northern Ireland (1998) and Portugal (1995, 1999) – New Zealand (1995) and South Africa (1998). Most recently, more ambitious laws concerning gender violence in general have been approved in Mexico (2006) and Colombia (2008). Other countries are likely to follow suit. Is this just a remarkable coincidence? Was it the product of local efforts by well-intentioned legislators or energised national feminist movements acting in striking coordination with one another? Apparently not. Developments in international law, as civilising a force as any ever experienced before, provided the required incentives and momentum.

In 1962, under the leadership of the Dominican Republic, the women's movements of Latin America and the Caribbean selected 25 November as the day to denounce violence against women. On that day two years earlier, three Dominican women activists (the Miraval sisters, Patricia Mercedes, Minerva Argentina and María Teresa) had been killed by the Trujillo dictatorship. Three and a half decades later, in 1997, the General Assembly of the United Nations passed a formal resolution recognising that same day as the 'International Day to Eliminate Violence Against Women'. Even though it was political violence in the Spanish Caribbean that prompted the earlier marker, various forms of gender violence, including intimate-partner violence, were unquestionably central to explaining the second landmark. During this period, intimate-partner and other modalities of gender violence had become a matter of increasing concern for the women's movement, the international community and individual states in the region and elsewhere. From 1975 to 1985, the United Nations Decade for Women, numerous feminist conferences, encounters and campaigns were organised around the world. Research and writing on gender increased dramatically, along with information about the condition of women and families (Chant and Craske, 2003: 5). As we have seen, by 1997 many Latin American countries had compiled statistics and evidence of the human rights and public health significance of intimate-partner violence. A host of international actions and policies on this issue were implemented. Much as in the case of protective international policies in favour of ethnic minorities, these international rules were gradually endorsed by numerous countries, eventually became binding, and determined the passage of copycat legislation in country after country (Uribe-Uran, 2007: 83–104).

The international feminist movement gained strength thanks to a series of global women's conferences, starting with that in Mexico in 1975 to mark the start of the 'United Nations Decade for Women'. This conference led to the establishment of the International Research and Training Institute for the Advancement of Women (INSTRAW) and the United Nations Development Fund for Women (UNIFEM), designed to provide the institutional framework for research, training and operational activities in the area of 'women and development'. Follow-up conferences were held in Copenhagen (1980), Nairobi (1985) and Beijing (1995). All of these conferences served to push forward 'global' efforts to promote the advancement of women and opened a worldwide dialogue on gender equality. Each conference developed strategic objectives and platforms, culminating in a World Plan of Action that addresses a variety of gender equality fronts targetting governments, international organisations, communities and individuals. An important component of the platforms and the World Plan is the issue of gender violence, starting with intimate-partner violence, which has rightly come to be understood as a 'global problem'.

By 1992, all of Latin America and the Caribbean had ratified the UN Convention on the Elimination of All Forms of Discrimination Against Women (CEDAW). Then came the Organisation of American States' Inter-American Convention to Prevent, Punish and Eradicate Violence against Women in June 1994 (better known as the Convention of Belém do Pará). By 1998, this multilateral treaty had been ratified by almost all countries in the region, and later Grenada (2000), Suriname (2002) and Jamaica (2005) followed. Following ratification, numerous signatory nations passed their own national laws on intimate-partner violence, several of which are described above. At no other time in the history of Latin America had intimate-partner violence been considered a human rights or public health problem of global dimensions worth addressing through comprehensive legislation, specialised state and civil society institutions, and mass campaigns. It goes without saying that feminist mobilisation through the years was indispensable in making possible many of these developments, although the specific understanding of these dynamics is beyond the scope of this chapter (Dore, 1997; Chant and Craske, 2003: 19–45).

The passage of patriarchy from private to global regulation is a truly structural transition, likely to have greater impact on patterns of gender relations than liberal and modernised versions had in the past. Howver, one must not forget that patriarchy and the violence associated with it have for centuries been structural (cultural, social, economic, political) conditions – 'habitus', to use Bourdieu's expression – of world societies . The ongoing transition is likely to be protracted and likely to face all kinds of hurdles, because habitus is hard and costly to break.

3

Judging Violent Crimes: Patterns of Sentencing in Modern Argentina, 1878–1948

RICARDO D. SALVATORE

Universidad Torcuato Di Tella, Argentina

In the political and institutional history of modern Argentina the question of social order and political stability has been examined in relation to a few leading actors: ruling elites, dominant political parties, the executive, Congress and organised labour. Between 1880 and 1916, elite political control was said to be dominated by a closed political coalition that reproduced itself in office through the use of electoral fraud, federal interventions in the provinces and the outright repression of competing political groups (Alonso, 1993; Botana, 1979). This situation changed somewhat after the electoral reform of 1912, which brought a middle-class party, the Unión Cívica Radical, into government. Since the 1890s, with the emergence of radical workers' ideologies (socialism, anarchism and anarcho-syndicalism) and a militant working class, this elite became concerned about the challenge that this new actor represented to the established social order (Munck 1987: 34–90; Suriano, 2000, 2001; Camarero and Herrera, 2005). More importantly, mass immigration Argentina (1890–1930) was said to be affected by a new 'social pathology' that seemed to corrupt social norms and interactions among the lower classes: the problem of a rising criminality, as construed by newspapers, legal agents, and criminologists.

After the mid-1880s, concern with controlling the multiple aspects of deviance (crime, madness, alcoholism, vagrancy, prostitution, anarchism) grew, promoted by a new medical view of social problems, best exemplified by the emergence and consolidation of Positivist criminology (Terán, 1986; García-Alejo, 1991; Salvatore, 1992; Salessi, 1995; Rodríguez, 2006; Marteau, 2003). While it could be argued that early criminologists and police reformers paid more attention to theft and swindling than to criminal violence, in the 1920s and 1930s the emergence of organised criminal bands and the widespred use of firearms in robberies and interpersonal conflicts promoted the notion that Argentina was turning into a more violent society (Caimari, 2012). Rising union activisim during the First World War and the first violent nationalist blacklash against immigrant workers in 1919 (a pogrom called the 'Tragic Week') made social and political commentators think that there was a convergent upward movement of political and criminal violence (Seibel, 1999).

Conventional historical wisdom has minimised the role of the judicial system during the República Conservadora (1880–1916), arguing that the police (and at moments of danger, even the army) was really in charge of repressing social protests. Revisionist historiography has moderated this claim, presenting the governing elites as willing to cope with the new challenges posed by the 'workers' question' (Zimmermann, 1992, 1995; Suriano, 2000). The repressive laws aimed at evicting anarchist agitators from Argentine soil (1902 and 1910) were followed later by legislation that protected children and women in industry, reduced the working day, established Sunday rest and provided compensation for work accidents. These reforms, which included the increasing mediation of the executive in labour conflicts, were said to have pacified the social order in the sphere of productive relations, reducing the influence of the more militant factions of organised labour (mostly anarchist unions) in favour of more conciliatory and reformist unions.

Did public violence increase or decrease between the transition from the 'oligarchic republic' and the more democratic, populist administrations of the Unión Cívica Radical (UCR)? What about the evolution of violence in the 1930s and into the first years of the Peronist administration? Unfortunately, at the moment, the unreliable nature of statistics about violent crime makes it impossible to give a definite answer to this question, and the impressionistic evidence in this regard is contradictory. On the one hand, there are indications that sustain the existence of a 'civilising process' in matters of interpersonal and state violence; after 1880, the number of public executions became negligible, as courts commuted the few death sentences to long-term prison terms, and, according to Mantilla (2013: 121–138), there were only five executions between 1880 and 1920. Duels among elite men, in vogue in the late nineteenth century, declined abruptly after 1920 (Gayol, 2008). Moreover, at least in the major cities, the police increased their presence and surveillance of individuals and families (Ruibal, 1990; Barreneche and Galeano, 2008; Galeano, 2008). On the other hand, growing concerns about the spread of firearms, new sensational crimes such as kidnappings and bank-robberies, and the recurrent eruptions of street violence on election day or during political demonstrations point to the persistence of violence as a privileged means of dispute resolution and social interaction.

Few historians have attributed to the judiciary an important role in crafting the social order and the political stability that emerged between the federal compromise of 1880 and the advent of Peronism in 1945; the exceptions are Zimmermann (1999), Barreneche (2001), Palacio (2004) and Sedeillán (2009). Recent cultural studies of the intersection between crime, the police and the press have underscored the importance of popular illegalism and alternative interpretations of justice (Caimari, 2007a). Elsewhere, I have argued for a reconsideration of this view, presenting a more balanced view of the intervention of higher courts in the 'processing' of socio-political violence (Salvatore, 2009, 2010). Although Congress gave the executive exceptional legislation to deal with foreign labour agitators, and the police confronted recurrently diverse manifestations of collective action, the courts managed to maintain some minimal individual guarantees to protesters. In this chapter, I aim to extend this analysis to common crimes and examine the active role played by criminal courts in the maintenance of social order.

Judges and courts played a crucial role in tempering the violent impulses emerging from civil society and in providing greater legitimacy to government. Criminal courts processed and punished the violation of legal norms according to legal codes and procedures and, by doing so, communicated to potential offenders the costs of violating the rules. To the extent that these messages were consistently transmitted to society – by proportional penalties and consistent sentencing patterns – they played a 'civilising role' that could have contributed to the amelioration of interpersonal violence. Judges, it is often argued, 'speak through their sentences'; in a system dominated by inquisitive, written judicial procedures, criminal sentences constitute messages to society. Relatives and friends of the accused and the victim can learn about and discuss the sentences passed and the arguments that led to those decisions; reports in newspapers and magazines feed the public interest in leading cases, contributing to disseminating information about legal procedures. One way or the other – considering sentences too lenient or too harsh – public opinion passes judgment on the inadequacy of penal sentences. If this is so, the consistency in judges' sentencing patterns can provide clear messages to society about the gravity of certain offences and the penalties that accompany specific crimes.

Consistency in sentence patterns is crucial for this communicative interaction between government and governed. If judges apply more severe penalties to poor felons than to rich felons, the legitimacy of the ruling order is open to question; similarly, if judges are insensitive to the punitive demands of society against violent offenders (murderers, rapists, arsonists and kidnappers), imposing penalties that are considered too soft, a sense of injustice will grow in popular opinion. Conversely, harsh penalties applied to particular political actors (for instance, deportation of anarchist activists) can undermine the legitimacy of the ruling order. From the state perspective, judicial actors should pursue a delicate balance between duress and equity to generate the consent of the governed (Garland, 2001; Roberts and Hough, 2005; Pratt, 2007).

Much ink has been devoted to the construction of the view that, in Argentina, in the past as well as in the present, the judicial system was undermined by corruption, political favouritism and social insensibility. More importantly, the brutal repression of military regimes in the 1970s has naturalised the notion that illegality and impunity have been characteristic of Argentine public culture. Scholars have argued that the violation of legal norms is a natural condition of Argentine society and culture, and that judicial authorities have failed in their constitutional mandate to control the other powers and to administer 'justice' (Nino, 1992; Abós, 1999; O'Donnell and Méndez, 1999; Gargarella, 1996). More often than not, these generalisations are the extrapolation of a few criminal cases improperly resolved or left untried; but they cannot be extended, without further evidence, to the experience of the criminal justice system as a whole.

An informed socio-legal history should attempt to provide some historical perspective to these blanket statements and to examine whether the judicial system, through its actual practices, has showed any bias in its sentencing pattern over time. If the criminal justice system has followed the rule of trying each felony according to its particular circumstances and passing sentence according to codified penal law, one should expect that average sentences for a given felony would remain stable over time. If the diffusion of prior rulings (jurisprudence) acts as a self-correcting mechanism, we should expect that the range of variations of penalties would tend to decline over time. If this does not happen, we can speak of bias in the pattern of sentences, in relation to both law and jurisprudence. Consistent sentencing patterns tend to enhance the legitimacy of the criminal justice system.

This chapter deals with two interrelated issues: the consistency over time of the pattern of criminal sentences and the question of proportionality between crimes and penalties. In the absence of significant reforms to the penalties associated with a crime, one would expect average sentences for each felony to remain relatively constant over time. That is, that a homicide, whether committed in 1890 or in 1940, would be punished with a similar average prison term, consistent with the upper and lower boundaries established in the penal code. The second issue relates to the very existence of consistency between the criminal code and contemporary social mores, in the sense of punishing more severely those crimes that society considers more aberrant, brutal or dangerous. The Penal Code that guided the sentencing of judges during most of the period under consideration clearly showed a strong proportionality: aggravated homicide was punished with a life sentence (*prisión perpetua*), simple homicide received eight to 25 years in prison, and unintentional murder (*homicidio preter-intencional*) one to three years.

The proportionality between felonies and penalties was one of the main features of the 1886 Penal Code. This was a central argument deployed at the time of the enactment of the code, subsequently underscored by different expert commentators (Castilla, 1889; Drago, 1887). Penalties in the code reflected a progressive increase in prison terms, according to the gravity and importance of the offence: from defamation to assault, from assault to fraud, from fraud to homicide, prisons terms increased, reflecting the growing moral condemnation of society. Additional rules strengthened the proportionality between felonies and penalties: Attempted felony deserved a penalty that was one-third to one-half of the same felony, when actually carried out. A second important feature of the Penal Code was the reduction of judicial discretion, via the establishment of minimum and maximum penalties for each felony. Once the felony had been characterised – and this was very much the product of the *sumario* instruction – the judge had a relatively limited choice regarding the punishment to apply to the particular case under consideration. The Penal Code established a series of attenuating and aggravating circumstances that could reduce or increase the penalty, within the minimum and maximum boundaries established in the same code.

Hence, the Penal Code served as 'algebra' of felonies and penalties to which the judges were supposed to adapt their decisions. This double-entry matrix between offences and prison terms guaranteed the accused the principle of equal penalty for the equal crime, while ensuring society the certainty that a given prison term should be granted for those who had committed a crime specified in the Penal Code. This was expected to deter potential offenders from committing illicit activities. In principle, a judge had to establish the facts, determine the existence of a felony, identify its author or authors, classify this felony according to the Penal Code, and issue a sentence within the upper and lower boundaries determined by the code. Typically, the prosecutor argued for aggravating circumstances and requested a penalty closer to the upper boundary, while the defence presented proof of alleviating circumstances that could reduce the penalty to the lower boundary. Thus, unless the judge systematically sided with the prosecutor, it was likely that the average sentence issued would be at a midpoint between the minimum and maximum limits established in the code.

This, as we shall see, did not happen in the city of Buenos Aires and its surroundings between 1878 and 1948. Evidence provided by the register of sentences for those prisoners who entered the National Penitentiary shows that, on the contrary, prison terms increased over time, for violent crimes as well as for other types of crimes. Although this result should at this point be considered as tentative, the finding itself is so striking that it merits a preliminary investigation as to its feasibility and possible determinants. The hardening of penalties in modern Argentina – a span of time covering the period from Avellaneda's government to the first Peronist administration – is a novelty in social history that needs to be examined carefully. For, if confirmed, it would reinforce the proposition that judges, through their sentences, responded somehow to the increasing demands of Argentine society for more punitive sanctions.

Drawing on these new data, this article seeks to examine the treatment of violent crimes by criminal courts in Buenos Aires and surrounding areas. In particular, it concentrates on the attributes of certainty, proportionality and fixity of penalties, as they evolved in judicial practice. Apparently, judges passed sentence with increasing duress for felonies that earlier, at the time of enactment of the Penal Code, had been considered not so problematic or dangerous. Were they responding to the demands of a society increasingly concerned with crime and its pernicious effect on social interaction? In the absence of substantial revisions of the Penal Code, what were the legal mechanisms through which judges could increase the penalties for felonies?

The Data

The data examined comes from the Registro de Testimonios de Senten-cias, a tabulated register – now preserved in the Argentine Penitentiary Museum – that transcribed (limited) information about the sentences of all those prisoners entering the National Penitentiary. The purpose of these registers was to serve as a quick reference guide to prison administrators when, by order of judges or lawyers, they needed to consult what the prison term was to which a given convict had been sentenced and the exact date when he was due for release. These registers contained basic information about the prisoner, the felony and the sentence term; with this information, prison administrators could then search for the actual sentence, which was transcribed in a different register, the Testimonios de Sentencias.[1] Since there are quite a few collections of first-instance sentences for this period in Argen-tine archives, this source is quite important. For, in spite of their limitations and biases, the records of the National Penitentiary present the possibility of a long-term study of sentence patterns. The large sample of inmates whose information was retrieved (13,370) allows for sufficiently large samples per quinquenium (890 observations on average), which, in turn, ensures fairly unbiased estimates of average sentence terms.

---

1   Unfortunately the Testimonios de Sentencias (where the full sentences appear) are only complete for the period 1878–1911. More recent sentences appear to have been preserved separately – not in bound volumes – making its compilation and statistical processing difficult, and only fragmentary. Sandra Gayol (2000) has used these records for qualitative information. As far as we can tell, there has been no attempt at a quantitative study of sentence patterns for this period.

The Penitentiary of Buenos Aires, built in 1876 and inaugurated the following year, was a modern institution of containment and reform, modelled on US institutions. Since the early 1900s, a group of positivist criminologists took control of its administration and introduced 'modern' reforms: individual follow-up and treatment; classification of inmates according to conduct; and the use of work and elementary education as instruments of rehabilitation (García Basalo, 1979; Salvatore and Aguirre, 1996; Caimari, 2004). To this extent, the Penitentiary, later called National Penitentiary when it came under federal jurisdiction after 1880, was a peculiar institution. In 1905, the principles of 'modern penology' were extended to the Penitentiary of Sierra Chica, in the south of Buenos Aires province; both prisons then contained felons of similar 'dangerousness'. The other important prison in Buenos Aires city, the Prisión Nacional, was built to contain felons undergoing criminal trial, placed under preventive detention. Naturally, many of its detainees remained in prison for shorter terms than in both penitentiaries for, once sentenced, they were transferred to the National Penitentiary, to Sierra Chica, or to other provincial prisons. Women prisoners, usually sentenced for misdemeanours, went to the Carcel Correccional de Mujeres (Women's Correctional Prison); for this reason, my findings refer exclusively to male convicts.

Considering the country as a whole, the administration of prison sentences was fragmented into nineteen provinces and four national territories (under federal administration). Consequently, we should not expect the sentence pattern to be the same across provinces. The diversity of criteria used by provincial judges and the uneven distribution of legal information and jurisprudence in the provinces conspired against homogeneity in sentence patterns across the country. In comparison with seventeen other federal prisons, the National Penitentiary had a higher percentage of long-term prisoners. This could be related to the 1922 provision that allowed federal prisons in the provinces to send some long-term prisoners to the National Penitentiary. It also relates to the fact that, in the provinces, people sentenced by the correctional system were held usually in the same facility as people sentenced by criminal courts.

Almost all sentences issued after 1924 were expressed in prison terms. Whereas the Penal Code distinguished between three different types of prison sentences – *reclusión* (imprisonment with forced labour and no parole), *presidio* (imprisonment in a penitentiary) and *prisión* (imprisonment, without forced labour, in any prison) – commentators make clear that in practice these distintions were not maintained (Moreno, 1922: 327). Those sentenced to *reclusión* could be employed in public works, those sentenced to 'prison' could not. Felons convicted to 'prison' (*presidio* and *prisión*) had to perform work within the prison, if appropriate facilities (workshops) were available. Before the reform of 1902, the Penitentiary admitted detainees sentenced to other types of penalty: arrest, forced labour, and banishment. Almost all penalties refer to cases of wounding and other physical injuries, not to homicides or other grave crimes; these penalties practically disappeared after 1902. The death penalty, abolished in the 1922 reform, was in practice very unusual: we have found only two cases for the whole period of 1902–1924. As mentioned above, based on newspaper evidence, Mantilla has found only five deaths by execution in Buenos Aires during the period 1877–1922. Other felons sentenced to death had their sentences commuted by the courts.

Potential Biases

The sentences of the inmates of the National Penitentiary present the advantage of a common and homogenous registration for a sufficiently long period of time (1878–1948). However, there are some risks involved in this choice. First, the National Penitentiary seems to have admitted more dangerous delinquents than other federal prisons. In part, this was due to the existence in the city of the Prisión Nacional, a detention facility used to hold felons under trial. Although the National Penitentiary also contained *procesados*, these prisoners were of course not included in the register of sentences, which only annotated those convicts with a firm judicial sentence. These felons spent their 'preventive detention' in this prison or in the various police stations of the city, being sent to the National Penitentiary after their sentence was issued. This might explain why the National Penitentiary had few convicts sentenced to terms less than two years. It is quite likely that people arrested for misdemeanours carrying sentences of between two months and a year went to other prisons and not the National Penitentiary. Second, it is possible that the prison bureaucrats in charge of this summary register annotated the felony as it appeared in the front page of the judicial proceeding (*carátula*). It is also possible that, in the actual sentence, the judge further characterised the crime as more or less grave than on the title-page, or that, if various felonies were involved, only the most important was annotated. This is one of the deficiencies of this register: the lack of sufficient detail about attenuating and aggravating circumstances prevents us from controlling average sentence terms for these factors. It is possible, then, that a rise in sentence terms for the same type of felony was in fact a result of increasing aggravating circumstances (for instance, the use of arms in cases of robbery), while the attenuating circumsntances either remained the same or became more difficult to prove.

The register does not provide information about the jurisdiction where the sentence was issued. For the early years, it is clear that the majority of cases came from the city of Buenos Aires and its surroundings; however, over time, prisoners came from judicial districts further from the city, including the interior provinces. A 1922 decision allowed provincial authorities to send some felons sentenced to five years or more to the National Penitentiary, in cases where the province did not have the appropriate facilities to hold them. If this was the case, a bias in the composition of the sample – in the direction of longer sentences – could be expected; however, the extent of this bias cannot be assessed with the available information. These are good reasons to think that the inmates of the National Penitentiary represented a distribution with a greater proportion of long-term sentences than other federal prisons. Nonetheless, the criminal sentences covered in the registries of the Penitentiary constitute a unique collection that could be used to study the sentencing pattern of Argentine criminal courts, provided there is external corroborating evidence. Further investigation is required to check the extent to which the pattern of sentences examined is typical of judicial decisions issued in different provinces of Argentina.

The Main Hypotheses

It is proposed here to examine the validity of the following hypotheses:

(i) Actual sentence patterns showed a hardening of judicial decisions about violent crimes.

(ii) The increased severity of penalties was a generalised phenomenon that extended also to crimes against property and crimes against public order.

(iii) The alleged proportionality embedded in the Penal Code was violated in practice, with sentences revealing a greater degree of judicial discretion than intended by the legislator, and

(iv) Violent crimes (homicide, wounding, rape, and so on) received similar sentences to robbery, fraud and various offences against public order.

If this was the case – that is, if the available evidence corroborates these hypotheses – then there was a generalised 'penalty inflation' in modern Argentina that may have corresponded with the increasing gravity of criminal offences. The fact that this increase in penalties was generalised to most types of crimes may indicate that the judiciary was not just responding to a perceived increase of violence in society, but were probably concerned with the more general problem of social order. Extending harsher penalties for the same crime, in the absence of substantial reforms in penal legislation, assumes that over time judges adopted stricter rules for admitting evidence about attenuating circumstances and made the proof of aggravating circumstances easier to accept in court. Given the lack of evidence on this question, we can neither accept nor reject this conjecture.

Sentence Patterns for Violent Crimes

During the period examined (1878–1948), the sentences passed for violent crimes became harsher. In Table 3.1, we see a number of felonies that, by definition, require violence. They are divided into three groups: (i) homicide; (ii) assault, robbery, and use of firearms; (iii) sexual crimes. The results clearly show that, for all crimes involving violence, the average term in prison was substantially longer for the period 1925–1948 than for 1878–1901. The exceptions to this rule (aggravated homicide and assault) involve felonies with too few cases to be considered indicative of a trend. The severity of penalties increased significantly for the most common violent crimes, that is homicide, robbery, use of firearms, and rape. The average term in prison for homicide increased by 72 percent (from 10.6 to 18.3 years); the average sentence for robbery rose by 96 percent (from 2.6 to 5.1 years); the average prison term for 'abuse of arms' increased by 147 percent (from 1.7 to 4.2 years); the punishment for rape rose by 63 percent (from 5.5 to 9.0 years). In the language of economists, the cost of committing violent crimes went up significantly in modern Argentina.

Table 3.1 reflects changes in the legal categories. In the first period, some cases of simple homicide were labelled as 'deaths'; it is likely that these crimes coincided with accidental deaths or 'preter-intentional' homicide. The category of 'death' later disappeared from the records. At first, the penal officers found no reason to separate the homicide of children from other homicides; only after 1924 were cases of child murder registered separately. Similarly, the category of 'aggravated homicide' (*homicidio calificado*) appeared only in the third period; it is possible that the emergence of this new category was contemporaneous with the labelling of certain murders as 'simple homicide', a category non-existent for the first two periods. The category of 'woundings' (*heridas*), appropriate for a time when most injuries were caused by knives, was replaced later by the more general category of 'injuries' (*lesiones*), referring to all kinds of body injuries and wounds. With regard to robbery, we see the emergence of two new categories: 'gang robbery' and 'aggravated robbery'. This was probably a result of the new phenomena of organised crime and the operation of gangs in the city.

We should examine more closely the three major types of violent crimes: homicides, bodily wounds, and rape. Our estimates show clearly that the penalty for simple homicide increased from 10.6 years in the period 1878–1901 to 14.2 years in 1902–1924, rising to 18.3 years in 1925–1948 (Figure 3.1). The gravest type of homicide, aggravated homicide, received sentences a little below the maximum penalty, life sentence. In order to be able to calculate average terms of prison, I have arbitrarily assigned 40 years to the category of 'perpetual prison' (life sentence); this might slightly over-estimate

Table 3.1.   Mean Penalties for Violent Crimes

Felony	Average prison term (years)					
	1878–1901		1902–1924		1925–1948	
Homicides						
Homicide (simple)	10.6	(679)	14.3	(1277)	18.3	(1038)
Double homicide	5	(1)	32.2	(19)	29.6	(33)
Triple homicide		(0)	40	(1)	40	(5)
Death	15.9	(34)		(0)		(0)
Aggravated homicide		(0)		(0)	36.2	(16)*
Child homicide		(0)		(0)	5.3	(7)
Homicide by imprudence	2	(1)	1.4	(5)		(0)
Attempted homicide	7.6	(35)	9.1	(33)	8.4	(31)
Simple homicide		(0)		(0)	11.8	(19)
Infanticide	2.2	(2)	25	(2)		(0)
Parricide	40	(1)	25	(0)		(0)
Assault, woundings and robbery						
Assault	8.8	(18)	4.5	(6)	6.5	(2)*
Use of arms	1.7	(117)	2.4	(365)	4.2	(40)
Armed resistance to authority	0.8	(91)	3.4	(322)	3.9	(172)
Woundings	2.7	(121)	4,5	(3)		(0)
Bodily injuries	0.8	(534)	1.7	(936)	3.7	(73)
Grave bodily injuries	3	(2)	5.3	(9)	4.9	(64)
Robbery	2.6	(527)	4.3	(588)	5.1	(366)
Aggravated robbery		(0)		(0)	6	(97)
Gang robbery		(0)		(0)	7.6	(23)
Attempted robbery	1.9	(47)	3.4	(103)	4.1	(66)
Sexual crimes						
Rape	5.5	(14)	7.3	(60)	9	(89)
Attempted rape	2.5	(2)	6	(5)	6.5	(22)
Rape of a minor	3.7	(4)	6.5	(5)	7.5	(21)
Dishonest abuse		(0)	1.7	(2)	4.5	(11)
Corruption of minors (prostitution)	2	(2)	4.8	(6)	7.3	(76)
Sodomy	6	(1)	9.5	(2)		(0)
Rapto (kidnapping)	1	(1)	12.2	(5)	4.9	(7)
Secuestro (kidnapping)		(0)		(0)	2.8	(3)

Source: Archivo Penitenciario Argentino, Registro de Testimonios de Sentencias, 1879–1948.
Note: Numbers of cases in parenthesis.

the average prison-term for homicide. The average penalty for 'double homicide' (32 years) in the second period is similar to the average between 'double homicide' (29.6 years) and aggravated homicide (36.2 years) in the third period. The penalty for the least serious form of homicide, attempted homicide, increased likewise from 7.6 to 8.4 years in average.

The 'hardening of sentences' extended also to other felonies involving violence; wounding, injuries and threats definitely followed this trend (Figure 3.2). All felonies classified under this category received, on average, prison terms of one year and two months during 1870–1901, and one year and ten months during 1902–1924. In the third period (1925–1948),

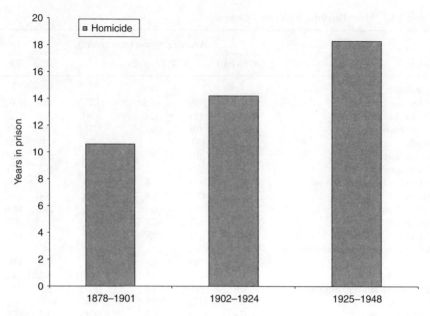

Figure 3.1.   Penalty for Homicide Over Time

there was a significant 'penalty inflation', wounding, injuries and threats receiving sentences of four years and five months on average. Making a threat to another person could cost six months in prison in 1878–1901, but it carried a penalty twelve times higher in 1925–1948 (six years and two months). Discharging a firearm cost the felon one year and eight months in prison during the first period, and four years and one month during the third period (2.4 times as much). Causing injuries or wounds to another person was punished during 1878–1901 with a term of eight months on average, but in the period 1925–1948 the same offence could keep the felon in prison for three years and seven months (five times as much).

Prisoners condemned for rape were few, but the length of sentence which they faced increased significantly from the opening of the Penitentiary (1877) to the mid-1940s (Figure 3.3). The average prison term rose from 5.5 years in 1878–1901 to nine years in the period 1925–1948. In the latter period, the number of rapists in prison, though small in comparison to other types of delinquent, was almost 10percent of the whole prison population. In terms of overall numbers, below rapists came those condemned for inducing young girls into prostitution ('corruption of minors'); the sentence for this felony increased even more than that of rape, rising from two years (1878–1901) to 7.3 years (1925–1948) on average. The campaign against the 'white slave' traffic, which had started around the time of the First World War, escalated in the 1930s, after the prostitution ring 'Zwi Migdal' was discovered and its

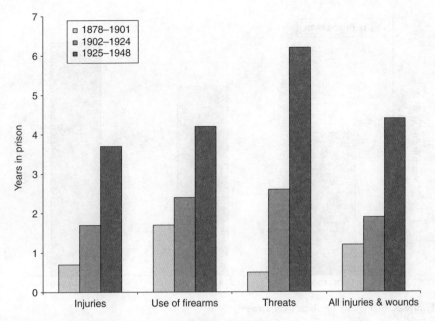

Figure 3.2. Penalty for Injuries, Use of Firearms, and Threats

members arrested or deported. It is likely that the increased visibility of this threat to morality moved judges to increase the severity of penalties imposed on pimps (Guy, 1994).

Penalty Inflation

The increase in the penalties given for the same felony – a phenomenon we could call 'penalty inflation' – was quite generalised. It affected crimes against the person, crimes against property (such as larceny, theft and swindling), as well as felonies against public order (such as resisting arrest, currency fraud, tampering with public documents and infractions against gambling laws). The average penalty for crimes of honour and of a sexual nature (rape, bigamy and corrupting minors) also went up. This generalised increase in penalties for all types of crime may indicate a rising judicial intolerance for violent crimes. However, it is more consistent with the evidence that judges were toughening their position vis-à-vis criminal activities in general. The cost of committing a crime increased for all types of felonies – larceny, theft, fraud, resisting authority, rape, dishonest abuse, and the falsification of money or lottery tickets – during this period Table 3.2.

The increase in the severity of penalties was quite remarkable. The ten crimes for which the average sentence term changed the most are shown in Table 3.3. The penalty for frequent crimes, such as armed resistance to

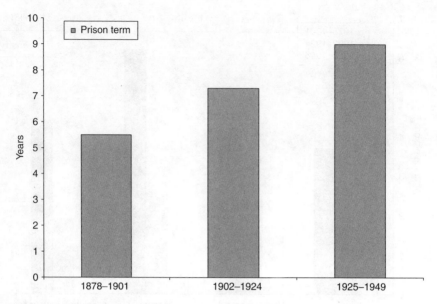

Figure 3.3.   Penalty for Rape over Time

Table 3.2.   Mean Penalty by Type of Crime

	Prison term in years		
Type of crime	1878–1901	1902–1924	1925–1948
Against the person	5.8	8.1	16.3
Against property	1.5	3.1	4.1
Against honour and sexuality	4.6	6.1	7.4
Against public order	1.6	2.5	3.6

authority and bodily injuries, increased more than three times. The penalty for 'corruption of minors' increased by more than double. Average sentence terms for robbery, homicide and rape also increased, but to a lesser extent (from 60 to 90 percent); the same could be said about attempted murder and grievous bodily injuries. The judicial system, without major changes in the legislation, managed to respond to the increasing demand from government and society for increased security of person and property.

The increased severity of penalties, as inferred from the data of the National Penitentiary, was not a product of a particular set of legal reforms, nor did it emerge at a particular point in time. It was, rather, the result of many individual decisions by judges over the long-run. Figure 3.4 presents an estimate of the trend in average penalties (measured in prison years) over the whole period 1878–1948. While it is clear that the first fifteen years of the

Table 3.3. Percentage Increase in the Severity of Penalties* (From 1877–1901 to 1924–1948)

Rank	Felonies	Percentage increase in penalty
1	Armed resistance to authority	388
2	Bodily injuries	363
3	Corruption of minors	265
4	Use of arms	147
5	Attempted robbery	116
6	Robbery	96
7	Homicide	72
8	Rape	64
9	Grave bodily injuries	63
10	Attempted homicide	10.5

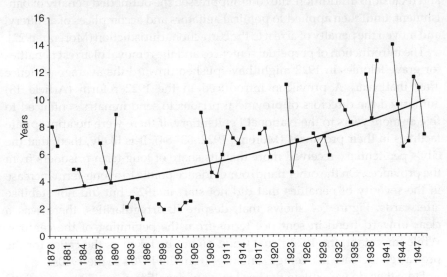

Figure 3.4. Estimated Trend of Average Penalties (1878–1948)

enforcement of the 1886 Penal Code saw a decline in average penalties, from *c.*1908–1910, average penalties began to rise, and continued, with ups and downs, throughout the time of the first Peronist administration. The long-run trend is definitely upward.

Possible Explanations

The first question to examine is whether there were changes in penal laws that might explain this hardening of sentences. According to Rodolfo Moreno's commentaries on the antecedents to the 1922 Penal Code, between 1886 and 1922 there were only minor changes in the penalties attributed to a particular felony. While the 1886 code had established eight types of penalty (death, *presidio*, penitentiary, imprisonment, arrest, banishment, in-habilitation, and fines), the reform of 1903 (Law 4189) added the penalty of deportation. The inclusion of this penalty was related to the need to repress 'foreign agitators'; in fact, this penalty was already established by the Law of Residence of 1902, specially designed to deal with anarchist labour organisers. The 1906 draft reform, never enacted, proposed the abolition of the death penalty, which was later incorporated into the Penal Code of 1922. In compensation for this, the reformed code introduced the penalty of life imprisonment or reclusion. This meant that the old penalty of imprisonment for an 'indeterminate time' could now be substituted for life imprisonment. The 1922 reform tried to simplify penalties establishing only two sanctions of 'deprivation of freedom': prison and reclusion. In addition, the code suppressed the outmoded penalty of banishment, until then applied to political agitators and accomplices of adultery, and moved the penalty of arrest to the correctional jurisdiction (Moreno, 1922).

The introduction of perpetual sentences and the removal of arrest penalties for grave felonies in 1922 might have pushed upward the average sentence after that year. A provision introduced in the 1922 reform (Article 18) authorised the directors of provincial prisons to send inmates sentenced to five or more years to the National Penitentiary, if there were no appropriate facilities in their provinces (Moreno, 1922: 83–84). It is likely, then, that the city's penitentiary received more than its share of long-term prisoners from the provinces. On the other hand, our evidence points to a long-term increase in the severity of penalties that did not start in 1922, but did not stabilise afterwards. Figure 3.4 shows that, despite its irregularities, there was a clear upward trend in sentence terms from the beginning of the century. While important, the 1922 Penal Code cannot be taken as the cause for the protracted increase in average sentences from the 1870s to the 1940s.

How then do we explain the hardening of penalties over a 70-year period? There are two possible readings of these results. One is congruent with the idea of the 'civilisation of crime' (Johnson and Monkkonen, 1996). To the extent that society attributed a greater value to life and rejected the use of violence to settle interpersonal disputes, judges translated into their sentences these new sensibilities, raising the penalties for crimes involving violent actions. How could they do this, if penal laws remained basically unchanged with regard to penalties? In practical terms, this would mean that judges were increasingly reluctant to accept alleviating circumstances and more willing to side with the prosecutor on the existence of aggravating circumstances. Pressed by a society increasingly revolted by violent crimes, judges tended to pass sentences closer to the upper limits established in the Penal Code.

A second possible interpretation refers to the reality of crime. It is possible that, over time, homicides became more gruesome and cruel, involving pre-meditation and the use of excessive violence. The generalised use of fire arms and the formation of gangs in the 1920s and 1930s could have created situations in which judges thought that they needed to issue harsher sentences. This second interpretation fits into the frame of the 'modernisation of crime' hypothesis, traditionally associated with the processes of urbanisation and industrialisation (Zehr, 1975; Shelley, 1981; Hewitt and Hoover, 1982). One variant of this interpretation argues that it was the increasing organisation of criminal activity and the more frequent resort to violence as means to commit crimes that triggered efforts to reform the legal statutes, so that crimes would be punished with greater severity. While Congress was unable to gather the majorities required to pass these reforms, judges interpreted the message of society and gave exemplary sentences to crimes of a 'modern type'. In a recent book, Lila Caimari (2012) has shown how, in the 1920s and 1930s, organised bands, with automobiles and firearms, gave rise to a new alarm among the population of the city of Buenos Aires about an alleged 'crime wave' and sustained the emergence of a new figure, the so-called *pistolero criollo* (literally 'creole gunfighter'). She also discusses the 1932–1933 attempt to reform the penal code, introducing tougher penalties against violent crimes, including the death sentence.

A third possible explanation relates to the question of order, that is, the perception that tougher penalties for crimes would bring greater stability to the social and political order. Judging by the ten felonies whose penalties increased the most, one is tempted to conclude that this order was menaced by the growing presence of organised crime (in particular prostitution rings), by the use of firearms to resist arrest and by men's generalised resort to violence to resolve personal disputes. New and more violent forms of robbery (gangs using automobiles and automatic weapons) and ever more sophisticated forms of fraud (counterfeit money and forged documents) complemented the picture of changing criminality in the city of Buenos Aires. Caimari has argued that the kidnapping of a young man from an aristocratic family in 1932 (the Ayerza case), committed by a 'mafia' gang based in in Rosario, created a crime panic that led to the discussion in Congress of a proposal to increase the penalties for violent crimes. The 1933 draft law, though not sanctioned by both chambers, included the legalisisation of the death penalty, abolished by the 1922 Code (Caimari, 2007b).

Also important were the changes in judicial practice. It is conceivable that proofs for attenuating circumstances became more unlikely to be admitted in court and, conversely, that technological improvements and a more spe-cialised police force increased the availability of proof relating to aggravating circumstances. The more precise and extensive identification of delinquents and the sharing of information about recidivist offences among different levels and jurisdictions of the justice system might have contributed to

Table 3.4.   Sentences 1870–1948, Ordered by Duress

Rank	Felonies against the person	Mean penalty (years)	N =
1	Multiple homicide	40	6
2	Aggravated homicide	36.5	17
3	Parricide	32.5	2
4	Double homicide	30.1	53
5	Death	15.9	34
6	Homicide	14.8	2,992
7	Infanticide	13.6	4
8	Simple homicide	11.8	19
9	Attempted homicide	8.4	99
10	Child homicide	5.3	7
11	Homicide by imprudence	1.5	6

increasing sentences. Changes in the rules for adding up penalties or for combining felony charges should also be considered. By the 1930s, as I have argued elsewhere, the spread of Positivist criminology had permeated the judicial system (Salvatore, 2005). It is likely that clinical advice about a felon's 'dangerousness' might have inclined judges to increase the prison term. At this point, we cannot assess the extent to which this factor affected sentencing patterns in Argentina.

Proportionality and Judicial 'Arbitrio'

Was the harshness of actual sentences proportional to the gravity of the offence? An initial intuitive way to test the proportionality of sentences would be to rank them according to their harshness. Results for homicide for the whole period are presented in Table 3.4; according to these averages, there was clearly some proportionality. Multiple homicide and aggravated homicide carried penalties substantially heavier than simple homicide; the latter in turn carried penalties larger than attempted homicide or homicide by imprudence. While one charge of murder would produce sentences averaging fifteen years, two charges of murder would give the felon about 30 years in prison.

However, exceptions to the rule of proportionality were salient. For example, it is not clear why murdering a child would 'cost' one-third (5.3 years) of the penalty of murdering an adult (11.8 years), or why the crime of parricide would be punished less severely than aggravated homicide (*homicidio calificado*). Cases labelled as 'death', some of which turned out to be accidental deaths, produced slightly greater penalties (15.9 years) than cases branded as 'homicide' (14.8 years) or 'simple homicide' (11.8 years). This result could be influenced by the catch-all nature of this category of crime. In its treatment of infanticide, the literature tells us that Argentine

Table 3.5. Proportionality of Penalties (1878–1948)

	(a) Attempted	(b) Accomplished	(a)/(b)
Homicide	8.4	14.8	0.57
Woundings	n.a.	2.8	n.a.
Threats	2.9	4.5	0.64
Rape	6.1	8.1	0.75
Larceny	2.6	2.1	1.24
Robbery	3.3	3.9	0.85
Swindling	2.8	3.9	0.72

courts declined from harsh to soft penalties depending on the delicate balance between shame and the duties of motherhood (Ruggiero, 1994). Our evidence suggests that this felony was punished more severely than child murder and almost as harshly as adult homicide. This unusual result merits further investigation.

The Code of Criminal Procedures of 1888 established that an attempt to commit a felony would be punished with a prison term from a third to a half of the penalty for the actual crime. This was apparently not the case; attempted murder carried a penalty that was 57 percent of that for murder, while an attempted threat was punished by a prison term that was 64 percent of that corresponding to a completed threat, and attempted rape carried a penalty 75 percent of that of the actual crime. As Table 3.5 shows, the proportionality rule was systematically violated: all penalties reported were above the 50 percent mark.

This evidence raises serious doubts about the proportionality and fine calibration of penalties and, more generally, about the very existence of a ranking of penalties according to an implicit moral ordering. Figure 3.5 presents estimated confidence intervals (of relative confidence around the mean or average) containing 95 percent of the expected frequency. The results clearly indicate that the range for discretionary decisions was remarkably broad and, more importantly, that the penalties for different types of felonies overlap each other. It is true that homicide started with a higher penalty than any other felony, and that the smaller penalty for rape was higher than that applied to many forms of crime against property; but for most of the felonies ranked, there was a remarkable overlap in penalty intervals, revealing a high degree of substitutability between felonies, an outcome probably not planned by the legislators. In this situation, a person accused of larceny could receive the same sentence as another accused of swindling. A felon accused of attempted robbery had a good chance of getting the same sentence as one accused of corrupting a minor. Similarly, a potential murderer had a significant probability of getting the same prison term as a swindler. The same could be

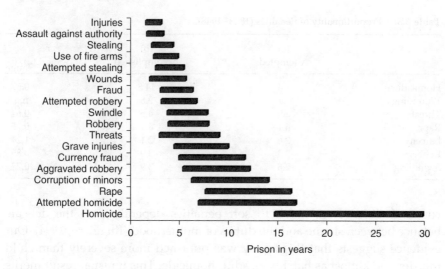

Figure 3.5.   Confidence Intervals around the Mean (Average Penalty)

said about a rapist and a thief. Thus, the broad range between minimum and maximum penalties gave judges such a strong power of *arbitrio* (discretion) that it militated against the proportionality between crimes and penalties.

The Penal Code provided judges with a sufficiently broad discretion in terms of prison terms; apparently, they did significantly extend the boundaries established in the code. Table 3.6 presents the actual minimum and maximum sentences passed by judges, and compares changes from the first to the third period. An astounding range of variation characterised the sentence pattern for those imprisoned in the National Penitentiary. As this evidence indicates, during the first period (1878–1901) at least one person received only two months of prison for murder, while others received life sentences (again equated with 40 years in prison in the calculations). This situation did not change at all during the third period (1924–1948), in which the spread of jurisprudence might possibly have reduced the number of arbitrary decisions. With time, judges introduced the notion of 'aggravated homicide', which carried a minimum penalty of ten years. Yet even in these cases, the range of discretion was wide: sentences varied from ten years to life. There was some improvement in cases of attempted murder. At first, sentences varied from six months to life; in the third period, the range of variation was reduced somewhat, from two to twenty years.

For the felon who had to spend twenty years in prison for an unrealised murder, the rigour of Argentine justice might have seemed a little extreme. Worse was the case of the felon who was imprisoned for life for wounding (*heridas*): it is possible that such wounds led to the later death of the victim, but, even so, his penalty was excessive when compared with those who

Table 3.6. Maximum and Minimum Effective Penalties

	1878–1901			1924–1948		
	Minimum	Maximum	Range	Minimum	Maximum	Range
Homicide						
Double homicide			n/a	12	40	28
Homicide	0.17	40	39.8	0.29	40	39.7
Aggravated homicide			n/a	10	40	30
Simple homicide			n/a	2	20	18
Death	1.5	40	38.5			
Attempted homicide	0.5	40	39.5	2	20	18
Injuries and wounds						
Grave injuries			n.a.	1	15	14
Injuries	0.08	18	17.9	0.33	25	24.7
Wounding	0.04	40	40.0			n.a.
Use of firearms	1	9	8	1.5	25	23.5
Threats			n.a.	2.5	16	13.5

spent only one to three months in prison for a similar felony. After 1925, judges ceased to use this category, labelling it as either assault with firearms or bodily injuries. The judicial discretion applied in these two felonies was appalling: a felon could be given from eighteenth months to 25 years in prison for shooting other people without causing them injuries, but, if they caused bodily injuries, the penalty varied in the same way, from four months to 25 years. The cost of threatening another person could bring the accused a minimum sentence of two years and six months, but there was also the possibility of being punished with sixteen years in prison.

It may be that minimum and maximum penalties exaggerate the actual degree of judicial discretion. To evaluate whether judges passed sentences consistent with a declining degree of discretionary power, we can use a more precise measure: the standard deviations from the mean. The results, reported in Table 3.7, show little change in the discretionary power of judges. An accused could expect a penalty 8.6 years greater or lower than the average during the period 1902–1924 and a penalty of 10.8 years above (or below) the average penalty during the period 1925–1948. This variation was certainly smaller than the 12.3 years above or below the average of the period 1870–1901, yet still they represented a significant degree of discretion placed in the hands of judges. This wide margin of penalty variation – which implied the unpredictability of trial outcomes – was not only the attribute of homicides, but of many other felonies as well. Measured in terms of coefficient of variation (CV), the level of judicial discretion concerning the punishment of homicide was quite high at first but later declined significantly. The CV of average penalties for homicide went from a high of 1.14 during 1878–1901 to

Table 3.7.   Standard Deviation from Mean Penalty

Felonies against the Person	1878–1901	1902–1924	1925–1950
Homicide			
Double homicide		9.6	10.7
Simple homicide			4.1
Homicide	12.3	8.6	10.8
Aggravated homicide			10,2
Death	15.1		
Attempted homicide	10.6	6.4	4.5
Injuries and wounds			
Grave injuries		2.3	27
Injuries	1.2	1.9	3.3
Wounds	5.3		
Use of firearms	0.9	17	3.7
Aggression		1.2	
Threats	1.1	1.2	5.3

levels of 0.60 and 0.56 in the following two periods. The standard deviation for bodily injuries (*lesiones*) and for the use of firearms grew larger over time. Only in cases of attempted homicide was the standard deviation of penalties significantly reduced (from 10.6 to 4.5 years).

One would expect that, in the long-run, as the knowledge of leading criminal cases and procedural rules spread among prosecutors, defence attorneys and judges, the range of variation of penalties would decrease. Our evidence, however, indicates quite the contrary. How can we explain such different rulings for apparently similar cases and felonies?

At this point, we cannot control for socio-economic differences among the accused. Hence, we cannot answer the question as to whether harsher sentences were associated with the poorer social condition of the accused. Two institutional practices, however, seem to have influenced the pattern of sentences. One was the combination (*concurso*) of charges and penalties; the other was the recidivist condition of the accused. In cases of homicide, the *concurso* with the other felony raised the penalty from 14.2 to 23.6 years on average; that is to say that courts punished this circumstance severely, making the penalty closer to that for aggravated homicide. In cases of wounding and bodily harm, the *concurso* with another felony doubled the average penalty, raising the prison term from 1.7 years to 3.7 years. The other special circumstance, recidivism, suffered from under-registration. Very few cases mention the fact that the felon was a recidivist. The National Register for Reincidence, created in 1936, extended to the national level and systematised a practice that started in the late 1910s in Buenos Aires: to provide judges with information about earlier offences of each felon. Indeed, in 1921, Rodolfo Moreno complained about the lack of a national register of recidivists (Moreno, 1922:

141). As the process of registration extended, it is reasonable to expect that a greater proportion of felons found themselves labelled as recidivist.

Concluding Remarks

New evidence on sentence patterns for felonies in Argentina, during the period 1878–1948, indicates that there was an increased severity in the penalties imposed on delinquents tried in criminal courts. This 'penalty inflation' was a generalised phenomenon, extending to crimes against the person, against property, and against public order. Although it could be argued that criminal judges considered themselves part of the 'civilising mission' to reduce the level of violence in society, the toughening of penalties seems to have obeyed a more general demand for order in society. This notion of order included the control and reduction of violent personal interactions, but was not limited to this. Harsher penalties were intended to raise the cost to potential violators of legal norms that could erode the authority of the state. From prostitution-ring leaders to labour agitators, from murderers to forgers of lottery tickets or paper-money, from store-thieves to those who defied the police with hand-held weapons, the judiciary defended the citadel of order and civilised sociability with increasing duress.

Ironically, the Penal Code that was supposed to reduce the degree of judicial *arbitrio* and the resulting unpredictability of colonial justice, ended up by placing a great deal of discretionary power in the hands of criminal judges (Bravo Lira, 1991). The reform of the Penal Ccode in 1922, which introduced life sentences in place of the (abolished) death penalty, might have contributed somewhat to this inflation of penalties. But the hardening of penalties cannot be wholly explained without examining judicial practices. It is possible that criminal judges listened ever more carefully to the advice of psychiatric and criminology experts about the 'dangerousness' of certain felons. It is also possible that judges imposed greater hurdles for the admission of attenuating circumstances (such as drunkenness) or that, in the absence of a good defence, they sided more often with the prosecutors. Finally, one could imagine a situation in which improved information about the background of delinquents might have aggravated the penalty for the accused. The media could have also contributed to raising the level of public awareness about violent crimes. Newspapers and magazines, bringing to the attention of state authorities new forms of robbery and assault, new ways of deceiving the public trust, might have contributed to creating a punitive reaction among the judiciary. All of these possibilities are at this point simply informed conjectures, open questions that call for a continued effort to study criminal prosecutions and conceptions of crime in modern Argentina.

4

Homicide as Politics in Modern Mexico

PABLO A. PICCATO

Columbia University, USA

This chapter is part of a larger attempt to understand crime from the point of view of Mexican civil society. In order to do this, it starts at the intersection of two traditions in the study of violence. One is embodied in the work of historians, such as Eric Johnson, Pieter Spierenburg and the late Eric Monkkonen, who expanded the range of sources, interpretive tools and chronological breadth of the study of crime, proving that a long-term examination of criminal trends is required for any effort to understand the broader impact and contemporary relevance of crime and punishment (Johnson, 1995; Monkkonen, 2001; Spierenburg, 1998, 2008). The second tradition engaged by this chapter consists of the scholarship of historians of Mexico, such as Carlos Monsiváis, Jorge Aguilar Mora and others, who try to look at homicide as an act always invested with meaning in the cultural and political history of the country (Aguilar Mora, 1990; Monsiváis, 1994; Meade, 2005; 'Punishment and Death', 2006). In order to respond to both bodies of scholarship, this chapter deals with statistics of crime, as well as the words and images produced around crime.

The thesis is simple: because of its frequency and its changing trends, crime is a central field in the relationship between civil society and the state in contemporary Mexico. Homicide in particular (how it was perceived, committed, explained) was a key theme in the definition of victim's rights and authorities' obligations, and in the public discussions about justice and transgression. In other words, all homicide in post-revolutionary Mexico is political homicide. The twentieth century saw many creative ways to kill, outside civil war. After the apex of violence, during the revolutionary decade from 1910, homicide rates decreased, yet remained high and prominent in everyday life. Individual and multiple homicides attracted inordinate amounts of attention, bringing together a massive public and generating debates, explanations and narratives in many different media. Discussions focussed on the usual questions (who did it? why? how?), but also on the larger meaning of homicides – as if each one of them contained an important message regarding the state of Mexican society, the legitimacy of its institutions, and the weaknesses and moral quality of its people. The focus on civil society allows me to bring out that territory of life that is not ruled by the state (in this case, through law, policing and punishment), or by the market, but instead involves the deliberate and critical participation of individual and collective actors. An analysis involving civil society cannot be reduced to psycho-social study of responses to, and performance of, murder; examining crime only as a pathology or as a transgression of the law denies a host of non-state actors any involvement in the resolution of conflict and loss derived from the crime itself (Cohen and Arato, 1992; Braithwaite and Strang, 2001; Forment, 2003).

The main expression of the significance of homicide for civil society is its ability to summon large and diverse audiences and turn them into one single public. This public can judge the performance of institutions and the state of social mores with a great degree of consensus, given the clear moral value of homicide – regardless of the political motivations of the actual crime or lack thereof.[1] Such discussion, open yet based on a shared agreement about 'reality' and moral value, is a central aspect of the process of political incorporation and democratisation, as it allows an increasing number of social actors, even if they are not part of the government and central party structure, to have an effect on politics and policy. Thanks to civil society's response to crime, people otherwise marginalised from public life claim stakes in the quality of governance and justice (Habermas, 1991; Guerra, 2000: 271; Warner, 2002; ICESI, 2010). With some optimism and in spite of many obstacles (including the political manipulation of moral panics), we can say that the process of political incorporation is a central feature of the evolution of twentieth-century Mexican politics, even as violence remains a central aspect of political and social life (Vaughan, 1997; Buffington and Piccato, 2009).

This chapter will specifically address the value of homicide as a source of meaning in the public sphere. A parallel effort, within the concern about civil society, could be developed around non-state prevention of, and responses to, crime (Piccato, 2005). I will examine here three bodies of evidence. The first is statistical, to get a sense of the size and direction of criminality during the twentieth century. The second is more clearly political: the letters written by family and friends of homicide victims to Mexican presidents, from the 1930s to the 1950s. The third kind of evidence pertains more fully in the

---

1   In contrast to Alan Knight's contribution in this volume, I am focusing on the effects of violence; in that regard, I am proposing that the distinction between political and non-political (or mercenary) violence, or between instrumental and expressive violence, is not essential.

public sphere, although it is structured by the previous two: the images, explanations and narratives that thousands of readers consumed in order to make sense of murder and the debates they generated. These sources, I contend, are not three different windows onto one reality but integral aspects of the study of homicide.

Statistical Evidence

Figure 4.1 reveals that homicide is indeed a long-term and serious problem in Mexico. The graph shows a generally stable number of persons indicted for homicide, which contrasts with the growth in the total number of crimes during the period for which we have consistent figures (Piccato, 2003); it should be noted that the database has been updated with data from the Instituto Nacional de Estadística y Geografía (National Institute for Statistics and Geography) (http://www.inegi.org.mx), and also that 'indicted', or *presunto*, refers to those suspects charged and imprisoned but not yet sentenced. Their cases constitute the most reliable figure available for compiling long-term series. Even though they may not represent the entire number of homicides, as

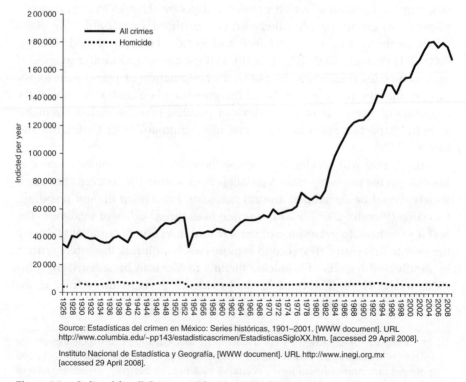

Source: Estadísticas del crimen en México: Series históricas, 1901–2001. [WWW document]. URL http://www.columbia.edu/~pp143/estadisticascrimen/EstadisticasSigloXX.htm. [accessed 29 April 2008].

Instituto Nacional de Estadística y Geografía, [WWW document]. URL http://www.inegi.org.mx [accessed 29 April 2008].

Figure 4.1.   Indicted for all Crimes and for Homicide. Mexico, 1996–2009

we will see below, indicted suspects are more important in public perceptions of crime than those found guilty, and certainly more visible than those not arrested. The contrast between the recent increase in violence, associated with the so-called 'war on drugs' and the stability of the total number of homicide indictments is striking. However, this impression can be deceiving on two accounts: first, as we will see below, the recent violence is not necessarily reflected by national judicial statistics and, second, public perception of the crime as an all-too-frequent problem in Mexican society is not new but was sustained throughout the century.

Figure 4.2, giving national rates for the most important crimes per total population shows a clear decline in homicide during most of the twentieth century. Although rates are high today, they are much lower than in previous years and immediately after the Revolution. In the capital, where the information is available, the rate of homicide sentenced per 100,000 inhabitants was 46 on average between 1885 and 1871 (only in Mexico City, contained by the Federal District), 31 in 1909, and rose to 37 in 1930 for the Federal District, decreasing thereafter (Dirección General de Estadística, 1890; *Anuario Estadístico*, 1895; Piccato, 2001: 79). This decline corresponds with that of criminality in general in the country, as can be seen in the trends of other

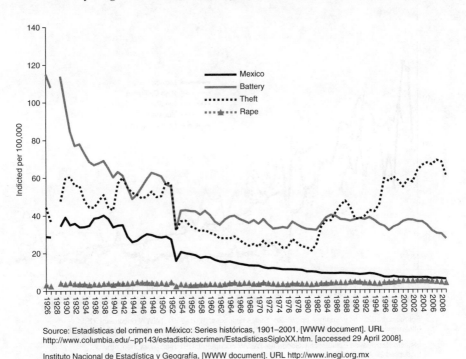

Source: Estadísticas del crimen en México: Series históricas, 1901–2001. [WWW document]. URL http://www.columbia.edu/~pp143/estadisticascrimen/EstadisticasSigloXX.htm. [accessed 29 April 2008].

Instituto Nacional de Estadística y Geografía, [WWW document]. URL http://www.inegi.org.mx [accessed 29 April 2008].

Figure 4.2. Indicted per 100,000, Selected Crimes. Mexico, 1926–2009

crimes. As in other contemporary societies, multiple socio-economic factors explain this broad phenomenon; education is one that I found to be strongly correlated with rates in Mexico. Literacy increased throughout the century, its correlation with lower rates seeming to reinforce the common notion that links violence with poverty and marginality. Yet this explanation is too broad and the link between poverty and violence is problematic, particularly when it refers to the notion of a 'subculture of poverty', associated with Mexican *machismo* (Lewis, 1961; Gutmann, 1994). By contrast, theft seems to have responded more directly to the socio-economic deterioration of the last decades of the twentieth century (Beltrán and Piccato, 2004). As Figure 4.2 shows, homicide seems to have continued a steady decline until the present.

Figure 4.3, in which selected states are compared, suggests that, even if homicide has been a stable problem throughout the twentieth century, it has changed places and trends in recent years. The Federal District, which had lower rates for most of the century, now has rates at the same level as the national rates, while states such as Sinaloa and Baja California, both clearly affected by the expansion of the drug business and correlated violence, seem

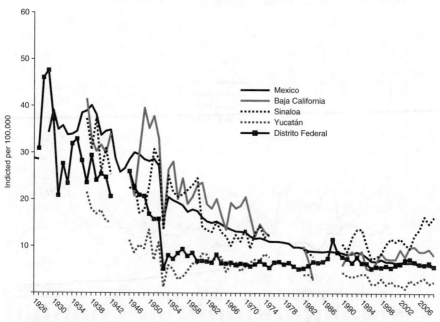

Source: Estadísticas del crimen en México: Series históricas, 1901–2001. [WWW document]. URL http://www.columbia.edu/~pp143/estadisticascrimen/EstadisticasSigloXX.htm. [accessed 29 April 2008].

Instituto Nacional de Estadística y Geografía, [WWW document]. URL http://www.inegi.org.mx [accessed 29 April 2008].

Figure 4.3.   Homicide Indicted, Rates per 100,000 Population. Mexico and Selected States, 1926–2009

Table 4.1.   Average Homicide per 100,000. Selected States

Period	Mexico	Baja California	Sinaloa	Yucatán	Distrito Federal
1990-2009	7.06	7.94	11.55	2.74	6.37
1926-2009	17.71	17.34	16.27	6.4	12.43

Sources: Pablo Piccato, "Estadísticas del crimen en México: Series históricas, 1901–2001," http://www.columbia.edu/~pp143/estadisticascrimen/EstadisticasSigloXX.htm; data Instituto Nacional de Estadística y Geografía, http://www.inegi.org.mx

to have followed an upward trend since the 1980s, similar to that noted for Central America by Orlando J. Pérez in his chapter in this volume. Yucatán has remained, by contrast, a state with very low rates. In all of these states, and in the country as a whole, as shown in Table 4.1, the averages for the last twenty years are still lower than those recorded since 1926.

These figures are only a partial representation of the problem. Homicide is commonly held to be a good index of quantitative criminal tendencies, on the assumption that police and judicial authorities are more diligent in prosecuting it, while other crimes such as theft and rape can easily escape the attention of institutions. In the case of Mexico we have to take this with a pinch of salt. Many homicides are not investigated and go unpunished. Figure 4.4 compares the evidence from judicial sources with that from health authorities counting homicide as a cause of death. The number of deaths reported as homicide by forensic sources is consistently higher than that from judicial statistics. Part of this might be the result of cases in which a corpse leads to an investigation but not to an indictment. In any case, the difference, an average of 65 percent more for the country between 1926 and 2005, and 91 percent more for the Federal District, suggests that justice only reaches a limited number of cases. This is a greater problem in certain places, such as the northern border in recent years: in Nuevo Laredo, during 2004, there were 130 reported cases of homicide but only eleven indicted for the crime (INEGI, 2005; INEGI, 2006a; INEGI, 2006b). The work of other researchers suggests that the number of crimes never reported or prosecuted is very high, although it is not clear whether this situation has worsened in recent years because of the lack of long-term victimisation surveys (Greenberg, 1989; Zepeda Lecuona, 2004; Escalante Gonzalbo and Aranda García, 2009).

Table 4.2 presents all indicted rates and the rate of homicide as cause of death, according to public health authorities. It suggests a steep increase in 2008 but represents the same long-term decline – although at levels comparable to other countries in Latin America, as noted by Pérez. There is no evidence, however, that the lack of prosecution for murder could explain this recent rise: most likely, if we consider the contrast between homicide as cause of death against judicial indictments and the qualitative evidence of the sections

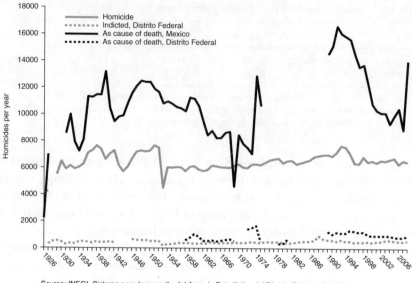

Source: INEGI, Sistema para la consulta del Anuario Estadístico del Distrito Federal, Edición 2006. [WWW document]. URL http://www.inegi.gob.mx/est/contenidos/espanol/sistemas/aee06/estatal/df/index.htm [accessed 29 April 2008].

Figure 4.4.   Homicide According to Judicial and Public Health Sources, Mexico and Federal District, 1926–2009

that follow, the problem of impunity has been constant throughout the century.

This lack of investigation and punishment for murderers explains in part why the decline in murder rates is not echoed by a decrease in public concern about the problem throughout the century. If we examine the ways in which homicide has been depicted, explained and discussed, famous cases and the evidence of impunity seem to have had more impact than any statistical analysis. The increasing use of guns, rather than the traditional knives, also partly explains the difference between trends and perceptions (Quiroz Cuarón Gómez Robleda, and Argüelles Modína, 1939).

Murder and Petitions

Homicide was a consistent presence throughout the twentieth century, and it was often associated with impunity by the public. Murders had political repercussions because they invited civil society to question the response of the state. This gave a kind of political agency to victims that is not found in other crimes – not until recent times, at least, with police abuse, rape and kidnapping the clearest examples, as we will see below. These demands, usually addressed to the president, came from individuals (the aggrieved

Table 4.2.   Indited for Homicide and Homicide as Cause of Death per 100,000. Mexico, 1926-2009

Year	Indicted	As cause of death	Year	Indicted	As cause of death	Year	Indicted	As cause of death
1926	28.80	15.49	1961	16.20	29.24	1996	6.89	15.70
1927	28.59	47.02	1962	15.35	25.26	1997	6.76	14.48
1928	N.A.	N.A.	1963	15.02	21.68	1998	7.21	14.44
1929	34.27	N.A.	1964	15.34	21.82	1999	6.73	12.77
1930	39.11	N.A.	1965	14.73	19.80	2000	6.72	11.07
1931	34.96	50.71	1966	14.11	19.19	2001	6.51	10.47
1932	35.76	58.13	1967	13.65	19.51	2002	6.60	10.16
1933	33.82	45.21	1968	13.19	19.12	2003	6.49	10.04
1934	33.95	40.65	1969	13.12	9.86	2004	6.51	9.14
1935	34.59	44.73	1970	13.02	17.52	2005	6.54	9.61
1936	38.52	61.46	1971	12.13	15.65	2006	6.00	9.95
1937	38.95	60.17	1972	11.64	14.56	2007	6.15	8.30
1938	40.11	60.20	1973	11.79	13.27	2008	5.94	12.89
1939	38.15	59.17	1974	11.46	23.47	2009	5.67	N.A.
1940	33.75	67.04	1975	11.03	18.82			
1941	34.64	51.48	1976	11.02	N.A.			
1942	34.88	45.30	1977	10.99	N.A.			
1943	28.77	45.63	1978	10.85	N.A.			
1944	25.85	44.76	1979	10.65	N.A.			
1945	26.61	47.60	1980	9.84	N.A.			
1946	28.62	49.67	1981	9.85	N.A.			
1947	30.05	50.62	1982	9.64	N.A.			
1948	29.60	50.84	1983	9.04	N.A.			
1949	28.60	49.25	1984	8.96	N.A.			
1950	28.21	48.09	1985	8.90	N.A.			
1951	28.68	44.52	1986	8.85	N.A.			
1952	27.15	42.18	1987	8.98	N.A.			
1953	15.81	37.87	1988	8.89	N.A.			
1954	20.50	37.20	1989	8.78	N.A.			
1955	19.80	35.52	1990	8.62	17.87			
1956	19.34	33.72	1991	8.29	18.19			
1957	18.76	32.46	1992	8.45	19.49			
1958	17.37	30.91	1993	8.79	18.41			
1959	17.87	33.08	1994	8.49	17.77			
1960	17.54	31.95	1995	7.77	17.14			

Sources: Pablo Piccato, "Estadísticas del crimen en México: Series históricas, 1901–2001," http://www.columbia.edu/~pp143/estadisticascrimen/EstadisticasSigloXX.htm; data Instituto Nacional de Estadística y Geografía, http://www.inegi.org.mx

relatives, many of them mothers) but also from corporative organisations, such as unions or neighbours' associations; examples include a mother denouncing a policeman freed after killing her son (Estrada Aguirre, 1969), and letters from taxi drivers (González, 1959), chauffeurs (Lucero, 1955) and Trabajadores de Caminos (1936). Letters usually centred on justice, the oldest trope in the petitions of Mexican subjects to their authorities, yet the individuals or associations that demanded justice never failed to mention the political implications of their appeals. The archives of Mexican presidents, particularly from Lázaro Cárdenas (1934–1940) to Adolfo López Mateos (1958–1964), held at the Archivo General de la Nación, contain a large number of letters demanding justice after homicides that went unpunished. They come from all states and they make for a large number of documents: an average of 1,189 files per six-year presidential period. If we take the number of indicted persons as a reference, 3 percent of all homicide cases found their way to the president's desk. While President Porfirio Díaz, before the 1910 Revolution, usually limited himself to responding to similar letters by stating that he could not intervene in judicial matters, post-revolutionary presidents took a more active role, forwarding the letter to the Procuraduría (Attorney General's Office) of each state, following up on certain cases, and even offering additional security for relatives of victims threatened by freed murderers. Thus, Manuel Avila Camacho instructed the Mexico City Chief of Police to instruct a suspect, Manuel Sáenz de Miera, to stop bothering the mother of a homicide victim (Romo Castro, 1942).

Letter-writers ranged from the wealthy foreigner demanding justice to the humble mother, such as Balentina Esquevel, who denounced the local bosses who killed her son and shot her in the leg, yet escaped punishment because they offered 'beer and a good lunch' to the prosecutor (Esquivel, 1940). Some of these letters offer detailed narratives of the aftermath of the crime – in contrast with judicial records only concerned with its causes. Refugio Carbajal, for example, wrote to president López Mateos in 1961, demanding justice for the murder of his son Antonio by one Luis Barrón. Referring to his deceased son, Refugio wrote that 'he told me himself' the details of the murder and the attempts to make it look like an accidental electrocution. The son asked the father to use his entitlement as a veteran of the Revolution to have the murderers pay for the education of his orphaned children. The letter quotes the ghost of the son: 'do not forget this, dear father, because until there is a solution I will continue bothering you' (Carbajal Flores, 1961).

Testimony from the spirit of the victim could perhaps seem the only certain truth, because complainants and most local judicial and police authorities were powerless in the face of violent individuals , local *caciques* or wayward officials. Everyone knew that policemen, prosecutors and judges could be bought. The figure of the *pistolero* (in reality part bodyguard, part policeman, part pure criminal) was widely associated with unpunished violence during the middle decades of the century. Even when *pistoleros* were involved in incidents of common crime, the implication was that they acted with the support or complicity of well-connected patrons. A lawyer characterised them as the 'best defined type of the born criminal', yet they were an essential element of the 'micropolitical violence' that pervaded the post-revolutionary period, according to Alan Knight in this volume (Langel, 1942: 1).

Homicide, however, gave enough courage to enough people to tell the president about some ugly realities. In 1958, a relative of his victim claimed that air force pilot Sergio García Núñez bragged that a judge was going to acquit him soon because he had received 50,000 pesos. Javier Torres Pérez wrote to President Ruiz Cortines that García Núñez was an example of those 'well-connected abnormals, *pistoleros*, inveterate murderers on the salary of your friends, who commit crimes every day and who, when they finally fall into the hands of justice, its action is impeded by corrupt judges and orders from powerful men that send such social degenerates as García Núñez to privileged prisons for the military [...] instead [...] of a true prison for dangerous schizophrenics' (Torres Pérez, 1958). Another suspect was paying 9,000 pesos per month to avoid indictment. All letters were more or less explicit about a basic political reasoning: the legitimacy of the president himself depended on his handling of such cases. Or, in the words of the letter just cited, 'the people get tired, Mr. President, of so many García Nuñezes' (Torres Pérez, 1958; Vélez, 1948). The difficulty in reaching the truth and justice through institutions, and the belief in the great power of the president, inspired these letters and prompted the half-hearted reactions of national authorities.

Only since the 1980s, as documented in the presidential archive of Carlos Salinas de Gortari (1988–1994), have these petitions come to be understood as human rights violations and associated with the mobilisation of 'civil society', particularly in the form of non-governmental organisations (NGOs) dedicated to seeking justice against sexual violence and the repression of dissidence. Even before the denunciation of 'dirty war' disappearances, torture and murder, scandalous police abuses in the 1980s put the language of human rights at the centre of political debates in the Mexican press. Feminist organisations raised the profile of rape (a persistently underreported component of police abuses) and, more recently, child prostitution (Monsiváis, 1994: 44; Lang, 2003; Cacho, 2005). Yet even in the earlier era, the letters examined above cannot be interpreted as anything other than critical expressions by civil society about the failure of the state's protection of citizens' security – but couched in the traditional language of petitions to the sovereign rather than the modern language of human rights. The continuity is clearer in contrast with other cases, such as that of Argentina, examined in this volume by Emilio Crenzel, where an institutional break and alternative narratives about terrorism provided a clear before-and-after for the use of that language.

Presidents responded in some cases because these letters were not mailed to them alone. Some complainants copied their letters to the press, for example Florencio Rodriguez Cárdenas, whose son died after a beating at the police station (Rodriguez Cárdenas, 1959). The growth of presidential power is the main thread of the narrative of presidential archives and of much of twentieth-century political history. But homicide opened up debates that were not easy to integrate into the political discipline built by the post-revolutionary regime (Gillingham, 2010). Even if relatively few murderers were at large because of their official position or connections, they were a stain on the reputation of the police and the judiciary, and a symptom of a president's limited power. When a case of grievous impunity was mentioned in the pages of newspapers, the game shifted in favour of victims. Keeping homicides quiet was therefore useful for suspects. The aforementioned García Núñez bragged that 'by explicit orders of the Presidency newspapers remain silent about everything concerning his case' (Gómez Pérez, 1958). He did not have an alibi, but he did have a media strategy. This was not always easy to achieve. Newspapers were the first place where one learned about a homicide, where murderers confirmed what only they knew, and where justice, or its failure, could be documented. Indeed, one man read a newspaper about the crime he had committed, although nobody had interrogated him (Anonymous, 1958), repeated in a similar case (Alexa et al., 2003).

Chapters by Christopher Boyer, Víctor Macías, Renato González Mello and the present author in a recent book on Mexican crime stories reveal how common cases of murder were invested with strong political meanings during the 1920s. Some of these cases led to further violence (as in the murder and kidnapping of the son of a Catholic leader in Zamora, Michoacán), or to public challenges to the legitimacy of a government (as in the jury trials of women who killed their husbands and were acquitted in Mexico City). Newspaper and radio audiences followed the jury debates and fiery defence speeches that led to the acquittal of María del Pilar Moreno in 1924 and María Teresa de Landa, Miss Mexico 1928, in 1929. The trial of José de León Toral and Concepción Acevedo, for the assassination of president-elect Alvaro Obregón in 1928, was staged and absorbed by public opinion in much the same way as the common crimes of Moreno and de Landa. This surely was a factor in the elimination of the popular juries in 1929, but police news continued to follow homicide investigations and trials with the same disregard about the proper distinction between politics and crime, as seen in the extensive coverage of the 1940 assassination of Leon Trotsky (Buffington and Piccato, 2009; Luna, 1993; Monsiváis, 1994: 18).

Before the 1929 consolidation of a fragmented political system under a single party, and the effective control of Congress by the presidency, public debates were quite open about themes that would later become harder to discuss. Although national political news remained contained by the main newspapers' loyalty to the presidential figure, local news media could be highly critical of local authorities. The national political elite remained largely in control of what the press said about them, but that was not always the case at the state or municipal levels (Scherer García and Monsiváis, 2003;

Piccato, 2010b). Media coverage and informal discussions about famous crimes shaped a field of public discourse that maintained a considerable autonomy from political power in subsequent years. In a few cases, these would involve members of the political class, particularly if they were killed, as in the murder of Senator Rafael Altamirano in 1959, at the hands of a former lover. The case was widely covered in *La Prensa* and other newspapers in Mexico City in March of that year.

Through the detailed information provided by police news (or *Nota Roja*), some particularly scandalous cases incorporated multiple voices and extended public discussion into multiple fields of public culture. The unanimous condemnation of those murders, recounted and photographed in gory detail, and the fascination with criminals' minds, explored in depth by reporters, created a broad public sharing a common sense of 'the facts' of reality – something not always available in other areas of public life. Indeed, Mexican newspapers of the twentieth century devoted much attention to crime news, and their coverage was not radically different, in terms of this moral consensus, across the ideological spectrum; interestingly, the opposite was the case in the German Empire (Johnson, 1995: 58–61).

The paradigmatic case is that of Francisco 'Goyo' Cárdenas, who strangled and buried four women in his Mexico City house in 1942. Housewives wrote to the president and newspapers, congressmen gave speeches demanding the reinstatement of the death penalty, and even female prisoners demanded swift justice. Psychiatrists, doctors and criminologists claimed authority over the penal law. Cárdenas was declared, in spite of his intelligence and education, mentally unfit to stand trial. Everyone knew and discussed his case, even if disapproval of the crimes seemed unanimous. Experts and lay people joined in a true 'interpretive feast', to use Carlos Monsiváis apt words (Monsiváis, 1994: 26; Meade, 2005). People insulted and threw stones at him as he was taken to the hospital or to prison, while some reporters treated him like a celebrity (Salgado, 1942). Political authorities remained cautiously silent: the death penalty was not reinstated, but he was not released until 1976, when he received applause in Congress as an example of a 'regenerated' criminal. The general balance of this case, in which, like many others, the guilty verdict was a minor aspect of the story, was to raise the profile of police news, in contrast with the uncertainty of the judicial process. While newspapers could follow a story over several days and provide readers with a wealth of detail about the case, judicial procedures were slow, recorded in writing, and taking place in the uninspiring location of court offices. Thus, newspapers tended to lose interest in a case after the suspect had been indicted or if the case was otherwise concluded. There was a narrative closure in the image of the suspect behind bars that was never found in the uncertainty of a long-postponed sentence issued by a judge.

Talking and writing about the crimes and mind of Goyo Cárdenas was not a veiled way to criticise President Manuel Ávila Camacho – as it was when defending María del Pilar Moreno, in her 1923 trial, during a massive military rebellion against President Alvaro Obregón. Yet the case of the serial killer provided broad publics the ability to talk about and judge the performance of representatives of the state, science and the law.

Press Images and Narratives

Why was the press able to amplify the political implications of murder? Homicide became the centre of public debates because it gave photographers, reporters and writers a clear grammar, many readers, and a relative autonomy to talk about Mexican society and government. Thus, we can best understand the political significance of homicide if we examine the rules and limits of Mexican journalistic depictions of murder (Kalifa, 1995; Pelizzon and West, 2010; Piccato, forthcoming).

Homicide attracted the interest of the mass media because its consequences could be depicted in a visual way impossible to emulate in other crimes. The twentieth century in Mexico, as in other places, witnessed the development of a visual language that filled newspaper pages with naked or decomposing cadavers, 'mug shots' of the suspects, and crime scenes with the objects and traces of death. Most researchers agree that photojournalism was the key to the popularity of newspapers such as *La Prensa* and weeklies such as *¡Alarman!*, and explains why police news was the journalistic genre that attracted most readers during the twentieth century. Their illustrations echoed the stark contrasts and frontal framing of forensic shots, but they added a sense of drama in conjunction with written narratives (Figure 4.5). Blood is abundant (thus giving its name to the genre: *Nota Roja*), but there is also information about the relatives of the victim (his brother in Figure 4.5) and the murder weapon (Monsiváis, 1994: 30–31; Stavans, 1993: 76–78).

These images were not just gore, but have a complex genealogy. Besides drawing heavily from the style of police investigations, police photographers also borrowed from other uses of the medium. Photography, along with mural painting, had developed a clear and effective political language since the 1920s, documenting and creating iconic images of the mobilisation of the Mexican masses and the inequalities of Mexican society. To illustrate that exchange we can compare Manuel Alvarez Bravo's 1934 photograph of a murdered worker (an image full of political meaning, taken from a political context) (Figure 4.6) with the image of a victim of a routine hotel murder in *La*

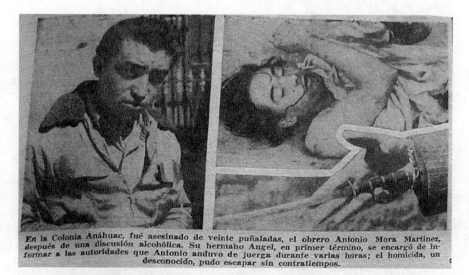

En la Colonia Anáhuac, fué asesinado de veinte puñaladas, el obrero Antonio Mora Martínez, después de una discusión alcohólica. Su hermano Angel, en primer término, se encargó de informar a las autoridades que Antonio anduvo de juerga durante varias horas; el homicida, un desconocido, pudo escapar sin contratiempos.

Source: La Prensa, 5 Jan. 1953, p. 23.

Figure 4.5.   Images of Nota Roja

Prensa twenty years later (Figure 4.7). Both are basically images of the crime scene. Even if Alvarez Bravo's photo was published in political magazines of the left, readers could not have failed to connect it with many similar images in which the dead body was the opening image of stories that often led to impunity – as suggested by the caption of Figure 4.5: 'the murderer, an unknown man, was able to escape without a problem'. Similar examples abound – a beaten victim's face (*El Universal Gráfico*, 1 September, 1942: 16), a naked female victim (*El Universal Gráfico*, 19 September, 1942: 1) – and the 'problematic' nature of the image within Alvarez Bravo's oeuvre has been analysed by John Mraz (2002) and Lerner (2007).

The Revolution, particularly since the 1913 military coup against President Madero, also provided plenty of images of death, for consumption in Mexico and abroad, as shown in the postcard in Figure 4.8. Many of these were published in *Nota Roja* magazines as part of historical articles about the Revolution. These stories usually dealt with assassinations and executions in the context of civil struggle, yet had many graphic and narrative traits in common with normal crime stories. Semi-interred bodies, like those of the victims of Goyo Cárdenas shown in Figure 4.9, also reminded readers of the many homicides in which the discovery of bodies was only the beginning of complex and uncertain investigations.

Not only police photographs but also *Nota Roja* articles had the ability to condense multiple, high and low influences, in a language that became accessible and popular, yet engaged readers in a critical exchange with

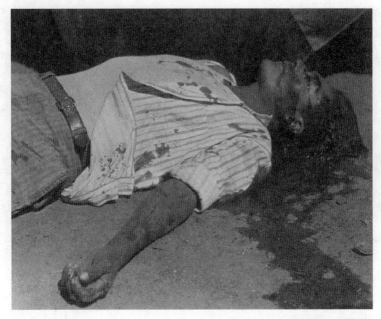

Figure 4.6.   Manuel Alvarez Bravo: 'Obrero en huelga asesinado', 1934 © Colette Urbajtel/Archivo Manuel Álvarez Bravo, SC

Source: La Prensa, 8 Jan. 1953, p. 1.

Figure 4.7.   Crime Scene, Victim, Suspects

the representatives of the state. As Monsiváis has noted, the narratives of *Nota Roja* continue the popular forms of transmission of information of the revolutionary *corrido* and oral tradition. According to Monsiváis (1994: 14, 42), the key to the success of the *Nota Roja* is the open-ended nature of its stories, similar to classic tragedies, in that speculations on motivations and fate are more attractive than any search for objective certainty about guilt or

The grave of a Federal officer executed in Juarez.

Source: The Grave of a Federal Officer Executed in Juarez, Postcard, 1913.

Figure 4.8. Postcards of Violence in Mexico

innocence. Yet the stories centred on homicides, often lasting several days, were not epic, chronologically direct narratives, as Monsiváis suggests, but more complex artefacts. They provided a wealth of detailed information gathered by the reporter and the photographer as soon as they entered the crime scene – often on the heels of police agents. Multiple articles, captions and images presented all the information to the readers, even if to do so they had to gather testimonies and evidence in advance of the police.

The 1954 image of the victim of a hotel murder in *La Prensa* mentioned above also exemplifies the effective combination of narrative and images in the *Nota Roja*. Closely cropped are the female suspect, held by a police officer, the administrator and owner of the hotel where the events took place, the two other suspects, also surrounded by police agents, the exact place where the victim fell and the body of the victim. The ensemble combines the gory shock of blood, the objectivity of the crime scene investigation and the shaming effect of 'mug shots'. The events, the consequences and the responsibility could not be depicted in a more direct and economical way. This case was quite straightforward, as the suspects were caught immediately and the victim was not a famous person. In others, where the initial mystery required the labour of detectives and reporters, these resources were also used and included diagrams of the crime scene and interviews with different actors.

The hotel staff were portrayed in an unflattering way in this image because they 'obstructed the job of reporters'. The illustration not only referred thus

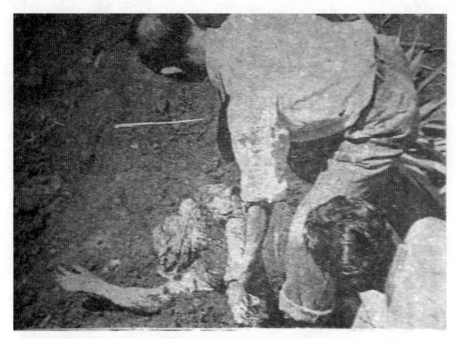

Source: Undated press clipping in Archivo Histórico del Distrito Federal, Sección Jefatura de
Policía, Serie Investigación y Seguridad, Servicio Secreto, caja 7, exp. 53.

Figure 4.9.   Victim of Goyo Cárdenas Disinterred

to the text (where the hotel administration tried to avoid the scandal and
delayed calling the police after the crime) but also to the implicit role of the
Nota Roja reporter, a that became central in the genre. Some reporters became
famous with their coverage of sensational cases, like that of Goyo Cárdenas,
which promoted reporter Güero Téllez to a position of considerable fame in
the profession. His reports were well written and included rapid dialogues,
similar to novels or short stories. The police reporter was closely identified
with the police; suspects sometimes took Téllez for a detective. Judges showed
reporters documents of the trial, allowed them to handle and photograph
evidence, and gave them complete access to imprisoned suspects (Téllez
Vargas and Garmabella, 1982). In one case, a reporter took hold of a fleeing
suspect. Other depictions of reporters presented them as young, modern and
well dressed, but the reality was that the police beat was not the most productive in a profession where those journalists covering the federal government
could receive thick cash payments and other incentives to remain loyal. Police
reporters, in contrast, were so close to the police that they often were associated with the abuses of policemen against citizens, when they did not become
detectives themselves, or carry police badges and guns (Marín Castillo, 1964:
28; Scherer García and Monsiváis, 2003; Rodríguez Munguía, 2007).

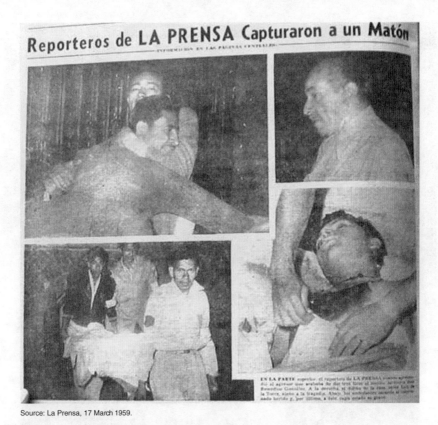

Source: La Prensa, 17 March 1959.

Figure 4.10.   Reporters of La Presna Capture a Criminal

It is commonly argued that the *Nota Roja* is a genre where moralistic opinion combines with scientific methods and morbid images to avoid dealing with the full political and social implications of crime. If we look at the specific stories of homicides, however, we find detailed narratives that faithfully convey the diversity of voices and opinions surrounding objective events. Readers had the right to know every detail and to have an opinion about the case based on fact, just like any detective or judge.

The political dimension of the *Nota Roja* is easy to see if we also read the columns and other news associated with it. Police pages contained opinions, reports and letters from readers about insecurity, police corruption and the failings of the justice system. Editors encouraged the active participation of readers in the course of stories. *La Prensa* interviewed readers, to ask them, for example, about the possibility of applying the death penalty, even in the extra-judicial form known as the *ley fuga* (shooting the prisoner while allegedly trying to escape, another trait of post-revolutionary 'micropolitics of violence', according to Knight). In the case of the Tacubaya barber shop,

Source: El Gráfico, 18 April 2007.

Figure 4.11.   Murder Victim with a Note

La Prensa offered a prize to the reader who submitted a 100-word letter containing the hypothesis about the killer's motivation that most resembled the truth, which was going to be revealed as soon as he was captured (*La Prensa*, 1934: 3). As one reader put it in a letter about an abusive landlord in 1952, *La Nota Roja* was 'the magazine that has defended the people of Mexico the most'.[2] Involuntary manslaughter, a staple of police news in the form of traffic accidents, reminded readers of the precarious safety of the streets and the ease with which those responsible escaped punishment and even the payment of damages to victims (*El Universal Gráfico*, 1947: 5). Recurrent 'purges' of the police were extensively covered starting in the 1920s.

In a way that was casuistic more than systematic, loaded with detailed information rather than broad programatic statements, yet in an effective language that reached thousands of readers every day, the *Nota Roja* became a space in the public sphere where civil society's concerns about justice and citizens' demands for state action against criminals found expression and, perhaps, a degree of impact on authorities' concern for efficacy.

Conclusions

Reading the secondary literature on *Nota Roja* in Mexico, I often came across references to Thomas de Quincey's ideas about murder as a fine art (Monsiváis, 1994: 87–88). At first, I dismissed the notion of murder as art as the facile device of taking an aesthetic approach to a phenomenon that needs first to be understood as what it is: a social problem with political and, yes, cultural implications. Certainly the *Nota Roja* has found increasing attention in recent years from a different audience: the photographs of Enrique Metinides are displayed and sold in art galleries, performance groups like SEMEFO play with forensic materials and references, and criminal stories inspire lavishly illustrated coffee table books (Villadelángel Viñas and Ganado Kim, 2008; Servín, 2010; Metinides, 2012).

Further research led me to think that there was something useful about de Quincey's provocative ideas. Beyond the possible attractions of blood effusion, homicide was a form of expression, an act full of meaning that sought and even created an audience, an object of criticism and multiple interpretations. Rodolfo Usigli's *Ensayo de un Crimen*, from 1944, the first

---

2   AHDF, GDF, Oficina central de quejas, caja unica, primer folder, clipping from *La Nota Roja*, no. 17, 13 September 1952, p. 2. See list of political achievements of *La Prensa* in one year of publication, 1.ene.1929, 2a sec., p. 5. Manuel Buendía's 'Red privada,' perhaps the most influential political column in the twentieth century and the reason for its authors assassination in 1984, was already published amid police news in *La Prensa*, 18 March 1959, p. 10. The arrest five years later of a police chief has not satisfied public opinon about the depth of the investigation (Monsiváis, 1994: 47). See also 'Mirador del D.F.' por Jose Angel Aguilar, also published in *La Prensa*. 'Vox Populi', published anonymously in *La Prensa*, reproduced neighbours' complaints about many urban themes and even their letters to the president demanding justice. *La Prensa*, 25 March 1959, p. 9.

and perhaps the best Mexican crime novel, explored the implications of this aesthetic view of homicide in the face of the ineptitude of the police: the main character, Roberto de la Cruz, imagines perfect murders but his victims are killed just before he can execute his plans. His work of disinterested art is never recognised by the press – a constant reference in the novel, sometimes quoted at length. De la Cruz decides to confess to the crime he did commit, but he is sent to a mental institution (the novel was based on actual cases, including that of Gallego: Stavans, 1993: 97–100). He is a frustrated author in a country where so many other, humbler people have the opportunity to achieve fame and power through crime. De la Cruz knew that homicide reached more readers than any other kind of news. Perhaps aesthetic value was not in the mind of most criminals, but they were certainly aware of the communicative value of the crime, and its broad repercussions in the relationship between state and civil society. The 'perfect homicide' is a fantasy, perhaps owed to de Quincey. A large number of offenders – around half in the United States, according to Monkkonen (2006) – get away with murder without any artistic pretension. A similarly high proportion of unsolved murders in Mexico has fuelled, during the twentieth century, the public perception of an increasing problem of murder, in spite of its decreasing rates. As the evidence discussed in the first section suggests, the frequency of murder was never so low as to be considered an acceptable and 'natural' aspect of Mexican life.

Homicide provided legitimate occasions to discuss the state, justice, society. The *Nota Roja* was an influential journalistic genre, beyond its gore and moralism. It forced the government to be responsive to civil society's demands in a way that preceded greater accountability in other realms. The increasing importance of human rights in the public sphere – first in political opposition, now in regards to the 'collateral damage' of the war on drugs – should be interpreted as part of this broader history of public debates about crime.

I would like to end with two by-products of this political history of common homicide. First, the massive demonstrations that took place in the summer of 2004: intended to protest against insecurity and rampant crime, they forced President Fox to respond, although in his characteristically tepid way. Strongly supported by business organisations and extensively covered by the media, the demonstrations conveyed the indignation of the Mexican public in the face of growing crime rates and several well-publicised instances of violence. 'A bunch of guys kidnapped my cousin and the bastards killed him', one participant in Mexico City declared, 'now what I'm asking for is the death penalty against them and if no one does anything we're going to take justice into our own hands'. Another warned that 'from this mobilisation onward, the ones that ought to be scared are the politicians, because they will see the power that civil society has when it demands attention to its problems' (*La Jornada*, 2004: 1–13; Buffington and Piccato, 2009: 3–21).

The other by-product is reproduced in an image from contemporary *Nota Roja*: a murder by *narcos*, one among thousands in recent years, communicates a clear message to rivals through a careful composition of the scene: the naked body, the dog and the note with large letters in the foreground. In another highly publicised case, the heads of executed victims were thrown into a restaurant in Michoacán. *Narcos'* deliberate use of media coverage is a counterpart to their frequent attacks against journalists – another increasing trend in recent years (Monsiváis, 2006; *Reforma*, 2 June 2007, 6 June 2007; Rodríguez, 2007; Piccato, 2012). The note in the image described above probably has to do with the internal struggles among drug trafficking organisations. Disputes among cartels have put a premium on perceptions of who controls the business in a city. But there was a broader message in the image: the state could do nothing about this and, we can be almost sure, the author of this homicide will not be punished.

This image summarises the changes in the practices of homicide that explain the gap between quantitative trends and the perceptions of public opinion. From the old *cantina* knife-fights of the early twentieth century, through the proliferation of guns after the Revolution and the exceptional but highly visible killings such as those of Goyo Cárdenas, all the way to the war-like violence of recent years, homicide has increased the sense of impunity. Petitions for justice by victims are no longer invested with the sense of political urgency that they used to have when presidents were considered more powerful. This does not mean, however, that the indirect victims of violence – a large sector of the population – no longer consider public safety important: the victim in the image described above might have been a *narco* himself (nobody will bother to clear his name in any case), but the collateral damage of images such as these reaches everyone.

Both middle-class protests and *narcos'* use of media stories and images of homicides anchor political disputes, incorporate large audiences, and reveal the limits of an historical perspective centred on the state. Stories and images made all homicides political because they expressed, when examined historically, changes in the state, corporative organisations and civil society. These changes, as other historians have suggested, had an impact on personal behaviour, specifically violence, but also on citizenship. The language of statistics, petitions and particularly *Nota Roja* created a field of public discussion that we would be too strict to call apolitical.

Acknowledgements

I would like to thank Laura Rojas for her support in this research and Pieter Spierenburg for his comments on an initial version of this chapter.

5

La Violencia in Colombia, through Stories of the Body

CRISTINA ROJAS AND DANIEL TUBB

Carleton University, Canada

This chapter explores a pivotal period (1946–1953) in Colombian history in which more than 200,000 mostly rural Colombians lost their lives and hundreds of thousands more were displaced from their homes in a complicated, multi-faceted, and geographically/temporally specific conflict that eludes simplistic explanation. Our aim is not to explain or locate the causes of the violence for, as French intellectual Daniel Pécaut (2001a: 558) contends, the excesses of *La Violencia* escape causal or instrumental explanations. The purpose of this chapter is to suggest, based on a review of a variety of readings of *La Violencia* in Colombia, that stories of the body, as outlined by Norbert Elias, Michel Foucault and Hannah Arendt, offer a useful lens through which to understand violence and the formation of citizenship at the dawn of modernity in Colombia.

In this chapter we take seriously the 'excesses of violence' in order to argue that *La Violencia* should be approached by analysing the technologies of government over the body, in order to grasp the conditions of possibility for the emergence of violence. Following Elias, we document how cruelty was made the object of public display, and terror became an instrument to control communities. Following Foucault, we argue that, in contrast to a normalised society in which individuals are perceived as capable of self-regulation, the perception among the elite was of a *pueblo* in need of physical and cultural improvement. Following Arendt, we ask how the mobilisation of biological imaginaries closed political spaces and generated outbursts of rage.

We propose the concept of tanatomo-power[1] to analyse the multiplicity of technologies of power over the body that made violence possible; these technologies included the tendency to govern the population under the

---

1   This is a combination of the words *tanatos* (the Spanish of the English thanatos, both from the Greek ϑάνατος) or destructive drive, and anatomy from the Greek *anatomē*, dissection, and *tomē*, cutting, with reference to the human body and the act of scrutinising.

perception of deviance rather than normality, the biological construction of antagonisms, declaring groups of population superfluous and the use of technologies of power centered on the surveillance of the human body. By taking an approach that concentrates on conditions of possibilities, rather than causal explanations, we want to move beyond essentialist explanations that attribute violence to the character of the population, or deterministic accounts that see violence as a necessary stage to modernity or as part of a desired revolution. Colombia's violence is discontinuous across time and geography; it manifested itself in multiple forms and it has been mobilised with different ends.

In this chapter we relate violence to the construction of collective imaginaries that closed the political space. We understand politics as the place where disputes are solved without recurring to violence while still recognising conflict.[2] We argue that violence was made possible through constructions of antagonisms as threats to be eliminated, rather than as political contenders. Moreover, certain imaginaries that made individuals superfluous or non-existent by referring to the colour of their skin or the weakness of the body as 'reasons' to deny voice, closed the space to negotiate their entering into political debates. Last but not least, the political space was closed when dominant groups perceived the *bajo pueblo* (low people), including peasants, Afro-descendants and indigenous peoples, as objects of improvement if modernity and progress were to be reached.

Our methodology uses interpretations of *La Violencia* developed by a selected group of scholars (Sánchez, 1985, 1992; Peñaranda, 1992; LeGrand, 1997; González, Bolívar and Vásquez, 2003). We examine these interpretations to make inferences about their potential contribution to the eruption of violence. We link the stories told about the body with the construction of imaginaries that closed the possibility of politics and, therefore, facilitated the emergence of violence. The first narrative centres on the (im)possibility of language; we analyse the books *La violencia en Colombia* (Guzmán Campos, Fals Borda and Umaña Luna, [1962] (2005)) – Mons Guzmán witnessed the

---

2 This understanding of politics is inspired by Arendt (1958) and Rancière's (1999) identification of the loss of a place with the loss of politics; for Arendt, politics make opinions significant and actions effective, while, for Rancière, the lack of place is also at the origin of politics, and he differentiates between police and politics – the former assign and distribute bodies to particular places and tasks, and determine which activities are visible and which are not, whose speech is understood and whose is merely noise (1999: 29). Politics breaks with the order of assigned places and tasks; political activity 'shifts a body from the place assigned to it or changes a place's destination' (1999: 30). Politics establishes disputes about the distribution assigned by police.

intensity of the violence as a priest in Líbano (Tolima) – and *Matar, rematar y contramatar* (Uribe, 1990) whose authors describe acts of cruelty over the body. Although this cruelty is presented as an emanation from personal frustrations or primordial desires, it also suggests that the disposition of bodies followed particular patterns suitable to interpretation. The second interpretation, based on the work of scholar Gonzalo Sánchez's (1991) *Guerra y política en la sociedad colombiana*, focuses on the (im)possibility of politics, as antagonisms did not take the form of contenders but instead appeared as deviants leading to the elimination of the transgressor; terror during *La Violencia* is analysed as a tactic on the part of the dominant classes. The third interpretation uses Daniel Pécaut's (2001a) *Orden y violencia* to describe the (im)possibility of representing social divisions. This impossibility is associated with the emergence of imaginaries which gave biological content to social divisions. The fourth interpretation, the (im)possibility of governing, is divided in two sections: one interprets Herbert Braun's 1985 *The Assassination of Gaitán* to describe the crisis in the technologies of governance resulting from the eruption of 'deviant' bodies into elite politics; the other, Mary Roldán's 2002 *Blood and Fire*, documents a case in which bio-politics is the prevalent mechanism of governance in what is perceived as the civilised centre, while tanatomo-power is employed to govern a periphery in order to contain blacks, indigenous and poor migrants from other regions. The last section outlines the (im)possibility of modernity by focusing on three articles that explain violence as the product of a struggle between the forces of modernity and tradition: Orlando Fals Borda (1985), Eric Hobsbawm (1985) and Camilo Torres (1985). This literature generally sees violence on the side of traditional forces struggling for modernity or revolution. We contend that the quest for modernity also contributed to the possibility of violence by declaring superfluous certain ways of living and denying them a political place as contenders worthy of consideration.

The History of the Body

Until the eighteenth century, penal repression was exercised primarily through corporal punishment displayed in public (Foucault, 1979: 8). Under Old Regime French law, the death penalty was imposed by drawing, quartering (dismemberment by horses), burning, breaking on the wheel, hanging, and decapitation. In 1762, the courts in Paris ordered 500 to 600 public humiliations and mutilations, and eighteen executions (Hunt, 2004: 44). Norbert Elias, [1934, 1978] (1994), Michel Foucault (1979) and Hannah Arendt (1958) focus on the body to explain the transformation towards the 'civilised individual' (Elias), the modern subject (Foucault), or 'the superfluous individual', also a product of modernity (Arendt).

For Elias, the 'civilising process' is characterised by its long-term duration, orientation towards the future, and its unplanned and unintended character; it did not happen without a certain order. Changes in feelings and emotions (psychogenetic) occurred concomitant with changes in societal structures (sociogenetic). The former were associated with the formation of a self-contained individual whose bodily functions were hidden from public vision, and whose conduct was controlled by feelings of shame and repulsion towards violence. A simultaneous sociogenetic change occurred during the process of state formation, as violence was progressively removed from public display. The monopolisation of physical violence by modern states pacified social spaces and imposed personal self-control. This pacification was possible because the removal of fear of sudden attack allowed individuals to suppress the impulse to attack the other physically. Elias was aware of the possibility of a decivilising process associated with the eruption of old fears. Civilised conduct would crumble 'if, through a change in society, the degree of insecurity that existed earlier were to break in upon us again, and if a danger became as incalculable as it was' (Elias, [1934, 1978] (1994): 253). Elias argues that this occurred in German society under fascism in the 1930s and 1940s.

Elias's 'civilising process' is distinctively a Western phenomenon; it 'expresses the self-consciousness of the West' ([1934, 1978] (1994): 3). Elias acknowledges that this consciousness was attributable to colonial expansion, suggesting that feelings of superiority were used as justification of Western rule over the non-European world. Despite this recognition, he believed that differences between Western countries and their colonies would be reduced with the spreading of Western standards of civilisation. This belief overlooked the fact that the process of civilisation in colonised countries was accompanied by narratives that, instead of removing fear of others, authorised violence in the name of civilisation (Rojas, 2002: xiii).

For Foucault (2003: 241) the analysis of the mechanisms of power over the body provides a grid of intelligibility to the social order. Modern societies are analysed in terms of the transformation of power. He calls the power that corresponds to modern societies 'anatomo-power' or disciplinary-power; it is a force that acts on the body by providing skills, promoting one's capacity for self-control, and facilitating one's performance in concert with others; it is a productive and a generalising power (Hindess, 1996: 113–118). Bio-power, a different modality of power, does not focus specifically on the body, but rather on life and populations, examines such factors as birth and mortality rates, and healthcare provision in improving life expectancy and the quality of life (Foucault, 1990: 139). With bio-power, life becomes a matter of state calculation, together with the emergence of norms as mechanisms of regulation to replace the use of force. For those that deviate from the norm, power tends to be more individualised, and it is over them that surveillance is exercised. Foucault (1979: 193) states 'the child is more individualised than the adult, the patient more than the healthy man, the madman and the delinquent more than the normal and non-delinquent [...] and when one wishes to individualise the healthy, normal and law-abiding adult, it is always asking him how much of the child he has in him, what secret madness lies within him, what fundamental crime he has dreamt of committing.' He acknowledges a combination of productive power and destructive power in the equation 'making live and letting die'. He differentiates this power from sovereign power which is 'take life or let live' (2003: 241). In his view, it is at this moment that the ritualisation of death began to fade away; instead of a spectacular ceremony, death becomes something to hide away, private and shameful (Foucault, 2003: 241–247). In the case of productive power, citizens are governed through freedom and improvements over life; political struggles over life are expressed in the language of 'rights': the right to life, to one's body, to happiness, to the satisfaction of needs, and to health (Foucault, 1990: 145). The 'letting die' refers to the elimination of forms of life identified as 'superfluous'. This relates to tanatomo-power, which, we will argue, took precedence over 'making live', bio-power, in the Colombian case. In a similar vein, Mitchell Dean (2002: 121) refers to the dangers of combining the productive bio-political powers of life and the living with the sovereign right to death.

Hannah Arendt helps us to relate technologies of power over the body, the impossibility of politics, and the emergence of violence. For Arendt, politics is a space of plurality where different perspectives converge, the space where citizens claim 'the right to have rights'. It is in a political community where individuals fight for equality and mutually recognise their rights: 'we are not born equal; we become equal as members of a group on the strength of our decision to guarantee ourselves mutually equal rights' (1958: 301). In her view, certain perceptions close the political space; one refers to the perception that people are driven by bodily needs such as the quest for bread, as the 'cry for bread will always be uttered in one voice'. Moreover, the cry for bread suppresses heterogeneity and difference: 'insofar as we all need bread we are indeed all the same [...] and manyness can in fact assume the guise of oneness' (Arendt, 1965: 89–90). As sameness abolishes plurality – a condition for politics – voicing concerns becomes unnecessary. She also poses a relation between the lack of voice, and the empowerment of leaders as organisers and spokesmen of the people. They tend to glorify the peoples' suffering, 'hailing the exposed misery as the best and even only guarantee of virtue' (1965: 107). A consequence is the dehumanisation of life as individuals are considered without dignity and lacking agency, which, according to Arendt (1958: 296), makes individuals superfluous by reducing them 'to the abstract nakedness of being nothing but human'. Her view of the superfluous individual inspired Agamben's *homo sacer*, defined as the one that 'may be killed and yet not sacrificed' (1998: 8) When people lose their 'place in the world which makes opinions significant and actions effective', forms of extreme violence are exerted on them, decreasing the possibility of representing their claims to the state (Arendt, 1958: 296). Or, if they do make claims, the claims are presented by authorities as a confirmation of their barbarian character and protest is criminalised. Moreover, devoid of political channels of expression, political resistance may sometimes become violent (Balibar, 2001: 18). We will argue that violence was the cumulative effect of the closing of political space due to the lack of voice, the loss of place and the perception of individuals as superfluous.

Spatiality and Temporality of *La Violencia*

The excesses of *La Violencia* make it difficult to identify its temporal and its spatial nature (Sánchez, 1992: 224). Early interpretations of the period identified the year 1930 as the origin of violence, when Conservative leaders accused the recently elected Liberal Party of assassinating members of the Conservative Party in the regions of Santander and Boyacá, accusations that later spread to other regions (Guzmán Campos, Fals Borda and Umaña Luna, [1962] (2005): 41). Some scholars choose 1936 as the year that violence originated, associating it with a frustrated modernity. Daniel Pécaut identifies it as the year of the Conservative Party counter-revolution in opposition to president López's modernising programme, the 'Revolution on the March'. Marxist interpretations tend to elect the year 1948, when the politician Jorge Eliécer Gaitán was assassinated, frustrating hopes of a social revolution (Sánchez, 1992: 83). Others argue that the violence was sparked by the presidential elections in 1946, which ended sixteen years of Liberal rule.

The statistics on deaths related to *La Violencia* suggest that the period encompassed a conflict on a massive scale that profoundly altered the way of life in many rural areas. While statistics are sparse, Oquist (1980: 6–11) contends that – based on the Colombian population figures from the 1951 census – of the 11.5 million people living in Colombia at the time, at least 1.5 percent (179,400 people) lost their lives during the period 1948 to 1966. According to Oquist's often-cited figures, the lowest estimate for deaths that can be attributed to the violence beginning in 1946 and ending in 1966 was 193,603, with the actual death toll likely to be far higher, as many deaths went unreported. Other estimates suggest that between 200,000 and 300,000 people died because of *La Violencia*. Nonetheless, the geographic and temporal breakdowns of these statistics show that the violence had a differential impact on the country over time and space.

The majority of fatalities related to the violence occurred between 1948 and 1950. Geographically, the violence had a profound impact in the departments of Valle, Antioquia, Tolima, and Western Caldas, with greater intensity in the North of Santander, Santander, Boyacá, and Cundinamarca (Oquist, 1980: 4). Focussing on departmental and annual statistics provides only an incomplete understanding of the particularities of the violence.

Apart from the events surrounding Gaitán's death and sporadic violence in the major cities, *La Violencia* was largely a rural phenomenon. Death occurred in isolated peasant hamlets and in the pathways between them. It occurred in the form of selective assassinations and massacres perpetrated by different groups: sometimes by Liberal and Conservative bands roaming the countryside; sometimes by neighbours within a community; sometimes by the police or army fighting Liberal or Communist guerrillas; and sometimes by criminal groups. Although soldiers, police, leftist guerrillas, right-wing paramilitary groups, neighbours, wandering criminals, and social bandits all perpetrated violence, the victims and the victimisers were almost always peasants. As to the question of banditry during *La Violencia*, Sánchez and Meertens (2001) unpack the ambivalent meanings of the term 'bandit' and argue for a distinction between social and political banditry.

In some areas of Colombia, such as the Eastern Plains and the south of Tolima, the violence could best be described as a guerrilla war; while in other areas paramilitary forces – known as *pájaros* (birds) or the *contrachusma* (literally 'anti-rabble') – roamed the countryside. In some cases, the catalyst was rivalry between villages and neighbours, while in others violence was the result of a conflict for the control of local politics. In some areas violence had a cyclical relationship to the coffee-growing season, as murders, robberies and assaults increased as coffee ripened and conflicts ensued over who controlled the harvest. In other areas, violence re-configured and concentrated property relations, as hundreds of thousands of peasants, Indians and Afro-descendents were forced to leave their land and migrate to the cities. An important characteristic of this period was the multiplicity of sites and types of violence involving interpersonal, social, economic and political dimensions. In this chapter, we show that these multiplicities of violence were also often connected with the perception of politics as violent.

As a consequence, the diversity of actors, places, temporalities and motives were encapsulated in the single name of *La Violencia*, a conflation that evokes several imaginaries. For some it refers to a background of terror. For others it is associated with the feeling of fear toward the other, be they a member of the opposite political party, or the fear that the elite felt toward the lower classes. For the popular classes, *La Violencia* becomes a synonym for an overwhelming actor that was responsible for taking their land and killing their family. The generalised use of the term *violencia* is part of the technology that we designate as tanatomo-power, as it allowed those who were responsible to be hidden, to govern through violence by using mechanisms of terror on the population, and to blame the population for the occurrence of the violence by accusing them of barbarism and uncivilised behaviour.

The Impossibility of Language

The corporality and terror of violence were analysed in the books *La violencia en Colombia* (Guzmán Campos, Fals Borda and Umaña Luna, [1962] (2005)) and *Matar, rematar y contramatar* (Uribe, 1990). The first book, authored by Mons Germán Guzmán, Orlando Fals Borda and Eduardo Umaña Luna, was based on documents produced by an official commission created by the government in 1958. The book aimed at the creation of a consensus that would put a halt to the still prevalent situation of violence. Contrary to the authors' expectations, the publication was the centre of angry debates among the public and political elites and the authors faced death threats (Guzmán Campos, 1986: 355; Fals Borda, 2005: 20–21). The book presents an overview of the different stages of violence by paying close attention to its geographical distribution, and the relationship between violence and the breakdown of institutions such as political parties, the police, and the army, as well as changes in the family, schools and even ludic activities. The book documents the effects of violence on mortality, migration and the judicial system.

The book turns its enquiry 'from the offices of managers or governors' towards the countryside, the 'space inhabited by the perpetrators of vio-lence (los violentos)' (Guzmán Campos, 1986: 351). Rejecting structural or functionalist approaches, it focusses on the 'human element' of the differ-ent groups implicated in violence: the displaced population, the guerrilla groups identified with the Liberal Party and their commanders, *cuadrillas* (gangs) who do not belong to a specific organisation but were anarchical and extremely violent, and the *pájaros* guerrilla organisations identified with the Conservative Party. The 'human element' is presented as common to all the groups said to be of peasant origin, illiterate, young, mestizo (although there were some blacks and indigenous peoples) and practitioners of Catholicism. The description oscillates between admiration and contempt, depending on whether the actors are described as having sensitivity to music, as good mem-bers of family and guardians of their home and honour, as hard workers, and as exhibiting political fervour and capacity for sacrifice. Following the pattern of modern historiography, the authors describe these groups as primitives without historical consciousness (Guzmán Campos, Fals Borda and Umaña Luna, [1962] (2005): 163). The role of women is limited to being supportive of the rebel groups; they usually appear performing maternal activities such as sewing and cooking. The exception is when they worked as spies, a role that caused their 'systematic extermination' (Guzmán Campos, Fals Borda and Umaña Luna, [1962] (2005): 163).

The book describes a variety of tactics to control communities. Groups dictated codes of conduct for the population and established structures of command. They printed orders (the *boleteo*) commanding the inhabitants to abandon a municipality. Groups also issued identity cards indicating whether the bearer could be left alive or condemned to die. Systems of financing included compulsory contributions and trafficking of women, a practice identified as unique to the Chocó region, with its majority black population. Each group created its distinctive language, dress code, and even instruments for killing that distinguished one from the other. Each had its own popular songs and anthems narrating the members' duty to use arms in order to liberate the people 'oppressed and violated by the law'. The songs praised the masculine image of guerrilla men who liberated women from oppression.

In a chapter entitled 'Tanatomanía of *La Violencia*', the authors describe how death was managed and instrumentalised by different groups: how all sides castrated the living and the dead, mutilated bodies, burnt, disembowelled, raped and killed. The authors use the term *tanatomanía*, a contraction of the Spanish *tanato* with *manía*, to refer to an obsession with death, its physical and sexual nature, the way that entire communities were liquidated. Violent practices are cast in psychological and corporeal terms, which, it is claimed, made the period almost unique.

Each group had its unique way of mutilating bodies. The authors describe these practices as a post-mortem reconfiguration of the body. The *franela* cut was particularly common in Tolima and practised by guerrillas; it involved a swift blow to the base of the neck with a sharpened machete to produce a deep hole that severed the muscles and tendons holding up the head. The *corbata* cut, practised by the *pájaros*, consisted of an incision made in the throat through which the victim's tongue was pulled out and left hanging. Decapitation involved the violent removal of the head, and its placement in the hands of the victim, resting on the pelvis or the chest. In some regions of Antioquia, the head was scalped so that the skull of the still living victim became visible. Ears and hands were removed to facilitate the counting of bodies. The 'flower vase cut' involved the stuffing of amputated arms and legs into the thorax cavity, after the victim's head had been removed. In some areas, bodies were diced as if preparing meat for *tamales*, a local staple made from corn boiled in banana leaves. In Llanos, victims were flayed alive. In Tolima, a favoured method was disembowelment, which involved cuts to the abdomen and the removal of the viscera. In other areas the quartering of the body became common, as did the inflicting of small cuts on the back, so that the still living victim bled to death.

Violence had a particular gender component: perpetrators used rape and castration to destroy the possibility of reproduction. Rape was employed by all sides; women and children were raped in front of their families. In some areas, such as Planadas, guerrillas took young women and raped them. In Miraflores, the authors report, an eighteen-year-old paraplegic girl was raped by fifteen men. Castration was common. In El Cocuy and Palchacual, 26 young boys were castrated, while in other areas testicles were cut off and placed in the mouths of the victim. In some areas, pregnant mothers were subjected to a caesarian, the fetus removed from the uterus and torn into pieces in the presence of the parents. After this, the mother was murdered.

Anthropologist María Victoria Uribe (1990, 2004) analyses the semantic meaning of massacres and mutilation. For her, death and mutilation were more than the physical act of ending biological life; processes of mutilation and dismembering were the language in which politics was conducted. Death was both a technology of destruction – the destruction of the life as well as the body – and an instrument to control survivors and their communities by instilling fear and generating terror. In addition, as terror was aimed at frightening people away from their land, it also created new institutions, reconfigured territories, and created local identities to the detriment of a national identity (Uribe, 2004: 89).

Uribe describes some general patterns of how violence was undertaken. The event often occurred late at night at the peasant's house while everybody was eating or sleeping. Soldiers banged on the door, and gathered all the men in the central courtyard. There they were killed. The military used a bullet or a sword, the guerrilla a machete, and the bandits and paramilitaries revolvers or knives. Although in some cases, women and children escaped, in others they were killed. Sometimes victims were tortured. When the perpetrator knew the victim, he or she received death threats, and when the victim was unknown, death came without warning. The next day, family members or community members would discover the bodies of the dead. Often, great care was taken in the presentation of the body, which Uribe describes as a corporeal stage management designed to terrorise, to instill fear, and to force the displacement of entire communities. Bodies were laid out in rows in the courtyard, with dismembered body parts scattered all over the place. In other cases, bodies were displayed at the crossroads of paths connecting different communities. Alongside these corporeal messages of terror, notes were left on trees, on the bodies, and on the walls of the homes of the dead, so that survivors knew clearly who had perpetrated the crime. Butchery and dismemberment became public spectacles in which mutilated corpses were displayed in carefully constructed public spaces, to be seen by survivors, passers-by and neighbours.

Michael Taussig (2003) reflects both on the categorisation and schematisation of death – found specifically in the diagrams used by Uribe, but just as easily in Guzmán's descriptions of cuts, on which Uribe's analysis builds – and searches for precision in the study of Colombia's violence. Taussig sees Uribe's diagrams as 'frightening and destabilising' images that are 'so detached from reality, so clearly, so strenuously unreal, yet nevertheless terribly real [. . .] that they acquire the haunting power of ghosts. Being so utterly without life, these diagrams of the outline of the human form create an emptiness that no mutilation or cartoon ever did' (Taussig, 2003: 130). Taussig suggests that 'in attaching a commonplace name to a transgressive act the act is somehow completed, dignified with a meaning [. . .] only to shatter that name and that meaning' (2003: 100). Thus, not only are descriptions of the violence necessarily incomplete, but there is also the risk that the relationship between these acts and the surrounding technologies of power, especially those originating among elites and powerful groups in state and society, will be obscured.

The Impossibility of Politics

Gonzalo Sánchez (1991), author of some of the most insightful studies on *La Violencia*, takes us a step further in understanding the relationship between tanatomo-power and the governing strategies of the dominant classes. In his view, they use terror as a strategy of control of the population. Political rivals are not conceived as antagonists but as deviations from the norm. As a consequence, social regeneration requires the annihilation of those transgressing the norm. Terror is not something that emerges by accident among the people; it is a deliberate policy that includes specific strategies, agents, organisations, rituals, instruments and chronology.

Although predominant, terror did not monopolise the political scene. Some resisted terror, as in the case of the guerrilla movement of the 1950s (Sánchez, 1991: 37, 1992). Areas dominated by the guerrillas also had their own codes of governance, for example those issued under the First and Second *Leyes del Llano* (Laws of the Plains), which Sánchez characterises as the most 'complete democratic project proposed by the armed movement'. Some of the 224 articles in these *Leyes* provided for establishment of groups to discuss community problems: the design of a war economy for the production and distribution of resources; the regulation of relations with the non-combatant population; and a programme of revolutionary instruction for the troops that included 'notions of civic culture, national history, courtesy (*urbanidad*), hygiene, reading and writing, and especially, knowledge of the motives and objectives of the struggle' (Sánchez, 1992: 97).

Questioning Marxists' interpretations of *La Violencia* (Kalmanovitz, 1974; Arrubla, 1978), as part of the process of primitive accumulation and the expansion of capitalism, Sánchez contends that the transformation into modernity emerged from below, through the mobilisation of an independent workers' movement in the 1920s, as well as through incipient peasant mobilisations and rural trade unions in the coffee economy. Sánchez, like most scholars, shares the perception that the division between Liberals and Conservatives was part of the traditional structure of society. He sees in Jorge Eliécer Gaitán a key figure in the mobilisation of popular classes against the oligarchy and foreign capital, and at the opening of the democratic space (LeGrand, 1997). This mobilisation occasioned a crisis of party politics (Sánchez, 1985: 797). The assassination of Gaitán in 1948 produced a revolutionary conjuncture that resulted in a failed revolution. As a response, the elites reasserted their control using party mechanisms from which *La Violencia* originated (LeGrand, 1997).

The Impossibility of Society

Daniel Pécaut searches for the origin of violence in the construction of collective mentalities that produce violence rather than democracy. His views are influenced by Furet and Lefort's insights on the institutionalisation of the social as a condition for democracy. In Colombia, the unity of the social was blocked by a natural division of the social body into two political sub-cultures, the Liberal and Conservative Parties (Pécaut, 2001a: 327). The programme of Liberal President Alfonso López's 'Revolution on the March' (1934–1938) represented the beginning of a modern bourgeois society. By introducing social and labour legislation, he aimed at establishing 'a new relation between the state and the people, founding a principle for the national cohesion' (Pécaut, 2001a: 134). López's aim was to further industrialisation and transform social relations in the countryside. Among his reforms, he set the basis for a modern regime of wages, the recognition of the social function of property, the state intervention in the economy and the modernisation of labour relations. López's Constitutional Reform of 1936 expanded citizenship to the entire male population, eliminating the requisites of literacy and property; the reform allowed religious and educational freedom. Although he proposed the introduction of civil marriage and divorce, as well as women's suffrage, these proposals were defeated. Notwithstanding, women were allowed access to university education as well as to hold public office. Law 45 of 1936 ended the discrimination between legitimate and illegitimate children, allowing both to claim inheritance and credit paternity (Tirado Mejía, 1981).

Pécaut contends that the opposition mounted by the Conservative Party and the private sector made modernity impossible; it was at this moment (1936) that the 'political began to unravel as violence' (Pécaut, 2001a: 317). Another factor contributing to the failure to constitute democracy was the entry of Jorge Eliécer Gaitán onto the political scene, which, Pécaut argues, did not introduce class concepts or revolutionary thought. Gaitán displaced the 'social' by giving a medical and biological content to social divisions (Pécaut, 2001a: 406). Pecaut's Gaitán fits well in our description of tanatomo-power, Gaitán's society was divided in biological terms between those 'without rights' and the oligarchy. Pécaut points out that Gaitán's mode of representing antagonisms dehumanised the contenders, as they became simply personifications of either enjoyment or suffering (Pécaut, 2001b: 65). Pécaut suggests that devoid of social content the programmes of the political parties – that is, regarding the orientation of the economy, or even social and cultural differences – the political was emptied of content. Because of this emptiness, the enemy acquired concrete characteristics, which he designates as 'pre-political', that stigmatised cultural, ethnic, religious, and socio-economic differences. He draws a conclusion similar to Arendt's: the use of biological imaginaries translated into the removal of political status from the masses. For Pécaut, the assassination of Gaitán left the masses without a leader, oscillating between passivity and rage, the rage erupting after Gaitán's assassination (Pécaut, 2001b: 71). Like Arendt, Pécaut's terror emerges as a product of the absence of language, as cruelty takes the place of language (Valencia, 1999: 161).

The Impossibility of Governing I

The analysis of Herbert Braun allows us to explore the presence of tanatomo-power, associated with the obsession with deviant bodies that closed the political space to the people, and increased the possibility for the spread of violence. According to Braun, Liberals and Conservatives shared a desire to govern the masses in accordance with a 'pre-capitalist ethos' founded on the belief that public figures were uniquely qualified to lead the people and that the masses threatened social order and civilisation (Braun, 1985: 20). The elite's aim was to encourage civilised comportment, and to raise the masses 'above the necessities of daily life, so as to ease their integration into society' (Braun, 1985: 22).

Like Pécaut, Braun did not perceive divisions among Liberal and Conservative leaders in programmatic or ideological terms. Their major disagreement was about how to direct the conduct of the people and how to preserve social hierarchies (Braun, 1985: 30; LeGrand, 1997). Gaitán's entrance into politics occasioned a crisis in the way the elite governed, not in the introduction of class divisions, as Sánchez contends. For Braun, it was Gaitán's lower-class origin and the dark colour of his skin that interrupted the elite's vision of government in the hands of a white elite. In his view the white elite 'became obsessed, not only with [Gaitán's] crude language and skin color, but with his teeth, his orifices, and even the perspiration that formed freely on his forehead and upper lip as he delivered his speeches' (Braun, 1985: 82). Cartoons in the main newspapers, such as *El Siglo*, show the fear inspired not just by Gaitán but by his followers, who were represented as naked Indians armed for battle, or as a black 'Gaitanista tribe' knifing (Arendt, 1965; Braun, 1985: 124).

Gaitán's speeches made bodily improvement a condition for reaching progress and modernity. He asked the peasants to take daily baths and brush their teeth, promoting movements known as the 'revolution of the soap' and the 'campaign of the toothbrush'. As Arendt reminds us, a focus on the needs of the body facilitates feelings of anger: 'When everybody had become convinced that only naked need and interest were without hypocrisy, the *malheureux* changed into the *enragés*, for rage is indeed the only form in which misfortune can become active' (Arendt, 1965). Moreover, she contends that the glorification of suffering makes misery the only guarantee of virtue; leaders tend to 'emancipate the people not *qua* prospective citizens but *qua malheureux*' (Arendt, 1965: 106–107). The following excerpt from a text written by Gaitán, entitled 'Biological and Social Reality of Men', illustrates how Gaitán conditioned democracy and citizenship on physical wellbeing and nutrition:

> Don't tell me that there is free will in an organism without nutrition; don't tell me that there is magnanimity in a body with [a] dysfunctional endocrine gland. Don't tell me that there are big achievements in a deficient liver[...] Our politicians forgot that man is a biological and physiological reality. And without nutrition in the cells and without a functioning and balanced organism, it is vain to speak of freedom, democracy, and national greatness. (Gaitán, [1946] 1968b: 473).

Moreover, the condition of illness and ignorance homogenised the people, blurring social divisions and political differences among them, while uniting them with their leader, in this case Gaitán:

> I don't find a difference between a Liberal and Conservative peasant ill with malaria; I don't find differences between the Liberal and Conservative illiterate [...] We are for the defence [of Liberal and Conservative

multitude] and we know that their needs are the needs we also feel; their outcry is the same that we cry out; their pain is the same that we felt yesterday and feel today [...] and against the embrace from the plutocracy we want to oppose the embrace of the forgotten Colombians. (Gaitán, [1946] 1979: 198).

Gaitán's state was a medical state, centreed on the management and regeneration of a population identified as deviant (Salvatore, Aguirre and Joseph, 2001: 84). Gaitán commonly depicted himself as a doctor performing an anatomy of the *pueblo*, advising the people on how to develop 'healthy and productive cells of the social organism' (Braun, 1985: 52). The state was not perceived as the guardian of a self-regulating population, which Foucault identifies as bio-power, but as one dominated by physical needs of the population:

> Under a pile of abstract concepts, we have forgotten the lives of men that love, suffer, have ideals [and] physiological needs. Under the abstract concept of freedom we have forgotten the free will of living men [...] Vindicate that man is our mission. It is not enough to assert that the man is submitted to the law. It is even more urgent to know that law is determined by man's needs [...] Thus the three main objectives of the state are the main aspects of man's life: Man is an organism that demands health, nutrition, and a clean house as conditions to live. Therefore, this is the first objective of the state [...] Our aim is the Colombian man suffering from malaria in hot lands; destroyed by lack of hygienic conditions in lowlands; malnourished everywhere; without hygiene, dress, shoes, and minimum medical conditions. (Gaitán, [1945] 1968a: 403).

Due to illness, individuals were deprived of a space in which to claim rights, which for Arendt was equivalent to making them 'superfluous'. With a similar argument, Gaitán dismissed workers' petitions for increased wages, as they could result in an 'increase in syphilis and alcoholism. An improved wage might be spent Saturday in taverns and brothels, and by Monday, children and mothers would not have food.' Politics was reduced to the satisfaction of bodily needs: 'today's politics is the life of our home, our room, food, bread, milk, meat and children. Everything else said is loathsome and a lie' (Gaitán, [1946] 1979: 473). As a correlate, Gaitán represented himself as the embodiment of the people ('I am not a man, I am the people') and as their only voice.

Gaitán was assassinated in Bogotá on 9 April 1948; that year the country was under the leadership of Conservative president Mariano Ospina Pérez (1946–1950). After hearing of his assassination, the *pueblo*, identified by the elite as *la chusma* (the rabble), burned churches, looted stores, derailed the trolley-bus system, and burned public offices. According to historian Braun (1986: 221–222), that day the crowd inverted social hierarchies: they dressed elegantly and furnished their houses with stolen articles; they collaborated and helped those in danger, while at the same time they reacted with hostility and desperation. The number of deaths was never made official – estimates fluctuate between 549 and 2,585 (Braun, 1986: 222) , but decomposed corpses were abandoned in the central cemetery as a testimony to the dangerous crowd (Roldán, 2002: 20).

In 1949 Laureano Gómez was elected president (for health reasons he served only until 1951, although he continued controlling the government through the acting president) in an election without the participation of the Liberal Party. His term in office is associated with the most intense period of violence. At that time, violence had spread to the rural areas; elites agreed that the *pueblo* was dangerous, and a war was waged against them. This war was accompanied by a racial discourse that attributed violence to indigenous ancestry and physical attributes. Unlike the nineteenth century, where racial exclusion was justified by the lack of civilisation (Rojas, 2002), racial exclusion was now medicalised, declared a cancer of *el pueblo*. Analysing the causes of *La Violencia*, a medical doctor wrote in the pages of the influential weekly news magazine *Semana*:

> [The country] is inhabited by descendants of the most fearful Indians that in remote times populated Colombia. We need only to study them superficially to know what we are dealing with. They live in extremely marshy (*palúdico*) lands and are friends of alcohol in the extreme. When they get drunk, the toxins begin to affect them and they become crazy [. . .] the only thing that matters to them is killing, and they do it without a second thought. (Braun, 1985: 254)

According to elite interpretations of the events on 9 April, it was the *pueblo* that committed irrational violence.

The Impossibility of Governing II

Mary Roldán's 2002 work on the geographies of *La Violencia* in Antioquia not only adds a regional element to previous interpretations, but suggests insights on the regional heterogeneity of *La Violencia*, as well as on the different strategies of government practised on those identified as 'deviant' compared to the category of 'normal', in this case white *antioqueños* living in the capital and central areas as opposed to the peripheral areas inhabited mainly by Afro-descendents and indigenous peoples. Her analysis focuses on Antioquia and describes the conflict over political, social, economic and cultural practices between the regional (departmental) and central states and the inhabitants of the peripheral regions of Antioquia, located in Urabá, Bajo Cauca, the north-east, and the Magdalena Medio. Our reading highlights the racial components of Roldán's analysis, in order to suggest how racial deviance from an imagined normalcy formed part of the technology of power, named tanatomo-power, which had violent consequences.

The language of racial difference allowed the departmental state and the regional elite to maintain colonial relations, as well as to ensure the displacement of peasants and recent settlers from lands in the departmental periphery. In the peripheral regions, land was concentrated, agribusiness and cattle ranches were dominant, landless migrants and seasonal workers were numerous, and extractive industries of mining and rubber prevailed over peasant farming. The language of race was used to justify murder, land seizure and rape against peripheral residents who were constructed as deviant, dangerous and criminal. Residents of these areas were dehumanised because they were constructed as deviating from a regional identity of *antioqueñidad* (the quality of being *antioqueño*). The identity of *antioqueñidad* dominated the central coffee areas and the city of Medellín. To be *antioqueño* was an imagined cultural identity, whose characteristics included discipline, hard work, whiteness, business sense, Catholicism and being from a coffee-producing region. Being *antioqueño* gave access to social and economic benefits provided by the local government and through private philanthropy, which was stronger in the Antioquia region. Residents in the peripheral areas of the department were imagined to be quite 'ethnically and culturally' distinct from this ideal (Roldán, 1998, 2002: 337–38). They were an internal-colonial other, labelled as 'non-*antioqueño*', *costeño* (coastal) and *negro* (black). Residents of the central regions saw those living on the periphery as 'everything they perceived themselves not to be: lazy, unruly, promiscuous, irreligious, and shifty' (Roldán, 2002: 37). Imagined differences included those in sexual relations, free unions rather than Catholic marriage; in labour relations, dominated by transience and seasonal migration, rather than sedentary homesteading; in the collective cultivation of land; in the 'tendency to embrace dissident political movements'; and in the practice of 'folk rather than institutionalised religion' (Roldán, 2002: 38). These differences became connected to ideas of 'deviance, criminality, and corruption', and were seen as threatening to the civilised identity of *antioqueñidad*. Violence and terror in the peripheral zones was a colonial development, as the regional state helped support the paramilitary in the pursuit of its economic and social goals. At the same time, entire regions and populations were dehumanised because of their imagined racialised construction.

In the central regions of Antioquia, Roldán argues, *La Violencia* never had a large impact because of the existence of a developmental state, which had been built up in the late nineteenth and early twentieth century. By the 1930s and 1940s, this state provided residents in the geographically central areas of the department with some social protections, including education, employment and public investment. However, Roldán suggests, access to these services was predicated on a variety of social, economic and cultural ties that included business associations, familial and kinship relations, and most importantly conformity to the imagined regional cultural identity of *antioqueñidad*. In the language of Elías, these central areas housed a self-contained bourgeoisie, imagined along the lines of *antioqueñidad*. Membership in the imagined community of *antioqueñidad* was constructed in the bodily terms of civilisation described by Elias, and in the racial language described by Foucault, being *antioqueño* became the arbiter of public and private repression and violence in the periphery. In Antioquia, the bodies on which the regional elites mandated terror were not distinguished along partisan lines; rather, terror was deployed to control those who deviated from an imagined socio-cultural normality.

The Impossibility of Modernity

A question arising from Roldán's analysis, and still not resolved in the literature, concerns the relationship between violence and the quest for modernity. The tension was in the mind of scholars, writing in the 1960s during the hegemony of modernisation theory, and those influenced by Marxist conceptions of history as transition to capitalism (such as Fals Borda, Eric Hobsbawm and Camilo Torres). A commonality of both tendencies is the argument that violence was the outcome of a struggle for modernity in a country immersed in traditional structures. In this contest, they argued, violence was exerted from below in the struggle against tradition. Although these interpretations recognise the agency of subaltern groups, they cannot escape a linear vision of history in which *La Violencia* appears as the necessary condition for a transition to modernity/capitalism. Moreover, this interpretation obliterates the violence that emerges from the tendency to install a single capitalist modernity in a culturally diverse country. In this section we want to take a step forward. We suggest that while Liberals' and Conservatives' perception of modernity differed, they agreed that it was impossible in a population marked by illiteracy, illness and peasant and indigenous ways of life. At stake was a project of physical, moral and cultural improvement of peasants, women, Indians and Afro-descendents into an industrial worker force. A disagreement emerged between the leaders about how to govern the 'low people', as documented by Braun and Roldán. We have referred to Gaitán's use of biological metaphors that suppressed politics. The technologies employed by President Alfonso López and Laureano Gómez closed the political space by focusing on projects of personal improvement, declaring non-modern modes of life 'superfluous'. They rendered these populations the object of intervention by designated experts: cultural missions for Liberals, and Catholic missions for Conservatives.

The Struggle for Modernity

Sociologist Fals Borda (1985), one of the authors of *La Violencia in Colombia*, described Colombia as a country that, in the twentieth century, was still dominated by a colonial mentality under the predominance of the church. In that country, indigenous peoples were treated like minors; it was a paternalism informed by religious beliefs. He called this ethos the 'sacred', which was not restricted to a religious connotation but rather to the survival of colonial structures. He saw the rise of Liberals in the 1930s, after almost 50 years of Conservative hegemony, and especially the reforms enacted by President Alfonso López, as modernising forces in the quest for secularisation, social security, land reform and labour legislation. In this account, Jorge Eliécer Gaitán was part of a modernising tendency; his assassination in 1948 put a halt to modernity. Violence, Fals Borda contended, was the 'irrational but effective' response from the population, mainly peasants from rural areas, against those who wanted to preserve the sacred order (Fals Borda, 1985: 28). In this interpretation, the passage to a true social revolution was frustrated partly because of the ignorance and lack of ideology of the 'low' people, which misled them as to their true enemies, and ultimately directed their violence against their neighbours and family (Fals Borda, 1985: 42). Notwithstanding, Fals Borda acknowledged that violence opened the room to a transition towards modernity and the defeat of the sacred; although, as he recognised, at a very high cost in lives and material losses. The historian Eric Hobsbawm (1985) endorsed Fals Borda's thesis; for him, Colombia witnessed the largest armed revolt of peasants in the Western hemisphere, with the exception of the Mexican Revolution. *La Violencia* was a frustrated revolution, as it was not accompanied by economic development, or by new and revolutionary social structures. Camilo Torres (1985), known as the 'guerrilla priest' (as chaplain of the National University, he joined the guerrillas in 1966 and was killed by the army a few months later) also saw in *La Violencia* the seeds of modernity. It allowed the integration of peasants into urban areas, the division of labour, and social mobility; it also opened the possibility of constituting a revolutionary peasant class.

Alfonso López Pumarejo's 'Revolution on the March'

López Pumarejo (1934–1938) combined elements of bio-power, opening the door to a concept of citizen rights, with perceptions of deviance, which combined projects of physical and cultural transformation. López Pumarejo attributed the lack of progress not to racial degeneracy but to ignorance and illness. The need, he said, was not for land or wealth, but 'to make [Colombians] more robust intellectually and physically in order to exert dominion over and take advantage of [the] territory. The consciousness of this need [led] the government to innovate in educational matters and to expand and improve hygienic and health services' (López Pumarejo, [1936] 2002: 147). His programme concentrated on the eradication of deviance or 'social wrongs' (*mal social*), such as illnesses, feebleness and malnutrition. During his term in office, the quest for modernisation was pursued through 'cultural missions', emphasising the biological and cultural strengthening of the population, mainly peasants in the rural areas (Sáenz, Saldarriaga and Ospina, 1997; Silva, 2005, 2006). Exhibiting truly missionary zeal, intellectuals participated in the programme of *cultura aldeana* (village culture), bringing cultural messages on good manners, the dangers of alcoholism, and the benefits of literacy (Sáenz, Saldarriaga and Ospina, 1997: 306). The project of cultural transformation included itinerant schools, book fairs and village libraries for small municipalities. The content of the books aimed at the creation of sameness instead of plurality; the book entitled *The Twelve Plagues*, available in every library, identified alcoholism, malaria, syphilis and leprosy as the most important problems of the population (Helg, 1987: 154). The project targeted life, which would be managed by the state, not based on their freedom but in their daily activies, as indicated in the following quotations from President López: '[M]y government understands education beyond schools for children [...] Education intervenes on life itself, using all the power of persuasion of the state, for its modification and improvement' (López, [1934] 1986: 219).

At the same time, programmes purported to attend at 'the kitchen and the dining table of peasants to teach them how to prepare their food and to take away the gluttony with which they approach nutrition [...] It is necessary to teach them simple lessons of hygiene and biological defense, and to create ambitions that are absent (López, [1934] 1986: 220). The ultimate end was the creation of habits of production and consumption required for capitalist expansion, as formulated by the interior minister Alberto Lleras: 'we aimed to raise the living conditions of the people, not only to serve better national firms [...] but also to have efficient consumers, that is, safer elements for industrial and agricultural progress' (Pécaut, 2001a: 229). The poor and the illiterate were identified as threats to be eliminated. Illiteracy, for example, was posed as a potential source of violence in need of eradication: 'We cannot continue building the life and reality of the republic over a vast layer of hopeless people [. . .] It is also not possible to think for a moment that the Nation would build its structures and organise its vital architecture based on people in permanent revolt against everything that is harmonious and that has stability' (Sáenz, Saldarriaga and Ospina, 1997: 292). 'Illiteracy has two deadly effects: it causes violent tensions because of the excessive distance between men, and, in addition, ignorance hinders the cultural and economic development of the country' (Helg, 1987: 212).

To manage this danger, educational programmes emphasised physical strengthening, as in the 'summer schools' (*colonias escolares*) programme under which 'weak' children were sent to other regions for 'physiological recovery' and education in 'community life', (López de Mesa, 1935: 35) and 'complementary schools' whose goal was to 'lift [the students'] lifestyle and get rid of vices and customs that form part of their [. . .] depressing ancestry' (Castro Martinez, 1938a, 1938b). Racial differences did not disappear from the debates, as in the case of the programme in Boyacá entitled 'defensive school', which proposed the 'defence of life', understood as racial improvement (Sáenz, Saldarriaga and Ospina, 1997: 99). Although created during the Conservative regime in 1924, the idea inspired López's education minister (Helg, 1987: 152). In 1934, the national conference of teachers discussed openly the importance of racial improvement for education (Sáenz, Saldarriaga and Ospina, 1997: 245).

Additional dangers referred to for the population were malnutrition, venereal diseases and alcoholism, identified as occurring mainly among the poor, Indians, Afro-descendents and women. The creation of the Department of National Hygiene and Public Assistance in 1931 was directed to the organisation of 'modern' hygienic campaigns; some targeted 'racial defense and improvement of race', while social assistance targeted the bettering of the sick individual [. . .] Hygiene is a social obligation, result of life in common and the needs of the conservation of the people', according to the medical doctor Juan de J. Peláez (Quevedo, 2004: 264). The campaign against *chicha*, an alcoholic drink made of corn and used by indigenous people and popular classes, is a good example of this; its consumption was associated with an illness referred to as 'Indigenous Sadness' (*melancolia indígena*) that was identified with the isolation, distrust and sadness of Indians from Cundinamarca and Boyacá. The medical doctor Jorge Bejarano argued that the explanation of the difference between European and Colombian workers was that the former '[has drunk] beer for centuries and our race [has drunk] *chicha*' (Márquez Valderrama, Casas Orrego and Estrada Orrego, 2004: 167). The promotional posters were more specific in the identification of the link between consumption of *chicha*, violence and race. One of the posters says 'Prisons are full of people that drink *chicha*' and portrays' a black man behind bars. The second portrays a hand holding a bloody knife with the legend '*Chicha* engenders crime'. Regulations enacted under Decree 1839 of June 2, 1948 and Law 34 of 1948 outlawed the manufacture of *chicha* in an artisanal manner; the reason was that 'one of the main factors contributing to political over-exuberance and crime is the use of alcoholic drinks, especially those of low quality and sold in places where its consumption is more prone to conflicts of all kinds' (Bejarano, 1940: 97).

Women were a special target of educational campaigns on issues such as health, hygiene and venereal diseases. Although the use of less repressive technologies was suggested, there was an increase in moral education and medicalisation of women's bodies. In the city of Medellín, social workers were named 'messenger angels' and sent to visit the homes of prostitutes, workers and peasants to 'spread the catechism of social hygiene'. The proposal of a 'nuptial certificate' was discussed, as well as the foundation of a eugenics laboratory where married couples could obtain free information on venereal diseases (Quevedo, 2004: 263–265).

It is not surprising that the reforms announced during the Revolution on the March were more a 'change in tone' than content, as is reflected in the lack of important social legislation on wages, benefits or conditions of bargaining (Stoller, 1995: 374). López did not introduce important social legislation before 1944–1945 (Pécaut, 2001b: 59). Even López's most progressive reforms, aimed at regulating labour conflicts and agrarian reform, did not reflect a strong commitment to establish social rights (Pécaut, 2001a: 315). A case in point is López's legislation on political rights, which was supposed to facilitate universal citizenship, at least for the male population. Catherine LeGrand (2008: 2) has documented how Decree 944 of 1934, which regulated Law 31 of 1929 on citizenship, particularised difference. Each identity card contained information on parents' names, which revealed whether the bearer was an *hijo legitimo* or *hijo natural*, the finger prints, the colour of the skin, the hair colour, the eye colour, the shape of the nose, mouth, lips, eyebrows, ears and forehead, as well as the external appearance – that is, whether they were dressed as someone with high status or as someone who was poor, and if there was any untidiness.

Laureano Gómez's Impossibility of Progress

When, in 1928, Laureano Gómez was invited to participate in the debate on the problems interfering with the country's progress, he stated that Colombia's cultural development could not attain civilisation. In his view, the racial composition did not ensure progress, because of the mix of Spanish,

Indian and black races. He perceived the blacks as existing in a permanent state of childhood, the 'savage Indigenous race' as totally indifferent
to the vigour of national life, resigned to misery and insignificance. He
called for a power that combined 'intelligence and artful device, passion
and surveillance, that minute upon minute combined favourable elements
and isolated the adverse' (Gómez, 1970: 40, 44–46). He saw himself as a
purifying knight, while his enemies named him a 'counter-revolutionary
inquisitor' and the 'creole Hitler' (Dix, 1971: 109; Henderson, 1988; Hylton,
2006: 37).

Gómez considered *Hispanidad* the golden age for Colombia. As several
authors point out, his speech was not that dissimilar from Gaitán's in its
anti-oligarchic rhetoric, its commitment to moral restoration and its distrust
of politicians (Dix, 1971: 109; Abel, 1973: 29; Pécaut, 2001a: 523). They both
catalogued politics as either pure or impure 'without a middle ground,
without commitment or complete rest; the only thing left is the call for
death' (Pécaut, 2001a: 524). Gómez introduced the opposition 'barbarism or
civilisation' to refer to the division between Liberal and Conservatives, and
presented politics as a battle between life and death. He characterised the
years of the Conservatives in power as a march towards politics: the protection
of life and impartial justice. On the contrary, the Liberal government that
started with President Olaya was designated as an era of political corruption
and annihilation of the political adversary. As early as 1934, he asked the
president 'to stop the bloodshed' (Gómez, 1981: 171–172). Narratives of terror
dominated Gómez's polemic against the Liberals as early as 1933, just three
years after Liberalism's ascent to power and thirteen years before *La Violencia*;
in this narrative he mobilised the fear of a return to a barbaric past, recalled
as consequence of the Liberal victory:

> During seventy-five years, efforts were made to civilise the people,
> to instill democratic feelings and republican principles, like respect for
> human life and social habits; the core of the barbaric man was eliminated
> [...] but in the past thirty months this peaceful land has been flooded
> with a series of crimes committed in the name of the Republic [...]
> A situation of terror has been established in most of the country [...]
> A disgusting and hateful scene of cannibalism garnished the so-called
> Liberal victory [...] What happened is not and will not be a victory: it
> is the unleashing of a dark, African, barbarianism, that hurts the honor
> of the Republic. (Gómez, [1933] 1981: 80–83)

Gómez dehumanised Communists and Liberals. He depicted the Liberal Party
as a monster with the form of basilisk, the mythological animal: 'Our basilisk
[the Liberal Party] walks with feet of confusion and ingenuity, with legs of

crime and violence, with an enormous oligarchic stomach, with [a] chest of anger, Masonic arms, and with a small, very small, communist head' (Pécaut, 2001a: 601). He contended that the Conservative Party fought against both liberalism and socialism because 'their lack of respect for religious beliefs of the people' (Gómez, [1933] 1981: 279). The Conservative Party, unlike the Liberals, adapted 'the Christian doctrine to the anthro-geographic and ethnographic conditions to the Colombian people' (Gómez, [1933] 1981: 893). He compared the struggle between the materialists, referring to both Liberals and Marxists, and the spiritual, as a struggle 'between violence and freedom' (Gómez, [1933] 1981: 809).

On similar grounds Gómez viewed modernity as oppressive, because of the primacy given to reason and the lack of attention to the primacy of the spirit and erasure of the evangelical doctrine. Extreme individualism, which engendered capitalism, was seen as equally oppressive, and was abhorred by the Conservative Party (Gómez, [1933] 1981: 811, 821). Moreover, he interpreted the re-election of President López as a 'declaration of war' which should be accepted as a crucial imperative. The disjuncture was between morality and life: ' [e]ither we accept the concept of fatherland, the concept of culture, the concept of morality deep-rooted in our consciousness or we renounce life [. . .] And this is an obligation to all of those who have children, an unavoidable duty because if, at the time of conceiving a child and bringing it into this world, they thought that it is a place of tyranny, corruption and scandal, a better decision would be not to have children. But given that you have them, we must defend our heritage, we cannot give it up' (Gómez, [1933] 1981: 615).

Conclusion

We suggest that *La Violencia* can fruitfully be understood by tracing the stories of the body. In this chapter, we have documented the presence of the technology of power that we designate tanatomo-power. It is a repressive power that acts on the body to eliminate those that are perceived as obstacles to progress. The peasant, the illiterate, the dirty and the sick all became the focus of this intervention. At best, subalterns are conceived (among other things) as ill, illiterate, racially inferior, demoralised and in need of close surveillance. At worst, they become obstacles to modernity, their status equated with superfluous individuals, devoid of the capacity to participate in politics. More important, they are seen as dangerous and threatening, while their protest is criminalised and feelings of fear dominate the political spectrum.

Drawing on diverse interpretations, we relate *La Violencia* to the impossibility of politics that resulted from conceiving people as deviants, who called for elimination of the antagonist. The situation was aggravated by the strategies of control employed by dominant classes, which consisted in the employment of narratives of terror. The use of biological imaginaries contributed to violence by declaring individuals 'superfluous', and as a consequence, their lives were put in danger. The belief that it was impossible to govern those identified as racially and culturally inferior meant that violence was directed towards the peripheral spaces and perpetuated with arguments of the lack of governability of the lower classes. Rather than attributing violence to the 'pre-political' partisan division of society, we emphasise that the identification of subjects with bare life and its individualised management through technologies that emphasise bodily needs, as illustrated in the speeches of the most influential leaders of the period, made individuals superfluous. Subsequently, they were expelled from politics, in the best cases, or deprived from the right to life, in the worst. The elite's homogenisation of multiple forms of violence into a single narrative that referred to the barbarism of the masses was another form of tanatomo-power that exposed the people to physical and political annihilation.

Last, but not least important, in this chapter we question interpretations of *La Violencia* as the product of a frustrated modernity where pre-political subjects revert to their primitive emotions and uncivilised behaviour. Rather than a process of history repeating itself, the adoption of a de-humanising language and the use of technologies of government emphasising death rather than life precipitated *La Violencia* as a project where governing the deviant and the irredeemable was declared impossible. We argue that it was these conditions that eliminate people from a place and that produced terror as the only possible language of politics.

Acknowledgements

The authors would like to extend their gratitude to the editors of the book, Ricardo Salvatore, Eric Johnson, Pieter Spierenburg, and also to Mitchell Dean, Catherine LeGrand, Richard Fidler and Herbert Braun, who read and provided valuable comments on an early draft of this chapter, as well as the anonymous readers who provided their comments. Any errors, of course, remain the responsibility of the authors. This research was possible thanks to a grant from the Social Sciences and Humanities Research Council of Canada.

6

Genocide and State Terrorism in Guatemala, 1954–1996: An Interpretation

CARLOS FIGUEROA IBARRA

Benemérita Universidad Autónoma de Puebla, Mexico

The case of Guatemala is paradigmatic of the enormous capacity for violence that can be unleashed by a state and ruling group faced with the threat of rebellion. Unlike countries such as Colombia where there are a variety of killers, in Guatemala the institutions of the state were mainly responsible for the extrajudicial executions and forced disappearances of approximately 200,000 Guatemalans (ODHA, 1998; CEH, 1999; Ball, Kobrak and Spirer, 1999). If we compare the case of this small Central American country with the crimes against humanity committed in other Latin American countries during the twentieth century, both in absolute and proportional terms Guatemala has the dubious honour of being number one.

According to data from the Commission of Relatives of those Killed and Disappeared for Political Reasons and of the Institute for the Study of State Violence in Brazil, there were 'only' 136 disappeared during the years of the military dictatorships, mostly between 1970 and 1975 (CFMDP/IEVE, 1995–1996). A preliminary report from the National Commission for the Protection of Human Rights in Honduras, records 'only' 179 cases of disappearances in the country between 1980 and 1993 (CNPDH, 1993). In Argentina, the report from the National Commission on Disappearances, entitled *Never Again* (see Chapter 7), records 600 cases of kidnappings before the military coup of March 1976 and 8,960 between that date and 1983. The great majority of the forced disappearances in Argentina were concentrated between 1975 and 1978 (Comisión Nacional Sobre la Desaparición de Personas, 1996). These 9,540 victims are from documented cases, especially in four years of the 1970s, during the counter-insurgency 'dirty war' carried out by the military dictatorships. In Argentina, these more than 9,000 cases are only a third of the 30,000 disappeared reported in conventional estimates.In the study of what happened during the genocide in Guatemala, it is not a question of repeating the syndrome noted by a specialist in the Armenian genocide: genocidal killing turns genocide itself into a unique experience for the victim (Dadrian, 2005: 75). Despite its cruelty, the genocide in Guatemala pales in comparison with the Armenian and Jewish genocides, as well as the experiences in the second half of the twentieth century: Iraq (1988–1991) with 180,000 dead, Uganda (1972–1979/1980–1986) with between 400 and 500,000 victims, Sudan (1956–1972) and South Vietnam (1965–1975) with similar numbers, Pakistan (1971) with between 1,000,000 and 3,000,000 dead, Rwanda (1994) with between 500,000 and 1,000,000 dead, and Kampuchea (1975–1979) with between 2,000,000 and 3,000,000 victims (Harff, 2005: 179).

Despite those shocking figures, it can be agreed that, with a territory of 108,000 square kilometres and a population from 2 to 10million during the internal conflict (1954–1996), 200,000 victims is a substantial number. It is the largest number in Latin America. This is one motive for my reflections on Guatemala and a powerful reason making such reflection necessary.

Violence, Terror, State Terrorism

In basic terms, violence is an act of power. But not every act of power is violent. Violence is an action that implies the use of physical force, or the threat of it, to impose the will of who is exercising that physical force or threat upon the person who is the object of that action. Thus, violence is an act of domination that expresses a social relationship, at least between the person that exercises it in the interests of an objective of power and the person who is victim of that action. Since violence is a phenomenon that has always existed, it is easy to be tempted to associate it with human character. But there is another answer to the origin of violence: that it is a product of socialisation. The first explanation is based on the assumption that a 'human essence' exists, and the second assumes that this essence has historicity (Figueroa Ibarra, 2001: 16).

One argument, worthy of the common sense that is often put forward, lends the violence an 'animal nature', or an irrational bad habit that alienates us from what is human. Again we find in this kind of argument a quite common way of thinking: transforming into natural that which is social (Figueroa Ibarra, 2001: 14). In reality, as Santiago Genovés says, the roots of violence are not something innately human, but are in the culture, nor are those roots found in the bad animal habits that we humans still have (Genovés, 1993: 83, 111). As a rational phenomenon, violence is a human trait, since 'only man can be violent' (Sánchez Vázquez, 1980: 427–480).

As an act of power, in the broadest sense every act of violence is a political act. Thus, politics is a sphere to which violence is closely linked, because it is almost implied by the very notion of power: the ability to impose one's own will on others, given a determined balance of forces. This is why there is no lack of people who define violence as a link in which one of those who is linked 'exercises his or her accumulated power' (Izaguirre, 1997: 3). Violence can be an act of domination and also an act of resistance. As an act of domination, violence is a means to impose privileges arising from power and wealth, while as an act of resistance it is also a means to avoid or destroy this imposition.

Just as not every act of power is an act of violence, not every act of violence is necessarily an act of terror. An act of violence becomes an act of terror when it has the premeditated purpose of destroying spiritually the victim or victims, by way of the fear it instills. Violence, like terror, seeks to destroy the will of the person (who is the target of this terror) to do or stop doing something. In the case of terrorism carried out as an act of domination, the violence seeks to destroy the victim's will of transformation (Figueroa Ibarra, 1991: 37). Like violence, terror can become an act of domination or an act of resistance. Not only those who resist commit acts of terrorism; also those that dominate do so. Furthermore, terrorism is probably an act of violence preferred by the strong and powerful (Chomsky, 2001). By terrorism, it should be understood as every act of violence that seeks to instill extreme fear in the adversary, and which is carried out by means of acts of violence that do not distinguish between civilian and military objectives (Figueroa Ibarra, 2002: 16). Indiscriminate violence carried out with the conscious objective of instilling extreme terror is the essence of terrorism. This definition is valid for those forces in civil society who resist by making use of this evil method, as well as those forces from the state level that use this method to subjugate people.

When we talk of carrying out actions of indiscriminate violence from the state level that seek to instill extreme fear, we are speaking of state terrorism. Generally these actions have counter-insurgency purposes, that is, they are carried out when there is a situation of intense or broad rebelliousness in a society and in a given territory. In these situations, the violence unleashed by the state is intrinsic to it at its most extreme, illegal and illegitimate levels.

The Legality, Legitimacy and Illegitimacy of State Terrorism in Guatemala

In normal times, Max Weber has stated, the state is just 'a relationship of domination that is maintained by means of legitimate violence'; the modern state is an association of domination with institutional character, which has succeeded in monopolising legitimate physical violence as a means of domination in a given territory (Weber, 1974: 45, 92, 184). Actually, a state can exercise violence, legally and therefore legitimately, if it goes along with the rule of law. If the state does so by resorting to methods that the law endorses and does so following the national and international legal conventions respecting human rights, according to legal theory and political science it may resort to acts of violence that are legal and thus in general considered legitimate. When a state carries out violent actions that become illegal, it risks losing legitimacy, or losing the acceptance and assent of civil society and of the citizenry in general. It is also a fact that things tend to happen, as in the case of regularities: when a state faces periods of rebellion of significant sections of society, it easily falls into illegality regarding the use of violence. In Guatemala, the illegality of the use of violence was manifest in the extreme methods of repression unleashed against the population; these can be described as acts of state terrorism.

As long as a state adhering to legality maintains an internal and external legitimacy, the violence carried out illegally through state terrorism easily becomes clandestine violence. Thus, in these circumstances, the state carries out violence through illegal acts that it seeks to hide. It does so because it does not want to lose legitimacy within the territory that it governs, as well as within the international community. The state that acts in this way violates its own legality, and this act makes it effectively an even larger criminal than usual. It might be that a state openly carries out terrorist forms of violence. Since democracy has become more and more a synonym of good government, open state terrorism tends to be carried out with less and less frequency. Only in those places where democracy is not a commonly accepted value can the state openly carry out acts of terrorism without fearing the loss of legitimacy.

In Guatemala, we have witnessed the above-mentioned regularities or things that tend to happen. Guatemala lies in a region of the world where democracy is usually a commonly accepted value. However, in the context of the Cold War, democracy, in the specific region close to Guatemala, often became an ideological tool wielded by Western capitalism against its communist opponents. Thus, illegal violence, or state terrorism, could not be carried out openly. Furthermore, in Guatemala there was no established democratic tradition, nor a long history of respect for human rights. For that reason, the existence of an internal conflict that developed into an armed one easily led the Guatemalan state to unleash the most abominable repressive actions. However, in order to not lose its national and international legitimacy, the Guatemalan state had to carry out repressive measures, mainly through clandestine means.

The Tools of Counter-Insurgency: Countryside and City

Open state terror always had more possibilities of being carried out in the countryside than in the city. This was because, during the twentieth century, the nation's capital was the epicentre of the political struggle. There, the decisive political events were determined in the nation's most recent history. In general, the cities were nerve centres that the state suppressed, but tended to act as the sites for clandestine state terrorism and, therefore, it kept the democratic cover for the reasons of legitimacy mentioned above. The cities, mainly the largest ones, were showcases where the state made efforts to show the population and the rest of the world that democracy was a fact and that the violence was the work of 'extremists'.

The extreme signs of structural weakness of the state, seen in the years of the Romeo Lucas García government (1978–1982), meant that these priorities were set aside in the process of building of hegemony – such priorities were established by the degree of difficulty of constituting this hegemony in urban settings – and, thus, open state terrorism tended to replace clandestine terrorism. Nevertheless, because the rural areas became the epicentre of social conflict in the second half of the 1980s, the countryside continued to be the scenario of the most open state terrorism. The Panzós massacre in May 1978, whose most spectacular precursor in recent times was the Sansirisay massacre in May 1973, was but the beginning of a long series of mass and selective murders in which the army, military police, treasury police and military commissioners (civilians attached to the army), as well as elite corps such as the 'Kaibiles', participated openly.

Many examples can be given of clandestine terrorism, given the impossibility of using open forms. During the larger part of the various military dictatorships, the Constitution became a material force only in those ways beneficial to the most powerful forces; the democratic and union freedoms in the Constitution had an uncertain existence and, at times they disappeared completely, because, despite union organising being permitted in word, union leaders and activists were murdered, kidnapped or disappeared. Tolerating the registration of a new political party with a democratic character alternated with the murder of its leaders. The officials of the military dictatorships spoke of university autonomy, but at same time implemented new forms of intervention in the universities, so it was not necessary to eliminate university autonomy: employees, teachers, students and workers were murdered, the university president was harassed, the facilities were bombed, and bodies were left on campus with signs of brutal torture, until finally the university institutions were largely dismantled. The division of powers that was constantly spoken of contrasted dramatically with the reality of a parliamentary façade and a president who was just the political power of the army high command personified. The regularity of the presidential, municipal and parliamentary elections contrasted with scandalous electoral fraud.

The state's need for this democratic façade explains why in large part the so-called death squads carried out the murders, kidnapping and torture. These squads, which arose between 1966 and 1967, were no more than far-right groups protected by the dictatorship or the army and police apparatus. In civilian dress, they carried out the worst infamies against workers, peasants, students, office workers and intellectuals. Given this situation, the clandestine organisations and regular repressive agencies murdered, in the seven months between 1966 and 1967, more than 4,000 people (Aguilera Peralta, 1969; Maestre, 1969). The Guatemalan state organised state terrorism by trying to appear above it all, and in these years more than ever the legality became a tool of verbal demagogy. This is why the Guatemalan state made what has been called 'the rupture with its own legality'.

State terrorism, whether open or clandestine, seeks to create, in multiple ways, a certain psychological effect among the people who are its victims. This psychological effect appears as a deep fear, which can even become paranoia, like a sensation of impotence and weakness in the face of the powerful and terrible repressive machine, a feeling of conformity such that one does not try to change what one already knows cannot be changed, a passivity in the face of inequality and oppression, and, lastly, an aversion toward all political or social organisations that reject or oppose the status quo.

In addition to the distinction between open terrorism and clandestine terrorism, it is important to include the difference between selective and mass terrorism. Selective terror was based on the careful selection of potential victims for extrajudicial execution and forced disappearance. Old lists of communists or communist followers, drawn up by the Committee for the Defence of the Nation against Communism, were probably used to draw up the death lists. One of these lists, with the suggestive title 'Special book for registering the admission and release of individuals of Communist leanings', turned over to the Committee for the Defence of the Nation against Communism, can be found in the Historic Archives of the National Police (AHPN, 1954–1955). Further, there are police records, lists of criminal histories and reports written by agents from different police agencies. Everything was combined with intelligence work that led the counter-insurgency planners to select victims with a high degree of accuracy.

Under the Lucas García government, the selective terror was preceded by a psychological campaign, which laid the foundations for the timing of the murder or disappearance. This psychological terrorism was implemented at first by means of the public appearance of organisations supposedly unrelated to the state, like the Anti-Communist Secret Army (ESA), which announced its plans to begin a campaign of extermination. The publication in the press of lists of people 'sentenced to death', the sending of threatening messages to homes or places of work, and phone calls in the small hours of the night that made clear to the target that each of his or her activities during the day was under surveillance, were some of the aspects of psychological terrorism. All of these were complemented with the photographs and news that every day were published about the discovery of brutally tortured bodies, or about men and women murdered in the street inside automobiles, on highways and in farm fields (Figueroa Ibarra, 1991: 38–39).

In the final days of the Kjell Laugerud regime (1974–1978) and during the Lucas García government, mass terrorism gradually became the main form of terror. Unlike selective terror, mass terrorism was relatively indiscriminate. The massacres of Indian peasants, carried out under the counter-insurgency scorched-earth policy, were clear examples of mass terror. But even despite its indiscriminate use, mass terror was linked with a process of selectivity. As I will explain later, the massacres were carried out based on a selection process preceded by intelligence work that determined which regions were more under the influence of the insurgents. In May 1978, in the last days of the Laugerud government, mass terror was used to contain a movement of peasant masses in Panzós (a region between the departments of Alta Verapaz and Izabal). This terror was renewed at a time when it was necessary to set a macabre precedent so that no revolutionary action would occur again, as with what happened with the massacre in the Spanish embassy in January 1980. Again, in June and August 1980, its purpose was to disarticulate various trade-union and mass organisations with mass kidnappings of union leaders. But during the seventeen-month de facto government of General Efraín Ríos Montt (March 1982–August 1983), mass terror reached its height (Figueroa Ibarra, 1991; ODHA, 1998; CEH, 1999).

It is fitting to conclude this part of the chapter by suggesting some additional hypotheses on the differences between the countryside and city regarding state terrorism and counter-insurgency. At first sight, it can be said that the Guatemalan state found it more convenient to carry out clandestine terrorism in the cities and open terrorism in the countryside. It has been said that the state did this because any repressive action in the cities was more visible, drew more attention, and therefore had more negative repercussions on its legitimacy. Likewise, selective terror tended to dominate in the cities, while in the countryside, particularly in times of heavy repression, it was easier for the state to carry out mass terror. Lastly, the national and international media did not really have access to what was going on in the remote rural areas. So, in these areas, agents from the Treasury police, sections of the army such as the regular troops, elite corps from the army such as the Kaibiles, or the civilian population organised by the state, such as the Civilian Self-Defence Patrols (PAC), and in general the various repressive agents of the state had no qualms in openly carrying out the most atrocious human rights violations.

Finally, it is also fitting to suggest the hypothesis that, in general terms, there was a kind of division of labour in the repressive tasks. The police agencies focussed on counter-insurgency in the urban areas; the army did likewise in the rural areas. Among other reasons, this may have been due to the very operative necessities that the internal armed conflict imposed; ultimately the insurgency had its strongest strongholds in the rural areas. But there also may have been the necessities born of legitimacy: maintaining the army permanently deployed in the urban areas might have generated a perception of extreme crisis of ungovernability, might have made more clear to people that they were living under the rule of a military dictatorship, and might have contradicted the official line that peace was being preserved and that it was the 'extremists' who wanted to upset things.

The Tools of Counter-Insurgency: Extrajudicial Execution and Forced Disappearance

For numerous reasons it would take too long to analyse in this chapter the enormous repressive capacity developed by the ruling classes and the state in Guatemala. Suffice it to say that the colonial legacy of plunder, racism and repression, together with the dictatorial traditions, the anti-communism as the ideological glue of the far right, the rise of the insurgency, and the counter-insurgency advisors from the United States mainly gave form to what has been called the culture of terror (Figueroa Ibarra, 1991, 2006).

It can be said that the social phenomenon that made possible the development of counter-insurgency in the form of large-scale state terrorism was the engendering in the Guatemalan state of a culture of terror that was also the result of the combination of various historical events. By culture of terror we mean the political culture that conceived domination as the unchallenged and unquestioned rule of state power, which thinks the solution to any kind of difference basically lies in the elimination of the other side, which imagines the society as a homogeneous space regarding thought and also as a heterogeneous environment in which class and race designate legitimate differences, which thinks citizenry as just a formality that covers a class reality that it has to maintain, and which, lastly, as a result of all of the above, considers repressive violence to be a legitimate tool to preserve the world shaped according to that imagery (Figueroa Ibarra, 2005).

The accumulation and sharpening of conflicts that capitalist development in Guatemala has generated gave rise to two opposed cultures through which the conflicts that this model generated were manifested. The permanent state instability meant that state terrorism took on an economic aspect, because, though it was an ancestral custom, it became a current necessity in the sense that it was an indispensable tool for giving continuity to an economic model of exclusion. This exclusion was manifest on both sides of the coin: a weak and unstable state and a civil society with tendencies towards rebelliousness. The combination of these two factors was the basic source of state terror as a structural and permanent phenomenon. The cyclical crises of this combination were the basic source of state terrorism as a conjunctural mass event.

Then, extrajudicial executions and forced disappearances were the basic instruments that the state and ruling groups used to deal with the rebelliousness sparked by a dictatorial regime and capitalist model of exclusion. The extrajudicial executions were linked to the selective terror (murder or disappearance of individuals or small groups of people considered specific targets), but it was also linked to mass terror. Apart from their evilness, the extrajudicial executions had the advantage of eliminating people that were active, or supposedly active, in subversive acts or in the opposition to the military dictatorship. By executing such a person a destabilising factor was eliminated.

But the population was also affected psychologically by the extrajudicial executions as well as the forced disappearances. They generated fear as long as everyone who had played any leading role or was an important activist in the democratic political parties, revolutionary organisations, trade unions, peasant leagues, and neighbourhood or student groups were presumed to be 'list-able', and therefore feared that they might be liquidated at any time. Probably, to liquidate a person, state terrorism had among its more valued criteria the determination that the future victim was active in opposition or subversive activities. But, as extrajudicial execution not only sought to liquidate but also to intimidate, it was very probable that the counter-insurgency leaders considered a future victim to be valuable when he or she was broadly known and esteemed and had a wide range of personal relationships. This was done for the simple reason that it created more fear among the people who knew the victim than among those who did not. On the other hand, in the case of the murder or disappearance of leaders, in a way, among broad sections of the people, it was possible to create a sensation of lack of protection, of leadership and, of course, of organisation. As long as the counter-insurgency sought not only to disarticulate opposition and subversive activities, but also to sow terror, it is quite probable that another criterion for selecting victims was the clear lack of active participation in political activities or other struggles. When the victim had no relation to political activities, this increased the terror among those with some degree of participation.

Regarding forced disappearances, it is necessary to begin by saying that it is quite probable that an important number of these disappearances in Guatemala were carried out in the context of some kind of violence unrelated to political violence. Nevertheless, when the statistics on terror are examined, the quantitative variations of forced disappearances in general coincide with the periods and regions of the country characterised by big societal confrontations, and thus it can be deduced that this has been true in the great majority of cases counted as forced political disappearances.

The forced disappearances in Guatemala during four decades were acts of power mainly carried out by state repressive agencies to stop the subversion of the political and social order imposed after the 1954 counter-revolution. With the forced disappearance of individuals, and even of groups of individuals, the political regime achieved several objectives: to dispose of the body and spirit of the disappeared person, avoid international discredit and internal upheaval caused by the existence of political prisoners, avoid this same discredit as a result of the increase in official figures on deaths for political reasons and, lastly, sow terror among the people and thus destroy the people's will for transformation. The basic objective of state terrorism, whether through extrajudicial executions or forced disappearances, was to obtain passive consensus in the face of the impossibility of achieving active consensus.

Thus, we can say that, using an extremely evil rationality, the military dictatorships and limited or restricted democratic regimes in Guatemala from the 1960s until the larger part of the 1990s carried out actions of terror, including the forced disappearance of individuals or groups. Two cases of collective forced disappearance were paradigmatic in the recent history of Guatemala. The first occurred on 21 June 1980, when 27 leaders and activists of the National Union of Workers were kidnapped in the union headquarters in downtown Guatemala City. In the second case, seventeen union and student activists were kidnapped on 24 August 1980 while in a meeting in a Catholic centre called Emaús, in the department of Escuintla (Ball, Kobrak and Spirer, 1999). The state violence followed a logic that rationally adapted the means (the terror) to the ends (political re-stabilisation and disarticulation of subversive activity). It can be accepted that this rationality was not based on humanist ethics, but it is not acceptable to deny the rationality of the monstrosities that the Guatemalan people have seen in the past four decades. For example, by having control over the body and spirit of the disappeared person, the state repressive agencies succeeded in obtaining the potential information needed by the counter-insurgency. By making total use of the body of the disappeared man or woman, the repressive apparatus turned torture into an enormously productive means to get the information it needed. This productivity was only limited by the pain thresholds (and also the convictions) of the victim, or by how much time the victim could hold up under torture before dying.

Probably many of the disappeared ended their lives without suffering physical torture. This also illustrates another act of perverse rationality. In this kind of situation, the objective of the disappearance is not to get the necessary information for carrying out the repression more effectively, but rather to eliminate the opponent without political cost, or to be able to freely eliminate the opponent, because if the opponent had been turned over to the judicial apparatus for punishment, it would not have been possible to do this. Until the systematic forced disappearances became part of the political violence, in the cases of opponents or subversives who were captured and imprisoned, they were freed after a certain time. Thus, the quantitative increase of forced disappearances went along with the clear decrease of the role of the political prisoner. In the last third of the twentieth century, in certain circles the phrase was popularized that 'in Guatemala there are no political prisoners, only disappeared persons'.

The kidnapping and disappearance of thousands of people was an act of political violence. It was an act of power, carried out mainly by the state repressive agencies, in order to stop the subversion of the political and social order that had been developing since the 1954 counter-revolution. With the forced disappearance of individuals, and even of groups of individuals, the Guatemalan state achieved several objectives: the necessary information for the counter-insurgency, the liquidation of political enemies, and the intimidation of the population overall. Thus, the forced disappearances were acts perpetrated essentially by the state or, in concrete terms, by military dictatorships and, from 1986, by the first civilian governments. This was not a capricious act but a political option, because the objective of the different regimes was to annihilate an enemy or make it negotiate within the very unfavourable balance of forces. So it is not surprising that a very important number of the disappeared were people who had decided to carry out peaceful or violent acts of resistance against the situation created in the country from 1954.

Lastly, regarding extrajudicial executions and forced disappearances as instruments of the counter-insurgency operating in the countryside and the city, it is surprising to see that the empirical references to the latter are overwhelmingly in the cities. Relatedly, it can be thought that these acts of forced disappearance seemed more news-worthy for the media than those carried out in remote rural areas. Ball, Kobrak and Spirer state the following: 'Testimonies and documentary sources from the data bank of the International Center for Research on Human Rights (CIIDH) establish that the violence had an alarming increase in rural areas in the late 1970s and early 1980s. The press in Guatemala missed this completely.' They go on to confirm the supposition made earlier concerning the considerable data on forced disappearances in the cities: 'few journalists who live in the capital have managed to report on the life of the majority of the rural population in Guatemala. Particularly, for reporters with no local contacts, it has been difficult to get to and enter the geographically – and culturally – isolated Mayan communities' (Ball, Kobrak and Spirer, 1999: 58–61).

However, irrespective of the fact that this may have biased the available empirical information, it might be hypothesised that again this has to do with the necessity of a state forced to wage a dirty war and at the same time conserve its strength, pressed to preserve its legitimacy. If it the hypothesis is plausible that, in the cities, any act of counter-insurgency involving terror had a higher political cost than that carried out in the countryside, then forced disappearances might have been politically more profitable. One of the advantages of forced disappearances is that the state that perpetrates them can claim innocence, or put forward many reasons for the disappearance of a person, not necessarily as a result of an action of counter-insurgency. There are numerous stories of relatives of disappeared persons that record the responses of the authorities to their desperate efforts when they were asking if their loved ones were charged instead of being disappeared: 'Perhaps they went to the United States without telling you', 'Maybe he went off with another woman?' or 'Your relative must be in the mountains with the guerrillas' (Figueroa Ibarra, 1999: 193).

The General Dynamics of the Insurgency in Guatemala: The Cycles of Terror

In an original argument about this kind of violence in Guatemalan sociology, an interpretation of state terrorism was attempted that viewed the level of violence as a direct result of the greater or lesser degree of capitalist development observed in a given region. The regionalisation of the country, based on the different degrees of capitalist development within it, and its correlation with the levels of terror, became crucial in this interpretation.

In summary, the argument goes as follows: in Guatemalan society the system of capitalist production has arisen unequally, and this has generated regions or zones with a greater or lesser degree of capitalist development; in those regions where capitalism has been clearly established, there is an extreme sharpening of class contradictions and, therefore, political violence becomes more likely, including, obviously, state terrorism. This interpretation was based on the analysis of the regions of the country that were affected by the rise of political violence. This analysis confirms that these regions coincided with those where capitalist production had developed more deeply and broadly. So, according to this interpretation, the terror was a predictable result in any class society with large social groupings with antagonistic political and economic interests, which were exacerbated by the sharpening of the contradictions generated by capitalism and resolved via the class struggle in its highest form (CIDCA, 1979: 40; Aguilera, Romero Imery et al., 1981). [1]

What happened in the period following the years covered in the aforementioned research and publication enabled us to know more about the general dynamics of the counter-insurgency. At the end of the 1970s and in the early 1980s, the figures on state terror indicate that the regions that previously had not been affected by state violence now were common scenarios of this violence. It is not accurate to argue that a lesser capitalist development generated a less acute class conflict and, therefore, that a marked development of this conflict generated a greater social confrontation.

With what happened in the 1980s it could be confirmed that state repression is something that in general terms has a directly proportional relationship to the level of disobedience or rebellion in civil society. From this we can draw a conclusion that perhaps is a valid regularity or tendency beyond the Guatemalan and Central American cases: the sharper the conflict, the greater the resistance of the people who suffer the most in society, and the greater the violence from the state. The explanation for the selective terror as a constant in the country's political life and for the big waves of mass terror is to be found in the persistence of rebellions in the second half of the twentieth century. Although among the victims of state terrorism in Guatemala there were people unrelated to the rebellions, it would be a historical injustice to say that essentially they were passive objects of dictatorial cruelty. The big waves of terror in the second half of the twentieth century were the necessary and inevitable response, according to the counter-insurgency logic, to important expressions of mass rebellion and uprising. Selective terror as a constant can be explained by the repressive habits, but also by the fact that in those years the opposition and subversive activities were a constant part of reality.

Since 1954, Guatemalan society has experienced two large insurgent cycles (1962–1967; 1973–1982) and three major waves of terror (1954; 1966–1972; 1978–1983). These periods in the political life of the country were clear signs of the crisis that was generated beginning with the 1954 counter-revolution. Terror as a constant in the political life of the country was the most palpable proof of the necessity of state terrorism for the perpetuation of the society in Guatemala. The first wave of mass terror occurred in the months after the overthrow of the Jacobo Arbenz government in 1954. In addition to the thousands of victims that it left (it is said that there were 3,000 dead and

---

1   It is useful to point out that the sociologist Jorge Romero Imery was one of the victims in 1982 of the extrajudicial executions in Guatemala.

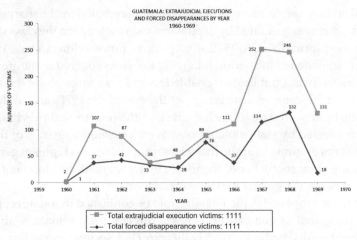

Figure 6.1. Guatemala: Extrajudicial Executions and Forced Disappearances by Year, 1960–1969

disappeared), it had a powerful effect that would become very useful in later years: the propagation of anti-communist paranoia.

The second wave of terror that occurred between late 1966 and 1971–1972 left thousands of dead and disappeared, along with the defeat and almost total destruction of the first guerrilla uprising. There are no records of the number of dead and disappeared for that period, but some estimates affirm that state terrorism murdered 18,000 Guatemalans, in order to annihilate a few hundred rebels (Torres Rivas, 1980). The characteristics of the terror at that time and the histories of horror can be found in the works of Aguilera Peralta (1969) and Maestre (1969). The second wave can be seen in Figure 6.1, which shows what happened in those years. It shows that the figures for the dead and disappeared began to increase in 1966, reached their high point in 1967, and began to decline in 1969. Regarding extrajudicial executions, this maximum seems to extend into 1968, but it also begins to drop the following year (Figueroa Ibarra, 2004, 2006).

The third wave of terror began in 1978, reached its height under the Efraín Ríos Montt government (1982–1983), and ebbed in 1984. In 1978, it began with the Panzós massacre in May, the violent breakup on 4 August of the mass demonstration for economic demands and democratic freedoms, and the murder of student leader Oliverio Castañeda de León on 20 October. Confirming the regularity or tendency mentioned above, the third wave of terror was a response to the rise of a second revolutionary cycle that began with the teachers' strikes in 1973. This cycle can be divided into two periods. The first is made up of the huge, mass urban and rural struggles between 1973 and 1978, which were dramatically crushed by the first phase of the big wave of terror, begun in 1978. This first phase , based particularly on

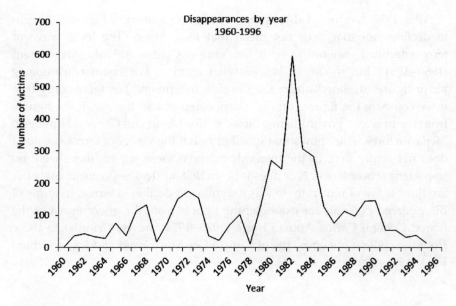

Figure 6.2.   Disappearances by Year, 1960–1996

selective terror, was aimed at mass, open and peaceful struggles. But there also was a contributing factor to unleashing the second period in this cycle: the widening of the guerrilla insurrection in the country between 1979 and 1982. This second guerrilla cycle was born of the reorganisation process and development of a new conception of the insurgent struggle that occurred within the insurgency after its defeat in the 1960s. In this new cycle, of particular importance was the re-insertion of a new detachment of rebels in the Ixcán area in January 1972 (Payeras, 1981).

In response to the widening of the revolutionary armed struggle, state terrorism increased in a phase of mass terror that, along with an important political realignment within the state, which began to be seen after the 1982 coup d'état, managed to force the revolutionary movement into a new stage of decline beginning in that year. An indication of the counter-insurgency behaviour regarding state terrorism can be seen in Figure 6.2 (Ball, Kobrak and Spirer, 1999; Figueroa Ibarra, 1999). This graph shows that, in the case of forced disappearances – and everything indicates that a similar behaviour can be seen in the extrajudicial executions – two big peaks can been seen in the case of counter-insurgency terror. The first is between 1966 and 1968 and after a declination between 1969–1970, rises again in 1972 and 1973, then declines up to 1977. In 1978, when the General Romeo Lucas García government took power, the counter-insurgency terror figures began to increase, until reaching very high levels during the General Efraín Ríos Montt government of 1982 and 1983.

After 1983, the forced disappearances figures shown in Figure 6.2 begin to decline, but that does not mean that they ended. The third wave of terror declined, beginning with the Vinicio Cerezo Arévalo government (1986–1991), but to say so is somewhat relative. The counter-insurgency terror figures declined under the Cerezo government, but this is only true if we compare the figures on the disappeared at that time with the figures from the previous governments, those of Ríos Montt and General Humberto Mejía Víctores. This shows that whether or not the waves of terror subsided does not imply that, in the intervals between these waves, there were no important acts of terror. Nor does it mean that, under the governments after the third wave of terror, there was a significant decline in terror. In terms of disappeared persons, for example, the figures from the government of the feared General Carlos Arana Osorio (1970–1974) are very similar to those from the civilian governments of Vinicio Cerezo Arévalo and Jorge Serrano Elías (1991–1993).

Strategy and Tactics of Counter-Insurgency, 1978–1986

To understand the general sense of the counter-insurgency strategy in the second half of the twentieth century, the first question that must be answered is related to its basic objective. Among the hypotheses developed along these lines is one that suggests that the genocide in Guatemala in reality was ethnocide. If this was so, the 150,000 extrajudicial executions and 45,000 disappearances would have been the result of a desire for what erroneously has been called 'ethnic cleansing'. In fact, the figures from the records on the terror in Guatemala show that the great majority of the dead and disappeared were people from the different ethnic groups existing in the country. Thus, inevitably, it is concluded that the great majority of the victims of terror were from the Mayan peoples. Even so, these figures do not show that the genocide in Guatemala was ethnocide with the aim of making the Mayan peoples disappear.

In reality, it was another basic objective of the state and ruling powers by carrying out both open and clandestine mass and selective terror as part of the weaponry in the counter-insurgency repertoire. The objective was to disarticulate the forces that opposed or sought to subvert the order bred by the Guatemalan military dictatorship. This order implied an economic and social model of exclusion, as well as a political and ideological regime of exclusion. The counter-insurgency terror was inexorably aimed at all those sections of the people in disagreement with this order, who opposed it, criticised it, conspired against it and subverted it, irrespectively of whether they were Indian or *ladinos* (as the mestizos are called in Guatemala), men or women, young or old, poor or well-off, or urban or rural inhabitants. If perhaps the genocide in Guatemala had ethnocidal consequences, this was particularly so because, in the third wave of terror, the greater part of those people who joined the subversive activities against the military and exploitative order came from the Mayan peoples. The counter-insurgency sought to annihilate, intimidate and disorganise the rebels, and it did so effectively, irrespective of ethnic group, gender, age, social position and geographic location. More than the dominance of an ethnic group, what the counter-insurgency defended was a complex model of privileges, pillage and oppression.

Having clearly determined its strategic objective, in general the counter-insurgency applied terror in an organised way and established tactical objectives. The counter-insurgency strategy must have begun to be forged in January 1978, when, as a result of the murder of Pedro Joaquín Chamorro in Nicaragua, a deep political destabilisation began to unfold, first in that country and later in El Salvador and Guatemala. Unlike what had happened previously, this political destabilisation was driven by broad sections of society who were putting forward revolutionary objectives. The triumph of the Sandinista revolution in Nicaragua in July 1979 sparked even more rebellion and the revolutionary thirst that fed it.

There were two periods in the third wave of terror. The first was characterised by terror aimed at destroying the mass movement and, therefore, at annihilating the mass organisations such as trade-unions, peasant leagues, squatter movements, and student and university associations. It is clear that the state terrorism at that time constituted a sharp response to the peaceful, open and legal struggles, which reached their height in October 1978. During this month, the urban masses, particularly in the capital, took to the streets in protest against the price increase for urban transport. State terrorism was used heavily to suppress the people. The tragic toll was 30 dead, 400 wounded and 800 arrested (Figueroa Ibarra, 2010: 72).

So, during the first period of this third wave of terror, approximately between 1978 and 1980, the overall function of state terrorism was to destroy the mass movement that arose in the 1970s, based on forms of struggle that were not necessarily armed or violent. Beginning in 1980, when the mass urban movement born in the 1970s was essentially disarticulated, state terrorism began its second period. Unlike the previous period of state terrorism, this time the emphasis was no longer on the mass organisations but was basically aimed against the insurgent organisations. From late 1979, repression was unleashed against the mass bases of the Guerrilla Army of the Poor (EGP) in the department of El Quiché. To stop this attack, the Robin García Student Front (FERG), the Committee for Peasant Unity (CUC) and other organisations responded with actions, which ended in the occupation of the Spanish embassy and the resulting tragedy on 31 January 1980.

A very important phase of this second period lay in the disarticulating actions carried out by the counter-insurgency in the infrastructure that the guerrillas had developed in the country's capital, for example the encirclement and suppression of the so-called urban 'cores' of the guerrillas, carried out in 1981. This offensive began in July 1981 and caused serious losses for the EGP and for the Organisation of the People in Arms (ORPA). This latter organisation recognised that, besides the destruction of the greater part of its urban infrastructure, the offensive annihilated 33 cadres of various ranks (Payeras, 1981). Besides the capital city, the insurgent organisations were based in various parts of the country and, unlike what happened in the 1960s, these regions were inhabited by Indian peoples. Thus, the counter-insurgency terror no longer involved only the central area of the country, particularly the department of Guatemala, where the nation's capital is located, but was much broader, including many departments, often those where previously the terror had been minimal. Given this situation, the first period of the wave of terror was aimed at annihilating the open, legal and peaceful struggles. The second period sought to destroy the guerrilla movement.

The periodisation and regionalisation of what happened between 1978 and 1986 show concretely which insurgent organisation at each point was considered to be a priority by the dictatorship. Clearly, in the first stages of this second period, the genocidal and scorched earth actions were the result of concentrating the military forces to attack those areas that (on the counter-insurgency map) appeared to be under the influence of the EGP. Among the 249 massacres recorded in 1982, 73 percent (which in absolute numbers meant 182) were carried out in the departments of El Quiché, Huehuetenango and Chimaltenango. In El Quiché alone, 80 were carried out, which amounts to 32 percent of all acts of mass terror carried out that year. The mass terror was very broad and deep in these regions, if we analyse the number of victims. As has been said, in 1982 the massacres left almost 7,000 dead (obviously this figure is only an indication, because only the recorded victims are counted). Of this total, the massacres carried out in those departments left 5,311 dead, which means 77 percent of the total victims of genocide in 1982. Furthermore, to strengthen this evaluation of the regionalisation of terror and its objectives regarding a particular organisation, the data on genocide and scorched earth policies in different towns in the departments of Alta and Baja Verapaz must be taken into account. In Alta Verapaz, 35 massacres were carried out (14 percent of the 1982 total) leaving 709 dead (10 percent of all victims) while in Baja Verapaz just seven massacres left 448 people dead (6.5 percent of all victims). Besides these departments, the genocide was not very significant in relative terms, although in some cases it was in no way insignificant. For example, in Sololá, eight massacres were carried out in 1982 that left 90 dead, while in El Petén four massacres left 228 dead and disappeared, and in

San Marcos and Escuintla, six massacres left 50 dead (Figueroa Ibarra, 1991: 231–261).

In 1983, evidence indicates that the Ríos Montt dictatorship varied its tactics of mass terror. First, the number of massacres and massacre victims dropped significantly. Some 82 massacres were carried out that year, which is a low figure compared with the 249 massacres the year before. The number of victims also dropped significantly, with only 957 recorded, while in 1982 there were almost 7,000. Second, the intensification of terror began shifting to other regions, even though the focus continued on El Quiché and Alta Verapaz. Of the total of massacres carried out in 1982, almost 30 percent were in El Quiché (24), while in Alta Verapaz sixteen were recorded (or almost 20 percent). Of the 956 victims of mass terror that year, 588 were concentrated in these two departments, which means almost 62 percent of the total; but other departments also began to feel the effects of the scorched earth and genocidal policies. In Quetzaltenango, six massacres left 51 dead, in San Marcos twelve massacres left 77 dead, and in Izabal one massacre left 30 dead. In particular, San Marcos and Quetzaltenango experienced a wave of selective terror during 1983, which was more significant that year than the mass terror. On the other hand, in all departments, a process of diversification of the mass terror actions took place, although on a minimal level. Thus, departments such as Sacatepéquez, Totonicapán, Retalhuleu, Jutiapa and Chiquimula, as well as Izabal, which in 1982 did not record any acts of mass terror (at least given the data we could get), in 1983 clearly became centres of state terror. Other departments, which in 1982 had been punished by this kind of terror, experienced less of it in 1983; examples of this were in Chimaltenango, Huehuetenango, El Petén, and Baja Verapaz.

The counter-insurgency's variations in tactics are clear in the analysis of the particular case of terror in the department of Baja Verapaz during 1982 and 1983. Even though the level of this terror there remained the same in 1982 and 1983, within it there were changes. So while, in 1982 the genocide and scorched earth policies in villages were applied in the north-west and central parts of this department, by the end of that year they had begun to extend toward the north-east. It seems that this shift was a result of the military priorities of the Ríos Montt government. Once they had finished the job against the most dangerous enemy, the EGP, the dictatorship began to attack enemies considered to be of less military importance, such as the Guatemalan Party of Labour (PGT). In October 1982, the army began a wave of massacres (between 20 and 30) in the municipalities of Cahabón, Senahú, Panzós and Lanquín, which continued into the beginning of the second half of 1983. For the same reasons, we can say that in 1983 the selective terror began to focus at first on San Marcos, Quetzaltenango and in the nation's capital, and later it turned the capital into its preferred scenario, at the same time as it was becoming the main form of terror. Lastly, in 1984, when the military dictatorship was headed by Mejía Víctores, it focussed on selective terror, although that did not mean that the mass terror had ended. In just the first three months of 1984, seventeen massacres were carried out leaving 200 dead (Figueroa Ibarra, 1991: 231–261).

The sense of all this periodisation and regionalisation of the counter-insurgency between 1978 and 1986 can be foretold. Beginning with the outbreak of a revolutionary situation in Nicaragua, the high command of the Guatemalan army must have proposed the annihilation of an internal enemy. This internal enemy was not of a regular nature, and thus not only were the insurgent organisations seen as military objectives, the mass organisations and civilian population, but also were viewed as the centres in which the insurgency was able to have a real or supposed influence.

Given this situation, broadly it can be said that the first tactical period of the counter-insurgency strategy was to disarticulate the mass urban movement that had developed in the 1970s. It focussed on this in 1978, 1979 and 1980. In late 1979, this focus was combined with the attack on the social base of the EGP in El Quiché and in 1981 proceeded to disarticulate the insurgent infrastructure in the capital. The targets of this offensive in the capital were the EGP and ORPA. In late 1981 it began to carry out scorched earth policies and massacres, which continued in 1983 and 1982 and whose main targets were the EGP and, secondarily, the other insurgent organisations such as the Rebel Armed Forces (FAR). The northern and central highlands became the preferred scenarios for mass terror, although this does not mean that the other regions went untouched. In March 1982, with the coup led by Ríos Montt, the state and army made a significant readjustment in their strategy, and the counter-insurgency terror was alternated with active efforts for legitimacy in order to re-stabilize the state (Figueroa Ibarra, 1991: 193–317). In 1984, the terror again became the focus in the capital and sought to disarticulate the clandestine network of organisations such as the PGT, which must have been considered of minor importance. From 1985, the mass terror declined and the focus shifted to selective terror, which would continue until the end of the conflict in December 1996. In this context, the strategy decisively shifted towards the establishment of a civilian government and democratic discourse, with which it sought to deprive the insurgency of a key argument: the existence of a military dictatorship. Formally the military dictatorship ended in January 1986, with the beginning of the Vinicio Cerezo government.

Legitimised Genocide and Terror in Guatemala

What occurred in Guatemala between 1954 and 1976 can be described as geno-cide. However,if we go by the legal definition adopted by the Convention of the United Nations Organisation on Genocide, the lawyers of the Guatemalan genocidal killers could argue that what happened in Guatemala does not qualify as such. There was no national, ethnic, racial or religious group that was destroyed totally or partially in an intentional way (Harff, 2005: 172). The case of Guatemala reveals the truth according to some specialists, but they also argue that the concept is problematic and tricky. Since the legal definition is exclusionary, in the Guatemalan case sometimes people who have argued that it was genocide have argued that the slaughter was aimed at 'disappearing' the different Mayan ethnic groups that exist in the country. Finally, it is argued, the great majority of those killed and 'disappeared' by state terrorism in Guatemala were people who belonged to these ethnic groups (Bjornlund Markusen, and Mennecke, 2005: 21–23, 47). The argument can be refuted with two equally true facts. First, an enormous number of victims were people who did not belong to any of these ethnic groups, that is that they were *ladinos*. Second, on the killers' side, there were enthusiastic Indian killers at many different levels of the genocidal apparatus.

Certainly Guatemala experienced much that was seen in the Armenian, Jewish and Rwandan genocides (Dadrian, 2005: 75–121). The slaughter was preceded by the creation of a negative otherness that generated the necessary conditions for legitimacy to carry out the massacres (Feierstein, 2000: 36–40). In the case of the region that includes Chiapas and Central America, the creation of a negative otherness manifest in the racism towards the Indian peoples was indispensable for legitimising the pillage and terror. The Indian was viewed by the ruling classes and *ladino* population – which arose beginning in the sixteenth century – as a lazy, dirty, two-faced, treacherous beast for whom there was only one remedy: the whip. But in twentieth-century Central America, especially after the insurrection in El Salvador in 1932, there arose a new negative otherness: communism. The new treacherous beast, equally two-faced and sneaky, sought to rob the honest citizens of the benefits of their efforts in favour of the state; it sought to rob them of their house in order to put several families in it, break up marriages and families, and even snatch away from parents the tutelage of their children, in order to cede it to the state. The anti-communist paranoia that the Cold War unleashed fitted perfectly into the extremist logic and totalitarian pretensions of the culture of terror. The Indians and communists embodied the otherness that had already been intolerable since before the beginning of the Cold War (Figueroa Ibarra, 2004).

The exclusivism of the legal definition of genocide has led some authors to develop other categories such as politicide (Harff, 2005) or gendercide (Jones, 2005). But if we set aside the legal definition and take up an inclusionary outlook, it is easy to detect genocide. The addition of the political and social groups to the national, ethnic, racial and religious groups, frankly, would place Guatemala on the list of countries where genocide is clearly obvious.

Also, this viewpoint is more solid if we base ourselves on the fact that the targetted group does not necessarily have to exist as such: it suffices that this group has taken form in the mind of the killer (Bjornlund Markusen, and Mennecke, 2005: 34, 40). What happened in Guatemala might seem to be a combination of the concrete existence of the group that was targetted for destruction (Indians and communists) and a subjective construct of them: the term 'communist' was applied with great flexibility to many individuals and social groups who hardly could be described as such.

The matter of negative othernesses is enlightening because genocide is only possible if it benefits from the passive or active legitimacy at least of part of society. This was examined by Eric Johnson (2002) when he studied the degree to which the German people knew of the genocide taking place in their own country, and concluded that it is very hard to believe that they were not aware of what was happening. The problem of the bonds of society and the counter-insurgency terror does not end with the question of the after-effects of the repression that continue to be felt among the victims, their families and society in general even after many years. In Guatemala, the fact must be directly confronted that, if the state was able to carry out the horrors recorded in the above pages, it was able to do so because there was a significant part of the society that passively, by simply looking the other way, or actively, by supporting and legitimating the terror, acted as a political prop for these actions (Calveiro, 1998; Figueroa Ibarra, 1999; Feiernstein, 2000).

The above text suggests that, when a state carries out violence that becomes illegal, it risks losing its legitimacy, or the acceptance and general assent of civil society and of the citizenry in general. But, what happens when this general assent is not lost or is not totally lost? What happens when at least a part of society actively intervenes with money and political support for these actions? Actually, you would then have to agree that the counter-insurgency terror not only was the work of a group of high-level military officers, but that there was also the involvement of a section of the business community. However, beyond that involvement, what happens when a section of society justifies the extrajudicial execution or forced disappearance of a person because he or she is a subversive or communist? The answer to these questions, and surely to others, must be given with painstaking care and precision in order to finish untangling the roots of the state violence in Guatemala. This is true because a good part of the origin of the counter-insurgency terror is to be found in the political culture that exists broadly in Guatemalan society; this political culture tolerates illegal acts of violence against certain people or groups of people as long as there is a consensus that they represent a danger. First, there were the members of different ethnic groups called, with racist disdain, 'Indians'. Then, there were the 'communists', however they might have been defined. Now there are delinquents, the *mareros*, that is, the members of the so-called *maras* (see Chapter 9 of this volume). The illegal actions carried out unofficially by police agencies, by death squads that probably operate within them, have a similar legitimacy to when in the past Indians and communists were assassinated. For better or worse, what is legal is not always legitimate, nor is what is illegal always illegitimate. In the sphere of vileness and evil, the extrajudicial executions of delinquents are legitimated by calling this legal monstrosity 'social cleansing'.

This subject, whose roots go back to the times of the dirty war in Guatemala, is very topical today. The press is already beginning to speak about it, saying that 'during 30 years the state was becoming criminal in order to defeat the subversive delinquency. Now, once more, a criminal state is being built to confront common criminals and organised crime' (Zamora, 2007). The worried journalist adds that 'the upper levels of the security forces in the Guatemalan state have always opted for efficiency and pragmatism and have proceeded to organise death squads composed of active police agents and professional goons contracted to murder delinquents, mafia gangsters and mareros'. It is discouraging that:

> these extrajudicial actions often have the support and sympathy of the people. In other words, they are popular causes, because the great majority of the people experience vulnerability and defencelessness when faced with criminality and are convinced that in the case of hard-line criminals there is no other way but to give them some of their own medicine. Hence, the desperation and fear of the citizenry ends up giving a certain kind of legitimacy to this variant of state terrorism. (Zamora, 2007)

This is the point at which Guatemalan society finds itself, at the beginning of a long road that remains to be taken. Along that road, on 28 January 2013, a pre-trial hearing started against Efrain Rios Montt for genocide and crimes against humanity.

7

The Narrative of the Disappearances in Argentina: The *Nunca Más* Report

EMILIO CRENZEL

CONICET, Argentina

The systematic disappearance of persons after the March 1976 *coup d'état* by the military junta, commanded by General Jorge Videla, resulted in two significant changes with respect to the intense history of political violence in twentieth-century Argentina. On the one hand, it turned the state's decision to exterminate its perceived enemies into an objective reality. On the other, it meant the clandestine exercise of political death. These characteristics also set the local military dictatorship apart from other Southern Cone dictatorships in the 1970s. In 1984, the commission appointed to investigate human right abuses recorded 8,960 cases of disappearances, 82 percent of which occurred in 1976 and 1977, during the first two years of the dictatorship (CONADEP, 1984).[1]

A Long History of Political Violence

The disappearances, however, were not an absolute departure from Argentina's political history. One cannot conceptualise the Argentine horror simply in terms of a 'breakdown of civilisation' (Huyssen, 2002: 17; Vezzetti, 2002: 13) given the political national history of the last century. Since 1930, in a political tradition that goes back to the nineteenth century, wide sectors of the society regarded military interventionism in the political arena as a 'matter of course'. With the influence of ideas from Catholic Integrism (a current that rejected communism, the principles of the French Revolution,

---

1 Human Rights organisations estimate there were 30,000 disappearances. In Uruguay, prolonged imprisonment prevailed; in Chile, disappearances represent one-third of the total murders; and in Brazil and Bolivia, fewer than 100 cases were recorded. On political repression in Uruguay, Chile and Brazil, see SERPAJ (1989); Comisión Nacional de Verdad y Reconciliación (National Commission of Truth and Reconciliation) (1991) and Arquidiócesis de San Pablo (Sao Paulo Archdioceses) (1985), respectively.

and changes in Catholic dogma and rituals), and prominence of nationalistic and conservative actors in public life, a culture marked by disrespect for the law and the rejection of otherness had emerged, a culture that privileged the use of violence to settle disputes. Furthermore, the use of torture had become a regular practice (Rodríguez Molas, 1984; García, 1995; Zanatta, 1996; Devoto, 2002).

In the 1940s, the emergence of Peronism polarised the political scene; the country divided into pro-Peronists and anti-Peronists – a process that continued after the 1955 *coup d´état* against Juan Perón. Parallel to this, in the context of the Cold War and the Cuban Revolution, whose influence was reflected in the ideas of the new Peronist and Marxist Left, the Argentine armed forces incorporated the Doctrine of National Security. Moreover, learning from the French experience in Indochina and Algeria, the governmental leadership thought that the 'enemy' could be located anywhere in civil society and, consequently, they perceived any social and labour conflict as a threat to national security. Hence, they did not hesitate to use torture as an instrument of military intelligence.

In 1966, the so-called Argentine Revolution seized the University of Buenos Aires and dismissed its faculty, stepped up censorship and fostered moral crusades against modern 'transgressive' practices embraced by young people (a more open sexuality, wearing long hair or mini-skirts, etc.). On 29 May 1969, in the climate of political radicalisation and student protests, student and labour militants took over the main streets of the city of Córdoba, defying the police and the military, to voice their demands and to call for the restoration of civil liberties in what would be known as the *Cordobazo*. After the *Cordobazo*, guerrilla organisations such as the Marxist Ejército Revolucionario del Pueblo (ERP; People's Revolutionary Army) and Montoneros (Peronist) appeared on the scene to combat the 'system's violence' and bring about social change.

Despite the amnesty for political prisoners granted by the Peronist government of President Héctor Cámpora, at the moment he took office (25 May 1973), the ERP guerrillas continued to operate. The Montoneros in turn, resumed their political violence soon after Peron took office on 12 October 1973, its militias becoming clandestine in the following year. Simultaneously, a paramilitary organisation, the Alianza Anticomunista Argentina (Argentine Anticommunist Alliance), was formed to threaten and/or murder political opponents, intellectuals, trade unionists and artists with ties to the Peronist or Marxist Left. On 1 July 1974, Perón died and was succeeded in office by his wife, María Estela Martínez de Perón. Political violence increased under the weak leadership of the new president, who clearly sided with right-wing sectors of the Peronist party. On 5 February 1975, by Decree No. 265, the President launched Operation Independence, authorising the armed forces to 'carry out any military actions that may be necessary to neutralise and/or annihilate all subversive element activities in the province of Tucumán' (National Executive Power, 1975). This north-east province was the epicentre of ERP guerrilla activities.

In October 1975 the Peronist government, with the opposition's approval, extended the military's involvement in the 'war against subversion' to the rest of the country through Decree No. 2772, issued by Provisional President Italo Luder (Boletín Oficial de Argentina, 1975). The idea that Argentina was a country at war was no longer limited exclusively to the armed forces and guerrilla groups, but became evident in the way that political violence evolved. From 1973 to 1976, there were 8,509 armed actions, 1,543 political murders, 900 disappeared persons and 5,148 political prisoners. Revolutionary and counter-revolutionary warfare experiences guided the practice of insurgent, state and paramilitary violence (Archivo CONADEP, 2010; Yooll, 1989). In this context, the armed forces overcame the isolation in which they had been since they stepped down from the government in 1973, and were able to establish themselves politically, as the only actor capable of restoring order.

In contrast to the Peruvian case, where the repression occurred under a democratic government (as described and analysed by Carlos Aguirre in this volume), in Argentina disappearances became the backbone of the anti-subversive war after the coup. Although 92 percent of the total disappearances occurred during the military government, the dictatorship always denied its responsibility for the practice, relativised the number of disappeared persons, or justified this practice as part of the 'war against subversion'. The leadership presented the disappeared as members of the guerrillas who had run away or died in combat, and the disappearances themselves as practices typical of the guerrillas or merely as isolated 'excesses' incurred during their repression (Bousquet, 1983: 61).

With time, the allegations by the disappeared's families attracted international attention. In 1976, Amnesty International and, in 1979, the OAS's Inter-American Commission on Human Rights visited the country after receiving thousands of accusations of human rights violations. The reports they produced were the first documents to request an end to the disappearances and the prosecution of the perpetrators (in practice, the Mothers of Plaza de Mayo had been demanding this since the beginning of the disappearacnes) (Amnesty International, 1977; Inter-American Commission on Human Rights, 1980: 17–18, 148–152, 289–291; Jelin, 1995: 119). The military dictatorship managed to prevent the dissemination of these reports and others with similar allegations (Mignone, 1991: 56–57, 111 and Novaro and Palermo, 2002: 281–282, 297–298).

The entire process of the disappearances comprised a sequence of violent actions that included public and secret instances. In general, the abductions took place in front of witnesses, whereas, in most cases, the captivity, torture and murder of the disappeared took place in a clandestine manner; Emilio Mignone, President of the Centro de Estudios Legales y Sociales (Centre of Legal and Social Studies) human rights organisation, created during the dictatorship, estimated that 72 percent of the abductions occurred before witnesses (Mignone, 1991: 67, 68). This procedure made it more difficult afterwards to reconstruct an integral picture of the sequence, to identify the state's responsibility, and to come to terms with the fact that the last phase in the sequence was murder – even for those reporting the crime (Yankelevich, 2004: 239–243; based on interviews with Meijide, 2004; and Calvo, 2005).

At the same time, a homogeneous style of criticism from the left emerged. Revolutionary arguments to denounce political repression, prevailing until the coup of 1976, were replaced by a humanitarian and moralistic narrative that called for empathy with the extreme suffering of the disappeared, placing the crime outside history. This narrative privileged the factual and detailed description of the violations perpetrated, and of the prisons, as well as the accuracy of the victims' and perpetrators' names. Those that had been affected by the repression were no longer presented as political activists. Instead they were characterised in terms of their basic identity data, such as their age and sex, and through comprehensive categories, such as their occupation, showing the indiscriminate character of the state's violence and the innocence of the victims.[2]

It was only after the dictatorship's military defeat in the Malvinas/Falklands War in June 1982 that the public silence about the disappearances was broken. The press published extensive and sensationalistic reports on the exhumations of the corpses of the disappeared carried out in public cemeteries, testimonies of survivors and perpetrators, and the reports produced by the human rights organisations (González Bombal and Landi, 1995: 156).

Upon taking office as President on 10 December 1983, the Radical Party's Raúl Alfonsín ordered the prosecution of both guerrilla and military junta heads. The provision was made under the framework of the so-called 'theory of the two evils', limiting the responsibility for political violence to the leadership at both extremes of the political and military divide, and designating state violence as a response to guerilla violence. It was also established that

---

2   About this type of narrative, see Laqueur (1989: 176–204). Markarian (2006) analysed the constitution of this narrative about political violence and its predominance among Uruguayan political exiles. Vezzetti (2002: 118) showed that this style of presentation was constructed as a way to face the dictatorship's stigmatising discourse.

those issuing the illegal orders for repression and those who had committed excesses during the fulfillment of these orders would be prosecuted, whereas those who had restricted themselves to obeying orders would be exempt from prosecution. The latter were assumed to have been unable to disobey because of the hierarchical military structure; nor could they have understood the nature of the situation, due to the prevailing ideological context (Official Bulletin, 15 December 1983: 4 and 5; Nino, 1997: 106, 107; Minutes of the House of Representatives, 5 January 1984: 422–424 and Orders 157 and 158, 13 December 1983). Finally, Alfonsín created the National Commission on the Disappearance of Persons (CONADEP), consisting of prominent figures without a political or military background, some of whom were members of human rights organisations. CONADEP was chaired by the writer Ernesto Sábato (1911–2011). Its function would be to receive and compile evidence about the disappearances, forward them to the judiciary, look into the *destino* (both 'fate' and 'the place where they ended up') of the disappeared, and issue a final report (National Executive Power executive order number 187, 15 December 1983, Official Bulletin, 19 December 1983).

CONADEP concentrated on and centralised the depositions about the disappearances submitted in the country and abroad during the dictatorship, received thousands of new ones from the families of the disappeared, as well as from survivors of that extreme experience and from perpetrators and witnesses. The committee inspected the 'Secret Detention Centres' where the disappeared had been clandestinely imprisoned, and also mortuaries and cemeteries, in search of information to determine their *destino*. The public report that the CONADEP produced was called *Nunca Más* (Never Again), and it gave rise to a new interpretation of the political violence that the country had undergone, proposing an intelligible narrative of the disappearances, a new knowledge about their magnitude, and ascertaining the responsibility of the armed forces for perpetrating them.

Nunca Más has since become an object of study from many perspectives. A first set of studies has examined its impact on the justice system during the transition to democracy (Funes, 2001; Kritz, 1995; Marchesi, 2001; Hayner, 1994, 2001; Grandin, 2005: 46–67). A second group of scholars has devoted itself to understanding the continuities and discontinuities in the representations and ideas about human rights violations that the report included (Basile, 1989; González Bombal, 1995; Drucaroff, 2002; Vezzetti, 2002; Corralini, Di Iorio, Lobo and Pigliapochi, 2003). This chapter will analyse *Nunca Mas*'s explicatory and narrative strategy, as well as its connections with the premises set forth by the Alfonsín administration in understanding the past exercise of political violence and also in relation to the human rights organisations' style of presenting their accusations.

Nunca Más: A New Narrative of Political Violence

The very cover of the report anticipates the style of the narrative. The wine-red colour of the book cover illustrates the blood that was spilled in the country. In the manner of street graffiti, on a red background and in white letters, a phrase summarises a statement that looks into the future and is set against the past that it rejects: 'Never Again'. From the start, the book (produced in fifteen days by Pablo Barragán) (Interview with P Barragán) suggests that political violence was the result of ideological extremes. This violence is not accounted for in historical terms, nor are the reasons that gave rise to it explained. Far from looking for its roots in national history, the report presents violence as a phenomenon transcending local boundaries (CONADEP, 1984: 7; Crenzel, 2011).

The report repudiates the violence prior to the coup (during the period 1973–1976), but emphasises the tone taken by the state's 'response' from 1976. Thus, the sequence of violence that it presents is contrary to the prevailing revolutionary imagination that justified 'popular violence' as a response to 'the system's violence'. In contrast, the report validates the military interpretation in which the state's action simply had the aim of confronting and defeating guerilla warfare. However, at the same time, the report contests this perspective by establishing a qualitative difference between insurgent violence and the disappearance of persons, and by this very same statement, establishes clearly the dictatorship's responsibility for the latter (CONADEP, 1984: 7). In this same sense, the report validates the knowledge construed by the military regime about 'terrorism',' but it establishes the specific practice of the disappearances as deplorable state crimes. Thus, the report dismisses the possibility of producing a new public truth about guerrilla violence and accepts the military narrative of such violence (CONADEP, 1984: 10–11).

In this way, *Nunca Más* reproduces the view of the Executive Orders that both the guerrilla and military leaderships should be prosecuted, limiting the responsibility for the exercise of political violence to these two actors. It does so using an 'impartial' language ingrained in the law, summoning truth to cooperate in the establishment of justice and requesting that the search for justice and reparation should not produce any hatred or resentment, or detract from the primacy of politics in generating national reconciliation (CONADEP, 1984: 10–11).

By limiting the dictatorship's responsibility for the disappearances, the report cuts out the past and defines its object: the illegal actions of the armed forces after the military coup of 1976. Although it does mention, at a later point, the existence of disappeared persons in 1975, under Isabel Perón's administration, this recognition is confined to the prologue (CONADEP, 1984: 16, 58, 299, 383). Thus, the report proposes an institutional periodisation of violence on the basis of the dichotomy between 'democracy' and 'dictatorship' that silences the political and moral responsibilities of the Peronist administration, the armed forces, the political parties and the society for disappearances produced before the 1976 coup.

On the contrary, the disappearances are presented as a product of a 'state of the state' (or 'state within the state') The dictatorial state exerts violence on life with impunity; it has the scope of a network and the depth of capillaries, while society is depicted in a dual position, but always innocent. Society is a possible victim and an outside observer that, if it had justified the horror, might be considered an accomplice of the prevailing terror (CONADEP, 1984: 9). Thus, the prologue of *Nunca Más* proposes a 'we' that is external to the exercise of state violence and terror, an 'imagined community' (Anderson, 1997) of citizens who are external to the internal antagonisms that marked Argentine society. The report projects this image onto the past in the above-mentioned terms. Yet, in establishing that the law is the golden rule of political struggle, the report also projects the primacy of law to the present and into the future.

In spite of these statements in the prologue, the corpus of the book proposes a shared responsibility of the perpetrators of the disappearances and other social groups. In particular, it highlights the complicity of the judiciary with the armed forces, but also mentions that of the educational authorities, factory supervisors and managers, and even companies (CONADEP, 1984: 379, 397). However, except in the case of the judiciary, the responsibility of other actors is always presented in private terms, never on an institutional basis. Thus, when describing the role of the Catholic Church, the report emphasises that the bishops 'repeatedly condemned the repression' and 'described [the methods used] as sinful', while it regrets 'the participation of some members of the clergy who consented or validated – with their presence, their silence and even their justificatory words – these very actions' (CONADEP, 1984: 259). Finally, the report does not mention the attitudes adopted by big corporations, the political class and the union leadership.

Possibly, because of the profile assumed by the 'we' in *Nunca Más*, the question about how the horror was possible does not come up. The questioning is restricted to the judiciary's inability to tackle the violation of the law. On the contrary, *Nunca Más* proposes as its central question a prospective interrogative: how to prevent this from happening again? (CONADEP, 1984: 9, 15). The absence of the question of how the horror was possible is complemented and reinforced by the absence of references to any sort of continuity with practices developed by successive dictatorships and political actors during the second half of the twentieth century (Cavarozzi, 1988: 37–78). The absence of this question is also underscored by the failure to mention cultural values pertaining to the country's political history, in relation to which the expectation that this horror will not happen again could be read as idealistic or unreal. In the report, the hope of these events never happening again is embedded in the continuity of the present, the restored democratic order.

Nunca Más proposes an image of vastness and unpredictability about those who could be the object of disappearance, depending on the vastness of the definition of the 'enemy' (CONADEP, 1984: 9–10). This proposition tends to detach the exercise of horror from all rationality. On the other hand, the report presents the disappeared as a heterogeneous and inclusive group, but with boundaries. It limits them to those who fought injustice, participated in proletarian struggles, opposed the dictatorship or attempted to change the social order. But it also mentions 'the friends of these people and the friends of friends, plus others whose names were given out for motives of personal vengeance, or by the kidnapped under torture' (CONADEP, 1984: 9–10).

In spite of this vastness, the persons mentioned all have one attribute in common: they are foreign to guerrilla warfare. This boundary, set in the prologue, is transcended in the course of the book, when political activists become included. In most of the testimonies (64 percent), the report simply includes their names, and it describes them as 'people or human beings' in 16 percent of the cases. Likewise, it calls them 'the kidnapped, the detained, the disappeared, the imprisoned or the prisoners' – only in 16 percent of the cases does the report mention their political activism (Corralini, Di Iorio, Lobo and Pigliapochi, 2003). Within this small subset of victims, their belonging to a certain sector of activity (for example, their trade or occupation) is described, and only in a negligible proportion of cases (3 percent) is their political participation mentioned; yet this appears always far away from the guerrilla groups.

On the other hand, the report gives the personal information about the disappeared including, in most testimonies, their first and last names, and in only a few cases, just their initials. The latter occurs in cases of disappeared women who were victims of sexual violence (CONADEP, 1984: 49–52, 67, 155, 191, 211 and 317). Whereas, on arrival at the camps, the names of the disappeared were substituted by a number, *Nunca Más* gives them back their names and their basic identity data. Interestingly, while, in Nazi camps, the number assigned to the prisoners was tattooed on their arms, the identification number of the disappeared in Argentina also replaced their identity, but was only recorded in their memories. These different forms of identity replacement are linked, I think, to the different premises held by the two determinations to exterminate: the bodily and unavoidable record of those 'guilty of being,' in the case of the Nazi genocide, and the changeable record, embedded in the memory of the captives, for those 'guilty of doing' in Argentina. Additionally, the report classifies the disappeared by age and sex, revealing a predominance of young men. Almost 82 percent of the disappeared were between the ages of sixteen and 35, and 70 percent were men (CONADEP, 1984: 294). It also presents their distribution by profession or occupation: workers (30.2 percent), students (21 percent), employees (17.9 percent), professionals (10.7 percent), teachers (5.7 percent), self-employed and others (5 percent), housewives (3.8 percent), conscripts and security force subordinate personnel (2.5 percent), journalists (1.6 percent), artistic activities (1.3 percent) and clergy (0.3 percent). Thus, the report highlights the importance and the majority of the disappearances amongst workers and students. The names are listed in only three types of cases among the disappeared: journalists, clergymen, and lawyers. This selection emphasises the violation of the law, the detainees' lack of opportunity to defend themselves, or to express ideas and principles that were constrained by the state order that upset their lives (CONADEP, 1984: 296, 375).

The scope with which the report features the disappeared and the restrictions that it establishes around their commitments are also reflected in the second chapter, 'Víctimas' (The Victims). Its sections combine the different above-mentioned demographic and socio-occupational variables and include specific sections on journalists, clergymen, conscripts and union workers. The other subtitles 'Niños desaparecidos y mujeres embarazadas' (Children and pregnant women who disappeared), 'Adolescentes' (Adolescents), 'La familia como víctima' (The family as victim), 'La represión no respetó inválidos ni lisiados' (The repression respected neither the sick nor the disabled), reinforce the image of the wide scope of the disappearances as well as their helplessness and 'innocence'. (CONADEP, 1984: 345–346) By mentioning these attributes, and by taking up the narrative created by the human rights organisations, the report depicts the disappeared as innocent victims, because of their 'foreignness' to guerrilla warfare and politics. Thus, the claim rests on the moral condition of the disappeared rather than on the universal and inalienable character of their rights (Novaro and Palermo, 2002: 489).

In this fashion, *Nunca Más* re-established the humanity of the disappeared, presenting their names, ages, sex, and professional and occupational activities. This makes for an abstract humanisation, presenting their lives generically and clouding their condition as concrete historical beings, their own political will, and all attributes that would remind us of the actual confrontations that divided Argentine society. Thus, the report gives a new political significance to the identity of the disappeared, counter to the dictatorship's perspective, which identified them as guerrilla members. At the same time, it renders them apolitical by presenting them as innocent victims, ignoring their political activism.

On the other hand, the identity of the perpetrators is amply recorded in the testimonies, which mention over 400 names. In six out of ten cases, their status as members of the state's armed forces or law enforcement agencies is explicit, it seems, based on Corralini, Di Iorio, Lobo and Pigliapochi (2003). Regarding their values, the report shows the repressive coordination of the dictatorships in the Southern Cone and explains at the end, and in a few pages, the doctrine that guided them (CONADEP, 1984: 265–276). Because of this expository strategy, the political arguments are subordinated to the pure description of the violations and emerge as their corollary, not as their pre-condition.

In spite of this, the report defines the scope and depth of the crime, classifying it as a 'crime against humanity' or as 'genocide' The use of hell-related metaphors to describe the experience of disappearance complements these statements (CONADEP, 1984: 7, 8, 9, 11, 247). Through them, the report highlights the violation of the religious and political principles held in the Western world and upholds, by opposition, the very humanity of man. This interpretation of the violations debunks, from inside their own sphere, the dictatorships' discourse that justified their actions as the defence of the values of 'Western and Christian' civilisation (CONADEP, 1984: 8, 15, 347–139).

The Restoration of the Reality of the Crime

Nunca Más attempts to restore the very same materiality of the crimes denied time and again by their authors. The reconstruction of the facts is based on an expository strategy that combines the presentation of the disappearances as a system, the practices that they entailed, and their embeddedness in a meaningful framework that made them intelligible. In this process, the report produces a new knowledge about the magnitude and scope that the disappearances reached in the country. For this purpose, the narration goes through the same sequential rationale of the disappearances: abduction, torture, secret captivity and extermination. Thus, the public and clandestine moments of the crime of disappearance are articulated in a single narrative. Its truth is sustained by a realistic and detailed description of the disappearance system and its stages, on the basis of testimonies and primary sources produced by various actors. This strategy, therefore, combines the objective and the subjective reconstruction of the facts from different viewpoints.

On this basis, the report proposes a constant confrontation with the explanations for the disappearances provided by the military. The text describes the abduction operations and sets them in space and time, and details the different forms of violence exerted against people and objects. It establishes the military and police composition of the 'task forces' that perpetrated them and shows the materiality of the Clandestine Detention Centres, specifying their location and characteristics. Through this, the report restores the space and time coordinates of the facts, socialises the topography of horror, and breaks the secret around it and its consequence: its social normalisation.

Nunca Más describes the systematic character and the multiple shapes of torture. It mentions children and even babies who disappeared with their parents, as well as children born in captivity. Their identities were faked and they were adopted by families of the military or police personnel, or their acquaintances (CONADEP, 1984: 63, 303). Likewise, the report establishes the widespread physical elimination of the disappeared, presenting various forms of death. Contesting the voice of the military, it points out that murders were often concealed as deaths resulting from 'non-existent confrontations or attempted escapes'. In many cases the corpses of the disappeared 'were destroyed to prevent their future identification' by throwing the captives, still alive, from military planes into the sea or lakes or rivers, by burying them in anonymous ditches in public cemeteries under the label NN, or by incineration (CONADEP, 1984: 137, 224–226, 234–246 and 480).

On the other hand, *Nunca Más* sheds light on a quantitative dimension of the disappearances (8,960 cases) that was unknown until 1984 (CONADEP, 1984: 293). The figure is presented as a provisional record, for the authors warn that 'many disappearances have not been reported because the victims have no families left, because the families prefer not to report them or because they live in places far removed from urban centers' (CONADEP, 1984: 293 and 479). However, the report does not include among the disappeared those persons whose corpses were found and identified, nor those that survived clandestine captivity (Hayner, 2001: 302). It also establishes the number of Clandestine Detention Centres, detected at around 340 – a figure that until then was unknown even to human rights organisations; earlier, there were only partial descriptions of the main clandestine centres (Duhalde, 1983: 96–102 and 163–166). This information, in addition to the list of these places, their location and distribution, reconstructs the magnitude and scope of the clandestine system at a national level. The fact that they were mostly located in military or police units completely undermines the military's denial of responsibility for the disappearances.

In presenting the major stages involved in the disappearances and in describing them in detail, revealing the systematic character of their exercise and blaming the armed forces, *Nunca Más* becomes an integrated narration that debunks the interpretative monopoly exercised until then by the perpetrators of the disappearances. As has been said, the dictatorship had denied the existence of disappearances, dismissing them as mere 'errors' or 'excesses' committed in all wars. *Nunca Más*, however, holds the armed forces responsible for the disappearances, and refutes their exceptional character, presenting them as the result of a system of extermium planned by the military juntas (CONADEP, 1984: 16 and 17).

The report exposes the truth about the disappearances by including multiple testimonies and documents from different voices, which, in combination, acquire a new dimension. The fragmented character of the public and clandestine moments of the crimes, the division of tasks among perpetrators, the concealment of their identities behind 'war names', and the deliberate destruction of files and buildings presented a new challenge in terms of reconstructing events. Only a narration that would combine testimony and document, that would be collective and from the inside, would be able to recompose the scene and its protagonists with enough emotional and argumentative strength.

The narrative is mainly built on the basis of the allegations made by the survivors and the families of the disappeared. Of the approximately 379 testimonies that the report included, 59 percent correspond to survivors, 20 percent to individuals who witnessed a disappearance, 15 percent to relatives of disappeared individuals, 4 percent to friends or acquaintances of disappeared individuals, and 2 percent to perpetrators (Corralini, Di Iorio, Lobo and Pigliapochi, 2003). CONADEP operates by breaking down each testimony into fragments. Thus, the narrative establishes a general pattern that incorporates each single case as long as it is similar to the next. In spite of this instrumental use and the de-structuring of the testimonies as narrative units, these voices manage to put forward a heart-wrenching drama, which would not have been the case in an encyclopedic approach to the extermination.

Families start their narrative with the abduction, revealing its impact on their bodies and their homes, and tell of their fruitless search and accusations made before the authorities. The survivors reconstruct, in many cases, their experience from bodily memory. Through the evocation of sounds, smells, sights or tactile impressions, they describe their abduction, the tortures they went through, the spaces where they were held captive, the names of the perpetrators and other fellow captives (CONADEP, 1984: 60–61). Their role in this reconstruction is also revealed by the inclusion of maps and photographs depicting the camps recognised by them and CONADEP, which by virtue of that same act, become visual evidence that supports their statements and the report itself (CONADEP, 1984: 73, 76, 82, 85, 88, 91, 94, 109, 112, 115, 121, 124, 127, 133, 141, 153, 156, 168, 171, 174 (maps); 70, 79, 97, 100, 103, 106, 118, 130, 138, 144, 147, 150, 159, 162, 165, 177 (pictures)).

Also, the repeated references to places, dates, circumstances and names in the testimonies restore the reality and truthfulness of what came to pass, and they recompose the spatiality and temporality of these occurrences as well as the identity of those affected (Sarlo, 2002: 151; Halbwachs, [1925] 2004). However, in their testimony, the survivors also reveal the complexity of their own situation and their uniqueness with respect to their peers in other experiences of the kind;. in almost all of the cases, the survivors were freed by their own captors and faced, as has been pointed out, not only guilty feelings for having survived, the imprints of horror in their bodies and consciences, the stigmatisation of the regime, or the rejection of a society that could not, or did not want to, listen to them. They were also the object of suspicion and anathema from others reporting the crime However, *Nunca Más* never presents their ethical dilemmas or passes judgment on their attitudes during their captivity.

The fragments of testimonies, mediated by CONADEP, become a collective and inter-subjective narrative of high emotional weight and great narrative complexity. They express the objectification of an extreme reality; they embody the violence suffered by the disappeared by reiterating, in a quasi monophonic tone, a single narrative. The iterative effect alters the individual character of the testimony. At that moment, the testimonies become estranged and deprived from their uniqueness and become part of a public memory. The voices of the families and survivors occupy a position grounded on an otherness that is cognitively and emotionally affected by the impact of the violence exercised by the state. In spite of this, unlike the denouncing tone exhibited before the 1976 coup, no desire for revenge becomes apparent in the report, nor does it reveal any kind of singular political commitment. Even the word *compañero* (comrade), commonly used in Argentina to refer to lefist activism, is only mentioned by the survivors to refer to those who shared the work, study or captivity with them, and in only a few cases, union activism. The language that prevails in their testimonies, on the contrary, is frequently referential, containing few digressions. They become integrated in the public space evoking the assaults they went through without expressing hate, resentment or an epical tone, all of which were typical characteristics of the accusations before the coup (Basile, 1989: 48).

The testimonies of those directly affected by the disappearances – key pieces of the narrative of the report – convey the same accusatory narrative tone prevailing amongst those affected by the disappearances; the testimonies acquire a truth value in a text created by a state commission. This is not only markedly original with respect to the place that testimony as a genre used to occupy in Argentine narrative, as an expression of marginal or counter-cultural outlooks, but also with respect to the specific disparagement of and disregard for these voices under the dictatorship. At the same time, the experiential character and the realistic style of the testimonies, the proliferation of details, and their assertive structure exclude fiction or fantasy from the narrative, investing it with verisimilitude in the face of a generalised disbelief about the possibility of planning and execution of cruelty and horror (CONADEP, 1984: 15). Besides, CONADEP takes on the role of spokesperson, based on 'that which we have heard, read and recorded in the course of the research', proposing itself as a meta-witness of the testimonies, with its authority guaranteed by its official character (CONADEP, 1984: 7, 160, 161).

However, *Nunca Más* is not limited to incorporating these voices. It also includes the testimonies of the perpetrators of the disappearances. Rather than emerging as a result of the accusations of those affected, their narratives become integrated, on an equal basis, with other voices, as part of one single narration. Although the perpetrators represent only 2 percent of the testimonies, their words confirm the truthfulness of the testimonies of families and survivors (CONADEP, 1984: 132, 164–166, 175, 197–199, 202, 203, 214, 216–217, 228, 238, 253–259; Corralini, Di Iorio, Lobo and Pigliapochi, 2003). Likewise, the report includes testimonies of 'involuntary witnesses' to one or more stages of the disappearances: neighbours who witnessed abductions, the appropriation of the disappeared's goods; people who lived near the camps and heard gunshots and screams of horror, or saw corpses leaving the location, as well as maimed human remains inside bags; or civilians that helped to realise the disappearances, such as a group of mortuary workers who received corpses with evident signs of torture and participated in their clandestine burial in the city of Córdoba (CONADEP, 1984: 167, 225, 244, 245, 316; with letter to Videla, analysed in Crenzel, 2004).

In this way, the variety of statements produces a new product inside the text, a chorus of testimonies that transcends the partiality of personal experience, and at the same time, confirms its truthfulness through the voice of the others. This chorus presents a series of images whose structure would be unintelligible without its parts, but whose force transcends the sum of them, managing to propose a 'unitary representation' of the disappearances (Basile, 1989: 50). This choral game shows the systematic character of the disappearances, their stance as a collective process of national scope. This inter-subjective network creates the notion that what happened was not due to the reasons put forward by the military, or to eventual or random events, but that it was part of an atrocious, regular and hidden 'normality'.

The report reveals still other mechanisms for validating the facts that confirm and complement the testimonies. On the one hand, it incorporates scientific knowledge, whose neutrality before the occurrences places it beyond all doubt, and whose social validation and legitimacy is prior and independent. This technical rationality, this professional knowledge and its controllable, verifiable and renewable operations guarantees the truthfulness of direct experiences in documenting the narrative and sets it apart, through these restrictions, from literary narration. This scientific knowledge is implied by the mention of the architects who inspected the camps with the survivors and drew maps of them; the photographers who documented these inspections; the lawyers who organised the evidence, and, indirectly, through the inclusion of graphs of various kinds, pie-charts and bar charts of the type frequently used in scientific research (CONADEP, 1984: 25, 29, 294, 295, 296, 297, 298 and 300). It is also manifest in the manipulation of knowledge that was then cutting-edge in the country: the use of an information technology system to record the disappeared and detect changes in the physiognomy of children; genetic tests to determine their descent, and forensic anthropology techniques used to identify the corpses found. The mention of the international science institutions that validated their use further strengthened the legitimacy of these techniques (CONADEP, 1984: 184, 293 and 322).

On the other hand, truthfulness is established through the inclusion of data from military sources themselves. These documents, such as the books recording duties for the military service or entrances and exits, refute the military's arguments about the escape or desertion of the conscripts reported as disappeared. Others reveal the orders issued by the dictatorship to face grassroots protests, censor the press or simply order the abductions (ibidem: 275–279, 322, 361, 365, 367, 375). Complementing this, the report includes statements by military chiefs that justified their actions, or denied the existence of disappeared persons. Thus, it shows their fallacy when faced with the evidence that had been gathered (CONADEP, 1984: 55, 56, 402, 474 and 475).

Finally, CONADEP plays a part in the construction of the sense of truth of the narrative. On the one hand, its voice is descriptive and didactic. It operates as a prologue to the testimonies and mediates them without resorting to artifices. In general, it asserts when describing, but it includes an indication or a conjecture when faced with uncertainty amidst certain developments. The conclusive assertion and the rhetorical interrogation propose a pact to the reader: nothing that is not proven will be ascertained, and doubts about the occurrences will be taken into consideration. In fact, CONADEP did not include in the report certain facts mentioned in the testimonies that, if judged, could arouse public disbelief, such as the skinning of live captives or the rape, after her murder, of a captive woman by tens of soldiers (Aragón interview, 2003; Mansur interview, 2004). The report also proposes the validation of the narrative by presenting its work in detail, the interviews held, the visits to the camps, the cemeteries, the mortuaries and the hospitals, the trips made to hear the reports, and the cases it took to court. This link between the construction of truth and legal proof is reproduced throughout the text by presenting the testimonies and the documents with a file number (CONADEP, 1984: 447–450 and 451–459).

The Ties Between Truth and Justice

CONADEP clarifies in *Nunca Más* that its mission is not to determine criminal responsibilities, but the report proposes two dissimilar readings on this issue. On the one hand, it establishes the military Juntas' responsibilities for the planning of the disappearances (CONADEP, 1984: 8). On the other hand, it presents the list of camps by each of the forces under their control and the distribution of the disappeared by military jurisdiction, suggesting the responsibilities of its chiefs. Finally, the report highlights that 'all signs of dissatisfaction inside the armed forces and the security forces with the methods used for the detention and elimination of people were brutally punished [. . .]; any attempt to escape the repressive structure, which the participants called the "blood pact" would mean persecution or even elimination' (CONADEP, 1984: 253–239, 300).

These considerations might imply that the book's view reproduces the distinction supported by President Alfonsín regarding the various levels of responsibility. That strategy had been seriously questioned in the debate in the Senate, in February 1984, when Elias Sapag, from the Movimiento Popular Neuquino, proposed that the authors of 'atrocious and aberrant actions' be excluded from the claim to due obedience (Senate Minutes, 9 February 1984: 318). However, *Nunca Más* confronts the official distinction that proposed to restrict criminal action to those who committed excesses by warning that 'the cases transcribed are not those that constitute excesses, for such excesses did not exist if we understand by that the incurrence of isolated actions, especially aberrant [. . .] [for] the aberrant was common and widespread practice. The [supposedly] "especially atrocious actions can be counted by the thousand," so they are the "normal actions"' instead' (CONADEP, 1984: 15, 16 and 481). In turn, by this very assertion, the report denies Sapag's argument, proposing that only egregious and heinous acts could not be justified on the basis of the argument of obedience to authority. The report elaborates on that position with the statement that it is necessary 'to carry out legal research into the integration of the task forces in the repressive structure' thereby expanding legal action onto the middle and lower ranks of the armed forces, which the government attempted to exclude from the legal inquiry (CONADEP, 1984: 16, 223, 256, 481).

Nunca Más was quickly projected into the public sphere and found echo in society, awakened dormant public sensibilities and 'shocked' the population with its revelations. The 40,000 copies of its first edition, issued in November 1984, were sold out in just two days. Between that date and April 1985, when the trial of the members of the military juntas started, 190,000 copies were sold. The readers of the report vividly recall the actual moment when they bought the book and how they showed it proudly to friends and acquaintances. That action changed the way in which some of them, in particular professionals, reacted to the information they had about the disappearances. This experience took place within intimate circles, as knowledge of the disappearances was considered dangerous and it was not something that was openly talked about. As Michèle Petit (2001: 48) notes, in certain cases a text has the effect of liberating something that was held silently by its readers. A different group found in the report an integrated account of the repression of which until then they had only had a fragmented knowledge. A very small number read the book as a way of challenging their own denial or justifications of the crimes.

But no matter what their profile was or how much of the report they read, none of the readers recall having doubted the truth of the account. This was so even among those who considered that it 'omitted a condemnation of guerrilla violence'. Most found it revealing, in particular in terms of the scope of the disappearances and the systematic nature of their practice, and, therefore, they claimed that it reconfigured their perspective on the subject and led them to believe in the need for the state to prosecute the perpetrators. The severity of the crime and the systematic targeting of 'innocent' people who were defenceless thwarted in their opinion any justification given for these practices. The respondents also recall that reading the report heightened their rejection of all forms of violence.

It could be held that, in contrast to what occurred in other extreme experiences, the report entailed an immediate political intervention that prevented the events of the past from being silenced or forgotten, and that it confronted the dictatorship's discourse, which denied, relativised or justified the existence of disappeared people. Despite differences, the act of reading the report reconfigured, to various extents, the knowledge and interpretation of state violence and the identity of the disappeared, gave a sense of shared knowledge to information that had been kept silent, or revealed a scarcely or partially known universe, while promoting practices aimed at regulating private and public actions, the demand for justice and the repudiation of political violence.

In the same way, the influence of *Nunca Más* was evident in the trial of the military juntas. The prosecutor, Strassera, went on to condemn both guerrilla organisations (calling them terrorists) and 'state terrorism'. The ruling handed down in the trial, based on the evidence of *Nunca Más*, condemned guerrillas and found that the members of the juntas ignored the legal instruments that they had at their disposal and conducted instead an illegal repression through clandestine procedures. Item 30 of the ruling extended the scope of criminal action to include superior officers who commanded the military zones and sub-zones into which the country had been divided for repressive purposes, and any who had orchestrated kidnapping operations or committed abhorrent acts. This item, then, echoed the *Nunca Más* call to expand the investigation to members of the 'task groups'. In sum, the report changed individual and social perceptions about political violence and revealed the emergence of a new sensibility in public and private spheres, in Norbert Elías's words, a correspondence between psychogenesis and sociogenesis in the development of social processes (Elias, 1987).

Conclusions

This chapter has shown how *Nunca Más* proposed a new reading of the past of political violence in Argentina that is distinct from the revolutionary narrative prior to the coup and the dictatorship's justification or denial of their crimes. CONADEP's foundational reading combined the premises of Alfonsín's administration to have the exercise of political violence stand on trial, with the discourse of human rights organisations forged during the dictatorship to report violations to human rights.

The report considered the disappearances as a violation of the moral, religious and political principles of the Western world. It presented the disappeared as subjects of the law, rejected violence as a way to solve political conflicts and imagined democracy as the guarantee that horror would not be repeated. The report's recommendations demanded from the state the redress to the affected, the repeal of repressive laws, the materialisation of justice, the establishment of the disappearances as crimes and a guarantee that human rights would be respected (CONADEP, 1984: 477 and 478). In this way, the report included the past within the general principles of the political order restored in the country in 1983. However, it put forward the 'foreignness' of the disappeared with respect to politics and insurgence, deriving their innocence from that. This aspect reveals the limitations of this foundational narrative of restored democracy, relative to the universal defence of civil rights. At the same time, the omission of the responsibility incurred by political parties shows the difficulties of Argentine society, which are still undeniably present, to reflect upon these sorrowful events in complex terms.

In keeping with the presidential orders to prosecute guerrilla and military chiefs, *Nunca Más* established a periodisation of political violence, positing insurgent violence as a precedent to state violence and the disappearances as the exclusive responsibility of the dictatorship. The report proposed the 'foreignness' of civil and political society with respect to both. Finally, it incorporated into its narrative, in a privileged position, the testimonies of families and survivors, in order to reconstruct the materiality of the disappearances, and to integrate their public and hidden stages. Thus, it officially consecrated the humanitarian narrative forged by these actors during the dictatorship, setting it in the framework of a new reading of the past.

Through the articulation of the Executive's premises and the humanitarian narrative forged during the dictatorship, *Nunca Más* proposed a new 'emblematic memory' of the past of political violence, to be acknowledged and to be deployed in the public scene. This notion refers to the configurations that, in the public arena, provide interpretative sense to think of, and evoke, the past, integrating personal memories and concrete experiences, and that, backed by legitimate spokespeople, resonate in the society (Stern, 2000).

The strength of the constellation of meaning that the report combined is revealed in three key dimensions. First, before *Nunca Más*, the dictatorship's perspective had not been denied by an integrated narrative, with emotional, argumentative and symbolic strength, supported by the weight of the testimonies and the official word. The report installed a new public truth about the disappearances confronting the denial, justification and relativisation of the crime by the military.

Second, *Nunca Más* would soon turn into an instrument of justice by becoming the key evidentiary corpus in the trial of the military Juntas in 1985.

Third, the report became an unprecedented publishing success and the canon for the collective memory about the disappearances. By 2010, *Nunca Más* had sold 515,330 copies and had been translated into English, Hebrew, Italian, Portuguese and German, and was incorporated into schools to transmit this past to the new generations.

Finally, *Nunca Más* would acquire outstanding importance in the politics of justice during transitions from authoritarian to democratic regimes when imagined by governments and human rights organisations, as a vehicle for navigating the political violence that these societies went through in the 1970s and 1980s. Even the reports of several truth commissions created in the Southern Cone had as a title 'Never Again' (Sikkink, 2008). The phrase 'Never Again' was, and is, used as a symbol of commitment to the truth; it connotes justice and memory and it is proposed as the name for a future museum dedicated to this period. Nevertheless, the phrase also acquired a different meaning. Political and social groups reproduced it in a literal way, but simultaneously deployed it with an exemplary meaning, derived from their own readings of this past of political violence and dictatorship.

8

Punishment and Extermination: The Massacre of Political Prisoners in Lima, Peru, June 1986[1]

CARLOS AGUIRRE

University of Oregon, USA

On 18 June 1986, prisoners accused of belonging to the Peruvian Maoist guerrilla movement known as 'Shining Path' organised a synchronised mutiny in three prisons in or near Lima (two for men and one for women), took a few hostages in each of them, and presented the authorities with a 25-point petition that included demands ranging from ending abuses and mistreatment inside the prisons to stopping the 'disappearance' of persons, an already common practice in the state's counter-subversive campaign. By the time of the riots, the revolutionary war launched by Shining Path was about six years old, had already caused thousands of victims and millions of dollars in damages, and had triggered a brutal response on the part of the state, with widespread human rights violations, including extra-judicial detentions and executions, the ordinary use of torture and the massacre of innocent people, mostly in highland and Indigenous communities. The ongoing war had also produced thousands of prisoners accused of belonging to the Maoist group, and prisons had become potentially explosive scenarios of the war. Although the worst moments in the confrontation between the Shining Path and the Peruvian state were yet to come, Peruvian society was under considerable stress in June 1986.

The mutinies organised by Shining Path prisoners were carefully planned not only to occur simultaneously but also to coincide with the presence in Lima of dozens of foreign leaders who were coming to participate in an International Congress of Socialist and Social-Democrat parties, scheduled to start on 20 June, an event that the ruling party, Alianza Popular Revolucionaria Americana, or American Popular Revolutionary Alliance (APRA), and its young leader, President Alan García Pérez, expected to use as a showcase for their still young administration and the aspirations that García Pérez had of

---

1   All translations in this chapter are by the author.

becoming a leader of international dimensions. Not only prominent foreign political leaders, but also hundreds of journalists had arrived in Lima to attend the event. Shining Path wanted to use this opportunity to amplify its attacks against the government, embarrass the young and ambitious president, and denounce (and test) what they called the administration's 'genocidal' plan against political prisoners.

As soon as the news of the mutinies reached the highest levels of the Aprista administration, the president called an emergency cabinet meeting that also included the top military commanders of all three armed institutions (collectively known as the Comando Conjunto de las Fuerzas Armadas (CCFFAA; Joint Command of the Armed Forces). A series of decisions were made at that meeting, the most important being the determination to restore 'the disrupted national order' 'with energy and decision to reach the expected goals in the shortest possible time' (Presidencia de la Republica, 1986). The ultimate responsibility for conducting the operations to put down the mutinies was placed in the hands of the three armed institutions (army, navy and air force), one in each of the prisons affected by the mutinies, although it was also envisaged that the Guardia Republicana (GR), the police branch in charge of the prison system, would have to play a role.

The three prisons that were the scenario for the mutinies were the penal island of El Frontón (that had been recently re-named as San Juan Bautista), a few miles off-shore from Callao, the port just west of Lima, where an estimated 160 inmates accused of belonging to the Shining Path occupied the Pabellón Azul (Blue Pavilion); the Lurigancho prison (officially the San Pedro penitentiary), located in one of the most populous districts in Lima, whose Industrial Pavilion hosted 124 'terrorists'; and the Santa Bárbara women's prison in El Callao that hosted 64 female Shining Path interns. In all these prisons, Shining Path inmates occupied special areas, separate from common prisoners.

By the end of the day, on 19 June 1986, 124 inmates in Lurigancho, that is all of the Shining Path inmates, had been killed; at least 120 of the 160 El Frontón inmates had also died; and in the Santa Bárbara women's prison two Shining Path inmates had lost their lives. There were also a few military casualties and one of the hostages at El Frontón died. Most Lurigancho and El Frontón victims had been either shot after surrendering, or died as a result of the bombing of the Pabellón Azul, in the case of El Frontón. Altogether, close to 250 political prisoners had been killed, in what constitutes the deadliest massacre of political prisoners in Latin American history.

How could this happen? How and why did a democratically elected government, whose leader had promised to combat the insurgency while being respectful of human rights, opt for a military solution to a situation that could hardly be considered a threat to the security of the prisons, the government, or the 'national order'? True, this was a provocation by the Shining Path, but it was neither unprecedented nor particularly belligerent. The militarisation of the crisis was the most tragic decision made at that cabinet meeting, and the responsibility went directly to the President of the Republic himself. But equally tragic was the fact that, at no point during the unfolding of the events, did civilian or military authorities make any meaningful effort to prevent the massacre. This chapter attempts to elucidate the reasons behind what Shining Path activists called (even before it happened) a 'genocide', and what came to be officially and euphemistically known as *los sucesos de los penales* ('the prison incidents').[2]

The Shining Path and the Maoist Revolution in Peru

Shining Path is the nickname for the Communist Party of Peru, a Maoist revolutionary organisation that was born out of the multiple divisions within the Peruvian left in the 1960s and started an armed struggle in May 1980. After the Sino-Soviet split in the early 1960s, a pro-China group called Bandera Roja (Red Flag) saw the desertion of an even more radical faction, led by a philosophy professor, Abimael Guzmán, that gave birth to a party that claimed to be the 'real' Communist Party of Peru and whose initial base was the Universidad San Cristóbal de Huamanga, in Ayacucho, one of the poorest regions of Peru, where Guzmán began to recruit professors and students. The nickname, Shining Path, came from one of the slogans used by the party's university branch, 'Por el sendero luminoso de José Carlos Mariátegui' (Following the Shining Path of José Carlos Mariátegui), referring to the Marxist intellectual who is considered the founder of Peruvian communism. The name, however, was never officially embraced by the leadership or the members of the party (Degregori, 1990, 1996, 2013; Palmer, 1992; McClintock, 1998; Stern, 1998; Gorriti, 1999; Taylor, 2006).

Small cells worked in both ideological and military training throughout the 1970s in preparation for the armed struggle. Their ideology (known to its followers as 'Pensamiento Gonzalo' or 'Gonzalo Thought', after Guzmán's *nom de guerre* 'Gonzalo') was a mixture of Maoism with the ideas developed by José Carlos Mariátegui in the 1920s.

---

2 Although Shining Path referred to this episode as 'geneocide', I prefer to use the term 'prison massacre' instead of 'genocide'. It has become common in political debates to refer to waves of repression (such as those in Chile, Argentina or Central America) as 'genocide'. Scholars, however, disagree as to which cases would warrant the use of such a descriptor (Chapter 6 in this volume deals with the case of Guatemala). There are other interventions in this debate (Higonnet, 2009; Esparza, Huttenbach and Feierstein, 2010; Vezzetti, 2012).

On 17 May 1980, on the eve of the first presidential election in seventeen years, which would bring to an end a twelve-year military dictatorship, Shining Path announced the beginning of its armed revolution. Their goal was to destroy the rotten, exploitative and corrupted state, and to initiate what they thought was going to be the first step in the world's communist revolution. Shining Path's ideology and political strategy were extremely violent and confrontational, consciously seeking the polarisation of Peruvian society, and openly rejecting any possibility of negotiation with the state or the formation of political alliances with even the most progressive sectors of the legal left. A sort of 'everything or nothing' strategy informed Shining Path's almost fanatical crusade against the Peruvian state and what they considered its accomplices: legal political parties, non-governmental organisations (NGOs), and labour and peasant unions that did not yield to Shining Path's authoritarian and radical tactics.

During the next twenty years or so, but especially during the period 1980–1992, a bloody confrontation would take place between the Shining Path and the Peruvian armed forces. The 2003 report by the Peruvian Comisión de la Verdad y Reconciliación (CVR; Truth and Reconciliation Commission) concluded that almost 70,000 Peruvians lost their lives, the majority of them of indigenous descent (CVR, 2003a). The CVR report also documented the atrocities committed by all sides in what can truly be described as a contest between alternative forms of terror and intimidation. The Shining Path used a combination of guerrilla warfare, selective assassinations and indiscriminate terror to advance their agenda. They killed state authorities, military officers, police agents, labour and community leaders, NGO workers, individuals accused of abusive behaviour in villages and towns in the Andes, and others. They perpetrated some of the worst massacres committed by insurgent groups in the history of twentieth-century Latin America. In fact, according to the CVR, 54 percent of all the deaths during the war can be attributed to the Shining Path, the highest percentage among all Latin American revolutionary and insurgent groups. The Peruvian state responded with ever growing ferocity, usually by engaging in systematic abuses against not only Shining Path activists but also innocent people. The CVR concluded emphatically that:

'The fight against subversion reinforced among members of the police forces pre-existing authoritarian and repressive practices. Torture during interrogation and undue detentions, which had been common in their actions against common criminals, acquired a massive character during the counter-insurgent campaign. In addition, the CVR has confirmed that the most serious violations of human rights by members of the police forces included extrajudicial executions, forced disappearance of persons, torture, and cruel, inhumane and degrading treatment of individuals. The CVR condemns in particular the extended sexual violence against women' (CVR, 2003d: 360–361).

Most of the victims of the systematic violence applied by both the Shining Path and the forces of the state were members of indigenous communities. The rivalry between the two groups, although also fought in the terrain of ideas, propaganda, symbolism and political agendas, became essentially a contest between two forms of intimidation and coercion, as several scholars have argued.

'The Shining Trenches'

As the war unfolded, Peruvian jails and prisons began to be filled with individuals accused of being members of the guerrilla. According to the CVR, at least 20,000 people accused of belonging to 'terrorist' groups entered Peruvian jails and prisons during the period of war (1980–2000). Many of them were completely innocent people, and most never received a judicial sentence. A network of prisons throughout the country was used to host Shining Path suspects, but gradually most of them were concentrated in Lima, especially in the Lurigancho prison (still one of the largest and most overcrowded prisons in Latin America) and El Frontón penal island (established in the early twentieth century, closed in the 1970s, but re-opened in 1982). Later, other prisons were also used, most notably the Canto Grande high-security prison on the outskirts of Lima, and the Yanamayo prison in the highlands of Puno, in southern Peru, where inmates endured freezing temperatures and brutal isolation. Top leaders of the movement, including Abimael Guzmán after his capture in September 1992, would be secluded in special cells located in the basement of the naval base of Callao. Women were held in the Santa Bárbara prison in El Callao and later in the Women's Prison in Chorrillos.

From the very beginning of the war, prisons were seen by the insurgents as 'shining trenches of struggle' (luminosas trincheras de combate'), as Shining Path documents began to call them, quickly becoming arenas of confrontation with the state as well as spaces for different forms of political activity (Rénique, 2004). Shining Path staged a famous prison escape in Ayacucho, for instance, as early as 1981. In the largest and most secure prisons, such as Lurigancho and El Frontón, Shining Path's strategy sought to gradually 'liberate' the prison space they were held in, seeking to minimise both the state's control over their time and routine, and the possibilities of becoming victims of what they openly denounced as a 'genocidal plan' to exterminate them. While they clearly succeeded at liberating prison space from state control, they could not avoid the ferocity of state retaliation, most brutally in the form of prison massacres such as those that took place in October 1985, June 1986 and April 1992.

Shortly after El Frontón was re-opened to host Shining Path prisoners, journalist Gustavo Gorriti visited the so-called 'Blue Pavilion', the cellblock that housed them, and wrote a report in *Caretas*, the main political weekly magazine in Peru. Gorriti was impressed by the iron discipline shown by the 252 inmates whom he encountered and by the fact that they already controlled the internal space of the pavilion. Murals with revolutionary slogans and pictures of their leader, Abimael Guzmán, for instance, adorned the pavilion's walls (Gorriti, 1982). Two years later, in October 1984, a reporter for the *Oiga* weekly magazine also visited El Frontón, which he called 'Shining Path's Liberated Territory' (Barraza, 1984). He found about 400 inmates who exercised complete control over their daily routine without any interference from prison authorities or guards, except for the times when the doors were opened (6 a.m.) or closed (6 p.m.). Prison officers were no longer conducting searches (*requisas*) or even performing roll calls (*conteos*), and food preparation was carried on by the inmates, not by prison employees. During the daytime, Shining Path inmates, according to the report, could step out of the cellblock and bathe freely in the ocean without any supervision (escaping was almost impossible because of strong ocean currents). Inside the pavilion, and especially after the 6 p.m. curfew, inmates held assemblies, received indoctrination lectures, chanted their hymns and slogans, and even conducted military exercises. During the weekly visits by their relatives and lawyers, Shining Path inmates were in charge of the logistics, sometimes organising festivities and celebrations, and even allowing some visitors to stay overnight. Attempts by prison authorities to exercise greater control over visits, by issuing IDs to the inmates' relatives (*carnetización*) were defeated by Shining Path inmates. Even more seriously, they were able to dig tunnels and build underground shelters in the Blue Pavilion using construction materials that were introduced with the consent of prison authorities (Cristóbal, 1987: 58). A similar degree of control of their own space was also acquired in Lurigancho's Industrial Pavilion. Lawyer Martha Huatay, an outspoken defender of accused Shining Path prisoners and later a prisoner herself, described the functioning of prisons under Shining Path control as 'a monument and a spark of what collective work could do in a new society' (Huatay, 2002: 33).

How did Shining Path prisoners manage to secure control of their own cellblocks inside the prisons? Studies about political imprisonment in different societies show how political inmates tend to be exceptionally well organised and disciplined, and capable of developing structures of relative autonomy that allow them to resist the power of the prison system, strengthen their morale and preserve their cohesion (Buntman, 2003; Neier, 1995), but what Shining Path prisoners accomplished is well beyond any other case of which I know. Video footage from TV news reports and two documentaries

(*People of the Shining Path*, a 1992 documentary by the British Channel 4 and *Régimen Penitenciario* (2002), by the CVR) confirms what the journalistic reports quoted above depicted: except for external security, they controlled all aspects of their daily life. How could this happen? On the one hand, the functioning of prisons in Peru left much to be desired in terms of efficiency and security. There was a time, also in the 1980s, when the internal order of the Lurigancho prison was in the hands of prisoners, governed by the structures of hierarchy developed within the criminal population, as described in a fascinating book by anthropologist José Luis Pérez Guadalupe (1994). Poorly paid guards and employees, corrupted authorities, and a general state of abandonment characterised Peruvian prisons in the 1980s. A series of riots organised by common criminals, some of them quite deadly, had shocked the country, but little was done to reform the system. When Shining Path members began to fill the prisons, their discipline and determination sharply contrasted with the overall conditions of prisons and the situation of most common criminals; not surprisingly, they were able to challenge and subvert the rules that the state attempted to impose on them.

Shining Path inmates started by enforcing an iron discipline and an almost religious mystique among their fellow activists, something that was in fact a characteristic of the party as a whole. Prisoners who were not willing to yield to the authority of the party were either expelled from the cellblock or subjected to constant harassment and violence. Whenever a prison authority or guard attempted to implement measures that Shining Path considered unfair, restrictive or arbitrary, they and their families were threatened with retaliation. Not only guards, but even higher authorities preferred not to risk their, or their relatives', safety because they knew that the insurgents were capable of identifying their residences and whereabouts, and could cause a great deal of harm. Shining Path inmates also convinced prison authorities that they were indeed willing to fight until the end if they attempted to impose drastic measures against them. It was clearly a contest of wills. *Requisas*, for instance, were strenuously resisted, with Shining Path inmates threatening that, if they attempted new searches, it would lead to a situation of 'total confrontation' in which they were willing to die. Not surprisingly, the El Frontón authorities decided to discontinue them.

Prison mutinies were a common tactic used by Shining Path prisoners to negotiate their conditions of incarceration and obtain from the authorities certain privileges. There were eight such instances before June 1986, and all of them were solved after negotiations between inmates and the authorities, which always included concessions on the part of the authorities or the promise of improvement in prison conditions. We must clarify, however, that the fact that Shining Path inmates controlled their own cellblocks or that the authorities were forced to accept certain conditions does not mean that prisoners necessarily enjoyed a comfortable life or were free of harassment and even violence from prison personnel. They were still vulnerable in many ways. They suffered from shortages of water, food and medicines, for instance, and their relatives were mistreated during weekly visits or harassed, and treated as suspects by police and prison employees. Prisons, thus, were always on the brink of erupting into violence and, as such, they mirrored the war going on outside their walls. But riots and negotiations almost always ended with prison authorities surrendering a piece of their power and Shining Path inmates gaining increasing control over their lives, time and space. While, from a certain perspective, this was a sign of weakness on the part of state and prison authorities, the truth is that they were willing to go that way in order to avoid a much more serious confrontation.

The *Oiga* reporter had ended his 1984 article with an ominous question (and prediction):

> Will the final hour arrive? Everybody is prepared: the terrorist inmates, the guards, and the prison employees. The latter say that they are ready to put an end to the 'liberated territory' of the Shining Path in El Frontón with the use of paralysing gases that would cause no victims. But they are afraid that the Guardias Republicanos would intervene to take revenge for the victims of the Shining Path that belonged to their institution. When will the ticking bomb explode? (Barraza, 1984: 35)

The first sign that things began to change with the new Aprista administration would come just a few months after its inauguration in July 1985. On 4 October 1985, a riot erupted in Lurigancho when the authorities attempted a *requisa*. About 30 prisoners were killed during the operation to put down the mutiny. A few days later, delegates of Shining Path inmates and prison authorities agreed to honour the July 1985 accord of 24 points, signed by the previous administration. While negotiation was still possible, as the signing of a new document illustrates, the government signalled that it was less willing to yield to the Shining Path's strategy of confrontation and challenge. Tensions were heightened when the APRA government announced the transfer of Shining Path prisoners to the new high-security Canto Grande prison. Shining Path denounced this as part of a 'genocidal' plan put in motion by the 'fascist' state, and made the decision to resist it to the point of death. On 7 June 1986, a communiqué written by female Shining Path inmates 'secluded in this dark concentration camp of Callao' denounced the 'genocidal plan against political prisoners'. The transfer to Canto Grande was viewed as an attempt to isolate them from their relatives and to apply 'total annihilation'. Speaking for themselves, but also for their fellow male inmates, they announced that they were 'willing to resist and let the blood pour in El Frontón,

Lurigancho, and El Callao' (Cristóbal, 1987: 17–18). Antonio Díaz Martínez, a prominent member of the Shining Path, denounced, two days before the mutiny (he obviously knew of the preparations for it), 'the new genocidal plan that the government is preparing against inmates in various prisons' (Mora, 2003: 11). Unfortunately, the events that unfolded shortly afterwards would tragically fulfil their prophecy.

In the perception of large sectors of the public opinion, on the other hand, the state was too tolerant with 'subversion'. The dirty war was imposing its logic to the conflict and the voices demanding respect for human and legal rights for Shining Path inmates, and other suspects were increasingly being questioned as the insurgents' attacks escalated. The picture emerging from media reports about the state of prisons was alarming for both state authorities and the general public: there was too much leniency with 'terrorists', who used prisons to indoctrinate activists, prepare new attacks and challenge the authority of the state. The president of the CCFFAA saw El Frontón as 'a center where subversive or terrorist acts could be planned' (CVR: 2003c: 240). Both sides seemed to be ready for a violent clash when the mutinies erupted in June 1986.

The Dirty War

The overall confrontational strategy pursued by the Shining Path – total war against the Peruvian state and its allies – included a conscious tactic of provoking the harshest response on the part of the Peruvian state: this would show what actually lay behind its façade and would convince the population of its 'genocidal' nature. A fierce response by the state was actually welcomed by the Shining Path, as they believed that it served its political and military strategy. 'The forces of reaction are dreaming when they try to drown the revolution in blood. They should know that they are nourishing it, and that this is an inexorable law', declared Guzmán in 1988 (Guzmán, [1988] 1991: 45). On 23 March 1986, during a meeting with Shining Path cadres, Abimael Guzmán ordered them to 'induce the genocide. This is the mandate of the IV Plenary [of the party] [...] Let's destroy their [the government's] plan. And as we destroy their plan, they will apply genocide!' (CVR, 2003c: 239). After the events of June 1986, Abimael Guzmán would admit that one of their tactics was 'to induce the forces of order into greater repression' (CVR, 2003e: 14).

The progress made by the Shining Path in its military strategy and the increasing number of terrorist attacks and selective assassinations, coupled with the seeming inability of the state to stop them, led to growing frustration and the conviction among members of the armed forces, certain sectors of the political establishment and at least part of the general public that the only way to end subversion was to utilise *mano dura* (firm hand): harsher counter-subversive tactics, intimidation methods and brutal repression. The niceties of the rule of law and the respect for human rights were increasingly seen as obstacles in the fight against terrorism and a luxury that Peruvian society could not afford. Various massacres of people considered suspect were committed during the Belaúnde administration (1980–1985), and the number of victims of political violence spiralled after the December 1982 decision to send the army to combat the guerrillas. From 47 in 1982, the number of victims considered to be members of Shining Path grew to 1,398.

Simultaneously, the number of injured suspects taken alive decreased dramatically, which clearly reflects a deliberate tactic of getting rid of 'terrorists' without mercy. The disappearance of people and the use of clandestine burial sites became common practice (Flores Galindo, 1994: 323–324). General Luis Cisneros Vizquerra, Minister of War, described the situation in the following terms:

[The Army] would have to kill both terrorists and non-terrorists because [that] would be the only way to guarantee their success. They kill 60 people and maybe there are three senderistas [among them] [...] and most likely the police will say that the 60 were terrorists [...] I think that it would be the worst choice and that is why I'm opposed to the Army entering into this struggle until it is strictly necessary. (González, 1983: 50)

The army did indeed enter the war, and the 'worst choice' became a reality. After a top naval officer, Carlos Ponce Canessa, was killed by the Shining Path on 5 May 1986 (a little over a month before the June 1986 prison mutinies), the Minister of the Navy, Julio Pacheco Concha, stated: 'The subversives should know that they have caused a deep injury to the Institution and to the entire country, and they should know that they have woken up the lion' (CVR, 2003c: 237). Although the new administration of García Pérez promised to be respectful of human rights in its efforts to end subversion, the situation did not improve. A massacre of innocent people in Accomarca, during which a two-year old child was thrown into a fire, an act justified by one of the perpetrators, Lieutenant Telmo Hurtado, because 'at that age they [the indigenous inhabitants of the Peruvian highlands] are already terrorists', led to the dismissal of three army officers, but other similarly brutal actions did not generate any meaningful response on the part of the government (Haya de la Torre, 1988: 16). The army was allowed a free hand to employ its own tactics, which included systematic and indiscriminate violence against civilians and innocent people, especially in the highlands. Frustration with the lack of progress in the war against the Shining Path led to demands for swift justice, the application of the death penalty, and other radical measures. Conservative commentator Manuel D'Ornellas had stated on TV just a few days before the June 1986 riots that prisons were 'subversive centers' and that inmates should be 'annihilated' (Cristóbal, 1987: 173). When asked about the Shining Path's decision to die if necessary in order to avoid their transfer to Canto Grande, General Cisneros Vizquerra said: 'I think we should satisfy their wish [to die]. It is one of the few satisfactions we could grant to the subversives. If they prefer that, let them sign a document and let's proceed. The state will satisfy their personal wishes' (Cristóbal, 1987: 30).

Even President García had declared, when asked about a wave of strikes in the country, that his patience had reached the limit. This was on 23 May 1986, less than a month before the massacre of prisoners (Cristóbal, 1987: 101). When the mutinies erupted in June 1986, very few voices within the state were willing to speak in the language of dialogue, tolerance or patience, and public opinion seemed to share the same impatience towards subversion. Isolated voices were raised in an effort to stop the spiral of violence. A public statement signed by prominent Peruvian intellectuals – Gustavo Gutiérrez, Antonio Cornejo Polar, Alberto Flores Galindo, Max Hernández, Mirko Lauer, and many others – and entitled *United for life* (*Unidos por la vida*) was published on 15 June 1986. 'The voices that demand eye for an eye are growing', they warned, and asked Peruvians to unite behind the defence of life against the forces of both *senderista* violence and indiscriminate repression (Cristóbal, 1987: 23). Tragically, their invocation was not heard, and just a few days later more ominous signs that the eye for an eye approach was gaining momentum would shock their conscience.

Official and media depictions of the Shining Path contributed to the demonising of its members and sympathisers, and made the repeated calls for harsher responses to their insurgency look more acceptable. Insurgents were almost always described as 'terrorists', with other terms such as insurgents, revolutionaries, rebels or subversives considered soft, or even sympathetic to their cause, and thus gradually obliterated. The visual display of the effects of its violent actions in TV and other media – destroyed buildings, bridges, or electrical towers, suffering victims, bloody attacks against innocent people – helped reinforce the depiction of them as inhuman murderers who had no political agenda and were only interested in causing damage and destruction. They were constantly referred to as enemies of the fatherland, as a minuscule group of insane people in a war against the entire nation. This campaign was quite successful, because of the Shining Path's own brutality and terrorist methods but also because of the (real or attributed) ethnic background of most Shining Path members and suspects, who were seen as indigenous or *serranos* (people from the highlands) and, thus, dangerous, deceitful, and undeserving. Although the main leaders of the Shining Path and many of its members were 'white' or *mestizos*, the fact that the insurgency started in Ayacucho, one of the areas with the largest percentage of indigenous population, and many of its members were Quechua-speaking and had indigenous racial features, contributed to the widely held perception of 'terrorists' as 'Indians' and, thus, to reinforcing the notion that Shining Path actiivists were sub-human, savage, and undeserving of the protection that the law (in theory) accorded Peruvian citizens (Aguirre, 2011). As cultural critic Jean Franco has emphasised, the widespread view of Indians as 'alien to modernity' greatly contributed not only to state indiscriminate repression against peoples of indigenous descent, but also to popular support for harsh repression against the Maoist movement (Franco, 2006).

Calls to protect their human rights were dismissed as signs of weakness or open collaboration with the 'enemy'. Peruvians of all walks of life who suffered in one way or another from their actions were clearly willing to justify each and all forms of repression against Shining Path militants. There was no other way of eliminating subversion, they seemed to believe, than using the strongest (even if illegal) weapons available to authorities. As the war moved to Lima, the capital of the country and the centre of political and economic power, that idea became much more entrenched in the minds of various sectors of Peruvian society. Although few people could have predicted what happened in Lima's prisons on 18–19 June 1986, the scenario was ripe for a tragedy of enormous proportions.

The Unfolding of a Massacre

As stated above, the mutinies started simultaneously in three prisons in the Lima-Callao area. At Lurigancho, the mutiny started when one penitentiary agent was taken hostage at 6 a.m.[3] Judicial authorities arrived to inquire about the situation, but were unable to make any progress in solving the situation. Tension began to mount, as more GR troops were sent to the prison and relatives grew impatient as a result of the cancellation of visits. Penitentiary agents were reassured by the rebels that the hostage was being well treated. Around 11.30 a.m. the rebels presented to a prosecutor (*fiscal*) a 26-point platform, showed him the hostage, and announced that he would be freed only if their petitions were satisfied. In the next few hours, a series of attempts by prison and judicial authorities to convince the prisoners to end their mutiny did not lead to changes in the situation. Around 2 p.m.,

---

3　In the text that follows, I summarize the events using information contained in the report written by the Peruvian Congress's commission formed in the aftermath of the massacre (Ames, 1988; CVR, 2003c: 234–263; CVR, 2003e).

military commanders were notified of the government's decision to bring in the army to reestablish order in Lurigancho, with support from the GR, and military personnel began to be mobilised towards the prison. At 5.15 p.m., the CCFFAA issued a series of directives to the GR, detailing the objectives of the operation: to recover control of the prison, to rescue the hostages (referred to in the plural, although there was just one), to recover weapons seized by the rebels (who actually had none) and to facilitate the transfer of inmates to Canto Grande. It was also decided that it was going to be the duty of the GR to intervene in the Industrial Pavilion, with the army providing critical support in the use of explosives to facilitate such mission. A total of 159 GR troops were chosen to carry out the mission. A government-sponsored Peace Commission, formed in 1985, arrived at Lurigancho but could not talk to the director or the inmates and left the prison after 30 minutes. In the meantime, a series of communications indicated the mounting level of impatience among several military authorities. It is clear that military and GR commanders felt compelled to demand a more rapid intervention: they had been instructed to try to solve the crisis as soon as possible, but lack of coordination and of a well-thought plan made the operation much more difficult.

Around 8 p.m., the director of the prison made contact with the rebels, who told him that they would rather die than suspend the mutiny to negotiate with the authorities. The order to start the attack against the Industrial Pavilion was given to Army General Jorge Rabanal Portilla, who was in charge of the operation, around 8.40 p.m.. The GR would execute the plan, and an army unit (CEC 501) was going to be available in case they were needed. The director of the prison asked for a written order, but he was told to leave formalities aside. GR and army troops arrived in Lurigancho around 9 p.m.

It was only around 10 p.m. that an actual plan began to develop. The idea was to have CEC 501 open two holes (*boquetes* or *forados*) in the Industrial Pavilion's walls to allow GR personnel to enter the building, rescue the hostage and force the rebels out. Shortly after midnight, a final contact was made by the prison director with the rebels, with no results. They were told that a military operation was about to start, but the rebels responded that they already knew the army's 'genocidal' intentions. The final operation started around 12.30 a.m. Two explosives opened only a small hole, and GRs began to shoot through it. Army commanders began to throw grenades, while snipers began to fire towards the Industrial Pavilion from nearby locations. Additional explosives were used to try to open bigger holes, without positive results. At 1.40 a.m., Colonel Cabezas, commander of the GR's anti-subversive unit, arrived at the scene. More powerful explosives brought by the army were able to finally open a huge hole. When GRs entered the Industrial Pavilion, inmates attacked them with home-made weapons, but a group of GRs, under the command of Lieutenant Jorge Loyola Felipe, was able to enter the pavilion, rescue the hostage, encircle the rebels and force them to surrender. There were already about 30 inmates dead as a result of the exchange of fire during the attack. The survivors began to leave the pavilion through the hole. When the hostage left the pavilion, police members mistakenly took him for a rebel, and began to hit him violently, until somebody recognised him.

It is at this point that surrendered inmates began to be executed by a GR squad, commanded by Colonel Cabezas. As soon as they left the Industrial Pavilion, they were asked to lie on the floor and were shot in the head. The executions were witnessed by members of the army unit, GRs and penitentiary agents. The order had come, apparently, from Colonel Cabezas. GR Corporal Roque David Huanca Condori declared that he saw 'how the interns from the Industrial Pavillion were leaving; some did it crawling, others stooped, and others with their hands over their heads; later I have seen how these interns were executed' (Ministerio del Interior, 1986). GR guard Baltazar Ramos Paival also saw members of the GR and the army 'shooting at interns that were lying face-down on the floor'. GR guard Félix César Romani Yactayo stated that 'the officers that shot against the interns that were lying on the floor were about 15 to 20, including GR and army personnel'. Another GR guard, Marco Antonio Rimapa Jiménez, reported that, as the inmates left the Pavilion they were surrounded by members of the GR and the army, and that he heard the order to kill them: 'elimínenlos' ('eliminate them!'). He added that one officer ordered other guards to 'see who is alive', and whoever was found alive was killed, but he could not identify who actually fired the shots. Other witnesses confirmed that members of the army also participated in the massacre, shooting against injured and surrendered inmates. GR guard Pedro Quilla Mendivil testified that he saw that 'about thirty subversives were taken out and were lying on the floor with their hands behind their necks; under those circumstances, GR and army personnel on their own initiative decided to shot and kill them, [and] that nobody, neither Colonel Cabezas nor the Army commanders attempted to impede [the executions]'. He actually testified that he saw Cabezas shoot two subversives. Another guard asserted that he heard a rumour saying 'just do it, we are protected by the government' ('actúen nomás, estamos amparados por el gobierno'). GR guard Máximo Retuerto Moreno said that he thought that the order came from Cabezas because 'he witnessed the events' and he saw Cabezas shoot an inmate who was holding his hands against his neck two metres away. GR Lieutenant Justino Campos Alarcón testified that he asked Cabezas (without knowing that it was him, since he was wearing a mask) who had given the order to kill, but that Cabezas only responded with expletives. When Cabezas tried to leave, Campos removed his (Cabezas's) mask, and only then he was able to identify the Colonel. Campos even apologised to him. Penitentiary

Agent Willy Ríos also offered a first-hand account: 'There must have been more than one hundred. A lot of them were leaving [the Pavilion]. All of them were alive. They left with their hands behind their necks. They had surrendered, they were giving themselves in. They took all of them out, they left little by little.' Later, he continued, it was ordered that the terrorists return to the pavilion and then that they should leave in groups of five. They were ordered to kneel and asked for the whereabouts of Abimael Guzmán. As they did not respond, 'I saw a GR guard shoot one of them in the head. He did the same with the other four that were on their knees [. . .] When I saw this I felt repugnance.' He told another agent: 'Hey, they are killing them, they are killing them.' A policeman, in tears, told him that they were being forced to kill, but that he did not want to do it, and stayed with Ríos (Ramírez, 2003).

By dawn, all Shining Path prisoners who had surrendered had been executed. Ríos gave a reporter his impressions: 'At dawn I was able to enter the scene. I was shocked. All the terrorists were dead. There were piles of them. It was a mountain of corpses, a sort of human pyramid. It was a macabre spectacle' (Ramírez, 2003).

At El Frontón, on the other hand, rebels took three hostages, all of them members of the GR, and seized their weapons (three G3 rifles and one FMK-3 automatic rifle). Attempts were made to establish a dialogue with the rebels, but they did not respond. At 2.30 p.m., the Peace Commission arrived and spoke to the rebels through an amplifier, invoking them to end their mutiny. When they got no response, they left. Between 3 p.m. and 4 p.m., a special naval squad called FOES arrived on the island. Deputy-Minister of the Interior, Agustín Mantilla, also arrived and remained in El Frontón for the entire duration of the operation. The attack against the Blue Pavilion started around 5.15 p.m. Two rockets were launched to open a hole that would allow the troops to enter the pavilion. Rebels were well-protected by internal structures which they had built, and responded to the firing using the weapons they had seized, injuring several members of the navy. Inmates never stopped singing and shouting their hymns and slogans ('Long live the armed struggle, President Gonzalo, Communism!') and insulting marines ('mass murderers, cowards') (Poccorpachi Vallejos, 2002). But this was clearly an uneven battle. More powerful explosives were used and a hole was finally opened at 6 p.m. Exchange of fire continued. At 8 p.m. more army and GR troops arrived. One inmate was able to leave the pavilion and told officers that the prisoners who wanted to surrender were being stabbed by Shining Path prisoners. He also told officers that there were ditches used by the rebels to protect themselves against the attacks. The exchange of fire and fierce resistance on the part of Shining Path prisoners continued. At around 3 a.m., FOES took over the operation, under the command of Rear-Admiral Luis Giampietri. They began using much more powerful weaponry. One more time the rebels were asked to surrender, but once again they refused. At some point, FOES forces were replaced by marines, under the command of Rear-Admiral Vega Llona. At about 6.00 a.m. the final assault started and marines finally entered the Blue Pavilion around 8.30 a.m., shooting and throwing grenades.

There were still prisoners resisting the assault, many of them injured. Testimonies of Shining Path survivors described the carnage: there were inmates who had been decapitated or had lost arms and legs. One of them, who had lost both legs, begged to be killed. It was about 2 p.m. when the surviving inmates finally surrendered. They threw away their weapons, released two of the hostages (the other had been killed in the exchange of fire), and began to leave the pavilion. They were ordered to lie on the floor, but some of them were removed from the group and then executed. Witnesses have stated that inmates who looked like leaders were among those picked for execution. Others were found in the tunnels, taken out of the building and shot, while others were stabbed with knives in different parts of the body. Testimonies of both Shining Path survivors and GRs coincide in the description of what happened. An anonymous marine who was present blames Vega Llona for giving the order to execute prisoners: 'Mátenlos' (Kill them!) is what he would have said (Anonymous, 2003). According to Jesús Mejía Huerta, who miraculously survived the massacre, the bodies of those executed were thrown into ditches, showered with fuel and burned.

But then another decision was made: to completely demolish the Blue Pavilion. There are contradictory versions as to who gave the order. Deputy-Minister Mantilla is mentioned by several witnesses as the person who ordered the demolition (Haya de la Torre, 1988: 32; CVR, 2003a). Attorney General Elejalde was present on the island when the demolition started, along with a member of the Supreme Court, but they did nothing to stop it, even if they knew that there were inmates still alive inside. Several powerful explosions were heard. The building collapsed, burying both dead and alive prisoners inside the Blue Pavilion. That was considered the end of the operation. Officially, there were 34 survivors. The rest, 117, were dead, 90 of them executed after they had surrendered. Three marines were dead and five were injured. One of the hostages also died (CVR, 2003e).

In the Santa Bárbara prison, the air force was in charge of the operation. Their entrance was swift and much easier than in the other two prisons, because they found virtually no resistance. A GR officer blindly shot against the cells from where Shining Path inmates were insulting and harassing the troops, killing two inmates (Haya de la Torre, 1988: 47).

The bodies of most victims of the massacre were never returned to their relatives for proper burial. Only four out of the 97 recovered bodies from El

Frontón were identified. They were secretly buried in several cemeteries in localities near Lima.

The Aftermath

President García Pérez praised the armed forces for a job well done and added that 'the operation's outcome is regrettable, but it has demonstrated to the country that the authority has been imposed' (Haya de la Torre, 1988: 49). The CVR concluded that the government already knew about the extrajudicial executions when they issued the congratulatory declaration. The government and the armed forces issued various statements that contained false or misleading information. On 19 June, for instance, the CCFFAA's press office informed the country that 'many of them [died in Lurigancho] due to asphyxia and burnings that occurred inside the fortifications they had built and that they refused to leave, offering resistance with explosives, fire guns, and cutting instruments for twelve hours'. The same communiqué declared prisons as 'military zones', with the clear goal of placing the investigation in the hands of a military tribunal and preventing civilian and judicial authorities and political opposition leaders from entering it (Cristobal, 1987:160). This was clearly an anti-constitutional measure that reveals the intention of covering up the massacre.

Initial reactions by political leaders and public opinion seem to coincide in their satisfaction with the 'solution' which the government had found to the crisis, lamenting the loss of lives but basically expressing their support for the energy used to put down the mutinies. A daily newspaper summarised these sentiments with the following headline: 'From their own medicine' (Cristóbal, 1987: 97). Even leftist opposition leader and Mayor of Lima Alfonso Barrantes gave the impression of endorsing the official version of the events: 'The mutiny had to be put down', he declared to a local newspaper (Elejalde, 1986). 'Those who mutinied are the ones that violated the law', he told another paper, suggesting that the government had done the right thing in swiftly eliminating the rebellion (Elejalde, 1986). Attorney general Elejalde did not hesitate to state that 'the lives of those that surrendered were respected' (Elejalde, 1986). Archbishop of Lima Augusto Vargas Alzamora concurred: 'I wouldn't condemn the government' ('No me atrevería a condenar al gobierno') (*Oiga*, 1986). Gradually, though, human rights activists, victims' relatives, opposition leaders and independent journalists began to unearth the truth, and began to raise their voices in condemnation of the massacre (Cristóbal, 1987). The independent weekly magazine *Caretas* (in no way sympathetic to the Shining Path) called the government's actions 'deliberate extermination' ('exterminio deliberado') (Cristóbal, 1987: 63). The government, after its initial complacent statement, finally admitted that some 'excesses' had been committed and promised both a full investigation and sanctions to those that may be found guilty. President García Pérez visited Lurigancho (but not El Frontón) and emphatically declared: 'Either the ones responsible for this or I will have to go' ('O se van todos los responsables o me voy yo') On 24 June, the president spoke to the nation, insisting that the outcome was 'terrible but inevitable', admitting that between 30 and 40 inmates in Lurigancho had been executed by GRs, and announcing an investigation. Later, he called the GRs 'assassins' and demanded a 'historical sanction' against those responsible for the murders (Haya de la Torre, 1988: 57).

The official investigation was placed in the hands of a military tribunal, which found Colonel Cabezas and 52 GR personnel responsible for the execution of inmates in Lurigancho. But the army, which was in charge of the operation along with the GR, was relieved, by both García and the military tribunal, of any responsibility (Haya de la Torre, 1988: 37). The report of a special commission named by the Minister of the Interior concluded: 'There is clear evidence to conclude that there have been excesses in the intervention of the police in these events' and found responsible, among others, Colonel Cabezas and 52 members of the Anti-Subversive unit under his command. It also found responsibility on the part of Martínez Lara and other officers who, even if they did not participate in the executions, 'from their locations they saw the excesses committed against the prisoners that left alive from the Industrial Pavilion and did not adopt effective measures to impede them' (Ministerio del Interior, 1986: 32). In El Frontón, the tribunal found no blame for the Navy in the massacre, despite an internal investigation report that blamed Vega Llona for the decision to execute prisoners and destroy the Pavilion (Vega Llona was murdered by a Shining Path squad in La Paz on 9 December 1988). The sentence, issued on 6 July 1987, stated that the navy had fulfilled the mission given to them and that it had respected the life of the 34 inmates who had surrendered. The collapse of the Blue Pavilion, the military judge concluded, should be attributed to the weakening of its structures resulting from the changes made by the inmates themselves and the detonation of explosives stored by the prisoners inside the building (CVR, 2003e: 77). Later, a commission formed by the Peruvian Congress and presided over by a member of the opposition, Senator Rolando Ames, ended up issuing two reports. Both agreed on the reconstruction of the facts, but disagreed on the attribution of responsibilities. The minority report, signed by Ames and other members of the opposition, suggested that political responsibility should reach the president and his cabinet for making a series of decisions that allowed the massacres to happen. The Congress approved the majority report that, not surprisingly, denied any responsibility on the part of the president and his cabinet. In 2003, the CVR report shared the conclusions of the minority report, attributing 'serious political responsibility' to García Pérez and his cabinet members (CVR, 2003c: 261).

Explaining the Horror

The collective decision made by the government and the commanders of the armed forces to militarise the problem, without serious concern for the lives of the prisoners, and their reluctance to even attempt a different solution to the crisis were the driving force behind the unfolding of this tragedy. Agustín Haya de la Torre (1988: 39) put it this way: 'The motivation to intervene militarily determines and precipitates everything.' This decision was coupled by an almost desperate preoccupation with solving the crisis at the earliest possible moment, which came from the highest authority: the President of the Republic. The signals were clear: he wanted a swift operation. According to the President of the CCFFAA, 'there was a direct interest on the part of the President of the Republic that the intervention started as soon as possible' (CVR, 2003e: 54). Lieutenant Loyola declared that, once the operation was over, Colonel Cabezas told him that 'there are times in which you don't like the orders, but you have to obey them', and added that one day he would understand that 'if the President so orders, what can we do?' According to journalist Augusto Zimmermann, during a breakfast he had with President García Pérez and Minister of Justice González Posada on 16 June 1986, two days before the massacre, the president had asked, as if thinking aloud, 'What would happen if we get rid of all the Senderistas?' Then he answered his own question (which he later denied: Alava, 2003): 'Nothing, absolutely nothing'. While the responsibility of the president continues to be debated in legal and political terms, he certainly sent a clear message to the effect that he expected this crisis to be solved quickly and militarily, not through dialogue or the use of peaceful measures to dissuade the insurgents.

Although the imminent arrival of dozens of foreign visitors, and the impending inauguration of the Congress of socialist and social-democrat parties undoubtedly contributed to that sense of urgency, much more important in the decision to militarise the conflict and demand a quick 'solution' was the perception that doing otherwise would send a wrong message and that the time had arrived to 'satisfy' the subversives' 'wishes', as General Cisneros Vizquerra had put it, or to give them 'some oftheir own medicine'. A swift solution was in tune with the president's loss of patience and the disregard for human lives stemming from perceptions about their inhumanity and undeserving nature. If 'terrorists' were winning the war because, as many thought, of the lack of energy on the part of the state, then this was the time to give them a lesson. The mutinies had to be put down at any cost. As many commentators have emphasised, at no time did the government make any meaningful effort to minimise the loss of life or to conduct the operation following strictly legal procedures.

Officers in charge of the operation knew (or expected) that the use of extreme force and the disregard for human life were not going to be questioned and that, if they were, they could get away with it. They felt reassured that they were doing the right thing. They interpreted the orders as meaning a 'direct military' operation and a 'combat action', as Army General Guillermo Monzón Arrunátegui stated (CVR, 2003c: 247). After all, civilians had put the solution of the crisis almost entirely in their hands. In an interview after the June 1986 events, Deputy-Minister of the Interior Agustín Mantilla undoubtedly trying to minimise his own role in the massacre, declared that, when the Navy took control of the El Frontón island, 'we [i.e. the government] had nothing, absolutely nothing to do there' (Cristóbal, 1987:106). The Attorney General (Fiscal de la Nación) was present on the island when the bombing of the Blue Pavilion started and did nothing to stop it. According to the CVR, judicial and penitentiary authorities were prevented from exercising their functions and were excluded from any decision about the management of the crisis. 'The haste demanded from the Armed Forces and their lack of experience in this kind of situation prevented an adequate preparation of the operations; this, along with the 'military' character of the operation, brought about an improvised and violent intervention that caused unnecessary injuries and deaths among the rebels and the armed forces' (CVR, 2003c: 248).

Putting down the mutinies thus became a military operation: the government chose the cruellest, the harshest and the most punitive solution. Senator Armando Villanueva del Campo, an important leader of the ruling party, justified the decision by saying that 'there was no alternative' (Cristóbal, 1987: 188), but clearly there were other possible avenues to solve the crisis. Former member of the Peace Commission Diego García Sayán lamented that other methods were not used: 'Was it, he wondered, to satisfy the thirst for revenge within military institutions, instead of pursuing an effective project to pacify the country?' (Cristóbal, 1987: 323). And when asked whether the armed forces went out with the intention of killing, he responded affirmatively (Cristóbal, 1987: 323). Agustín Haya de la Torre (1988: 34), then a member of the opposition (and now a member of APRA), condemned the fact that 'the goal was to eliminate them'. After the events, Fernando Cabieses, a member of the Peace Commission, admitted that their efforts in trying to avoid the massacre were 'childish'. 'This was a battle that was already coming', he added ('una batalla que ya se venía') (Cristóbal, 1987: 187).

Thus, on the part of state officers, an authoritarian, militaristic reaction, shared by civilians and army officers alike and nurtured by frustration with the lack of success in the war against the Shining Path and a perception of 'terrorists' as undeserving and sub-human, led to the unfolding of the tragedy. Prisons were seen as spaces where the state had surrendered its authority and the insurgents had taken advantage; mutinies like the ones that erupted in June 1986 reinforced the perception that prisoners were being too defiant and that it was time to restore order and authority.

But the massacre also responded to Shining Path's strategy of confrontation and provocation. They pushed the government's tolerance to the limit and consciously and explicitly inserted the 'genocide' option within their strategy. A communiqué issued by prisoners' relatives after the massacre stated that 'this was a planned rebellion ('rebelión preparada') because they knew that the genocide was coming' (Cristóbal, 1987: 227). Indeed, they seemed to work to make it happen. They prepared for it, and when they saw it coming, they felt that it was the realisation of a plan and the fulfillment of a prophecy: if they died, it was for a cause, and their death would further confirm that they had been right.

Historian Pablo Macera wrote shortly after the events that this was 'the greatest political victory for the Shining Path' (Macera, 1986: 39). Was this actually the case? The insurgents lost 250 members (in a way, they had already lost them, because they were locked away in prisons from which it was very hard to escape, and many had received lengthy sentences), but they won a moral victory that reinforced the mystique among their members: 18 June became the 'Day of Heroism' in Shining Path's calendar. Accounts given to the CVR by survivors of the El Frontón massacre highlighted the heroism and resolution of Shining Path prisoners. One of them (Nicolás) emphasised how 'arrancamos lauros a la misma muerte para gloria del Presidente Gonzalo, del Partido, de la Revolución' ('we took honour in death, for the glory of President Gonzalo, the Party, and the Revolution'). They had resisted as the Party had taught us, we had agitated and sung our song "We are the initiators", which is very appropriate: "If we die in battle with our bodies mutilated, if we die in battle with our bodies in pieces (*desgarrado*), death will be welcomed, because it is a dignified death (*muerte digna*)". [. . .] They have not silenced us even in our agony [. . .] My morale is now higher, my class hatred is stronger now, to annihilate this genocidal regime' (CVR, n.d.).

On the other hand, the massacre did certainly prove to be a serious moral and political defeat for the government, but it was only temporary and, with the exception of Colonel Cabezas and the GR guards acting under his command, everybody else was shielded from any legal responsibilities. In the long run, the massacre did not erode the legitimacy or popularity of the García Pérez administration, and it definitely did not decrease the population's support for harsh measures and *mano dura*. A year later, the government's decision to nationalise the bank system would generate a much stronger response on the part of large sectors of the population and the political opposition. Clearly, economic decisions were much more important in the imaginary of the population than 'excesses' in the anti-subversive war that targetted Shining Path prisoners. The voices condemning the massacre and demanding both an investigation and punishment of the perpetrators were few and almost muted.

Shining Path, ultimately, did not significantly improve its image as a result of this massacre. It gave them cohesion and reinforced their mystique; it allowed Guzmán to insist that they were going in the right direction by combatting a genocidal state, and it confirmed them in the conviction that this was a war to the death with the 'fascist' state. But, in the larger context of a society under the stress of the war, the events of 18–19 June did not translate into more sympathetic views of the insurgents. The massacre was just one more incident – a horrendous one, indeed – in a long list of atrocities committed by the state and the insurgents during the war. In fact, the June 1986 massacre did not trigger a wave of indignation among the Peruvian public. Sadly but not surprisingly, the imposition of brutal state repression seems to have been approved by large sectors of the population. A poll taken in Lima shortly after the massacre showed that 75 percent of people supported the government's handling of the prison crisis, although that percentage declined sharply later, when more complete information about the atrocities was revealed (Flores Galindo, 1988: 245). Opposition parties and media, as well as human rights activists, forced the issue and the government had to at least offer the impression that it did not condone the 'excesses' and that it was willing to punish those responsible for them.

However, there was no wave of indignation among large sectors of the population, certainly not one comparable to the reaction to the brutal assassination by Shining Path, in February 1992, of María Elena Moyano, a leftist grassroots organiser in a shanty town in Lima. In the latter case, massive demonstrations of popular indignation repudiated Moyano's murder. Popular sensibility did not visibly express a similar condemnation of the prison massacre in June 1986. I suggest that the war brought to the surface what I would call a popular version of authoritarianism, one that was not actually new – it has been historically applied to children, delinquents, women, slaves, students, domestic servants and other subaltern groups – but that acquired a new dimension in the context of a war that was causing destruction, suffering and the forced relocation of people. Shining Path was blamed for all this, so the massacre was interpreted as an appropriate and justified way of dealing with 'terrorism'. This 'popular authoritarianism' would be even more perceptible during the Fujimori administration (1990–2000). Popular support for *mano dura* was readily available for Fujimori from ordinary people, eager to get quick solutions to their daily torment of having to deal with assassinations, blackouts, strikes and other forms of Shining Path violence. It actually increased as Fujimori was able to show 'results'. His April 1992 closure of the Peruvian Congress and judiciary, which led him to his dictatorial and anti-constitutional rule (known as the *auto-golpe*), as well as his 'success' in the war against subversion – much of it resulting from the use of extrajudicial mechanisms, such as torture and the disappearance of persons, for which he has since been condemned to 25 years in prison – were backed, at least temporarily, by a majority of the Peruvian population (Burt, 2007).

What we can call a 'clash of authoritarianisms' found its deadly climax in Lima's prisons in June 1986. The Shining Path's political project implied a top-down, authoritarian and fundamentalist view of society, to be imposed by the use of violence even against innocent, ordinary and working-class populations. The state's response made use of similarly violent and authoritarian methods. State repression included intimidation, assassination, illegal executions, disappearance of persons, massacres of innocent people and a general disregard for the rule of law and the protection of human rights of all individuals involved. Many scholars have not hesitated to refer to this clash as a 'dirty war'. The massacre of Shining Path prisoners revealed the militaristic conception with which the state responded to the insurgency, but also the brutality of Shining Path's political methods. At the end, Peruvians confronted a twofold tragedy: first, 250 people lost their lives in one of the deadliest prison massacres in world history and, second, in the perception of most Peruvians –and certainly that of state administrators – it did not really resonate as a real, regrettable tragedy.

Conclusion

As the war launched by the Shining Path in May 1980 escalated, prisons became also arenas of struggle, *luminosas trincheras de combate* (literally, 'shining trenches of struggle'), as they called them. Prisons were not isolated or marginal components of the Shining Path's overall political struggle; quite the opposite. They consciously used prisons as weapons in their radical confrontation with the state. In other words, instead of symbols of their defeat, prisons became arenas of struggle and even weapons to advance their cause. Shining Path did this by dramatically exploiting the aura of horror and resistance that surrounded the prisons so that the outside world would not overlook what was going on inside their walls. Denunciation campaigns about the atrocities that political prisoners faced became not only a way of forcing the authorities to change those conditions, but also – and probably more importantly – a means for undermining the legitimacy of the government. Simultaneously, the heroism and fortitude of political prisoners were widely publicised by the party, in an effort to demonstrate that, despite the ferocious repression, they were still strong and willing to persist in their struggle.

At the same time, though, the radical and confrontational strategy used by the Shining Path – the 'everything or nothing' kind of approach – and the way in which its goals and its members were demonised in media and public opinion debates, made it much more vulnerable to state repression. Shining Path's success in controlling prisons turned out to be one of the main justifications for the extremely violent response by the García Pérez administration (and, later, the Fujimori administration): prisoners were seen as too defiant and prison conditions were denounced as too lenient, so the government decided that this situation should come to an end and that it was time to apply *mano dura*. It seems as though the Peruvian state did not manage to escape the vicious circle in which it was trapped, the pendulum that oscillated between leniency and brutality.

Finally, it is revealing that the worst massacre of political prisoners in Peru happened under a democratically elected government. This gloomy corroboration speaks to the fragile nature of civilian rule, the restrictive observance of democratic and civil rights, especially for the most vulnerable sectors of the population, and the pervasive influence of a militaristic approach to social and political issues. Peruvian 'democracy' – the one that allowed the massacre to happen, and the one that refused to punish the perpetrators – failed to show its moral superiority vis-à-vis those that were trying to destroy it.

9

Gang Violence and Insecurity in Contemporary Central America

ORLANDO J. PÉREZ

Central Michigan University, USA

Gang activity constitutes one of the most serious problems of crime in Central America. Since the end of the 1980s, a period of armed conflict:

> gang violence has evolved from a localised, purely neighbourhood-based security concern into a transnational problem that pervades urban enclaves in every country in the region. The two predominant Central American gangs, Mara Salvatrucha (MS-13) and the 18th Street gang (Barrio 18), while originating in the Los Angeles region of the United States, have capitalised on globalisation trends and communications technologies to acquire arms, power and influence across the United States, Mexico, and Central America. (USAID, 2006)

Gang activity has developed into a complex, multifaceted, and transnational problem. This chapter will explore the origins and consequences of youth gang violence for contemporary Central America, focussing particular attention on the transnational and multidimensional nature of the problem.

The Latin American region has the dubious distinction of having the highest rates of crime and violence in the world. Homicide rates usually are considered to be the most reliable indicator of crime, because few murders go unreported. According to an extensive study (by the World Bank) of homicide rates for 1970–1994, the world average was 6.8 per 100,000 (Fajnzylber, Lederman and Loayza, 1998). The homicide rate in Latin America is estimated at 30 murders per 100,000 per year, whereas it stands at about 5.5 in the United States and about 2.0 in the United Kingdom, Spain and Switzerland. The Pan American Health Organisation, which reports a lower average for Latin America as a whole, of 20 per 100,000 people, says that 'violence is one of the main causes of death in the Hemisphere [. . .] In some countries, violence is the main cause of death and in others it is the leading cause of injuries and disability'. (Acemoglu and Robinson, 2001: 938–963). However, according to the United Nations Global Report on Crime, health

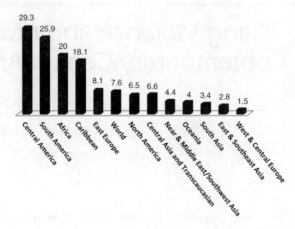

Figure 9.1.   Intentional Homicide Rates per 100,000 Inhabitants by Region and Sub-Region

statistics as a basis for measuring homicide significantly under-report the total homicide levels; health statistics data are based on the classification of deaths made by physicians rather than by the police. According to the United Nations (UN) comparison, health-based homicide rates average about half those of Interpol or UN statistics (Newman, 1999: 12–13). In the region, there are 140,000 homicides each year, although not all of the countries in the region face the same magnitude and type of violence. In the 1990s, Colombia, faced with epidemic problems of drug trafficking and guerrilla violence, had one of the highest homicide rates anywhere (around 90 homicides per 100,000 inhabitants), whereas, in contrast, Chile, despite a history of political conflict, displayed homicide rates no greater than five deaths per 100,000 inhabitants (Organisación Panamericana de la Salud, 1996). According to this and other indicators, violence in Latin America is five times higher than in most other places in the world (Fajnzylber, Lederman and Loayza, 1998). Moreover, according to Gaviria and Pagés, the homicide rates are not only consistently higher in Latin America, but also the differences with the rest of the world are growing larger (Gaviria and Pagés, 1999).

Figure 9.1 presents data that shows that Latin America has the dubious distinction of having the highest rates of crime and violence in the world (Geneva Declaration Secretariat, 2008). Within the Latin American region Central America exhibits the highest rates of homicide.

Crime Victimisation and Insecurity in Central America

Figure 9.2 indicates that homicide rates in Guatemala, El Salvador and Honduras have increased steadily since the early 2000s, despite significant efforts by national governments to apply *mano dura* policies that emphasise

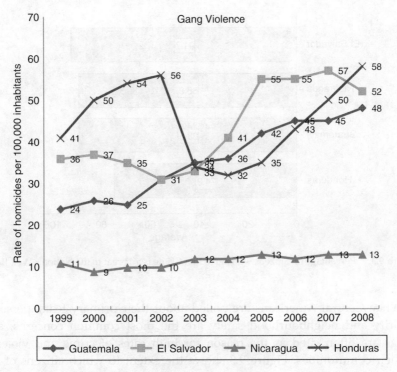

Figure 9.2. Central America: Homicide Rates (1998–2008)

law enforcement and punishment, including extensive use of the armed forces to repress gang and other criminal activity.

At its core, *mano dura* necessitates curtailing individual rights and re-empowering the military and police. These sets of policies normally include deploying the military for internal policing, in addition to lengthening prison sentences, suspending due process guarantees and other protections for alleged criminals, and aggressively arresting youths suspected of gang membership.

The evidence shows that criminal activity has not been disrupted by these strategies; instead, gangs and other criminal networks have increased their level of organisation, technological sophistication and international links. Moreover, because *mano dura* policies have led to the incarceration of growing numbers of at-risk youth, they have created prison conditions that facilitate the organisation of prison gangs, and that increase youths' risk of continuing involvement in gang-related activities. In El Salvador alone, police records show that some 60,000 young people were jailed as a result of the *mano dura* policies; Salvadoran police estimate that more than 10,000 of some 14,000 suspected gang members arrested in 2005 were later released for lack of evidence against them (Pérez, 2011).

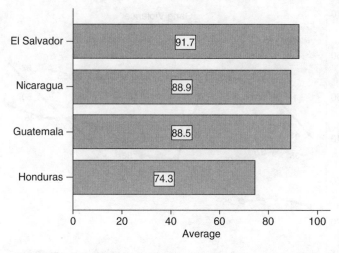

Figure 9.3.   Percentage of Citizens who agree that Crime is a Threat to the Nation's Well-Being

When Central Americans are polled about their primary fears, personal security and neighbourhood safety are the most common concerns, and gangs are often cited as the reason for high rates of crime and violence in their communities. Figure 9.3 shows the extent to which citizens of the region consider crime a threat to the nation's well-being (the data are derived from a series of surveys conducted by the Latin American Public Opinion Project (LAPOP: http://www.lapopsurveys.org); the surveys are of national probability employing a multi-stage cluster design with a minimum of 1,500 cases, conducted in early 2008). Overwhelming majorities in each nation indicate that crime is a threat to the country.

Figure 9.4 shows the percentage of citizens in the Central American countries who express fear that they will be victims of crime in their neighbourhood. The data indicates that over 40 percent of those surveyed in Honduras and El Salvador fear falling victim to a crime in their neighbourhood. Close to 40 percent express the same feelings in Guatemala. Citizens in the country with the lowest homicide rate, Nicaragua, exhibit the lowest level of fear of becoming victims of crime.

The differences between the vast majorities who say that crime is a threat to the nation and who express fear of becoming victims of crime reflect the dichotomy between evaluations of the national condition, which is affected by media coverage and more remote perceptions, and feelings related to the respondent's neighbourhood, which could be seen as safer than other places. Nonetheless, the fact that more than a third of respondents say they fear becoming victims of a crime in their own neighbourhood should indicate the seriousness of the crime problem for nations in Central America. As we

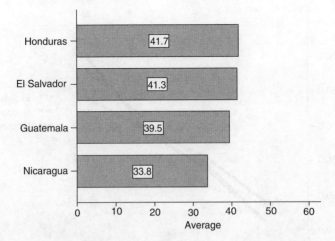

Figure 9.4. Percentage of Citizens who Express Fear at being Victims of Crime

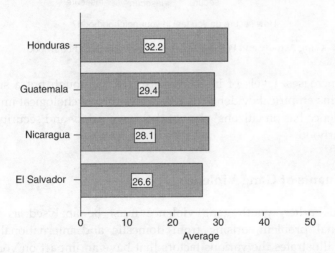

Figure 9.5. Percentage of Respondents whose Neighbourhood is Affected by Gang Activity

will see below, gang-related activity constitutes a particularly difficult and serious threat to the security and stability of democracy in Central America.

Figure 9.5 indicates the percentage of citizens who say that their neighbour-hood is affected by gangs. We can observe that nearly a third of respondents in Honduras and Guatemala indicate their neighbourhoods are affected by gang-related activity. More than a fourth of Salvadorians say that their neighbourhood is affected by gangs.

The relationship between perceived gang activity and fear of becoming a victim of crime is very close. Figure 9.6 shows the impact of gang violence on the sense of security in respondents' neighbourhood. As perception of gang

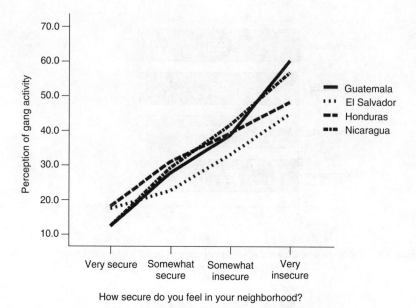

Figure 9.6.   Gang Activity and Perceptions of Security in the Neighbourhood

activity increases, levels of insecurity also rise; although not a surprising finding, this empirical evidence demonstrates the psychological impact that gang violence has on citizens' view of their own safety and security in their neighbourhood.

Determinants of Gang Violence

As stated earlier, youth gang violence must be analysed as a multi-dimensional problem, arising from domestic and international factors. Table 9.1 illustrates the various factors that have an impact on youth gang violence in the region.

Gangs are therefore the product of diverse social factors that express themselves in a variety of life conditions. In the end, these factors are responsible for shaping the conditions within which young people live and permit the emergence and growth of gang activity. For example, poverty is relevant only if it exists within an environment of social injustice and exclusion (Cruz, 2004). In a similar way, the Central American civil wars (Guatemala in 1960–1996 and El Salvador in 1980–1992), which have been mentioned by government officials and the media as the precursors of an army of youngsters ready to use violence, cannot explain entirely why hundreds of young people became involved in gang-related activity years after the war ended and without any historical memory of its violence. The first studies conducted on the

Table 9.1. Elements Associated with the Central American Gangs

Relational level	Causal category	Specific elements
Social	Social exclusion	Precarious socio-economic conditions
		Communities lack basic services
		Lack of educational opportunities
		School expulsion or dropout
		Unemployment or underemployment
		Culturally defined models of personal relationships
	Culture of violence	Patterns of teaching/learning violence
		Society's permissiveness regarding the use of weapons/availability of weapons
	Rapid and disorganised urban growth	Urban congestion
		Lack of recreational spaces
		Poor or non-existent community services.
	Migration	Youth adopt gang culture outside their country
		Youth return to their country without supportive infrastructure
		Deported criminals
Community	Lack of social capital	Lack of trust between community members.
		Lack of citizen participation in community affairs.
	Drugs	Drug consumption
		Drug traffic
Family and friends	Domestic problems	Dysfunctional families
		Neglect by the parents and/or guardians
		Family history of violence
	Friends	Gang members in the community
		Gang members in schools
Individual	Dynamics of violence	Cycle reinforces and reproduces violence
	Lack of individual or collective identity	Violence a means to create identity
		Absence of positive role models

Source: adapted from Cruz, 2004 and 2005

emergence of youth gangs did not show any evidence that those who fought during the civil wars in El Salvador and Guatemala were any more likely to engage in gang activity (Levenson, 1989; Argueta, 1992). The war's contribution also is questioned because Nicaragua, which suffered an armed conflict, does not have the type of gang problems that affect other Central American nations, and Honduras, which did not suffer an internal civil war at all, faces one of the most severe forms of youth gang violence. This does not mean that the wars had no impact whatsoever on the rise of gangs; the armed conflicts contributed by creating other conditions that would later favour the development of gangs in the region. They helped to generate an exile community in the United States and the subsequent migration that contributed to the diffusion of gang culture (Smutt and Miranda, 1998). Additionally, the civil conflicts aggravated a culture of violence that existed in Salvadorian and Guatemalan society and made weapons more accessible. Central American gangs did not develop in a vacuum. Gangs are the heirs of urban juvenile groups that developed in the socio-economic conditions of urban areas, and were transformed by those conditions and by political decisions, from juvenile groups engaged in petty crimes to transnational criminal networks involved in drug trafficking, money laundering and serial murders. Therefore, gangs are a result of the social, political and economic environment that the population of the region has experienced in the last two decades or more. This environment represents, on the one hand, the confluence of several demographic and social conditions: the average age of the population, the level of poverty and inequality, the unequal access to educational opportunities, lack of health coverage, scarce housing, little or no safe recreational spaces; on the other hand, it is the product of the reciprocal effects of political and security decisions taken to combat the problem, which have made the situation worse. In other words, gangs in Central America are the result of social dynamics, where not only the identity of gang members and their environment matters, but the manner in which society tackles the phenomenon (Cruz, 2005).

While gangs across the region share similar origins and characteristics, there are key differences. Each particular case generates a series of conditions that determine the gang's behavioural dynamics. This explains the differences encountered in the behaviour of the *clikas* (cliques) that make up the basic organisational structure of gangs. Thus, normal behaviour for some members in one country could be considered 'unthinkable' for fellow members in another country. For example, a practice known as 'Running the South', which means to establish alliances between enemy gangs inside penitentiaries, could be acceptable in prisons in the United States and, recently, Guatemala, but it would be nearly impossible to establish in countries such as Honduras or El Salvador. In the latter, gang activity is dominated by the 18th street gang (Barrio 18) and Mara Salvatrucha (MS-13), making collaboration in prison less likely; moreover, government policy perpetuates this polarisation inside prisons.

Strocka argues that the organisational structure of youth gangs varies across and within countries (Strocka, 2006). While some gangs, for example the Salvadoran *maras*, display clear leadership and a well-developed hierarchical structure, 'others, such as the Brazilian *galeras cariocas*, are more egalitarian and less cohesive. The age of youth gang members also varies widely, ranging from as young as seven to about 30 years old. Although the overwhelming majority of youth gang members are male, both all-female and female-led youth gangs reportedly exist in a number of Latin American countries, including Mexico, Nicaragua, Guatemala and Peru' (Strocka, 2006: 135–136).

Moreover, the reasons that youth gangs are established, as well as the functions that they perform, vary widely. Some gangs, such as the Brazilian *quadrilhas*, pursue primarily economic interests, while others, like the *pandillas* in Peru, fulfil mainly social functions (related to the achievement of a positive social identity, control over territory and neighbourhood protection). Youth gangs also differ significantly in terms of their involvement in illegal and violent activities. The Costa Rican *chapulines*, for example, are centred mainly on pleasurable pursuits, such as playing football and consuming alcohol and drugs, and only occasionally engage in petty crime. The Salvadoran *maras*, on the other hand, are extremely violent and extensively involved in armed robbery, assaults and homicides. Some youth gangs, such as the Nicaraguan *pandillas*, are mainly territorial and tend to have strong ties with their local communities. However, other gangs, such as the Brazilian *quadrilhas*, have only weak relationships with their local communities and are indiscriminate in the scope of their criminal activities (Strocka, 2006).

In the cases of Guatemala, El Salvador and Honduras, gang activity is primarily polarised by Mara Salvatrucha (MS-13) and Barrio 18 gangs, which are the most well organised and violent gangs in the region. According to the police, the gangs in the region are divided into three overall groups, and, while there is a degree of permeability between these groups, particularly between juvenile criminal gangs and organised criminal gangs, their activities and modus operandi are distinct. This typology is as follows:

  (i) Juvenile gangs (age range 9–20 years old):
      There may or may not be an organisational hierarchy; they engage in minor crimes (petty theft, burglary, fighting amongst themselves, and so on); they serve as a breeding ground for more sophisticated gangs; the majority still live at home.
 (ii) Juvenile criminal gangs:
      They possess defined organisational structures; they are used by organised crime and are capable of conducting more serious offences such as rape, larceny, homicide; most members have broken with family ties.
(iii) Organised criminal gangs:
      These are transnational criminal organisations; they have elaborate organisational structures, spanning several countries; they are linked to transnational drug trafficking and money laundering criminal organisations; they engage in homicides, kidnapping, drug trafficking, money laundering, and so on.

Only MS13 and M18 belong to the third group. The vast majority of youth gangs identified by the police belong to the first category. Table 9.2 shows an estimate of membership in the four countries with the highest level of gang

Table 9.2.   Estimated Numbers of Gang Members (Comisión de Jefes de Policía de Centro América y El Caribe)

Country	Gang membership (predominantly MS-13 and 18th Street)
El Salvador	10,500
Honduras	36,000
Nicaragua	2,200
Guatemala	14,000
Totals	62,700

activity. The largest number of gangs, according to the police, is concentrated in Honduras. However, while the number may be less than in Guatemala and Honduras, El Salvador's gangs are probably the most violent in the region.

One of the major trends observed across the region is the declining age of entry into youth gangs (Cruz and Portillo, 1998). Another trend is the expansion of gang activity to rural areas. Gangs are no longer restricted to the big cities but increasingly emerge and operate in small towns and villages. Youth gangs are increasingly and more systematically involved in drug trafficking. As a consequence, the divide between youth gangs and organised narco-crime is gradually disappearing (Rodgers, 2003, Moser, Winton and Moser, 2005). Finally, another trend that has been observed, at least among Central American youth gangs, is their transformation into 'transnational' networks (Reguillo Cruz, 2005). In other words, youth gangs no longer operate only within the boundaries of a particular, relatively small neighbourhood, but increasingly extend their sphere of influence across cities, regions and countries.

It is commonly believed that deportees from the United States have contributed to the gang problem. According to numerous anecdotal accounts, some of those deported during the 1990s who arrived in the United States during the 1980s, and who had participated in Latino gangs in the United States, had minimal family or community ties in their home countries, and spoke limited Spanish. Consequently, their arrival may have facilitated the rise of gangs in El Salvador, Guatemala and Honduras.

The level of deportations is related to US immigration policies. Deportations rose significantly after 1996, when the US government passed two new laws: the Illegal Immigration Reform and Responsibility Act (IIRIRA) and the Anti-Terrorism and Effective Death Penalty Act (AEDPA). The first law expanded the offences for which a non-citizen could be deported. Previously, only a fairly limited class of aggravated felonies, including murder and drug trafficking, could be the basis for deportation. IIRIRA extended the list to 28 specific offences, including any crime of violence with a prison sentence of at least one year. Provisions of IIRIRA and AEDPA also greatly limited the number of deportation cases subject to judicial review and subjected many more to expedited removal processes (Hagan, Castro and Rodriguez, 2008).

In 2005, US law enforcement began to target transnational gang members for deportation in a programme known as Operation Community Shield. The programme was initially directed towards the Mara Salvatrucha, but was later expanded to cover other gangs. Under the programme until September 2008, 4,000 suspected gang members and associates had been charged criminally, and more than 7,000 were charged with immigration violations and deported (Vaughan and Freere, 2008).

Overall, the information available suggests that the large majority of deportees are not gang members. However, among the more than 200,000 people deported to Central America since 2004, at least a few thousand were members of gangs. Nonetheless, while US immigration policies may be a contributing factor in the proliferation of youth gangs in Central America, the main determinants of gang activity are related to socio-economic conditions that undermine family and community cohesion.

In order to fully understand the gang problem in Central America we must examine further each national case. While there are common social and economic problems shared by the nations of the region, there are historical and socio-political factors unique to each country that help explain the differences in the levels and lethality of gang activity. The analysis will focus on El Salvador and Guatemala, among the nations with the most serious gang-related problems.

El Salvador

The origins of El Salvador's violent gangs can be traced to the Salvadorians and their children who fled the country during the civil war of the 1980s. By 1990, over 700,000 had settled mainly in Los Angeles, California, and also in Washington DC, suburbs of New York City and in parts of Maryland, where they had formed their own gangs or joined existing gangs (USAID, 2006). Salvadorian youth gravitated in particular toward two gangs that became increasingly organised in US cities in the 1990s: the 18th Street gang (Mara Barrio 18), composed mainly of Mexican-American youth and named after 18th Street in Los Angeles, and the Mara Salvatrucha (MS-13), a gang formed by Salvadorian youth (Hayden, 2004; Cruz, 2005).

In 1992, the Peace Accord between the government and the Farabundo Marti National Liberation Front (FMLN) marked an end of the twelve-year war and the beginning of the flow of Salvadorians back to their country. In

1996, changes to US immigration laws expanded the reasons for deporting non-citizens, including lawful permanent residents. Although these deported immigrants were not identified as criminals or gang members at the time of deportation, some had been incarcerated in the California prison system. Some of these deportees were gang members, including members of the MS-13 and 18th Street gangs, and took many aspects of US gang culture back to El Salvador, including hand signals, insider language, styles of dress and propensity for violence. Salvadorian gang members learned much of their craft from the Mafia Mexicana, then the most influential gang in Southern California (USAID, 2006).

The failure of the post-war Salvadorian government to address the structural causes of the civil war and to construct effective democratic institutions meant that conditions on the ground in El Salvador were ripe for the spread of gang culture, especially in marginalised communities. In particular, reductions in government expenditures on social services throughout the 1990s served to limit young people's opportunities to pursue decent and dignified lives in El Salvador. Furthermore, the Salvadorian government pursued policies aimed at transforming its traditional dependence on the agricultural sector and promoting foreign investment and labour-intensive exports. However, growth in the export sector has not kept pace with the displacement of rural populations who depended on agriculture for their survival, and the Salvadorian economy has come to depend increasingly on remittances from abroad. Poor, marginalised youth in post-war El Salvador thus had few options for the pursuit of a decent life. In addition, generalised levels of violence in post-war Salvadorian society have remained extraordinarily high. The weaknesses of post-war criminal justice institutions also contributed to the expansion of the gang phenomenon by failing to establish the rule of law or provide for citizen security in the country.

Although it is difficult to pinpoint the exact number of gang members in El Salvador, rough estimates exist. The National Civilian Police, for example, estimate there are approximately 20,900 members, whereas the government's Consejo Nacional de Seguridad Pública (National Council on Public Security) calculates upwards of 39,000 members (22,000 in MS-13; 12,000 in the 18th Street (Barrio 18); and another 5,000 in other gangs) (Consejo Nacional de Seguridad Pública, 2008; *El Nuevo Diario*, 2011).

The factors that lead young people in El Salvador to join gangs are related to socio-economic conditions, and the failure of state policy to effectively deal with the underlying structural factors that generate gang activity. First, gangs often dominate the most marginalised urban areas. In some cases, poverty levels in these areas contribute to the ongoing activity of gangs. The breakdown of the family, social and community structures, lack of basic services, and lack of opportunities for jobs or recreational activities contribute to a climate of desperation that drives young men in particular to join gangs. Gangs in turn are able to control these spaces with little challenge from law enforcement. Second, in circumstances of high unemployment, gangs offer an alternative means to acquire goods, and they offer social acceptance to these otherwise marginalised youths. Third, there is a direct correlation between school dropout rates and gang activity. In many cases, youths have poor attendance records and dismal grades, which make their retention even harder. A total of 40 percent of Salvadorian children drop out of school before grade 5. Schools lack the resources, both in terms of infrastructure and curriculum, to provide an educational experience that could serve to incorporate young people into society and provide them with hope for the future.

The reaction of the state to this problem has at times made the situation worse. The state has responded to gang activity with hard-line law enforcement tactics. In the worst cases, there are arbitrary detentions, torture and extra-judicial executions (US State Department, Bureau of Democracy, Human Rights, and Labor, 2004). For the most part, these repressive tactics have not deterred gangs from forming and operating, but rather have spurred gangs to consolidate, sometimes coming into direct confrontation with the state.

El Salvador's civil war (1980–1992), one of the most devastating armed conflicts in Latin America resulting in the deaths of more than 75,000 people, left a legacy of violence that is still felt today. Approximately 30,000 soldiers, over 6,400 national police and other security forces, and over 8,500 FMLN combatants were demobilised as a result of the terms of the Peace Accords (Montgomery, 1995; Byrne, 1996; Lungo Uclés, 1996; LeoGrande, 1998; Wood, 2003). Thousands of trained fighters were without jobs and struggling to exist, and thousands of firearms were available. The war engendered a culture in which the use of violence became common and people often used violence as the first response to settle conflicts. Moreover, the demobilisation of paramilitary forces after the Peace Accords in 1992 left thousands of small-calibre arms on the streets. Weapons proliferation is made easier by little or no controls on weapons by the state, easy access to trafficking routes and the availability of weapons cached from the civil conflict. Gangs, therefore, have found easy access to all kinds of weaponry.

Finally, El Salvador serves as a critical point of trans-shipment of drugs originating in Colombia and destined for the US market. Drug trafficking has created sophisticated and well organised crime networks in the country. The resulting flow of drugs into El Salvador also contributes to higher levels of drug consumption and addiction, which in turn may lead to more gang violence (US Department of State, 2008).

In March 2012, El Salvador's two largest street gangs, the MS-13 and the Barrio 18 signed a truce. In return for stopping the violence between them, the Salvadoran government agreed to transfer 30 of the gangs' leaders from a maximum-security facility to other prisons around the country, increased visitation rights and removed the military from various jails. The truce was brokered by an ex-guerrilla and former congressman, Raúl Mijango, and a military chaplain, Bishop Fabio Colindres. They had negotiated in secret for months prior to the announcement, under the auspices of the Security Minister at the time, retired army general David Munguía Payes. The first hundred days after the truce was signed showed a 50 percent decline in homicides (InSight Crime, 2012). Subsequent reports showed the trend of homicides maintaining their nearly 50 percent drop (InSight Crime, 2013). Despite the dramatic decrease in homicide rates, doubts remain as to the long-term effects of the truce. Surveys have shown that a majority of Salvadorians express little confidence in the truce, and are very sceptical of the gangs' motives. Additionally, analysts have questioned the effects of the truce on overall law enforcement efforts to control transnational criminal networks. Douglas Farah, of the Center for International and Strategic Studies, has argued that gang leaders 'are beginning to understand that territorial control and cohesion make it possible for them to wring concessions from the state while preserving the essence of their criminal character' (Farah, 2012: 1).

Guatemala

Guatemala signed Peace Accords in 1996, ending a 36-year civil conflict that left over 200,000 people dead and hundreds of thousands more maimed and internally displaced (Aguilera Peralta, Bran and Ogaldes, 1996; Torres-Rivas, 1997; Sieder, 1998; Azpuru, 1999; Jonas, 2000; McCleary, 1997; also Figueroa Ibarra in this volume). However, the transition from war to peace has not been a painless passage and peace continues to remain elusive. Since the accords were signed over a decade ago, Guatemala has earned the dubious distinction of being one of the most violent countries in the region and the world, with homicide rates comparable to those in war-torn African countries. The homicide rate in Guatemala was 47 per 100,000 people, compared to 5.7 per 100,000 in the US (USAID, 2006).

Violence is not a new phenomenon in Guatemala. The civil conflict was characterised by high levels of violence, much of it state-sponsored or institutional, the effects of which continue to manifest themselves in the country today. There are significant levels of economic, institutional and social violence in Guatemala. Organised crime networks exploit the weak rule of law to carry out their illicit businesses of money laundering, kidnapping and trafficking of narcotics, contraband, weapons and people (Azpuru, 1999; Jonas, 2000). Youth gangs have emerged on the scene as willing functionaries of these organised crime networks at one end of the spectrum and, at the other, as their convenient criminal scapegoats. Despite the end of the civil conflict, there are still incidents of institutional violence in the country, including police brutality and extrajudicial killings, as the state attempts to respond to mounting pressure to address high crime levels. Levels of social violence are also high in Guatemala, with a very high incidence of intra-family violence, including domestic abuse, child abuse and sexual violence, all of which contribute to perpetuating the cycle of violence within successive generations (Human Rights Watch, 2007: 206–210).

Youth under the age of eighteen comprise nearly half of the country's population. Many studies have correlated the 'youth bulge' factor with increased potential for violence (Fuller and Pitts, 1990; Goldstone, 1991). The majority of gang members in Guatemala are under 24 years of age. The average age of gang recruits appears to be on the decline, with youth as young as eight years old now joining gangs and taking on low-level functions such as serving as *banderas* (look-outs) and drug distributors in their barrios. According to the National Civil Police, there are over 400 *maras* in Guatemala, with about 14,000 members. The two largest youth gangs are the Mara Salvatrucha (MS-13) gang, with members comprising approximately 80 percent of the total number of gang members in the country, and 18th Street (Barrio 18), whose members comprise about 15 percent, and the remaining 5 percent made up of other smaller, copycat gangs (USAID, 2006).

A number of factors, socio-economic and contextual, create an environment for gang activity in Guatemala. To a great extent these factors parallel the problems that give rise to gangs in El Salvador. While rural Guatemala is by no means crime-free, crime levels, drugs and gang activity are most intense in urban and suburban areas of Guatemala. The lack of jobs in rural areas and the search for a better life have pushed many Guatemalans to migrate from rural to urban areas. Rapid urbanisation has concentrated the demographic group most inclined to violence – unattached young males. Gang members themselves largely come from poor, marginalised, urban areas, and are products of an environment characterised by overwhelmed and ineffective service delivery, social exclusion and weak social capital, disintegrated families, overcrowded living conditions, and greater population density (Cruz, 2004) (USAID, 2006). In 2000, the average number of children per household in poor urban areas of Guatemala was nearly five (Instituto Nacional de Estadística, 2005), resulting in large families, often headed by single mothers who must work long hours outside the home to sustain their large families. Fathers are scarce and, where they are a part of the family, alcoholism and domestic abuse are common. As families struggle to fulfil their most basic needs (food, shelter, electricity), other needs are neglected, such as healthy emotional bonds between parents and children, and the transfer of positive values.

While poverty is not the primary cause of crime and violence, it is one of several key factors; over 50 percent of all Guatemalans (and 76 percent of indigenous groups) live in poverty (World Bank, n.d.). The poor are disproportionately affected by gang violence. In many poor neighbourhoods, gangs are involved in extortion by forcing, upon threat of violence, local businesses such as taxi/bus drivers and small business owners to pay *impuestos de guerra* (war taxes).

Youth directly suffer the effects of poverty, which include unemployment, poor education and minimal access to high quality services. Guatemala suffers from the region's lowest public investment in social services and lowest tax collection base (less than 10 percent of GDP) from which to fund these investments. Guatemala scores consistently low on the United Nations' Human Development Indices, including infant mortality, life expectancy, and literacy (PNUD, 2006). Service delivery in poor, urban areas is increasingly characterised by increased law enforcement efforts to make arrests, but much less so by improvements in service delivery in the areas of health, education and other critical social services.

Drug consumption is practically a given with gang members. The drug trade is linked to inter-gang violence to control the drug market in local barrios. Drugs are often the motive behind robberies and assaults , intra-family quarrels between drug users and their families, and the murder of drug addicts by vigilante groups perpetuate an environment in which violence is taken for granted (Moser and McIlwaine, 1999).

The survivors of Guatemala's civil conflict inherited a legacy of institutional violence, hostility and injustice that continues to affect the daily lives of Guatemalans (Amnesty International, 2002; Sieder, Thomas Vickers and Spence, 2002). There exists a widespread culture in Guatemala that violence is an acceptable means of resolving conflict and Guatemalans do not have faith in the state's ability to provide anything other than partial and arbitrary justice (Archdiocese of Guatemala, 1999; Schirmer, 1998). The conflict also ensured that weapons would be readily available.

Since the conflict ended, very few weapons have been taken out of circulation. Approximately 2 million arms are estimated to be in the hands of 36 percent of the civilian population. Of these, only approximately 253,500 are legally registered, according to the National Civilian Police. In addition, organised criminal groups are believed to have imported large quantities of arms (Moser and Winton, 2002). Finally, the rapidly growing number of private security firms in the country has also increased the number of firearms (Munaiz and Mendoza, 2007).

In addition, the justice and security sectors in Guatemala are weak, corrupt, overwhelmed and neglected. Judicial impunity has emboldened organised criminal entities and gangs. There are severe shortages of trained judges, resulting in individuals generally spending days in pre-trial detention before ever seeing a judge. Accused spend weeks, months and often years in pre-trial detention centres where conditions are often worse than prisons. Prisons are overcrowded and lack adequate rehabilitation programmes. Gangs routinely replicate in prison hierarchical and organisational structures exhibited on the streets. Gang leaders arrested are often able with little effort to continue dominating members in prison and commanding gang activity on the outside. The conviction rate in Guatemala, and other countries in Central America, is less than 10 percent for all cases where a complaint is filed (USAID, 2006). Police suffer from weak capacity and lack the necessary equipment and training to deal effectively with gang activity and other crime-related problems. The military is often used to supplement police work with the attendant problems of the militarisation of police work, which thus degenerates further into violations of human and civil rights, perpetuating a culture of violence and making gangs ever more lethal.

Police rarely carry out significant or efficient investigations, and often make arrests only if the perpetrator is caught *in flagrante*. Because of deficiencies in the work of the police, many of those arrested end up going free on technicalities or lack of evidence. In many cases, police send those whom they arrest immediately to pre-trial detention, which is illegal without an order from a judge. Police officers have been linked to the practice of 'social cleansing' against gang members, common criminals and people otherwise considered 'undesirable' – prostitutes, street children, transvestites and other such groups. Some vigilante groups have been known to be engaged in such crimes and have enjoyed a degree of police support. The police also have been accused of abusing people arrested for minor crimes, raping women on police premises and in prisons, torture and other practices that constitute clear violations of human rights (Guatemala Human Rights Commission/USA, Guatemala Peace and Development Network, and New York Office of the Rigoberta Menchu Foundation, 2003).

Conclusion

This chapter has examined the problem of youth gang violence in contemporary Central America, focussing special attention on the cases of El Salvador and Guatemala. The chapter has provided evidence of the magnitude of the problem; evidence suggests that the region is the most violent in the world and survey results show that citizens express overwhelming concern about the impact of crime on their societies.

Furthermore, the analysis has shown that Central American gangs are a multi-dimensional problem, a result of an evolving interaction of different factors that include social and political conditions, cultural and historical legacies, and personal and collective decision-making. The emergence of gangs is not limited to patterns of immigration or poverty. To understand the existence of these groups it is important (i) to understand the structures of Central American societies, and the way in which they interact with each gang member's social conditions, personal relationships and community dynamics; and (ii) how the gangs' actions and society's reactions contribute to the reproduction, limitation or reduction of the gangs' existence.

Gangs are, therefore, the product of ongoing social and historical factors. Gangs did not appear spontaneously, and will not disappear, unless the social conditions are addressed. This includes, but is not limited to, overcoming the social pathologies that exclude many young people from productive society; promoting education and social cohesion; improving urban planning; developing a strategy to include immigrants as productive members of society; encouraging community and local acceptance, and participation of former gang members; fighting drug trafficking and drug abuse; creating support networks for those with financial and social disadvantages; and increasing training and job opportunities.

The evidence is clear that the current emphasis on law enforcement has not succeeded. Gang violence is worse today than fifteen years ago. Recent efforts at establishing a truce between gangs in El Salvador, while controversial, provide an opportunity to start dealing with the underlying causes of the violence. The solution must include prevention, rehabilitation and incorporation of gang members into society.

Conclusion: Violence and the 'Civilising Process' in Modern Latin America

RICARDO D. SALVATORE

Universidad Tocuato Di Tella, Argentina

Norbert Elias's ideas about the 'civilising process' and its reversal, the 'decivilising spurs' – leading on occasions to the 'breakdown of civilisation' – have found little resonance in Latin American historiography until now. In fact, few scholars have engaged critically with his socio-historical works or pondered on the application of his concepts to Latin America (Aguirre Rojas, 1998; Zabludovsky, 2007; Scribano and Vergara Mattar, 2009). Others have criticised the Euro-centrism of his notion of civilisation or found his definition of violence too limited. L. Wacquant has critically applied the concept to the US Black Ghetto (Wacquant, 2001). Although delayed translations, the misunderstanding of his key concepts, and the emergence of new methodologies and currents in the laboratory of the historian may partly account for this neglect or lack of interest, there are certain peculiarities of Latin American historical transitions and processes that have made it difficult to think about the evolution of violence in the region in 'Eliasian terms'. In this concluding chapter, I examine some of these peculiarities; among them are questions regarding colonisation and imperialism, the political fragmentation of the post-independence period, the burden of inherited, historical periodisations, and the existence of great racial and social inequalities. In order to adapt Elias's conceptual tools to the conditions of Latin American history, certain precautions and adaptations are needed. In this chapter, I discuss many of the chief obstacles and problems confronting a history of violence that would be sensitive to Elias's theory about societal development. While underscoring the vast nature of such an undertaking, I try to rescue some findings of existing historiography that underscore the current relevance and importance of Elias's theories and concepts.

Latin America at this present moment is characterised both by democratisation and globalisation, as well as by a massive outburst of numerous types of violence, political and criminal, domestic and public, instrumental and expressive, individual and collective. For these reasons it seems to be an

excellent time to reconsider Elias's ideas about monopolies of violence, pacification, social interdependencies and the repression of aggressive impulses as
societies 'modernise' over time. It may indeed be that the 1960s marked a shift
between a previous long-standing era of repressing violent impulses (prior to
1960 in Latin America) and the emergence of multiple signs of 'decivilising'
tendencies in the most recent period. The emergence of guerrilla warfare
and state terror in the 1960s and 1970s, the massacres of indigenous peasants
in Guatemala, Colombia and Peru in the 1980s, and the recent outbursts
of gang warfare, paramilitary activities, the killing of women, kidnappings
and narco-violence in various parts of the continent are clear signs of an
exponential growth of violence in Latin American social and political life.

A history of violence related to the ideas of Elias does not yet exist for
Latin America. Yet there is a wealth of discrete findings about violent crimes,
punishment, state building, military and police forces, forms of sociability,
and other related issues that could serve as the bases for such a history. It
is beyond the aim of this modest chapter to summarise historical findings
about violence, sensibilities, state formation and sociability in the region.
With the bits and pieces of historical evidence now available, it would be
premature to test the relevance of Elias's concepts of 'civilising process' and
'decivilising reversals' for the history of Latin America. Yet, within the wide
mosaic of Latin American historiography, there are some historical findings
relating to Elias's themes that seem particularly useful. By pointing out these
findings, I will attempt to show that a greater cooperation and exchange
among historians of the region, with a well-designed research agenda, could
produce significant generalisations about the long-term evolution of violence
and aggressive impulses in Latin America.

Elias and the Civilising Process

To Norbert Elias, the transformation of violence in European societies was a
process that affected first the long-term sensibilities of elites. Only gradually
and imperfectly did this process disseminate new patterns of conduct and
emotions among the lower classes. Bloody medieval feuds were gradually
transformed into sports-like competitions among knights and, with the formation of 'court society', men of the nobility were compelled to control their
emotions and expressions. In particular, the new court etiquette prevented
nobles from openly expressing rage and from exerting violence on others.
The regulated duel developed as an aristocratic way to resolve problems
of honour with minimal bloodshed. The court society of France during
Louis XIV's reign presented Elias (1994) with a model in which a successful
state monopoly over violence compelled nobles to change their conduct and
manners in the direction of self-control of emotions and expressions.

A process of destructive competition among warriors and knights ended with the incorporation of knights into royal courts, an outcome that granted absolutist monarchs a greater monopoly of violence, as well as increased sovereignty over distant provinces of the kingdom. Large mercenary armies of the king replaced the knightly armies of the nobles. Transformed into courtiers, the nobles ceased to be considered as a threat to the crown. These are, in a nutshell, the key ingredients of Elias's account of the transition from a warrior ethos to a 'court society' (Lasch, 1985).

Although concerned with Europe in general, Elias concentrated his analysis on England, Germany and France. The emergence of parliamentary culture in England and of court society in France constituted the two alternative ideal types in the transition towards more peaceful social and political interactions. England represented a case in which a long-term process of state formation, the greater intensity of social interdependencies made possible by commerce, and the increasing balance of power between the crown and the landed and commercial interests created the basis for peaceful social interaction. Elias attributed great importance to the formation of a parliamentary culture, in which rhetorical confrontations gradually replaced violence as a means for resolving political disputes. The 'parliamentarisation' of political conflicts was a chief instrument of pacification in England. At the level of social interaction and culture, this pacification manifested itself in the regulation of violence in popular sports and in the transformation of certain forms of hunting into sports (Fletcher, 1997: 88–147; Zabludovsky, 2007).

With regard to France, Elias stressed the transformation of knights into courtiers as a result of the gradual imposition of royal absolutism. Etiquette and court manners tamed the aggressive tendencies of the nobility. As a means to attain economic and political gains, courtiers learned to moderate their behaviour in terms of manners, dress and speech. Outside the royal court, the ancient regime retained traditional forms of social interaction, with occasional outbursts of violence, in the form of peasant rebellions and religious wars. In Germany, by contrast, the warrior ethos remained dominant among the aristocracy and the state bureaucracy during the period of state centralisation. The unification of Germany in 1871 preserved the landed oligarchy, the military and the bureaucracy at the top of a rather hierarchical society. In Germany, the civilising process took the form of strict social hierarchies, adherence to honour codes and the obedience to state rules. Controls by others produced self-control. In Germany, the pacification of elite violence entailed the consolidation of a militarist ethos of honour, distinction and manhood, consistent with imperial governance. The elitism of the German experience in controlling violent impulses, however, prevented its spread to the masses.

Elias was quite aware of the possibility of reversals in the civilising process. He acknowledged that the Weimar Republic was a clear case of a 'decivilising spurt', a peculiar political and social context in which leaders promoted the cult of hardness, severity and strength as a way to compensate for the weakness of the German nation. The need to restore Germany to its former position of great power status authorised aggressive impulses repressed during the imperial period. The humiliating defeat in the First World War, the fall of the Kaiser, and the fear of a Bolshevik take-over cultivated a violent ethos among members of the former German imperial establishment and among frustrated bourgeois youths. During the years 1919 to 1923, right-wing paramilitary groups (the Freikorps) exerted extralegal violence against opponents, turning political assassination into an almost 'acceptable' form of political action. The Freikorps' attacks, glorified in Ernst Jünger's novels, elicited an equally violent reaction from the working class and its organisations, leading to the generalisation of political gang violence in the streets. In the context of an intensified competition between left and right, between republican and anti-republican groups, the Weimar state lost its monopoly over the control of violence (Fletcher, 1997: 134–44). The Nazi racial state was, to Elias, an extension and intensification of forms of violence and ideological perspectives formed during the Weimar Republic.

Elias conceived the civilising process as the combined result of two major forces: sociogenesis and psychogenesis. The former related to the macro-social dimension, the latter to the terrain of emotions and sentiments, to the psychological structures of men and women. The gradual containment of aggressive impulses was then the double result of the state taking an ever greater control of public violence, while individuals learned to moderate their violent reactions and to appreciate the feelings of others. In addition, greater social interdependencies, associated with the extension of market relations, produced a slow transfer to social interactions devoid of violence. Elias's notion of a 'civilising process' alludes to long-term changes in human sensibilities, as well as to processes of state-formation, the dissemination of exchange relations, and the trickling-down of certain predispositions and conducts of elites to other social classes. This brief summary of a more subtle and sophisticated theory is meant only as a reminder of the general outlines of Elias's theories. My purpose is to examine to what extent this framework of ideas is applicable to the context of Latin American history.

Multiple Types of Violence

Scholars of Latin America have studied violence as a multi-dimensional reality. Some have focussed on the violence brought by Europeans to indigenous peoples, others on everyday violence and the culture of poverty, still others on the logic of revenge of indigenous communities, and a final group on the violence implicit in representations and discourse (Scheper-Hughes, 1992; Biron, 2000; Robins, 2005; Beckerman and Valentine, 2008). Studies of contemporary and past situations of capitalist exploitation and foreign domination had pointed out the existence of structural violence (Davies, 2006, 2009). Historians of crime and justice have centred their attention on criminal violence, examining crime itself, as well as the way that crime is construed by expert and non-expert discourses. But violence is clearly a much vaster phenomenon that transcends the boundaries of what is prohibited by criminal codes. Scholars have turned their attention to a variety of types of violence. Domestic violence, community lynching, paramilitary violence, police brutality, narco-violence and increasing middle-class fears about violent criminality are some of the most common topics in the vast array of contemporary scholarly contributions about violence (Huggins, 1991; Stern, 1995; Rojas, 2002; Taussig, 2005; Snodgrass Godoy, 2006; Dammert, 2009).

The contemporary profusion of forms of violence warrants using the word violence in its plural form. Colombian historian Cristina Rojas (2002: xxii–xxiii) distinguishes between *La Violencia* (singular), an unstructured and de-centred civil war between followers of the Conservative and Liberal parties in the period 1949–1957, and *las violencias* (plural), the contemporary juxtaposition of different forms of violence, including the organisation of drug-related private armies, the expansion of self-defence groups and death squads, and the 'clean-up' operations directed against petty criminals, prostitutes, vagrants and homosexuals. Perhaps this anarchic overlapping of multiple violences characterises the contemporary moment in Latin America. This makes the contemporary attention of anthropologists, political scientists, sociologists, literary critics, and economists to the study of violence in its multiple variants (*las violencias*) understandable.

For a historical inquiry interested in the long-term variation in individual sensibilities and forms of state control of violence, it is important to distinguish first between political and criminal violence. In appearance, these two types of violence are motivated by distinct objectives: political versus economic. But scholars have shown that the borders between the two are not so clearly demarcated and are often transgressed. For example, anti-insurgency state groups often act as organised crime, committing robberies and property fraud, and the same can be said of guerrilla groups (Isla, 2007). Political instability and conflict can facilitate the expansion of criminal activities, while the rising public antipathy towards criminality could easily translate into punitive demands in the political sphere. Clearly, both types of violence produce an impact on public opinion and the collective consciousness. While intensified criminal violence can create crime panics and punitive waves, political violence weighs heavily on the formation of collective memory. In moments of panic about criminality, newspapers invite readers to consider that a collection of criminal acts constitute an alarming tendency that generates personal and neighbourhood insecurity. In processes of democratisation and reconciliation, publicists, political parties and state functionaries bring public attention to the violence committed by a past dictatorial regime or by guerrilla activities. Guided by national reports of special commissions, the public discusses whether past terrorist activities by state or private armies were systematic or simple 'excesses'.

We need also to distinguish between instrumental and expressive violence: the former committed to attain an economic or political objective, the latter committed to transmit a message while eliminating an 'enemy', 'danger' or 'threat'. Like mafia violence, the killings by death squads, army patrols, or guerrilla groups contain a surplus of expression: legends, mutilations or messages to the media that try to explain the demonic character or extra-territoriality of the killed 'enemy'. In the history of Latin American societies, instrumental violence is more common than expressive violence, yet civil wars, social revolutions and racial massacres – however rare – tend to provide surprising evidence of internal divisions and hatred within the social body that merits special investigation. Even after finding evidence of a long-term amelioration of instrumental violence, historians should be attentive to the persistence of hate language and extermination rhetoric to make balanced evaluations about the 'civilising process'.

This in turn relates to the distinction between individual and collective violence, that is, between interpersonal aggression and mass killings. In principle, the two phenomena appear clearly distinct: interpersonal aggression being monitored through statistics gathered at police stations, hospitals and judicial centres, while mass killings require national commissions or judicial inquiries, after being reported by the press. Not only are the jurisdictions for judging these violent acts different, but also the crimes themselves merit different labels ('genocide' or 'mass murder' versus 'homicide'). Clearly, a 'civilising process', in Elias's sense, would require both a reduction in the homicide rates over the long run and a less frequent occurrence of mass murder (with a lesser number of victims) for whatever reason. Unfortunately, history rarely presents us with declining tendencies for both types of violence. It may in fact be more typical to find that a reduction of homicide or crime rates corresponds with a recurrence of moments of ethnic cleansing, intensified murder of females, or wars of extermination of limited duration. How can one explain these situations?

Waves in instrumental political violence, if not escalated into full-blown revolutions, tend to be short-lived. Well before people get 'accustomed' to kidnappings, disappearance, and torture based on political reasons – as is the case with terrorism by the state or by paramilitary organisations – there is usually a regime change that brings back some basic civil and political liberties. To this extent, we need to treat the 'cultures of fear' produced by the leftist guerrillas, terrorist states, and paramilitary groups as temporary conditions that might affect permanently the psychic state of victims, but rarely the general sensibilities of the whole population; cultures of fear leave traces in societies that have suffered their impact, but it is not clear whether these societies tend to lower their threshold of tolerance and naturalise events of violence, or whether, because of these terrifying experiences, they become more determined to ensure that organised political terror never happens again. Claims that certain periods of unusual state violence had created 'barbarism' or naturalised violent interactions among ordinary citizens should always be looked at with suspicion. It is more a statement about Otherness than a truthful or credible characterisation of the psychic condition of the governed. In Argentina, arguments about the persistence of violence committed by the so-called *mano de obra desocupada* (unemployed labour), referring usually to members of the police and armed forces with prior experience in the military dictatorship, should be treated with care; the argument is more about how these professional killers continue to remain free in a democratising society or, at other times, about the potential transformation of these ex-repressors into heads of criminal gangs. Rarely do those presenting these arguments assert that the mere fact of having acted as a torturer or murderer makes them sociopaths; there is no scientific evidence that ex-torturers or murderers have an irresistible 'craving' for torture or murder.

Spanish Colonisation and the Civilising Process

The historian who tries to test Norbert Elias´s concepts and propositions in the history of Latin America faces – at least – two important difficulties. One refers to the fact that Hispanic America did not have a 'feudal era'. The other stems from the fact that all current nations in the region had previously experienced Iberian colonialism. The lack of a feudal experience – although there was a time, in the 1960s and 1970s, when some scholars entertained the idea of residual 'feudality' in contemporary Latin American societies (Laclau, 1972; Carmagnani, 1976), this idea has long been abandoned (Stern, 1988; López-Alves, 2000: 16–17) – undermines the comparison between Europe and Latin America to the extent that the long-term evolution in levels of aggression and violence cannot find its exact parallel of origin. The problem of colonialism has more extensive implications. Although there were important interconnections between Europe and the American colonies regarding the processes of state formation, religious conversion, economic activities and forms of culture, Spanish colonisation brought forth institutions, practices and forms of sociability that were different from those experienced in Europe.

Similarly, although many historians speak freely of an *'ancien régime'* in the colonies of the Spanish empire, the analogies are only metaphorical. Historians recognise that a great gap separated the European *ancien régime* from the different colonial situations of Hispanic and Portuguese America. The lifestyles of vice-regal bureaucracies and of elite Peruvians and New Spaniards during the period 1570–1800 bear little resemblance to the sociability of European courts. The problems involved in colonial governance in Spanish America were different from those facing dynastic crowns in Europe. The Spanish crown had to exert dominance in situations where, in part because of distance from the metropolis, colonial authorities felt entitled to act independently ('obedezco pero no cumplo'; 'I obey but do not comply'), responding to local interests. As a result, the importance of the incorporation of warriors into courtly society, a crucial long-term socio-genetic process for Elias, does not have a parallel in Hispanic America.

It would take a leap of imagination to ascribe the processes of colonial state-building in Spanish America (the Toledan reforms in Peru and the reforms by Mendoza in New Spain) to the social dynamics described by Elias as the transition from a 'warrior society' to a 'court society' in Europe. What mattered in Peru and New Spain was the consolidation of a colonial state apparatus that could arbitrate the different interests in contention (indigenous communities, church, landowners, miners and merchants) without relinquishing its commitment to the colonial goals of evangelisation, tribute collection and territorial defence. We know that the Spanish colonial government established an innovative racially fragmented sovereignty, where the 'Republic of Indians' stood side by side with the 'Republic of Spaniards'. If labour exploitation and evangelisation were the two most important relationships between colonisers and colonised, it is proper to ask what kind of 'social habitus' emerged from such interactions.

A second, and perhaps more insurmountable, challenge refers to the fact that early modernity came to Spanish and Portuguese America in the form of conquest and colonisation. Colonisation entailed a protracted 'civilising impulse', which included vast operations such as the evangelisation campaigns, the reduction of indigenous populations in cities, and the re-organisation of production in mines, haciendas (landed estates), and plantations. All these colonial 'designs' contemplated some kind of control of conduct: the Toledan reforms were an exercise in total governmental control in ways similar to the Jesuit missions in Paraguay, and were intended to change indigenous peoples into obedient subjects of the crown, good Christians, industrious labourers and docile tribute-payers. It is hard to imagine that colonised Indian pueblos were ever 'free' to express their emotions. They had the Spaniards (*hacendados*, *regidores* (local councillors), priests, and so on) to control their actions, their dress, their speech, and so on.

To this extent, it is fair to argue that, at least in the first 200 years of Spanish and Portuguese rule, the imposition of a colonial order was achieved through violence and coercion. Spanish colonial authorities and their religious auxiliaries carried into the colonies a 'civilising mission' that included evangelisation, the reduction of indigenous populations to pueblos, and the imposition of both servile labour and tribute. Some or all of these innovations involved habit-forming practices that may have congealed into a 'colonial social habitus' (Calhoun, LiPuma, and Postone, 1993: 61–88). The Jesuits' missions in Paraguay, in particular, could be thought of as an intense exercise in behavioural modification in which missionaries tried to transform the work discipline, the sensibilities and the belief system of Guaraní indigenous peoples. Yet it is impossible to disassociate violence – corporal punishment, isolation, forced labour – from these disciplinarian experiments.

During the colonial period, but particularly during the late sixteenth and seventeenth centuries, the very consolidation of hybrid forms of governance, which included European institutions and pre-existing indigenous forms of representation, produced a long-lasting pacification. It is largely agreed among colonial historians that, apart from the great Andean rebellions of the 1780s, the colonial state experienced few outbursts of open resistance. According to McFarlane (1995), the Spanish colonial regime was characterised by a long-lasting peace and stability, interrupted every now and then by small revolts that, more often than not, ended up in negotiation and accommodation with colonial authorities. The judicial institutions played an important role in mediating social conflicts, and to the extent that it was possible, gave indigenous peoples and other members of the *castas* (mixed-race) the possibility of raising complaints to government (Stern, 1982). Moreover, the colonial state at the local level was committed to keeping the ideal of a well-ordered and pacific social interaction among town residents, something the Spaniards called *policía*. Could we consider this part of a 'colonial civilising process'?

Viewed in this way, the relationship between colonisation and violence is two-pronged. On the one hand, colonisation necessitated the perpetration of violence on the subjugated indigenous populations – a violence that was at first overwhelming but declined afterward – in order to produce subordination to Spanish authorities, some degree of conformity and deference to colonial officials, a transformation of everyday practices among the colonised, and a radical change in their religious beliefs. On the other hand, the consolidation of state colonial rule, with its consequent monopoly in the use of force, was translated into decreased levels of state violence. Indigenous peoples were compelled to constrain their aggressive impulses: they were prohibited from wearing swords, drinking alcohol or riding horses. To be sure, some exemplary public punishments had to be applied periodically in order to remind the colonised who was in power. Yet, by and large, the level of state repression exercised by the colonial state in the central areas (New Spain and Peru) was significantly lower in the 1750s than it had been in the 1570s.

In the context of Spanish colonisation, Elias's understanding of the 'civilising process' must necessarily undergo important modifications. The translation from 'European feudal' to 'Spanish colonial' alters significantly the nature of the comparison, forcing us to adapt the meaning of the concept. In colonial Hispanic America, any restraint of aggressive impulses on the part of indigenous subalterns must be placed in the context of a relationship of domination–subordination that was itself resistent to change. The same goes for the potential behavioural changes observed among the Spanish colonial elites in American territory. Their 'entitlements' to inflict violence on others were part of a power relationship that included their own subordination to colonial authorities and the imperative to control their own impulses vis-à-vis their peers, other *peninsulares* (Spanish-born). Institutional historians would argue that everyone's conduct, of indigenous *comunales* (non-elite Indians), of *peninsulares*, and of *castas*, was perfectly regulated by the legal and adminis- trative machinery of the colonial state. Rigid regulations kept the conduct of each colonial *estamento* (estate, or rank) within limited bounds. In the face of important transformations in racial mixture, tribute obligations and personal freedoms, it is possible that these over-regulated systems of caste behaviour were resisted, not enforced, or became outmoded over time.

It is well-established that the first decades of conquest involved substantial levels of violence. Those who have estimated the loss of life of indigenous peoples have spoken of a 'demographic collapse' (Crosby, 1972: 35–63; Baker and Kealhofer, 1996: 1–13). Others have called the devastating impact of conquest on the lives of indigenous communities 'genocide' (Stannard, 1992; Robins, 2005). After 1570, civil wars, insurgencies and colonial massacres gave way to a period of peace and stability, where the rebellions were quite infrequent and revolts usually localised and controllable. Could we call this a process of 'pacification', an American replica of the European 'civilising process'? A vexing problem with this interpretation is that the 'civilising impulse' of the evangelising crusades continued to bring violence and coercion to indigenous communities long after the initial 'genocidal impulse' had subsided. The forceful relocation of indigenous peoples also implied an unusual amount of violence. Francisco de Toledo relocated over 1.5 million Andeans into Spanish-style towns, which were later grouped into 614 administrative districts (*repartimientos*). The massive forced relocation made it possible to enforce uniform tax, labour and religious controls over Indian towns (Andrien, 2001: 49–56). This chief state-builder organised the infamous *mita* system, through which 13,000 Indian labourers were annually recruited from sixteen highland provinces and sent to the Potosí mines.

What about the particular form of 'civility' in the Hispanic American colonies, the city? The civilisation that Spaniards brought to their American colonies was profoundly urban in character; cities represented the centres of economic accumulation, social interaction and political organisation. Local governments provided a variety of services, including hygiene, civic works and law enforcement. During the Bourbon administrations, most major colonial cities had a corps of public officials in charge of policing. The *alcaldes de barrio* (neighbourhood policemen) had to keep public order, prevent public drunkenness, and avoid brawls and other scandals (Socolow, 1986). Did urban culture and institutions act to reduce aggressive impulses during the colonial period?

Following Elias's Footsteps

What kind of a history of violence would best serve to cross-examine Elias's thesis about the 'civilising process'? First, it should be a history concerned with the long-term evolution of violence. Spontaneous, spasmodic or episodic events of violence should not be part of the inquiry, unless they help the historian to reflect upon popular sensibilities to violence. Rather, our attention should focus on changes in patterns of violence over periods of time exceeding three generations. Second, our interest should concentrate not just on violence itself but on the effect of violence on people's sensibilities and emotions. We should be able to grasp the joy, apathy, rejection, shame or revulsion that the acts of violence in the past provoked. Third, historians should be able to connect long-term changes in sensibilities and emotions towards violence with processes of state formation and, in particular, with the gradual imposition of a monopoly of violence by the state. A history sensitive to Elias's theoretical propositions would necessarily interrogate the extension of state sovereignty over civil society, including the expansion of state capabilities to discipline and punish, and the associated decrease in privately administered violence.

Fourth, Norbert Elias dealt extensively with the growth in social interdependencies, in particular those produced by the expansions of markets, urbanisation and the integration of national economies, as determinants of non-violent social interactions. Consequently, historians of violence should be attentive to the impact of the expansion of commerce and transportation on social interactions, associationism and the formation of a peaceful social habitus. Fifth, historians following Elias's footsteps should be concerned with the learning processes associated with the internalisation of norms of conduct that involve the attenuation of violence by individuals, families and small groups: that is, with the transmission among social classes and across the population at large of peaceful and harmonious behaviour and with the sensibilities that produce such behaviour.

This five-point research agenda presents historians with a huge field of inquiry. In a history of violence that incorporates Elias's major insights, long-term changes in state policing, transformations in people's emotions and sensibilities, stronger social interdependencies created by trade, travel and sociability, and the top-down transmission of rules of conduct are among the most important aspects to investigate. The documentary requirements of such a history are immense. In order to interrogate the fifth point in the agenda (the transmission and internalisation of rules of behaviour) historians may have to look at manuals of conduct or manners, elementary-school reading materials, the advice that mothers and fathers gave to their children, the 'rules of engagement' taught at police academies, city ordinances concerning dispute-resolution among neighbours, or the tactics used by battered women to reduce the incidence of domestic violence. Tackling points one to four in the agenda may prove an even more daunting enterprise.

At this point, such a history of violence does not exist for Latin America. Violence has been a prominent topic in the history of Latin America, but a history of violence immersed in the socio-genetic and psycho-genetic processes that Elias associated with his concept of the 'civilising process' has not been a priority for historians of the region. Although Elias's work has received more attention since the 1990s, his influence in Latin American historiography has been rather limited (Zabludovsky, 2007: 100–102). Elias's works have been more influential among sociologists than among historians; the few historians who have discussed his writings did it in a critical manner, usually dismissing the usefulness of his categories for modern Latin America.

One of the reasons why historians of Latin America have avoided critical engagement with Elias is the very concept of 'civilisation', incorrectly understood in its normative dimension. Elias warned his readers not to see the civilising process as the result of conscious will or enlightened reason. He conceived the civilising process as an observable constellation of social facts, generated by psychological and social processes. This objective process was not to be confused with the ideology of 'civilisation', a position of superiority dividing the civilised from the barbarian, often with the underlying intention of 'civilising the barbarian'. Enshrined in Sarmiento's *Facundo* (1998), the idea of civilisation has always been associated with its opposite, barbarism, the two poles of an inextricable contradiction upon which the progress or backwardness of nations depended. With the expansion of cities in Hispanic America, Sarmiento thought, barbarism would recede to a minimal expression; if this occurred, European habits and manners would displace the crude and violent traditions of the inhabitants of the Pampas and, thus, significantly transform the cultural geography of South America. Discredited as a neocolonial, Eurocentric category, this normative concept of civilisation has been the object of great criticism. Modern-day historians have been reluctant to use the concept of 'civilisation', for the category carries the burden of elitism and racial difference and is often aligned with European conceptions of modernity, progress and culture.

Influenced by the postcolonial turn, historians of Latin America have been more interested in studying the 'violence of civilisation' than in interrogating the long-term construction of sensitivities and emotions that made possible the amelioration of open, public violence. This position, the study of the violence implicit in processes of colonisation, Europeanisation and internal conquest, is absolutely reasonable and valid. The historian Cristina Rojas, for example, one of the few in acknowledging the importance of Elias's concept for Latin American historiography, also employed the concept of 'civilisation' as the imperialistic expansion of Europe's self-consciousness; her book *Civilization and Violence* (2002) focusses on violence as embedded in regimes of representation. To this extent, she treats violence not as an observable phenomenon, but as a product of discourse. The colonial/imperial question represents an important oversight in Elias's theory of civilisation that needs to be acknowledged and problematised. Nonetheless, the 'violence of civilisation' question should not obfuscate the search for long-term trends in the evolution of different forms of violence in Western societies and in its colonies, neo-dependencies and hinterlands. Societies undergoing colonisation, or being part of neocolonial or informal empires, could add interesting dimensions to Elias's concept of civilisation. Colonial situations generate at first a surplus of violence but, in the long-term, induce the formation of habits and forms of social interaction that are conducive to the amelioration of violence. This trade-off is seldom acknowledged by historians critical of colonialism and imperialism.

An additional reason for the reluctance of historians to embrace the work of Elias is the 'linguistic turn'. Contemporary historical sensibilities, attentive to the opacity of representations, the workings of gender and race, and the contested nature of meaning in all writing, conspire against the production of one-dimensional and linear 'national histories'. Current historiographical critique tends to see these national histories as expressions of larger trends in Western thought and sensibilities. When Elias wrote, he could speak of the German, English or the French nations without many qualifications, caveats, or embarrassment, as if these were pre-existing entities that could be grasped directly from historical sources. He dealt freely with the 'German', 'English' and 'French' social habitus, taking for granted the validity of such abstractions. Today, that possibility is obstructed by what we know about culture and representations (Young, 1991; Trouillot, 1995; Chakrabarty, 2000; Buck-Morss, 2009). The nation appears today as a contested category, diversely construed from different perspectives and positionalities, a signifier always in tension with what it is supposed to represent or signify. In Latin America, even as imagined communities, nations are still fragmented entities (in terms of territory, regional diversity, social inclusiveness, and racial and ethnic make-up), striving for some unity of purpose. Hence, it would be more reasonable to speak of regional or sub-national, instead of national sensibilities or social habitus.

Yet behind the debris of contradictory representations and beyond the skirmishes over the meaning of nationhood, one could still envision the Eliasian object of inquiry: long-term trends in sensibilities and emotions concerning violence. It is just that, in applying Eliasian conceptual tools to Latin American realities, the fragmentation of the region, its enormous social and cultural diversity, and the different patterns of economic, social and political development experienced by different nations should be given special attention. Once we clearly distinguish between the normative and the concrete in examining the 'civilising process', it should be clear that all subsequent forms of governance in the region (colonial, post-independent, modern), until the 1950s at least, had attempted to imbue populations with habits and norms that led towards the amelioration of the public display of violence. Whether the regulations, pedagogy and predicament of the states made a true impact on the governed populations is something that historians will have to establish for each country, region and relevant period. Similarly, once we recapture the 'civilising project' as part of the unfinished project of modernity – not of European modernity, but of all different modernities – and incorporate the processes of colonialism and neocolonialism within the scope of analysis, the question of the long-term evolution of violence would acquire renewed centrality.

Limitations and Obstacles

What are the chief limitations and obstacles facing an Eliasan history of violence in the region? The first of them refers to space. The great diversity within Latin America conspires against generalising about the existence or non-existence of a 'civilising process' within the region. Latin America is an enormous region, comprising twenty Spanish- and Portuguese-speaking countries or territories, and numerous sub-regions within each country. Each sub-national region shows particularities in terms of population, economic organisation, sociability, state capabilities and cultural influences. Historians often find generalisations about 'Latin America' problematic, preferring more spatially restricted historical narratives, such as national or sub-national history. Although North-Atlantic scholars have used large regions – Central America, Caribbean, Andean America, Southern Cone – as relevant categories to organise historical knowledge, these labels are also the subject of contention. Each research topic (youth gangs, death squads, duels, lynching, spouse killing, cruelty to animals, and so on) presents the historian of violence with a particular spatial dimension, sometimes sub-regional, at other times regional or even transnational, yet seldom national.

The second limitation refers to the time-framework. Historians of Latin America work with inherited periodisations. Some of them are quite general and, to this extent, widely accepted and used. Historians speak of a 'late colonial' period (1780–1810), a 'post-independence' period (1820–1850), a 'liberal transition' (1850–1880), and an 'era of progress' (1880–1930) (Jacobsen and Hans-Jürgen Puhle, 1986; Bethell, 1989). After this, the periodisation changes. Some historians adopt a European dichotomy between an 'inter-war period' (1918–1939) and a 'post-war period' (1945 onward). Others consider the 1930s as a transition period, after which important modernisations emerged. Any process after the late 1950s is considered 'contemporary' or 'recent' history, including the 'spiral of violence' and the military regimes of the 1960s through the 1980s. Finally, the 1990s with their neoliberal reform, increased unemployment and social inequality, in the context of increasing democratisation are thought of as the beginning of a new era called 'globalisation'. This is quite apart from the tensions about distinct schools of history regarding the integration between national economies and the world market and of particular nations into the world system; the different supra-national sovereignties and their legacies (Hispanic, British and American hegemonies) may have an influence on issues of violence among persons, social groups and nation-states, yet the magnitude and direction of this influence is at the moment difficult to determine.

A long-term history of violence should be informed by this tentative periodisation if it is to account for the parallel processes of political and economic development and for the ways in which these processes condition or facilitate the generation of violence. Yet the available periodisation presents some drawbacks. Since each period has been associated with a particular set of problems, the study of violence has been ascribed to these problems. Indeed, the transition from the late-colonial period to the immediate post-independent period presents problems of its own; similarly, the end of 'caudillo regimes', the consolidation of national constitutions and the emergence of liberalism constitute another historical landmark, while the label 'era of progress' has been profitably used by economic, social, cultural and political historians of the region. Meanwhile, other historians have used a more restricted period (1890–1914) to evaluate export-led development, positivist social thought, the emergence of modern political parties or the formation of a modern labour movement. After that the periodisation becomes less clear. For instance, the post-independence period comes with problems of banditry, *caudillismo*, and recurrent 'revolutions'. Similarly, in the 'era of progress' historians emphasise certain types of violence: police repression against workers, government efforts to control the opposition and policies to prevent the political participation of the masses. In most historical narratives of the 'long' nineteenth century, the question of political violence is paramount, simply because the core issue is the constitution of a national political order. In the twentieth century, historical narratives stress issues of economic and social rights, new agencies (workers, women and ethnic-racial minorities), and the influence of European ideologies. As a result, the spectrum of violence seems to expand to verbal, psychological and symbolic violence, while historical interest in physical violence declines. For the period 1930–1960, industrialisation, large cities, populist regimes, proto-welfare states, well-organised police forces, and an ideology of middle-class respectability present a panorama of pacified and ordered societies.

The problem with these particular thematic concentrations by periods is that they render long-term comparisons particularly difficult. Nobody has tried to compare the risk of violent death faced by a mass-production worker in the 1950s with that of an urban artisan in the 1850s for the same country or region. Yet this is precisely the type of question that an Eliasian history of violence demands. Posing this and similar questions opens up many possibilities of comparison, for the century between 1850 and 1950 changed significantly the economies, the societies, the politics and the culture of Latin American countries. To compare one state of risk with the other one should consider changes in the state's control of violence, in the residential patterns and mobility of the workforce, in the nature of occupations, in the sociability at recreation places, in the rhetoric of male honour, in the employers' use of coercion to solve labour disputes and in society's tolerance of open displays of aggression. Despite the differences that one expects to find over time, the research question remains valid: did increased social interdependencies, greater state control of the public space, the dissemination of basic literacy, and enhanced individual and social rights increase or decrease aggressive impulses and the overall production of violence?

An attempt to examine the long-term evolution of violence in the region presents necessarily important methological difficulties. How can one compare post-independence banditry with modern gang robberies of the early 1900s? Is it legitimate to compare the brutality of armies during the independence wars with the atrocities committed in late nineteenth-century wars? Was the Mexican Revolution a unique event or can it be compared with other socio-political revolutions? Can we compare contemporary Indian massacres (such as that unleashed in the 1980s in Guatemala by General Ríos Montt) with colonial or post-independence era Indian massacres (such as those that followed the 'Great Rebellions' of the Andes, the Caste War in Yucatan or the 'Conquest of the Desert' in Argentina)? In the contemporary period, sociologists, political scientists, anthropologists, and journalists have uncovered a striking array of types and perpetrators of violence (self-defence groups, death squads, popular lynching, drug-related violence, youth gangs, assassinations of women, and so on) that, by the lack of evidence or of historical interest, find little or no correspondence with the remote past. What is to be done in cases where there is no historical precedent?

Third, in addition to limitations in the spatial and temporal dimensions, a long-term history of violence should be attuned to major changes in the relations between elite and non-elite groups. Subaltern groups in Latin America vary in terms of ethnicity, race, gender, age, regional origin, occupation, rural–urban residency, and other factors. If we are concerned with the violence that dominant groups exert on subaltern groups, we should be aware of the existence of various subalternities, with distinct grievances and sensibilities. Each subaltern group would advance different claims against state institutions for the non-enforcement of rights and benefits promised in national constitutions and laws. Among these claims and grievances, none are more important than the freedom from physical violence and corporal punishment. The types of coercion available to elites vis-à-vis subaltern groups (women, children, immigrants, workers, racialised minorities, and so on) change over time and space and historians must be aware of this (Salvatore, 2000).

By and large, one could assume that, in some of the most advanced countries of the region, c.1940–1960, some basic rights were sustained by government (rights to life, expression, association, religion, and so on). In these countries, it was more difficult (or more ineffective) for elites to threaten subalterns with violence or corporal punishment. Yet, for an important group of countries, this assumption about basic human rights could prove deceptive, in particular during *La Violencia* in Colombia. The freedom from coercion was achieved at different moments in time by distinct subaltern groups. Focussing on the claims made by subalterns at critical moments (revolts, rebellions or revolutions) may help us to understand the extent of denial of rights and its variation across time and space. A variety of subalternities and changing repertoires of coercion available to elites would add complexity to the project of a long-term history of violence.

When the revolutions of 1848 broke out, some parts of Europe were still under serfdom, while in other parts workers had enjoyed personal freedom for a long time. In his account of the European civilising process, Elias failed to underscore this fundamental difference. We should not make the same mistake when evaluating the march of the 'civilising process' in Latin America. It is quite possible that 'measuring' the degree of freedom from physical coercion in different parts of South America at a given benchmark (let us say, 1914), one should be able to detect important differences across countries and regions. It would not be surprising to find that at that time the rural workers were better treated in Argentina than in Chile, in Uruguay as compared with Peru, and in the three republics in relation to the rest of South America.

Fourth, in regard to questions of social and political domination, practical disparities in relation to the legal system and social welfare policies, ethnicity and race are important dimensions to examine. The race factor has been more determining in the history of Latin American societies than in the history of Europe, where Elias centred his study of the civilising process. Countries such as Bolivia, Peru, Guatemala, Ecuador and Mexico remained, until late in the twentieth century, racially and ethnically divided societies, in which constitutional promises of equality before the law, basic civil rights, and equal opportunities to education were illusory or unattainable for members of the racial and ethnic subalternities. Hence, to talk of interpersonal violence or of homicide in general, without an analysis of ethnicity and race, would be meaningless. Any meaningful history of violence in the continent, particularly in those countries with severe ethnic and racial fragmentation, cannot overlook the violence committed by elites against ethnic-racial minorities, through direct private means and through the mediation of state agencies.

Examining the 'thresholds' of tolerated coercion or violence in different countries and regions is particularly important. By the 1910s, a Peruvian coastal planter could still inflict corporal punishment on his labourers, a 'liberty' not granted to landowners in coastal Argentina, Uruguay or southern Brazil. According to certain elites of the region, race was an important instrument in the laboratory of virtue. By the mid-nineteenth century, slave owners in Argentina and Brazil thought that whipping a slave with a sufficient number of strokes would change the servant's irreverent or rebellious behaviour (Salvatore, 2000); in Peru, elites thought that indigenous subalterns required harder punishment, for they appeared insensitive to pain (Aguirre, 2008).

Fifth, in the frontiers of nations, or in areas of weak or non-existent law enforcement, physical violence and personal insecurity tend to be more prevalent than in areas closer to the centre. As Roger Casement documented for the early 1910s, rubber entrepreneurs in the Peruvian Amazon used to send bands of armed men to 'hunt' for servile labourers among the selvatic indigenous tribes. Violent raids against forest villages were their labour recruitment system. The white and mestizo employees of the Peruvian Amazon Rubber

Company felt entitled to kill, torture, mutilate and rape indigenous peoples. Casement also denounced the fact that these raids produced the 'material' for a profitable trade in indigenous children (Goodman, 2009).

In Patagonia, on the southern frontier of Argentina, the central state failed to impose a monopoly of force, at least during the 50 years following the incorporation of these territories to the nation (1880–1930). In these southern lands, bandit gangs reigned supreme, kidnapping and executing their victims. The police, even using movable horse brigades and communicating through the telegraph, could hardly control such a vast territory. Legality was an elusive and ambivalent concept. While the police were often involved in illegal activities, major crimes remained unsolved. As a result, personal insecurity was high (Bohoslavsky, 2005, 2010; Rafart, 2008); in frontier areas, where the reach of the modern state was minimal, landowners and other proprietors could exercise forms of violence not tolerated in other regions of the same country. A true history of violence should be attentive to this 'grey area' of law enforcement, in which dominant groups and crime gangs were able to exercise forms of violence that, even at the time, were considered violations of basic human rights.

A history of violence that could include the violence committed against distinct subalternities, a history sensitive to ethnic and racial factors, and attentive to regional variations in law-enforcement would be sufficiently complex. Yet there are still other limitations that historians need to overcome. The availability of archive sources is a determinant conditioning any long-term history of violence in the region. Certain types of violence committed against workers, certain forms of criminal violence and certain forms of popular violence may be detected by reading the labour-union press, the 'red pages' of newspapers, or state regulations. Yet many forms of interpersonal violence would remain unrecorded. Domestic violence, a widespread form of violence, only occasionally appeared in the official transcript. Even in the most advanced countries of the region, where state capacities are the largest, an extended array of violent acts passed unrecorded. Violence against animals would not be reported to the authorities, unless the event offended middle-class sensibilities (cock-fights in Mexico City, for example). More salient than the lack of information about violent acts is the absence of evidence about the emotional impact of this violence.

Historians do their best, with the partial or fragmented evidence extant in official archives, to document past acts of violence. Criminal records and the crime pages of the newspapers are still the best available sources for historians. These records, however, contain little information about the emotional reactions of various social groups. In societies with an ample circulation of periodicals, journalists contribute to creating waves of panic about crime by using the appropriate combination of images, narrative and language (Caimari, 2004). If this is the case, the periodic press is not a particularly reliable source about people's sensibilities about violent crimes. Yet, the same literature emphasises that the success in terms of readership of these sensationalist newspapers lies in the impact that macabre crime stories have upon regular readers. The acts of violence that are most useful for examining emotional responses are often hidden from the public record. This is the case of gentlemen's duels and of violence against animals. Modern journalists avoid exposing members of their same social class who engage in duelling; over time, the reports about illegal cock-fights became less interesting to readers and ceased to be published. Yet, even when the evidence is sparse, historians are trying to tackle issues such as elite ritualistic violence (see my later discussion of duelling) and popular enjoyment in events involving violence against animals.

We will probably never amass sufficient reliable information for a comparative history of violence against animals. On the other hand, there are volumes of information about political violence, committed by state agencies, paramilitary organisations, guerrilla groups or political parties. More often than not, political violence is committed in order to produce some effect: political intimidation, electoral conformity, passivity in the face of repression, even emigration. The assassination of political figures disseminates fear among the population. When political murders become massive and repetitive – and to this extent, predictable or expectable – the psyche of a great number of people could be affected. In Argentina, during the 1976–1982 military regime, state terror is acknowledged to have produced political apathy, a reduced participation in the public space, and the privatisation of everyday life (Corradi, 1992).

Waves of political violence are perfectly identifiable in the history of Latin America. The methodological problem is how to compare and contrast this type of violence. Should we rank these events in numbers of casualties? Should we qualify these figures according to the brutality of killings? Should we put added emphasis on surplus or expressive elements that made the killings more terrifying? We know that national histories have processed some recent experiences with state terror and guerrilla warfare in sufficient detail. This is chiefly because these events have entered the territory of collective national memory in the processes of democratisation and the expanded demands for human rights. But in the past, we suspect that similarly terrifying massacres might have escaped the historian's or the journalist's gaze. Or, at least, we suspect that these mass killings did not receive the judicial or journalistic investigation that they deserve; for example, the relatives of the victims of the so-called 'Tata Dios Rebellion' of Tandil, Buenos Aires province, in 1872, complained that the Argentine judicial system did little to clarify these ethnic killings (Lynch, 1998).

Need all of these obstacles be overcome in order to build a long-term history of violence attentive to changes in sensibilities and state–individual relations? We need to examine the persistence or change of aggressive impulses, and the effects of formal and informal controls over individual conduct, preferably at the level of the sub-national region. The Central Valley of Mexico, the Argentine Northwest, the Venezuelan Llanos, or Chile's Norte Chico would be the appropriate units to consider in a long history of sensibilities and emotions regarding violence. Concerning time frameworks, it is useful to use the existing periodisations ('late colonial', 'post-independence', 'liberal transition', and so on) as possible institutional and socio-eonomic contexts (ideal types) in which the struggles for affirming or rejecting violent trajectories should be examined. In addition, we need to standardise the historical evidence (events, interactions, discourses, emotional responses, and so on) to make possible inter-temporal comparisons.

We need to be able to establish whether a member of the *villista* army (1911) was more brutal, destructive or emotionally detached than a member of the Hidalgo revolutionary army (1811). Comparability is the key to the Eliasan enterprise. This applies particularly to the issue of elite coercion over subalterns. We know quite well that slavery, peonage and industrial wage labour entail quite distinct forms of coercion and violence. These different examples of oppression generate different sensibilities to violence that can be compared across time and space. To speculate about differences and similarities of labour regimes, historians could use conceptual devices that explain the elites' rationalisation of either respecting or disregarding basic rights and freedoms of subalterns. Similarly, we know that the public and the private spheres present different possibilities for the exertion of violence. These distinct aggressions need to be compared in levels of intensity and frequency, psychological damage and societal acceptance or rejection.

Eliasian Themes in Latin American History

Latin American historiography presents certain moments, processes, and discussions that are relevant to the examination of Elias's propositions about elite manners, the civilising process and reversals from civilised social interaction. A short review of publications concerning the questions of state-building, elite manners and duels, and the contemporary explosion of violence attests to the relevance of Elias's ideas in the Latin American context. Let me mention in passing that the history of sensibilities and emotions, a central preoccupation for Elias, is only in its infancy. Most recent studies in this line of research have not focussed on aggressive impulses or the emotional response to violent acts, focussing instead on republican culture, religiosity, urban modernity and gender.

Some studies of sensibilities have dealt with the construction of heroes and its role for republicanism (Langue, 2008). The question of colonial religiosity in clandestine environments has also received some attention (Ferry, 2006; Sutton, 2007). So have the imaginaries of modernity in cities such as Rio de Janeiro and Buenos Aires (Velloso, 2008). Oral historians are exploring the world of sensibilities of immigrants in São Paulo (Antonacci, 2002). Pesavento (2007) has studied how a French painter could capture in his canvases the quotidian life and soul of Rio de Janeiro before the Regency. Gender historians have used this framework to reconstruct the lives of prostitutes in Mexico (Núñez Becerra, 2002). Works on colonial insults, the barbarisation effect of revolutions, or the mobilising power of rage and hope are equally rare. Studies by Albornoz Vásquez (2005, 2006) deal with 'injuries by words' among Chilean and Mexican colonial elites. Insults reveal that colonial elites reacted with rage to insinuations of low birth and racial mixture. Reinaldo Rojas (2007) has examined the debates among the Venezuelan elites of the 1860s in relation to the civilising or barbarising effect of 'revolutions'. Reed (2004) has argued that events-motivated emotions, such as hope and rage, played an important role in the making of the Nicaraguan revolution.

State Monopoly of Violence

The building of central states and the gradual monopolisation of violence by absolutist monarchs are moments crucial to Elias's understanding of the sociogenesis involved in the civilising process. In Latin America, the correlate to this process of centralisation and monopolisation must be located in the 'long' nineteenth century (1829–1930). Two processes demand our particular attention: the pacification and disarmament of *caudillo* armed forces and their replacement by professional national armies; and the end of regional rebellions that challenged the legitimacy of the central state. *Caudillo* leaderships were well adapted to the fragmentation of post-independence era political sovereignty (nations were subdivided into so many provinces, which in turn built regional alliances). Their supression and defeat were the necessary conditions for a process of centralisation and monopolisation of legitimate force in the national state. Yet, whether the new national armies were able to displace the threat of regional rebellions depended greatly upon the ability of politicians to form lasting national alliances.

In Latin America, there is an important body of literature on the emergence, consolidation and weaknesses of nation-states (Oszlak, [1982] 1997 ; López-Alves, 2000; Dunkerley, 2002). While the depth and diversity of research vary from country to country, the findings have been important. The relative success of state-building was associated with the characteristics of war (whether fought or not near the centre), with the ways that elites mobilised the rural poor (through political parties, *caudillo* armies or state bureaucracies), and with the type of coalition among propiertied classes, state officials and caudillos (López-Alves, 2000). The question of whether or not the national states were able to achieve a monopoly of legitimate force in the long nineteenth-century is still an unsettled issue. In most cases, it is easier to point out certain moments where a consensus exists about the consolidation of a centralist state than it is to ascertain the moment when the state obtained an effective monopoly of legitimate force.

Sociologist Miguel A. Centeno (2002b) has examined the role of wars in state-making in Latin America. He argues that, in spite of numerous and violent wars during the nineteenth century, these wars rarely led to the centralisation of state power, much less to an effective monopoly of legitimate force. In most countries, the centralisation of state authority preceded in various decades the establishment of internal peace and stability. Effective centralised authority and the dwindling of internal rebellions had to do more with the enhancement of state capacities (censuses, railroads, unified currency and taxation) than with the military mobilisations generated by major wars. Rather than being the cauldron of political stability and statehood, wars generated social chaos and regional fragmentation. Divisions within the elites, excessive regionalism and the lack of racial or ethnic cohesion presented serious obstacles to the consolidation of a strong central state.

Historians agree that the decolonisation of Hispanic America produced, not unity and centralisation, but political fragmentation. Viceroyalties were divided into various nation-states, and then the force of regionalism fragmented the polities even further into local autonomies. After independence, *caudillos* came to dominate the politics of the provinces, preventing processes of national unification for decades (Chiaramonte, 1997). Did this fragmentation of political sovereignty translate into less self-control of violent impulses? In my own work, I have found that Buenos Aires province managed to pacify the countryside during the Rosas dictatorship. The extension of policing to the countryside entailed greater control of violent crimes. The prohibition of the use of knives in taverns was more strictly enforced than historians had hitherto granted (Salvatore, 2003: 116, 118, 215–16). The image of a 'violent countryside' was more the result of a construction of romantic writers than a reflection of everyday life in rural Buenos Aires province.

The two signals of a centralisation of political power and of a process of monopolisation of violence, the withering of *caudillo* warfare and the end of regional rebellions, have been the object of analysis and discussion. These processes belong to the end of the nineteenth century. We could add a third sign of the monopolisation of violence by the state: the control of banditry. Although banditry thrived in the nineteenth century, it was rare in the second and third decades of the twentieth century. These indicators speak of a long-term success in the processes of state-making and centralisation that cannot be ignored. Yet, it remains unclear whether these processes had permanent effects on the formation of peaceful social interaction and the control of aggressive impulses.

Regional historians have portrayed the regimes of the turn of the century (1890–1910) as republics of 'order and progress', with limited franchise and elitist governments. Under these regimes, urban populations lived in reasonably peaceful environments. These elitist or aristocratic governments dispensed repressive violence against rebellious workers, insurgent peasants and indigenous peoples. The monopoly of force attained by these oligarchic republics (the Mexican Porfiriato, the Argentine 'conservative order', the Guzmán Blanco regime in Venezuela, or the Peruvian 'aristocratic republic') proved spatially and temporally limited. Because of their exclusionary politics, these oligarchic republics provoked social and political reactions that tended to undermine the established order. In Argentina, the farmers' revolts of 1893 and 1912, and the 1907 'strike' by urban tenants in Buenos Aires are indicative of these social reactions. The Mexican Revolution is perhaps the best example of the long-term unsustainability of a political regime based upon social and political exclusion. More importantly, the central states of oligarchic republics failed to subdue all regions and peoples within the national borders.

The Porfirian regime in Mexico is a case in point. While the regime ensured 30 years of peace and political stability, it was also responsible for the forceful relocation of Yaqui Indians and for the violent repression of workers' strikes in Puebla and Veracruz. Porfirio Díaz's creation of a police force to control the countryside, the *rurales*, served as a credible threat to potential political rivals and to peasant rebels. The image of Mexican *rurales* following the sinews of commerce to protect property and commodities in transit connects well with Elias's notion of growing social interdependences, rooted in economic transactions and specialisation, as a parallel process to the centralisation of power and the monopolisation of force by the state. The construction of a vast railroad network ensured that armed forces could be dispatched promptly to crush any revolts in the interior. First used to control banditry and to put down regional political dissent, the *rurales* were later utilised to repress the protests of industrial and mining workers. They acted as an effective and visible police force in the service of the dictator (Vanderwood, 1992: 119).

The birth of modern Argentina as a centralised nation-state is usually dated from 1880, after the 1879 'Conquest of the Desert', a military campaign led by Julio A. Roca that removed the remaining foci of indigenous resistance south of the Colorado river. The following year, the army's successful repression of the last rebellion against the federal government ended in an agreement to 'federalise' the capital city. The defeat of the militias of Buenos Aires province by the national army gave the new national government an effective monopoly over legitimate force. Buenos Aires province was subject to federal intervention and banned from raising military forces (Ferrari and Gallo, 1980; Sábato, 2008). The stability of the government that followed was the result of a political alliance of provincial governors in support of a new national party, the Partido Autonomista Nacional (PAN).

Similarly, the birth of a stable and centralised state in Chile coincided with the passing of the 1833 conservative constitution, inspired by the policies and principles of Diego Portales. After the defeat of the Peru–Bolivian Confederation in 1839, Chile emerged as the most successful and long-lasting experiment in republican government in South America. The war contributed to a growing sense of national unity, promoting the popularity of Chile's next president, General Manuel Bulnes, a war hero. Fearful of the role of the military in political order, Portales entrusted the control of public order to a civil militia. The passivity and ignorance of the disenfranchised working masses, Portales thought, were the true pillars of Chile's lasting social order.

In Peru, the construction of a central state was a highly contested process, with advances and setbacks. In the post-independence period, the struggles among *caudillos* who represented different regions and supported distinct commercial policies generated much political fragmentation and social disorder (Gootenberg, 1991). Trade and regional rivalries prevented the formation of a national polity until the late 1840s. Starting in 1845, General Ramón Castilla built the political and regional alliances that made possible a consensus about free trade and the beginning of a centralised state. When regional conflicts over trade policies subsided, the process of state-building began.

Historical traditions have tended to present narratives that are too neat about the relative success of each country in the consolidation of its nation-state. In Peru, historians have agreed on the inability of elites to build a unified nation due to the dualistic nature of Peruvian society (white versus Indian), itself a legacy of colonialism. In Chile, the prevailing view has emphasised a solid state, able to unify the Chilean nation since the times of Diego Portales (1830s). In Mexico, the nineteenth-century is seen as a period of protracted conflict and regional disunity, followed by an elite-controlled peace during the Porfiriato, and by the dramatic turmoil of the revolution. The post-revolutionary state, by contrast, appears as a successful experiment in integrating distinct social forces under a single national project (Mallon, 2002).

These stylised historical narratives leave important subaltern actors (in particular, indigenous communities) and alternative conceptions of citizenship out of the picture. Thus, the 'success' of the post-Portalian state in Chile is predicated on the dismissal of autonomist tendencies among the Mapuches in the south. Similarly, the 'success' of the post-revolutionary state in Mexico leaves unexamined the question of regions that remained marginal to national politics and of indigenous communities that resisted their integration into the Mexican nation. Despite the relative success in some centralising experiences and in nation-building, historians agree that the state in Latin America remained weak, unable to exert full sovereignty over the whole national territory, and thus also without an absolute monopoly of legitimate violence.

Even in the most stable and centralised national states (Argentina, Chile, Mexico), the state's ability to repress regional rebellions and forestall potential fragmentations of sovereignty was not complete. In Argentina, the so-called 'national territories' of the Chaco and Patagonia remained areas lacking in governmental and legal sovereignty until the 1950s. Nonetheless, the decline of militias and regiments raised by local *caudillos*, as well as the reduction in the number of rebellions against the federal government, must be taken as signs of something of a 'civilising process', whose impact on the repression of violent impulses among the population at large needs further investigation.

Duelling and Elite Manners

In Imperial Germany, according to Elias, the establishment of 'Good Society' was unified through the acceptance of honour codes stemming from military culture. The upper echelons of the state bureaucracy and the high bourgeoisie appropriated the warrior codes of the aristocracy and expressed them through the practice of codified duelling (Fletcher, 1997: 124). Recent scholarship has found that the revival of elite duelling in the late nineteenth-century was not an exclusively German phenomenon, but was extended to many European nations; among the lower class, Spierenburg has encountered a long-standing tradition of 'popular duels' (Spierenburg, 1998; 2008: 71–96). Among military officers and university students, duelling became a crucial means for claiming upper-class status. The right to demand 'satisfaction' meant being recognised as part of the elite. Over time, student fraternities lost their reformist spirit and came to accept social inequality and rigid social hierarchies. Rather than cultivate an empathy with others, student duelling fraternities reinforced the militaristic ethos, with its emphasis on toughness and a lack of pity. Elias's point is that the adoption by student fraternities of the warrior code, rather than ameliorating violence, strengthened obedience and hierarchy and, thus, favoured control by others. These forms of controlled aggression did not reach the masses, which continued to resolve conflicts through fist fights (Fletcher, 1997: 130).

Duelling was rare in Spanish America during the colonial and post-independence period. After 1870, however, the 'duel with all of its attendant protocol had become a well-established institution in many Spanish nations and remained so for a full half-century, sometimes longer' (Parker, 2001: 314). The emergence of duelling according to code was a modern phenomenon, contemporaneous with the emergence of export economies, rapid social and urban modernisation, and increased political competition among elites. The consolidation of codified duelling in Latin American cities was part of a larger process in which the region's elites tried to imitate the manners and lifestyles of European elites. In addition, duels served practical functions. With increased political competition, public reputations became an all-important value for a successful political career. An elite man could gain a public reputation by challenging another notable to a duel; to defend his reputation, an established public figure had to accept the challenge of his social equal.

The imitation of European elite manners and the increasing competitiveness of electoral politics were two chief factors in the spread of duelling in Latin America during the period 1870–1930. In Porfirian Mexico, Piccato (2010a) argues, duelling was crucial for the consolidation of political elites; it put on a plane of equality educated men of distinct professions, political persuasions and even social backgrounds. Questions of honour raised in Congress, or through the pages of the newspapers, could be resolved in duels. The adherence to strict rules guaranteed equality among the elites. For the sake of the equality of contenders, most duellists chose pistols over fencing, a choice that required less instruction. To this extent, duelling played an important part in the formation of Mexico's public sphere.

The practice of duels tended to ameliorate inter-elite violence in Mexico. Duelling until death was forbidden. Most duellists ended challenges with only minor injuries. To an extent, duelling replaced political competition based on the use of military forces. Conflicts between educated members of the political and military elites were successfully shifted to the 'field of honour'. This ritualised form of violence permitted the formation of a relatively peaceful public culture in Porfirian Mexico (Piccato, 1999). After the revolution, duels continued to serve as a means to protect the honour of public men, yet the social hierarchies upon which the *Pax Porfiriana* was based began to unravel. The eruption of masses into politics, the increased availability of weapons, and a decade of violent resolution of conflicts diminished the role of duelling as a regulator of inter-elite aggression.

By the same time, upper-class Argentinians avidly took fencing lessons, learned the etiquette of duelling, and elected *padrinos* (seconds), in order to join 'the society of satisfaction-seekers'. In modernising Argentina (1870–1930), claims to family ancestry or participation in older wars no longer gave men arguments to affirm their upper social status. Under the pressure of newcomers from the middling classes, most of them European immigrants, the elites accepted a certain degree of upward mobility on the basis of merit while, at the same time, they reinforced their allegiance to the code of honour. Men of social prestige had to demonstrate their courage, determination and good reputation in the field of honour. To form an honourable reputation, elite men, in particular those potentially eligible for public office, needed to be able to demand and grant 'satisfaction' from and to their peers. The increased number of duels coincided with the economic and social modernisation of the country, a process made possible after the federalisation of the capital city. The height of duelling occurred between 1880 and 1910 (Gayol, 2008: 107).

Though clearly devised as an instrument of social differentiation and as a mimicry of the manners of European elites, the fashion for duelling did bring about a greater control of passions among members of the Argentine upper-class. After 1880, shoving, cane strokes, punches and other forms of physical aggression were considered rude and improper once elites accepted the code of duelling. Men of social weight began to value a form of courage based upon courtesy and respect. Calm and serenity became key attributes of their class. To be accepted in a duel, a man of honour had to demonstrate that he had behaved honourably and without resort to violence (Gayol, 2008: 61, 72–73, and 92).

As in the case of Mexico, political competition was central to the increase in duelling in Argentina. The number of challenges increased around election time, when candidates used the press or the chambers of Congress to disqualify political rivals. Public men found themselves the target of various accusations and innuendoes by other public men. Corruption, cowardice, incapacity for public office, violent character and the inability to control women were the most common offences. These personal verbal offences often served as part of the 'grammar of political combat'.

It is clear, from the works of Piccato, Parker and Gayol that the civilising impact of duelling – the amelioration of open outbursts of violence – did not extend to non-elite groups. The rapid adoption of codified duelling was indeed a form of social differentiation between elites and non-elite groups. Defenders of duelling presented it as a form of gentlemanly ritualised and contained aggression, quite different from the *riñas* (fights involving fists or knives), *pendencias* (any kind of dispute or conflict) and *desafíos* (challenges to fight) of the lower classes. Rather than a civilising example to the lower classes, duelling was another instrument of elite differentiation. It required impressive expenditures and the mobilisation of a social capital not available to lower-class subjects. Workers shared with elites the culture of masculine honour, but did not try to distance themselves from physical violence. They usually defended their honour in spontaneous fights, using guns, knives or fists, around taverns, ballrooms or drinking places. Wounds and deaths were common outcomes of these encounters. The apogee of gentlemen's duels in Argentina coincided with the criminalisation and stigmatisation of 'popular duels'. Considered as the expression of crude passions (rage or the desire for vengeance), *riñas* showed the failure of lower-class men to control their emotions.

'Decivilising' Processes

Studies on the escalation of political violence and on the consolidation of repressive military regimes in the Southern Cone (in the late 1960s and 1970s) have touched on themes crucial to Elias's concerns. Among them, none is more important than the question of 'decivilising reversals', that is, moments in which learned sensibilities about non-violent conduct are un-learned and crude open violence regains its force as a regulator of social and political interactions. Scholars who have studied state terror in the Southern Cone have paid attention to issues of public sensibilities, private conduct and the psychological effects of state repression on daily life.

In dealing with the Argentine military dictatorship of the 1970s, sociologists and political scientists have tried to understand the conditions for the establishment of a 'culture of fear' (Corradi et al., 1992; Spektorowski, 2003). Anthropologists have examined the important transformation in language and communication that these oppressive regimes brought about. Feitlowitz's work (1998) on the 'lexicon of terror' is a good example. Diana Taylor (1997) has studied both the theatrical deployment of terror by the military and the psychological reaction of middle-class Argentinians. During the period 1976–1982, people ceased to perceive uncomfortable images or news about the 'dirty war' (a collective reaction Taylor (1997: 119–138) calls percepticide, concentrating instead on their private lives. Others have noted the deep religious undertones of the rhetoric of military chiefs and torturers, pointing to the ideologically laden dimension of the 'dirty war'. The military sought to incarnate the values of Christian-Western Civilisation, presenting the leftist guerrillas as the modern embodiment of the anti-Christ (Graziano, 1992).

By focussing on collective fears, the theatrical deployment of state terror, and the ideological and rhetorical impact of the anti-insurgency war, scholars have begun to understand important dimensions (psychic, language, public communication, social interaction) of the impact of state terror in quotidian life. Unfortunately, such comprehensive interdisciplinary research is lacking for earlier processes of state-sponsored violence, particularly during the long nineteenth century. Hence, long-term comparisons are, for the moment, unfeasible. Yet it is clear that the new studies on the guerrilla violence in the 1970s and the right-wing reaction'that followed had produced an attempt to integrate the situation of the Southern Cone republics with other cases of genocide (Vezzetti, 2002; Sarlo, 2004; Crenzel, 2008). To this extent, they are approaching the Eliasian problematic: is there a learning curve in the control of aggression at the social and psychological levels? Or are the present levels of violence and levels of tolerance to violence unknown in the past century?

Historians, journalists, political scientists and anthropologists have begun to draw hemispheric connections in the wave of violence unleashed since the 1970s (Rosenberg, 1991; Nordstrom and Robben, 1995; Grandin, 2004). The Argentinian *desaparecidos* (disappeared) present a case of systematic violations of human rights that invite the use of the word 'genocide'. Recent revisions of the dynamic of the 'spiral of violence' between left and right in the 1970s bear some comparison with the violence of the Weimar Republic. Yet contemporary experience in other parts of Latin America has shown even worse scenarios of 'decivilising reversals'. The massacre of indigenous peoples in Guatemala in almost 30 years of civil wars, the emergence of self-defence brigades spreading violence in the countryside of Colombia and Peru, the recent explosion of narco-violence in Mexico and the spread of youth violent gangs (*maras*) in Central America are all signs of new moment involving a fall into a 'decivilising reversal'. Middle-class fears about criminal violence, the so-called 'insecurity problem', pale in comparison with these other markers of 'decivilising' tendencies, and may be an integral part of a generalised failure to control aggressive impulses (Briceño-León, 2007; Kessler, 2009; Frühling and Tulchin, 2005).

State-Formation and the Question of Generalised Violence

The Latin American experience presents cases, such as the period of *La Violencia* in Colombia, in which all societal boundaries and psychic restrictions regarding violence seem to have disappeared. The War of the Triple Alliance (1865–1870), in which a vast proportion of the Paraguayan male population was exterminated, and the Chaco War (1932–1935), whose ferocity is said to compare with the Spanish Civil War, can be added as moments of unbounded, generalised violence. Maybe the Mexican Revolution does not qualify in this category, as much violence, as Alan Knight argues in this volume, was instrumental and, to this extent, not excessive. The massacre of Guatemalan indigenous peasants in the 1980s (see Figueroa Ibarra in this volume) certainly qualifies for this category. Perhaps one should add to this list the 'Great Andean Rebellions' of the 1780s. Although the density of historical research may differ, it should be possible to draw some comparison among these moments of generalised violence – clear moments of reversals or breakdowns of civilisation – and to see to what extent there has been progress or regression over two centuries. Whereas all comparisons involve some risk, we need to discuss under what circumstances the 'genocidal impulse' takes over the politics and social interactions of vast portions of national territories.

Viewed in retrospect, situations of generalised violence in the history of Latin America seem to be associated with conditions stemming from political and social transformations. This volume makes evident that political violence is central to our understanding of violent impulses and civilising processes. Processes of state-formation in particular appear as crucial to decoding the patterns of civilising and decivilising tendencies in the region. To evoke certain crucial problems relating to violent impulses and restrictions, I need to return to the question of periodisation.

For our purpose, the periodisation that matters is the one that refers to the process of state-formation. The expansion of institutions with a potential to transform people's conduct and sensibilities is crucial in this regard. I refer to certain institutions such as the police, the school system, universal military enrolment, municipal organisation and the judicial apparatus of the state. Institutions stemming from civil society, such as labour unions, *sociedades de fomento* (self-improvement societies or clubs), popular libraries, women's societies and religious organisations may also affect the formation of sensibilities and patterns of conduct. There is almost no accepted periodisation in regard to the formation of civil-society associations. However, with regard to the process of state-formation, some generally agreed periodisation does exist.

To start with, the wars of independence imposed on the societies of Hispanic America the militarisation of social life. Forced recruitment was massive and men from all conditions of life entered the armies of the emerging nations. Black slaves entered national regiments with the promise of obtaining their freedom at the end of the war. The whole war itself was long-lasting, produced large numbers of casualties, and was unusually cruel. In Venezuela, according to Blanco Fombona (Rojas, 2007), the *guerra-a-muerte* (war to the death), because of its cruelty and high level of violence, was seen as a continuity of the violence of the *conquistador* against indigenous peoples. For the same reason – its unusual brutality – the war between patriots and royalists in Chile was equally called *guerra a muerte*. In most countries, the independence wars empowered a patrician military elite, which, although liberal in its rhetoric, employed all sorts of corporal punishment, including the death penalty, in its effort to attain the respect of the troops and of the civilian population. In post-independence Argentina, most subaltern complaints against undue corporal punishment occurred in the context of demobilisation of the armies who fought in Chile and Peru.

After independence, the new Hispanic-American nations went through a period of 30 years of civil wars, internal political fragmentation, government by *caudillos* and the unsuccessful experiment with various constitutions. Civil wars, though intense, were not as massive as the independence campaigns, each battle involving perhaps 1,000 to 3,000 combatants. The lack of prisons and the mobile nature of the regiments imposed the necessity of executing the captured enemies on site. No prisoners were taken, meaning that all captured enemy troops were killed, usually with the sword or with the knife. As a result of their participation in the civil wars, subalterns learned to kill by *degüello* (beheading). This was true of the Argentine Confederation and also of neighbouring nations. Intimidation and terror were crucial weapons in the civil wars; hence, the victorious army (whether *unitario* or *federal*) used to show the decapitated head of a defeated chief mounted on pikes.

The death penalty (executions by shooting or hanging) was used frequently to deal with deserters, murderers and bandits. We do not know exactly how frequently, but this was probably more so than during the late-colonial period. The interpretation of this decivilising trend is straightforward. The new political regimes, endowed with little legitimacy and in charge of gigantic mobilisations for war, needed to impose severe penalties on enemy collaborators and reluctant patriots. Yet the hanging tree (or the shooting bench) was less active in the new Hispanic American republics than in contemporary England. Was this then a truly decivilising moment? Clearly, post-independence regimes, whether governed by a junta, a governor, a protector or a Directorate, imposed on the civilian populations unusual levels of taxation and recruitment, and were ready to use exemplary punishment to make their threats credible. But the states they controlled were quite weak, unable to carry these threats into effect.

Clearly, war casualties created great social suffering. To the extent that campaigns were more frequent, these sufferings tended to increase. Between 1830 and 1903 Venezuela experienced 39 revolutions, a situation of recurrent violence that promoted sentiments of hatred, destruction and vengeance. To historian Antonio Arraez (Rojas, 2007: 22), recurrent revolutions created a 'collective state of permanent rage'. Enemies had to be exterminated, otherwise they could do harm to family and friends. We do not know how extensive these kinds of collective emotion were. We know that Federalist crowds in Buenos Aires province burned *muñecos de Judas* (effigies of Judas) representing the hated enemies (the *unitarios*) as a commitment to exterminating them. However, beyond certain key moments of heightened animosity, rural communities learned to cooperate with each other, even with political enemies. Lynching cases were rare or unknown.

After 1850, and coinciding with the increasing connection of Latin American economies with the world market, new political alliances were able to sustain representative governments and the new constitutions began to be enforced. The new liberal leaderships were concerned with asserting the civil rights of white and mestizo populations, while giving some concessions to Blacks and mulattos. During this period, much institution-building was predicated on the need to introduce 'progress': elementary education, entice-ment of European immigration, property laws, railroad-building, banking, and so on. By promoting the dis-entailment of Indian communal lands, liberal regimes (in Mexico, Bolivia and other countries) stimulated private land-seekers to commit violence against indigenous peoples. Yet, on the other hand, we know that liberals started the campaign for the abolition of the death penalty and began to advocate 'more civilised' forms of punishment.

The enthusiasm for liberal reform soon gave way to more elitist and scientific ways of state administration. The Roca presidency in Argentina, the Porfiriato in Mexico, the Guzmán Blanco regime in Venezuela, are all examples of 'order and progress' administrations that pushed the region further on the road of export-led development. These regimes tended to strengthen basic state capacities that the liberal regimes lacked, among them centralised government, standing armies, modern police forces and more complex tax systems. Intellectual historians associate this period with the ideological hegemony of positivism, in its social evolutionary forms, while political historians talk about 'aristocratic republics' to the extent that the extension of state capacities went along with severe limitations in voting rights and mass political participation.

These oligarchic republics unleashed unprecedented violent campaigns against indigenous peoples. With regard to other subalterns (women, immi-grant workers, vagabonds, street children), the new administrations tried to provide modern solutions: institutionalisation, urban policing and some minor welfare provisions. For the population at large, the school system constituted the way to 'civilisation' and 'nationhood'. Only in the case of Argentina was an effective system of universal male conscription estab-lished. Where Black workers constituted an important part of the workforce, the states implemented new forms of control: military policing was the answer that Brazilian elites gave to the problem of urban disorder. In the largest countries of the region, the adoption of modern penitentiary regimes was accompanied by an abandonment of the death penalty, at least in its public, exemplary version, so much so that, by the 1930s, this punishment was regarded as a curiosity of a bygone era.

Late nineteenth-century wars, such as the War of the Triple Alliance or the First War of Independence in Cuba, or the War of the Pacific, were more violent and cruel than any confrontation in the past, chiefly because of improvements in military technology and of the large numbers of soldiers who participated in them. Historians customarily state that the atrocities committed by General Weyler in the Cuban War of Independence were unprecedented, implying that the famous Spanish general invented the 'scorched-earth' campaign. While politicians and statesmen tied these military confrontations to efforts in nation-building, the subalterns who had to fight these wars thought otherwise. Desertions in the War of the Triple Alliance were massive in Argentina, Brazil and Uruguay. The defeated nations were naturally sour about the loss of property and lives that these wars produced. Their intellectuals and politicians used these defeats to stimulate sentiments of nationality and promote national awakening. In Peru, Bolivia and Paraguay, the wars left permanent scars in the collective psyche, yet it is not clear that a pacifist ethos developed from these dramatic experiences.

After 1914, countries of the Southern Cone came to inherit some of the new currents of thinking prevalent in Europe and, to this extent, adopted radical varieties of political thought (such as anarchism, syndicalism, socialism, nationalism and fascism) bound to generate violent social conflict. Although the region was spared the 'total wars' that threatened to destroy European civilisation, such a degree of social antagonism generated violent confrontations between workers and the police, on occasions assisted by pro-order 'white guards'. To the extent that the new ideologies privileged violence as the instrument of social and political transformation, peace was at a discount. What (if at all) was the 'civilising legacy' of these confrontations? It is often said that the violent struggles and repression of the Tragic Week (July 1919) in Argentina produced two decades of labour peace or, at least, lower union activism. Outbursts of workers' resistance that elicited violent repression by the army occurred only in the periphery of the nation (the Patagonia strikes of 1921–1922 and the Chaco revolts at La Forestal). How generalised was the avoidance of violence in the 1920s and 1930s? And to what extent did less confrontational tactics reflect a change in workers' sensibilities? Had workers exchanged less open confrontation for more effective collective rights?

The interwar period, to the extent that it combined intense social conflicts with modern forms of state intervention, particularly on issues such as industrial relations, workers' rights, and public services, showed a further expansion of state capacities in countries that were already in the way of industrialisation and rapid urban growth. At some time in the 1930s, the most advanced countries of the region (Mexico, Argentina, Uruguay, Chile) started to introduce some social policies destined to generate 'social welfare'. To this extent, industrialising Latin American societies replicated Europe, without being pushed into the madness of total wars. Many authors have called this transition the 'inter-war period' for a reason. In the aftermath of the Second World War, the characteristic policies, conflicts and styles of statecraft of the period 1919–1939 became obsolete. Afterwards, social and political conflicts began to conform to the ideological divide created by the Cold War. To this extent, little by little the signs of a new decivilising epoch began to emerge.

The overthrow of President Arbenz in Guatemala in 1954 started a cycle of political interventions modelled on the new paradigm. From then onward, the region witnessed an increase in guerrilla activity and counter-insurgency operations, until, in the late 1960s, the Southern Cone had been colonised by military dictatorships. The Cuban Revolution stimulated many left-wing political parties and movements to seek revolutionary solutions, often involving armed confrontation. While social scientists still debate the implications of this 'spiral of violence', few would deny that, in comparison with the 1940s and 1950s, the late 1960s and the 1970s were a period of increased political violence, in which revolutionaries and repressors felt no moral or psychic restraints to committing assassinations, kidnappings, torture and rape. The incidences of police repression and impunity denounced by Rodolfo Walsh in the 1950s (in his famous non-fiction writings, *¿Quién mató a Rosendo?* and *Operación masacre*) would look like children's stories compared with the mass disappearances of the late 1970s (Walsh, 1981).

Contributors

CARLOS AGUIRRE is Professor of History and Director of the Latin American Studies Program at the University of Oregon. He is the author of *Agentes de su propia libertad. Los esclavos de Lima y la desintegración de la esclavitud, 1821–1854* (Pontificia Universidad Católica del Perú, 1993), *The Criminals of Lima and their Worlds: The Prison Experience, 1850–1935* (Duke University Press, 2005), *Breve historia de la esclavitud en el Perú. Una herida que no deja de sangrar* (Fondo Editorial del Congreso del Perú, 2005), and *Dénle duro que no siente. Poder y transgresión en el Perú republicano* (Fondo Editorial Pedagógico San Marcos, 2008). He is currently working on a project on intellectuals and military nationalism in Peru between 1968 and 1975.

EMILIO CRENZEL is Professor of Sociology at the University of Buenos Aires. He is the author of *The Memory of the Argentina Disappearances: The Political History of Nunca Más* (Routledge, 2011), *Los desaparecidos en la Argentina (1983–2008)* (ed.) (Biblos, 2010), *La historia política del Nunca Más* (Siglo XXI, 2008), *Memorias enfrentadas: el voto a Bussi en Tucumán* (Universidad Nacional de Tucumán, 2001), and *El Tucumanazo* (Centro Editor de América Latina, 1991). He has published many scholarly articles in several languages on justice, human rights, and the social memories of the political violence and dictatorship in Argentina.

CARLOS FIGUEROA IBARRA is Professor of Sociology at the Benemérita Universidad Autónoma de Puebla, Mexico. Among his books are *El proletariado rural en el agro guatemalteco* (Editorial Universitaria de Guatemala, 1980), *El recurso del miedo. Estado y terror en Guatemala* (Editorial Universitaria Centroamericana, 1991), *Paz Tejada. Militar y Revolucionario* (Universidad de San Carlos de Guatemala, 2001), and *En el umbral del posneoliberalismo? Izquierda y gobierno en América latina* (F&G Editores/FLACSO, 2010).

ERIC A. JOHNSON is Professor of Modern European History at Central Michigan University. Among his books are *Urbanization and Crime: Germany 1871–1914* (Cambridge University Press, 1995), *Nazi Terror: The Gestapo, Jews, and Ordinary Germans* (Basic Books, 2000), and *What We Knew: Terror, Mass Murder and Everyday Life in Nazi Germany* (Basic Books, 2005, co-authored with Karl-Heinz Reuband).

ALAN KNIGHT is Professor of the History of Latin America at Oxford University. Among his publications are *The Mexican Revolution* (2 vols, Cambridge

University Press, 1986), *US–Mexican Relations, 1910–1940* (University of California, San Diego, 1987), *Mexico: From the Beginning to the Spanish Conquest* (Cambridge University Press, 2002), *Mexico: The Colonial Era* (Cambridge University Press, 2002), and *Caciquism in Twentieth-Century Mexico* (Institute for the Study of the Americas, 2005).

ORLANDO J. PÉREZ is Professor and Chairperson in the Department of Political Science at Central Michigan University. Recently, he published *Political Culture in Panama: Democracy after Invasion* (Palgrave-Macmillan, 2011). Additionally, he is co-editor (with Richard Millett and Jennifer Holmes) of *Latin American Democracy: Emerging Reality or Endangered Species?* (Routledge, 2009), and editor of *Post-Invasion Panama: The Challenges of Democratization in the New World Order* (Lexington Books, 2000).

PABLO A. PICCATO is Professor of History at Columbia University. Among his books are: *The Tyranny of Opinion: Honor in the Construction of the Mexican Public Sphere* (Duke University Press, 2010), *City of Suspects: Crime in Mexico City, 1900–1931* (Duke University Press, 2001), as co-editor with Robert Buffington, *Reconstructing Criminality in Latin America* (Scholarly Resources, 2000), and *True Stories Of Crime in Modern Mexico* (University of New Mexico Press, 2009).

CRISTINA ROJAS is Professor of Political Science at Carleton University. She is the author of *Civilization and Violence: Regimes of Representation in Nineteenth Century Colombia* (University of Minnesota Press, 2002). She has co- edited with Judy Meltzer a Special Issue of *Citizenship Studies* on Narratives of Citizenship in Latin America (2013), and the book *Elusive Peace: International, National and Local Dimensions of Conflict in Colombia* (Palgrave/St. Martin Press, 2005). Her most recent articles have appeared in *Citizenship Studies, Globalizations and Third World Quarterly*.

RICARDO D. SALVATORE is Professor of Modern History at the Universidad Tocuato di Tella in Buenos Aires, Argentina. He is the author of *Wandering Paysanos: State Order and Subaltern Experience in Buenos Aires during the Rosas Era* (Duke University press, 2003), *Imágenes de un Imperio* (Sudamericana, 2006), *Subalternos, Derechos y Justicia Penal: Ensayos de historia social y cultural argentina 1829–1940* (Gedisa, 2010). He coedited, with Gilbert Joseph and Catherine LeGrand, *Close Encounters of Empire* (Duke, 1998). His forthcoming book, *Disciplinary Encounters: US Scholarly Engagement with South America, 1900–1945* deals with the role knowledge plays in the making of inter-American relations. With Carlos Aguirre and Gilbert M. Joseph he co-edited *Crime and Punishment in Latin America* (Duke University Press, 2001). More recently he co-edited with O. Barreneche *El delito y el orden en perspectiva histórica* (Prohistoria, 2013).

PIETER SPIERENBURG is Emeritus Professor of Historical Criminology at Erasmus University, Rotterdam. Focusing especially on crime, law and violence in early modern history, he has published, among other books, *A History of Murder: Personal Violence in Europe from the Middle Ages to the Present* (Polity, 2008), *Written in Blood: Fatal Attraction in Enlightenment Amsterdam* (Ohio State University Press, 2004), *The Spectacle of Suffering: Executions and the Evolution of Repression, from a Preindustrial Metropolis to the European Experience* (Cambridge University Press, 1984; reprinted 2008), and, most recently, *Violence and Punishment: Civilizing the Body through Time* (Polity, 2012).

DANIEL TUBB is a doctoral student in anthropology at the University of Carleton.

VICTOR M. URIBE-URÁN is Associate Professor of History and Law at Florida International University. He is the author of *Honorable Lives: Lawyers, Families, and Politics in Colombia, 1780–1850* (University of Pittsburgh Press, 2000). He has edited *State and Society in Spanish America during the Age of Revolution* (Rowman and Littlefield, 2001), and has co-edited with Luis J. Ortiz, *Naciones, Gentes y Territorios. Ensayos de Historia e Historiografía Comparada de América Latina y el Caribe* (Universidad de Antioquia, 2000).

References

Abel, C. (1973) *Conservative Politics in Twentieth-Century Antioquia (1910–1953)*. Occasional Paper III. St. Anthony College: Oxford.

Abós, A. (1999) *Delitos ejemplares: Historias de la corrupción Argentina, 1810–1997*. Buenos Aires: Grupo Editorial Norma.

Acemoglu, D. and Robinson, J. A. (2001) 'A Theory of Political Transitions'. *American Economic Review* **91**(4): 938–963.

Acuña, C., Bombal González, I., Jelin, E., Landi, O., Quevedo, L. A., Smulovitz, C. and Vacchieri, A. (1995) *Juicio, Castigos y Memorias, Derechos humanos y justicia en la política Argentina*. Buenos Aires: Nueva Visión.

Agamben, G. (1998) *Homo Sacer: Sovereign Power and Bare Life*. Stanford University Press: Stanford.

Aguilar Mora, J. (1990) *Una Muerte Sencilla, Justa, Eterna: Cultura Y Guerra Durante La Revolución Mexicana*. Mexico: ERA.

Aguilera Peralta, G. (1969) *La violencia en Guatemala como fenómeno político*. Facultad de Ciencias Jurídicas y Sociales de la Universidad de San Carlos de Guatemala: Guatemala, CA.

Aguilera Peralta, G. (1980) *El Estado, la lucha de clases y la violencia en* Guatemala. *Programa de Maestría en Sociología Departamento de Sociología y Ciencias Políticas Administrativas*. Universidad Iberoamericana: México, DF.

Aguilera Peralta, G., Bran, R. and Ogaldes, C. (1996) *Buscando la paz: el bienio 1994–1995*. Colección debate No. 32. FLACSO: Guatemala.

Aguilera Peralta, G., Romero Imery, J., et al. (1981) *Dialéctica del terror en Guatemala*. San José, Costa Rica, CA: EDUCA.

Aguirre, C. (2008) *Dénle duro que no siente: Poder y transgresión en el Perú republicano*. Fondo Editorial del Pedagógico San Marcos: Lima.

Aguirre, C. (2010) 'Terruco de Mierda: Insult, Stigma, and Torture in Peru's Dirty War and Beyond'. Lecture delivered at the University of Washington (Seattle), 26 February.

Aguirre, C. (2011) 'Terruco de m . . . Insulto y estigma en la guerra sucia peruana'. *Histórica* **35**(1): 103–139.

Aguirre Rojas, C. A. (1998) 'Norbert Elías: Historiador y crítico de la modernidad'. *Diálogos* **2**: 1–27.

Alava, A. A. (2003) 'El Frontón: un caso reabierto'. *El Comercio*, 8 July: 2.

Alberro, S. (1988) *Inquisición y sociedad en Mexico, 1571–1700*. FCE: México.

Albornoz Vásquez, M. E. (2005) *La Injuria de Palabra en Santiago de Chile, 1672–1822*. Coloquios: Nuevo Mundo Mundos Nuevos.

Albornoz Vásquez, M. E. (2006) *Decir los sentimientos que se viven en singular. La frustración y la cólera de un comerciante de telas que se creía buen padre. Cuidad de México, 1714–1717*. Nuevo Mundo Mundos Nuevos: Coloquios.

Alexa et al. (2003) *Bajo Condena: Literatura Carcelaria Femenina*. DEMAC: Mexico. DF.

Almandoz Marte, A. (2002) *Planning Latin America's Capital Cities, 1850–1950*. Routledge: London and New York.

Alonso, A. M. (1995) 'Rationalizing Patriarchy: Gender, Domestic Violence, and Law in Mexico'. *Identities* **2**(1–2): 29–47.

Alonso, P. (1993) 'Politics and Elections in Buenos Aires, 1890–1890: The Performance of the Radical Party'. *Journal of Latin American Studies* **25**(3): 465–487.

Alvarado-Zaldivar, G., Salvador Moysén, J., Estrada Martínez, S. et al. (1998) 'Prevalencia de la violencia doméstica en la ciudad de Durango'. *Salud Pública* **40**: 481–486.

Amado, J. (1962) *Gabriela. Clove and Cinnamon.* Avon Books: New York.

Ames, R. (ed.) (1988) *Informe al Congreso sobre los Sucesos de los penales.* Talleres Gráficos OCISA: Lima.

Amnesty International (1977) *Informe de una misión de Amnistía Internacional a la República Argentina.* Barcelona: Amnistía Internacional.

Amnesty International (2002) *Guatemala's Lethal Legacy: Past Impunity and Renewed Human Rights Violations 28 February.* Amnesty International, International Secretariat: London.

Amnesty International (2009) 'México: a dos años de aprobada, ley de protección de mujeres sin impacto en los estados'. 29 January. [WWW document]. URL http://www.amnesty.org/es/for-media/press-releases/mexico-dos-anos-ley-proteccion-mujeres-sin-impacto-20090129 [accessed 1 May 2011].

Anderson, B. (1997) *Comunidades imaginadas: Reflexiones sobre el origen y la difusion del nacionalismo.* Fondo de Cultura Económica: México.

Anderson, R. (1976) *Outcasts in Their Own Land. Mexican Industrial Workers, 1906–11.* Northern Illinois University Press: DeKalb.

Anderson, T. P. (1971) *Matanza: El Salvador's Communist Revolt of 1932.* University of Nebraska Press: Lincoln.

Andrien, K. J. (2001) *Andean Worlds: Indigenous History, Culture, and Consciousness under Spanish Rule, 1532–1825.* University of New Mexico Press: Albuquerque.

Anna, T. E. (1998) *Forging Mexico, 1821–35.* Lincoln: University of Nebraska Press.

Anonymous (2003) *La verdad del Frontón,* Centro de Información para la Memoria Colectiva y los Derechos Humanos, Document 100319, Frontón y Lurigancho – Exp. 643–86 CSJM.

Antonacci, M. A. (2002) 'Atravesando el Atlántico: Españolas en Sao Paulo'. *Historia, Antropología y Fuentes Orales* **28**: 3–31.

Anuario Estadístico de la República Mexicana (1895) Secretaría de Fomento: Mexico City.

Archdiocese of Guatemala (1999) *Guatemala Never Again! The Official Report of the Human Rights Office.* Recovery of Historical Memory (REHMI) Project. Orbis Books: New York.

Archer, C. (2003) 'The Year of Decision: Félix Calleja and the Strategy to End the Revolution of New Spain' in C. I. Archer (ed.) *The Birth of Modern Mexco.* Wilmington: SF Books, 1780–1824.

Arendt, H. (1958) *The Origins of Totalitarianism.* Harcourt, Brace and Company: New York.

Arendt, H. (1965) *On Revolution.* The Viking Press: New York.

Argueta, S. (1992) 'Diagnóstico de los grupos llamados "maras" en San Salvador. Factores psicosociales que prevalecen en los jóvenes que los integran'. *Revista de Psicología de El Salvador* **43**: 53–84.

Arquidiócesis de San Pablo (1985) *Brasil: Nunca Mais.* Petrópolis: Vozes.

Arrom, S. (1985) *Women of Mexico City, 1790–1857.* Stanford University Press: Stanford.

Arrubla, M. (1978) *Estudios Sobre el Subdesarrollo Colombiano*. Editorial La Carreta: Bogotá.

Ashby, J. C. (1967) *Organised Labor and the Mexican Revolution Under Lázaro*. Cárdenas University of North Carolina Press: Chapel Hill.

Asociación Mexicana Contra la Violencia Hacia las Mujeres, ACC (1995) *Encuesta de Opinión Pública Sobre la incidencia de la Violencia en la Familia*. UNFPA/COVAC/PGJ: Mexico City.

Asociación Probienestar de la Familia Colombiana (1990) *Colombia: Encuesta nacional de demografía y salud, 1995*. Profamilia: Bogotá.

Asociación Probienestar de la Familia Colombiana (2000) *Salud sexual y reproductiva en Colombia*. Resultados Encuesta Nacional de Demografia y Salud. Profamilia: Bogotá.

Asociación Probienestar de la Familia Colombiana (2005) *Salud sexual y reproductiva en Colombia*: Resultados Encuesta Nacional de Demografia y Salud. Profamilia: Bogotá.

Astorga, L. A. (2003) Drogas sin fronteras. Grijalbo: Mexico, DF.

Azpuru, D. (1999) 'Peace and Democratisation in Guatemala: Two Parallel Processes' in C. J. Arnson (ed.) *Comparative Peace Processes in Latin America*. Stanford University Press: Stanford, 97–126.

Azuela, M. (1974) *Páginas autobiográficas*. Fondo de Cultura Económica: Mexico.

Baker, B. J. and Kealhofer, L. (eds.) (1996) *Bioarchaeology of Native American Adaptation in the Spanish Borderlands*. University Press of Florida: Gainesville.

Balibar, E. (2001) 'Outlines of a Topography of Cruelty: Citizenship and Civility in the Era of Global Violence'. *Constellations* 8(1): 15–29.

Ball, P. K. and Spirer H. F. (1999) *Violencia institucional en Guatemala, 1960 a 1996: una reflexión cuantitativa*. American Association for the Advancement of Science (AAAS) y Centro Internacional para Investigaciones en Derechos Humanos (CIIDH): Washington, 58–61.

Baranda, A. (2007) 'Piden no difundir narcomensajes'. *Reforma*, June 6. [WWW document] URL: http://site.securities.com/doc.html?pc=MX&doc_id=140143967 [accessed 7 January 2011].

Barragán, S. (2005) 'The "Spirit" of Bolivian Laws: Citizenship, Patriarchy and Infamy' in S. Caulfield, S. Chambers and L. Putnam (eds.) *Honor, Status and Law in Modern Latin America*. Duke University Press: Durham, 66–86.

Barraza, G. (1984) 'El Frontón. Territorio liberado de Sendero'. *Oiga* 197, 15 de Octubre, 30–35.

Barreneche, O. (2001) *Dentro de la Ley, todo. La justicia criminal de Buenos Aires en la etapa formativa del sistema penal moderno de la Argentina*. Ediciones al Margen: La Plata.

Barreneche, O. and Galeano, D. (2008) 'Notas sobre la reforma de la policía en Argentina, siglos XIX y XX'. [WWW document]. *Cuadernos de Seguridad*. URL http://m.minseg.gob.ar [accessed 21 October 2012].

Basile, T. (1989) 'Aproximaciones al "testimonio sobre la desaparición de personas" durante la dictadura militar y la democracia argentinas'. *Cuadernos Angers-La Plata* 2: 45–63.

Bauer, K. J. [1974] (1992) *The Mexican War, 1846–1848*. University of Nebraska Press: Lincoln.

Beckerman, S. and Valentine, P. (2008) *Revenge in the Cultures of Lowland South America*. University Press of Florida: Gainesville.

Beirne, P. (1997) *Issues in Comparative Criminology*. Dartmouth Publishing Company: Brookfield.

Bejarano, J. (1940) *La derrota de un vicio. Origen e historia de la chicha*. Editorial Iqueima: Bogotá.

Beltrán, I. and Piccato, P. (2004) 'Crimen en el siglo XX: Fragmentos de análisis sobre la evidencia cuantitativa' in A. Rodríguez Kuri and S. Tamayo (eds.) *Los Últimos Cien Años, Los Próximos Cien Años*. Universidad Autónoma Metropolitana: Mexico City, 13–44.

Benjamin, T. (2000) *Revolución: Mexico's Great Revolution as Memory, Myth and History*. University of Texas Press: Austin.

Berenguer Visbal, A. M. (1986) *Violencia conyugal*. Editorial Colectivo Cuéntame tu Vida: Cali.

Berenguer Visbal, A. M. (1993) 'Violencia conyugal' in *Violencia Intrafamiliar Memorias seminario realizado en la ciudad de Medellín, marzo 10–12, 1993*. Impresión Litoarte Ltda: Medellín, 110–123.

Bergquist, C. and Penaranda, R. (eds.) (1992) *Violence in Colombia. The Contemporray Crisis in Historical Perspective*. SR Books: Wilmington.

Bergquist, C., Peñaranda, R. and Sánchez, G. (eds.) (1992) *Violence in Colombia*. SR Books: Wilmington.

Bernate Ochoa, F. (2004) 'El Código Penal Colombiano de 1890'. *Estudios Socio-Jurídicos* 6(2): 535–558.

Besse, S. K. (1989) 'Crimes of Passion: The Campaign against Wife Killing in Brazil, 1910–1940'. *Journal of Social History* 22(4): 653–666.

Besse, S. K. (1996) *Restructuring Patriarchy: The Modernisation of Gender Inequality in Brazil, 1914–1940*. University of North Carolina Press: Chapel Hill.

Bethell, L. (1987) 'Spanish America after Independence, c. 1820–1870' in L. Bethell (ed.) *Cambridge History of Latin America*. Cambridge University Press: New York.

Bethell, L. (ed.) (1989) *Latin America: Economy and Society 1870–1930*. Cambridge University Press: Cambridge.

Bethell, L. (1993) 'Argentina Since Independence' in L. Bethell (ed.) *Cambridge History of Latin America*. Cambridge University Press: New York.

Biron, R. E. (2000) *Murder and Masculinity. Violent Fictions of Twentieth-Century Latin America*. Vanderbilt University Press: Nashville.

Bjornlund, M. and Mennecke, M. (2005) '¿Qué es el genocidio? En la búsqueda de un denominador común entre definiciones jurídicas y no jurídicas' in D. Feiernstein (ed.) *Genocidio: La administración de la muerte en la modernidad*. EDUNTREF: Buenos Aires, 17–48.

Blanco, C. G. (2005) 'Los 'Zetas' y 'El Chapo' Guzmán'. 29 August [WWW document]. URL http://www. nuevamayoria.com/ES/INVESTIGACIONES/seguridad/050829.html [accessed ?].

Blok, A. [1974] (1988) *The Mafia of a Sicilian Village, 1860–1960*. Waveland Press: Prospect Heights.

Bohoslavsky, E. (2005) 'Sobre los límites del control social. Estado, historia y política en la periferia argentina (1890–1930)' in E. Bohoslavsky and M. S. Di Liscia (eds.) *Instituciones y formas de control social en América Latina*. Buenos Aires: Prometeo Libros, 1840–1940, 49–72.

Bohoslavsky, E. (2010) 'El brazo armado de la improvisación. Aportes para una historia social de los policías patagónicos (1880–1946)' in E. Bohoslavsky and G. Soprano (eds.) *Un estado con rostro humano*. Prometeo Libros: Buenos Aires, 215–242.

Bohoslavsky, E. and Soprano, G. (eds.) (2010) *Un Estado con rostro humano: Funcionarios e instituciones estatales en Argentina (desde 1880 a la actualidad)*. Prometeo Libros: Buenos Aires.

Bortz, J. (2008) *Revolution Within the Revolution: Cotton Textile Workers and The Mexican Labour Regime, 1910–23*. Stanford University Press: Stanford.

Botana, N. R. (1979) *El orden conservador. La política argentina entre 1880 y 1916*. Editorial Sudamericana: Buenos Aires.

Botana, N. and Gallo, E. (eds.) (1997) *De la República posible a la República verdadera, 1880–1910*. Buenos Aires: Espasa Calpe/Ariel.

Bousquet, J. P. (1983) *Las locas de Plaza de Mayo*. Buenos Aires: El Cid Editor.

Braithwaite, J. and Strang, H. (2001) *Restorative Justice and Civil Society*. Cambridge University Press: New York.

Braun, H. (1985) *The Assassination of Gaitán: Public Life and Urban Violence in Colombia*. University of Wisconsin Press: Madison.

Braun, H. (1986) 'Los Mundos del 9 de Abril, o la Historia Vista desde la Culata' in G. Sánchez and R. Peñaranda (eds.) *Pasado y presente de la Violencia en Colombia*. Fondo Editorial CEREC: Bogotá, 195–231.

Bravo Lira, B. (1991) 'Arbitrio judicial y legalismo: Juez y derecho en la Europa continental y en Iberoamérica, antes y después de la codificación'. *Revista de Histora del Derecho Ricardo Levene* **28**: 7–22.

Brehm, J. and Rahn, W. (1997) 'Individual-Level Evidence for the Causes and Consequences of Social Capital'. *American Journal of Political Science* **41**(3): 999–1023.

Brena Sesma, I. (1996) 'Ley de asistencia y prevención de la violencia intrafamiliar'. *Anuario Jurídico 1996, Nueva Serie*: 43–45.

Briceño-León, R. (2007) *Sociología de la violencia en América Latina*. Quito: FLACSO: Sede.

Bronner, F. (1986) 'Urban Society in Colonial Spanish America: Research Trends'. *Latin American Research Review* **21**(1): 7–72.

Browning, C. R. (2001) *Ordinary Men: Reserve Police Battalion 101 and the Final Solution in Poland*. Penguin Books: Harmondsworth.

Brunk, S. (1995) *Emiliano Zapata*. University of New Mexico Press: Albuquerque.

Brunk, S. (2008) *The Posthumous Career of Emiliano Zapata*. University of Texas Press: Austin.

Buck-Morss, S. (2009) *Hegel, Haiti, and Universal History*. University of Pittsburgh: Pittsburgh.

Buffington, R. (2005) 'La violencia contra la mujer y la subjetividad masculina en la prensa popular de la Ciudad de México en el cambio del siglo' in C. Agostoni and E. S. Guerra (eds.) *De normas y transgresiones: Enfermedad y crimen en América Latina*. Instituto de Investigaciones Históricas: México, UNAM, 1850–1950, 287–325.

Buffington, R. and Piccato, P. (eds.) (2009) *True Stories of Crime in Modern Mexico*. University of New Mexico Press: Albuquerque.

Buntman, F. L. (2003) *Robben Island and Prisoner Resistance to Apartheid*. Cambridge University Press: New York.

Burt, J. (2007) *Political Violence and the Authoritarian State in Peru: Silencing Civil Society*. Palgrave/Macmillan: New York.

Byrne, H. (1996) *El Salvador's Civil War: A Study of Revolution*. Lynne Rienner Publishers: Boulder.

Cacho, L. (2005) *Los demonios del Edén: El poder que protege a la pornografía infantil*. Grijalbo: Mexico City.

Caimari, L. (2004) *Apenas un delincuente: Crimen, castigo y cultura en la Argentina 1880–1955*. Siglo XXI: Buenos Aires.

Caimari, L. (ed.) (2007a) *La ley de los profanos: Delito, justicia y cultura en Buenos Aires, 1870–1940*. Fondo de Cultura Económica: Buenos Aires.

Caimari, L. (ed.) (2007b) 'Sucesos de cinematográficos aspectos: Secuestro y espectáculos en el Buenos Aires de los años treinta' in *La ley de los profanos: Delito, justicia y cultura en Buenos Aires, 1870–1940*. Fondo de Cultura Económica: Buenos Aires, 209–250.

Caimari, L. (2009) 'Anatomía de una ola delictiva en Buenos Aires, 1920–1930' in M. Sozzo (ed.) *Historias de la cuestión criminal en la Argentina*. Editores del Puerto: Buenos Aires, 144–153.

Caimari, L. (2012) *Mientras la ciudad duerme. Pistoleros, policías y periodistas en Buenos Aires, 1920–1945*. Siglo Veintiuno: Buenos Aires.

Calhoun, C., LiPuma, E. and Postone, M. (eds.) (1993) *Bourdieu: Critical Perspectives*. University of Chicago Press: Chicago.

Calveiro, P. (1998) *Poder y desaparición: Los campos de concentración en Argentina*. Ediciones COLIHUE: Buenos Aires.

Camarero, H. and Herrera, C. M. (eds.) (2005) *El Partido Socialista en Argentina. Sociedad, política e ideas a través de un siglo*. Prometeo Libros: Buenos Aires.

Campbell, J. C. (1986) 'Nursing Assessment for Risk of Homicide with Battered Women'. *Advances in Nursing Science* 8: 36–51.

Carmagnani, M. (1976) *Formación y crisis de un sistema feudal: América Latina desde el siglo XVI a nuestros días*. Siglo Veintiuno Editores: Mexico.

Carmagnani, M. (1984) *Estado y sociedad en América Latina 1850–1930*. Critica Editorial: Barcelona.

Castañeda, E. (2000) 'Los grupos de hombres contra la violencia de Nicaragua: Aprendiendo a construir una nueva masculinidad'. [WWW document]. *En pie de paz* 52: 74–79. URL http://www.sodepaz.org/nicaragua/GHCV.htm [accessed 1 May 2011].

Castellanos, L. (2007) *México armado, 1943–81*. Ediciones Era: Ediciones Era.

Castilla, E. (1889) *Notas al Código de Procedimientos Penales para la justiciafederal y los tribunales ordinarios de la capital y territorios nacionales*. Mariano Moreno: Buenos Aires.

Castro, Martinez J. J. (1938a) *Educación nacional: Informe al Congreso*. Editorial Bogotá: ABC.

Castro Martinez J. J. (1938b) *Colonia escolar de vacaciones: Informe al Congreso*. Anexo 1. Editorial ABC: Bogotá.

Caulfield, S. (2000) *In Defence of Honour: Sexual Morality, Modernity, and Nation in Early-Twentieth-Century Brazil*. Duke University Press: Durham.

Cavarozzi, M. (1988) 'Los ciclos políticos en la Argentina desde 1955' in G. O'Donnell, P. Schmitter and L. Whitehead (eds.) *Transiciones desde un gobierno autoritario, América Latina*. Vol. II. Paidos: Buenos Aires, Barcelona, México, 37–78.

CEH (Comisión de Esclarecimiento Histórico) (1999) *Guatemala Memoria del Silencio* (12 vols). CEH: Guatemala.

Centeno, M. A. (2002a) 'The Centre Did Not Hold: War in Latin America and the Monopolisation of Violence' in J. Dunkerley (ed.) *Studies in the Formation of the Nation-State in Latin America*. Institute of Latin American Studies: London, 54–75.

Centeno, M. A. (2002b) *Blood and Debt: War and the Nation State in Latin America*. Penn State Press: University Park.

CFMDP/IEVE (Comissão de Familiares de Mortos e Desaparecidos Políticos y el Instituto de Estudo da Violencia do Estado) (1995–1996) *Dossie Dos Mortos e Desparecidos Politicos a partir de 1964. Companhia Editora de Pernambuco. Goberno do Estado de Pernambuco*. Goberno do Estado de Sao Paulo: Pernambuco.

Chakrabarty, D. (2000) *Provincializing Europe: Postcolonial Thought and Historical Difference*. Princeton Univeristy Press: Princeton.

Chant, S. and Craske, N. (2003) *Gender in Latin America*. Rutgers University Press: New Brunswick.

Chiaramonte, J. C. (1997) *Ciudades, provincias, estados. Orígenes de la nación argentina, 1800–1846*. Espasa Calpe-Ariel: Buenos Aires.

Chomsky, N. (2001) 'Injusticia infinita. La nueva guerra contra el terror'. [WWW document]. *Perfil de La Jornada*, 8 November. URL http://www.jornada.unam.mx/2001/11/07/per-nota.html [accessed 13 September 2013].

Christiansen, T. (2004) *Disobedience, Slander, Seduction, and Assault: Women and Men in Cajamarca, Peru, 1862–1900*. University of Texas Press: Austin.

CIDCA (Centro de Investigación y Documentación Centroamericano) (1979) 'Marco general de la violencia en Guatemala'. *Revista Alero* 3(4).

CNPDH (Comisión Nacional de Protección de los Derechos Humanos) (1993) *Los hechos hablan por sí mismos. Informe preliminar sobre los desparecidos en Honduras. 1980–1993*. Editorial Guaymuras: Tegucigalpa.

Coatsworth, J. (1988) 'Patterns of Rural Revolt in Latin America: Mexico in Comparative Perspective' in F. Katz (ed.) *Riot, Rebellion and Revolution: Rural Social Conflict in Mexico*. Princeton University Press: Princeton.

Cobb, R. (1972) *The Police and the People: French Popular Protest, 1789–1820*. Oxford University Press: Oxford.

Cohen, J. L. and Arato, A. (1992) *Civil Society and Political Theory*. MIT Press: Cambridge .

Código Penal de los Estados Unidos de Colombia (1873) *Lei 112 de 26 de Junio de 1873. Por el Congreso de 1873*. Imprenta de Medardo Rivas: Bogota.

Código Penal de la República Argentina (1894) *Sancionado por el Honorable Congreso Nacional el 25 de Noviembre de 1886. Pedro Igon y Cía. Editores: Buenos Aires.*

Colombia. Congreso de la República (1837) *Código Penal*. Imprenta Oficial: Bogotá.

Colombia, Congreso de la República, *Código Penal de la República de Colombia, con las leyes adicionales y su apéndice* [1890]. *Rige desde el día 15 de Junio de 1891* (Bogotá, Imprenta Nacional, 1906). Law, 19, 1890, art. 591, no. 9. Código Penal de la Republica de Colombia [1890].

Colombia. Congreso de la República (1895) *Código civil colombiano expedido por el congreso de 1873 y adoptado por la Ley 57 de 1887*. Imprenta Oficial: Bogota.

Colombia. Congreso de la República (1906) *Código Penal de la República de Colombia con las leyes adicionales y su apendice. (Rige desde el día 15 de Junio de 1891)*. Imprenta Oficial: Bogotá.

Colombia. Congreso de la República (1996). *Law 294* (18 July). Imprenta Oficial: Bogotá.

Colombia. Congreso de la República (2000) *Law 599* (24 July). Imprenta Oficial: Bogotá.

Colombia. Congreso de la República (2004a) *Law 882* (2 June). Imprenta Oficial: Bogotá.

Colombia. Congreso de la República (2004b) *Law 890* (7 July). Imprenta Oficial: Bogotá.

Colombia. Congreso de la República (2008) *Law 1257* (4 December). Imprenta Oficial: Bogotá.

Colombia. Congreso de la República (n.d.) *Código Penal de los Estados Unidos de Colombia.* Imprenta Oficial: Bogotá.

Colombian Penal Code 1967 (1967) (trans. and with an Introduction by Phanor Eder). American Series of Foreign Penal Codes, No. 14. Sweet and Maxwell: London, South Hackensack.

Comisión de Asuntos Penales y Penitenciarios, Colombia (1937) *Cógido Penal, Ley 95 de 1936, Decreto 2300 de 1936.* Imprenta Nacional: Bogotá.

Comisión Nacional Sobre la Desaparición de Personas (CNDP) (1996) *Nunca Más.* Editorial Universitaria de Buenos Aires: Buenos Aires.

Comissao de Familiares de Mortos e Desaparecidos Políticos y el Instituto de Estudo da Violencia do Estado (CFMDP/IEVE) (1995–1996) *Dossie Dos Mortos e Desparecidos Politicos a partir de 1964.* Companhia Editora de Pernambuco, Goberno do Estado de Pernambuco: Goberno do Estado de Sao Paulo.

CONADEP (Comisión Nacional sobre la Desaparición de Personas) (1984) *Nunca Más. Informe de la Comisión Nacional sobre la Desaparición de Personas.* Editorial Universitaria de Buenos Aires (EUDEBA): Buenos Aires.

CONADEP (Comisión Nacional sobre la Desaparición de Personas) (1996) *Nunca Más.* Editorial Universitaria de Buenos Aires (EUDEBA): Buenos Aires.

Consejo Nacional de Seguridad Publica (2008) *Los costos económicos de la violencia en Centroamérica.* [WWW document]. URL http://www.votb.org/elsalvador/Reports/costofviolence.pdf [accessed 17 April, 2011].

Corporación Casa de la Mujer (1988) *Violencia en la intimidad.* Casa de la Mujer: Bogotá.

Corradi, J. E. (1992) 'Toward Societies without Fear' in J. E. Corradi, P. W. Fagen and M. A. Garretón (eds.) *Fear at the Edge: State Terror and Resistance in Latin America.* University of California Press: Berkeley, 267–292.

Corralini, J., Di Iorio, E., Lobo, A. and Pigliapochi, J. (2003) *Políticas de memoria: el Nunca Más.* Unpublished document.

Craske, N. (2003) 'Gender, Politics and Legislation' in S. Chant and N. Craske (eds.) *Gender in Latin America.* Rutgers University Press: New Burnswick., 19–45

Crenzel, E. (2004) *Cartas a Videla: una exploración sobre el miedo, el terror y la memoria.* [WWW document]. Université du Québec à Montréal (UQAM), Canada. URL http://www.chaire-mcd.ca [accessed 30 August 2013]

Crenzel, E. (2008) *La historia política del Nunca Más. La memoria de las desapariciones en Argentina.* Siglo Veintiuno Editores: Buenos Aires.

Crenzel, E. (2011) *Memory of the Argentina Disappearances: the Political History of Nunca Más.* Routledge: New York.

Cristóbal, J. (1987) *¿Todos murieron?* Ediciones Tierra Nueva: Lima.

Cronin, H. (1991) *The Ant and the Peacock*. Cambridge University Press: Cambridge.

Crosby, A. W. (1972) *The Columbian Exchange*. Greenwood Press: Westport.

Cruz, J. M. (2004) *'Pandillas y capital social en Centroamérica'* in ERIC, IDESO, IDIES e IUDOP (eds.) *Maras y pandillas en Centroamérica. Pandillas y capital social*. Vol. II. UCA Editores: San Salvador, 277–326.

Cruz, J. M. (2005) 'Los factores asociados a las pandillas juveniles en Centroamérica'. *Estudios Centroamericanos, Juventud y desarrollo en Centroamérica* **685–686**: 1155–1182 (November–December).

Cruz, J. M. and Portillo, N. (1998) *Solidaridad y violencia en las pandillas del Gran San Salvador: Más allá de la vida loca*. UCA Editores: San Salvador.

Cubano Iguina, A. (2002) '"Con arrebato y obsecación": violencia doméstica y otras violencias contra las mujeres en Puerto Rico, 1870–1890'. *Revista del Centro de Investigaciones Históricas* **14**: 129–145.

Cubano Iguina, A. (2004) 'Legal Constructions of Gender and Violence Against Women in Puerto Rico Under Spanish Rule, 1860–1895'. *Law and History Review* **22**(3): 531–564.

Cubano Iguina, A. (2006) *Rituals of Violence in Nineteenth-Century Puerto Rico: Individual Conflict, Gender, and the Law*. University Press of Florida: Gainesville.

CNVR (Comisión Nacional de Verdad y Reconciliación) (1991) *Informe de la Comisión Nacional de Verdad y Reconciliación. Secretaría de Comunicación*. Gobierno de Chile: Santiago de Chile.

CVR (Comisión de la Verdad y Reconciliación) (2003a) *Informe Final*. 9 Vols. CVR: Lima.

CVR (Comisión de la Verdad y Reconciliación) (2003b) *Informe Final. Volume V. Historias representativas de la violencia*. CVR: Lima.

CVR (Comisión de la Verdad y Reconciliación) (2003c) *Informe Final. Volume VII. Los casos investigados por la Comisión de la Verdad y Reconciliación*. CVR: Lima.

CVR (Comisión de la Verdad y Reconciliación) (2003d) *Informe Final. Volume VIII. Segunda parte. Los factores que hicieron posible la violencia. Tercera parte. Las secuelas de la violencia*. CVR: Lima.

CVR (Comisión de la Verdad y Reconciliación) (2003e) *Sucesos en los penales en junio de 1986 August*. Centro de Información para la Memoria Colectiva y los Derechos Humanos: Lima.

CVR (Comisión de la Verdad y la Reconciliación) (n.d.) *Testimonios sobre el genocidio Centro de Información para la Memoria Colectiva y los Derechos Humanos*. CVR: Lima.

Dadrian, V. N. (2005) 'Configuración de los genocidios del siglo veinte. Los casos armenio, judío y ruandés' in D. Feiernstein (ed.) *Genocidio: La administración de la muerte en la modernidad*. EDUNTREF: Buenos Aires, 75–120.

Dammert, L. (ed.) (2009) *Crimen e inseguridad: Políticas, temas y problemas en las Américas*. Santiago De Chile FLACSO: Chile, Catalonia.

Darnton, R. (1999) *The Great Cat Massacre and Other Episodes in French Cultural History*. Basic Books: New York.

Davies, D. E. (2006) 'The Age of Insecurity: Violence and Social Disorder in the New Century Latin America'. *Latin American Research Review* **41**(1): 178–197.

Davies, D. E. (2009) 'Los orígenes estructurales de la violencia y la inseguridad en América Latina: El caso de México' in L. Dammert (ed.) *Crimen e inseguridad: Políticas, temas y problemas en las Américas*. FLACSO Chile/Catalonia: Santiago de Chile, 225–254.

Davies, N. (1977) *The Aztecs: A History*. Macmillan: London.

De la Pascua, M. J. (2002) 'Violencia y familia en la España del antiguo régimen'. *Estudis, Revista de Historia moderna* **28**: 77–102.

Dean, M. (2002) 'Powers of Life and Death Beyond Governmentality'. *Cultural Values* **6**(1–2): 119–138.

Degregori, C. I. (1990) *El surgimiento de Sendero Luminoso: Ayacucho, 1969–1979*. Instituto de Estudios Peruanos: Lima.

Degregori, C. I. (1996) *Las rondas campesinas y la derrota de Sendero Luminoso*. Instituto de Estudios Peruanos: Lima.

Degregori, C. I. (2013) *How Difficult it is to be God. Shining Path's Politics of War in Peru, 1980–1999*. University of Wisconsin Press: Madison.

Devoto, F. (2002) *Nacionalismo, fascismo y tradicionalismo en la Argentina moderna*. Siglo XXI Editores: Buenos Aires.

Díaz, A. J. (2004) *Female Citizens, Patriarchs, and the Law in Venezuela, 1786–1904*. University of Nebraska Press: Lincoln.

Dirección General de Estadística (1890) *Estadística del ramo criminal en la República Mexicana que comprende un periodo de quince años, de 1871 a 1885*. Secretaría de Fomento: México, DF.

Dix, R. H. (1971) *Colombia: The Political Dimensions of Change*. Yale University Press: New Haven.

Dodds Pennock, C. (2012) 'Maas Murder or Religious Homieide? Rethinking Human Sacrifice and Interpersonal Violence in Aztec Society'. *Historical Social Research/Historische Sozialforschung* **37**(3): 276–302.

Donghi, T. H. (ed.) (1999) *Vida y muerte de la República verdadera (1910–1930)*. Espasa Calpe / Ariel: Buenos Aires.

Dore, E. (ed.) (1997) *Gender Politics in Latin America: Debates in Theory and Practice*. Monthly Review Press: New York.

Dore, E. and Molyneux, M. (eds.) (2000) *Hidden Histories of Gender and the State in Latin America*. Duke University Press: Durham.

Downing, T. [1940] (1996) *The Mexican Earth*. University of Oklahoma Press: Norman.

Drago, L. M. (1887) *El procedimiento criminal en la provincia de Buenos Aires*. Pablo E. Coni: Buenos Aires.

Drucaroff, E. (2002) 'Por algo fue. Análisis del Prólogo a Nunca más, de Ernesto Sábato'. *Tres Galgos* **3**: 20–35.

Duhalde, E. L. (1983) *El estado terrorista argentino*. Buenos Aires: Argos-Vergara.

Dulles, J. W. F. (1961) *Yesterday in Mexico: A Chronicle of the Revolution, 1919–1936*. University of Texas Press: Austin.

Dunkerley, J. (ed.) (2002) *Studies in the Formation of the Nation-State in Latin America*. Institute of Latin American Studies: London.

Duque, L. F. and Montoya, N. E. (2008) 'La violencia física contra la mujer en Medellín y demás municipios del Valle de Aburra, 2003–2004'. *Revista Facultad Nacional de Salud Pública (Universidad de Antioquia)* **26**(1): 27–39.

Edberg, M. C. (2001) 'Drug Traffickers as Social Bandits'. *Contemporary Criminal Justice* **17**(3): 258–277.

Ehrlich, P. R. (2000) *Human Natures*. Penguin Books: New York.

El Nuevo Diario (2011) 'El Salvador tiene 21 mil pandilleros, dice Policía'. [WWW document]. URL http://www.elnuevodiario.com.ni/internacionales/94837 [accessed 18 April 2011].

El Universal Gráfico (1947) 'Por vago y malviviente pasará una temporada en la Penitenciaría'. *El Universal Gráfico*, 2 January, 5.

Elejalde, C. (1986) 'Fiscal César Elejalde: Se respetó la vida de los que se rindieron', La Crónica, 20 June, 6.

Elías, N. (1987) *El proceso de la civilización Investigaciones sociogenéticas y psicogenéticas*. Fondo de Cultura Económica: Madrid.

Elias, N. [1934, 1978] (1994) *The Civilising Process*. Blackwell: Oxford.

Elias, N. (1997) *The Civilising Process* (trans. Edmund Jephcott). Polity Press: Cambridge.

Ellsberg, M., Lijestrand, J. and Winkvist, A. (1997) 'The Nicaraguan Network of Women against Violence: Using Research and Action for Change'. *Reproductive Health Matters* 5(10): 82–92.

Ellsberg, M., Peña, R., Herrera, A., Lijestrand, J. and Winkvist, A. (1998) *Confites en el infierno. Prevalencia y características de la violencia conyugal hacia las mujeres en Nicaragua.* Nicaragua: Red de mujeres contra la violencia/ Departamento de Medicina Preventiva y Salud Pública de la Facultad de Medicina UNAN-León/Departamento de Epidemiología y Salud Pública de la Universidad Umea, Sweden.

Escalante Gonzalbo, F. and Aranda García, E. E. (2009) *El homicidio en México entre 1990 y 2007*. El Colegio de México: Mexico City.

Escobedo, R. (ed.) (2007) *Rompiendo el silencio: Mujer víctima y victimaria*. Alcaidía Mayor de Bogotá: Bogotá.

Esparza, M., Huttenbach, H. R. and Feierstein, D. (eds.). (2010) *State Violence and Genocide in Latin America: The Cold War Years*. Routledge: New York.

Fagen, P. W. (1992) 'Repression and State Security' in J. E. Corradi, P. W. Fagen and M. A. Garretón (eds.) *Fear at the Edge: State Terror and Resistance in Latin America*. University of California Press: Berkeley.

Fajnzylber, P., Lederman, D. and Loayza, N. (1998) *Determinants of Crime Rates in Latin America and the World: An Empirical Assessment*. World Bank Latin American and Caribbean Studies series. World Bank: Washington, DC.

Fals Borda, O. (1985) 'Lo sacro y lo violento, aspectos problemáticos del desarrollo de Colombia' in Centro Gaitán *Once Ensayos sobre la Violencia*. Centro Gaitán/ Fondo Editorial CEREC: Bogotá, 25–52.

Fals Borda, O. (2005) 'Prólogo' in G. Guzmán Campos, O. Fals Borda, and E. Umaña Luna (eds.) *La violencia en Colombia: Estudio de un proceso social (Tomo 1)*. Editora Taurus: Bogotá, 25–33.

Farah, D. (2012) *The Transformation of El Salvador's Gangs into Political Actors*. [WWW document]. Hemisphere Focus, Americas Program, The Center for Strategic and International Studies, 21 June. URL http://csis.org/ files/publication/120621_Farah_Gangs_HemFocus.pdf [accessed 4 June 2013].

Farriss, N. M. (1984) *Maya Society Under Colonial Rule: The Collective Enterprise of Survival*. Princeton University Press: Princeton.

Federación Iberoamericana del Ombudsman (2008) *Colombia: Sancionada ley que protege a mujeres contra la violencia*. [WWW document]. 15 December. URL http://www.portalfio.org/inicio/noticias/item/2003-colombia-sancionada-ley-que-protege-a-mujeres-contra-la-violencia.html [accessed 1 September 2013].

Feierstein, D. (2000) *Seis estudios sobre genocidio: Análisis de las relaciones sociales otredad, exclusión y exterminio*. EUDEBA: Buenos Aires.

Feitlowitz, M. (1998) *A Lexicon of Terror. Argentina and the Legacies of Torture*. New York: Oxford University Press.

Ferrari, G. and Gallo, E. (eds.) (1980) *La Argentina del ochenta al Centenario*. Sudamericana: Buenos Aires.

Ferry, R. J. (2006) *Margarita Moreira: amores, amistades, y los grupos de cripto-judíos portugueses en México, siglo XVII*. Coloquios: Nuevo Mundo Mundos Nuevos.

Few, M. (2012) 'Medical Humanitarianism and Smallpox Inoculation in Eighteenth-Century Guatemala'. *Historical Social Research/Historische Sozialforschung* **37**(3): 303–317.

Figueroa Ibarra, C. (1991) *El recurso del miedo. Ensayo sobre el estado y el terror en Guatemala*. Editorial Educa: San José.

Figueroa Ibarra, C. (1999) *Los que siempre estarán en ninguna parte: La desaparición forzada en Guatemala (1960–1996)*. Instituto de Ciencias Sociales y Humanidades de la Benemérita Universidad Autónoma de Puebla/Grupo de Apoyo Mutuo (GAM)/Centro Internacional para Investigaciones en Derechos Humanos: México DF.

Figueroa Ibarra, C. (2001) 'Naturaleza y racionalidad de la violencia' in S. Tischler Vizquerra and G. Carnero Roqué (eds.) *Conflicto, violencia y teoría social. Una agenda sociológica*. Universidad Iberoamericana Golfo Centro y Benemérita Universidad Autónoma de Puebla: Mexico City, 13–28.

Figueroa Ibarra, C. (2002) 'Terrorismo y doble moral'. *Revista Bajo el Volcán* **4**(2): 15–28.

Figueroa Ibarra, C. (2004) 'Cultura del terror y guerra fría en Guatemala' in D. Feierstein and G. Levy (eds.) *Hasta que la muerte nos separe. Poder y prácticas sociales genocidas en América Latina*. Ediciones al Margen: Buenos Aires, 391–403.

Figueroa Ibarra, C. (2005) 'Veintiún tesis sobre la violencia política en Guatemala' in F. Escárzaga and R. Gutiérrez (eds.) *Movimiento indígena en América Latina: resistencia y proyecto alternativo*. Casa Juan Pablos, Gobierno del Distrito Federal, Benemérita Universidad Autónoma de Puebla, Universidad Nacional Autónoma de México, Universidad Autónoma de la Ciudad de México: México D.F, 117–132.

Figueroa Ibarra, C. (2006) 'The Culture of Terror and Cold War in Guatemala'. *Journal of Genocide Research* **8**(2): 191–208.

Figueroa Ibarra, C. (2010) *El recurso del miedo. Estado y Terror en Guatemala*. F&G Editores/Instituto de Ciencias Sociales y Humanidades 'Alfonso Vélez Pliego' de la Benemérita Universidad Autónoma de Puebla. Segunda edición corregida y aumentada: Guatemala.

Flanet, V. [1977] (1989). *Viviré si Dios quiere. Un estudio de la violencia en la mixteca de la costa*. Dirección General de Publicaciones del Consejo Nacional para la Cultura y las Artes: Mexico City.

Fletcher, J. (1997) *Violence and Civilisation: An Introduction to the work of Norbert Elias*. Polity Press: Cambridge.

Flores Galindo, A. (1988) *Tiempo de plagas*. Lima: El Caballo Rojo Ediciones.

Flores Galindo, A. (1994) *Buscando un Inca*, 4th edn. Lima: Editorial Horizonte.

Forment, C. A. (2003) *Democracy in Latin America, 1760–1900*. University of Chicago Press: Chicago.

Foucault, M. (1979) *Discipline and Punish: The Birth of the Prison*. Vintage Books: New York.

Foucault, M. (1990) *The History of Sexuality: An Introduction*, Vol. 1. Vintage Books: New York.

Foucault, M. (2003) *Society Must be Defended. Lectures at the Collège de France 1975–1976*. Picador: New York.

Franco, J. (2006) 'Alien to Modernity: The Rationalisation of Discrimination'. *A Contracorriente* 3(3): 1–16.

Frazer, C. (2006) *Bandit Nation: A History of Outlaws and Cultural Struggle in Mexico, 1810–1920*. University of Nebraska Press: Lincoln.

Friedrich, P. (1977) *Agrarian Revolt in a Mexican Village*. University of Chicago Press: Chicago.

Friedrich, P. (1987) *The Princes of Naranja: An Essay in Anthrohistorical Method*. University of Texas Press: Austin.

Frühling, H. and Tulchin, J. (eds.) (2005) *Crimen y violencia en América Latina: Seguridad ciudadana, democracia y Estado*. Fondo de Cultura Económica: Bogotá.

Fuentes, C. (1997) *A New Time for Mexico*. Bloomsbury: London.

Fuller, G. A. and Forrest, R. P. (1990) 'Youth Cohorts and Political Unrest in South Korea'. *Political Geography Quarterly* 9: 9–22.

Funes, P. (2001) 'Nunca Más. Memorias de las dictaduras en América Latina' in B. Groppo and P. Flier (eds.) *La imposibilidad del olvido. Recorridos de la memoria en Argentina. Chile y Uruguay*. Ediciones Al Margen: La Plata, 43–61.

Gabbert, W. (2012) 'The Longue Durée of Colonial Violence in Latin America'. *Historical Social Research/Historische Sozialforschung* 37(3): 254–275.

Gaitán, J. E. (1945) (1968a) 'Discurso Programa de su Candidatura Presidencial' in *Los Mejores Discursos de Gaitán*, 2nd edn. Editorial Jorvi: Bogotá, 391–406.

Gaitán, J. E. (1946) (1968b). 'El Hombre Realidad Biológica y Social' in *Los Mejores Discursos de Gaitán*, 2nd edn. Editorial Jorvi: Bogotá, 464–479.

Gaitán, J. E. [1946] (1979) 'Los Partidos Políticos en Colombia' in J. M. Eastman Vélez (ed.) *Obras Selectas*.Imprenta Nacional: Bogotá, 191–202.

Galeano, E. (1969) *Guatemala país ocupado*. México, DF: Editorial Nuestro Tiempo.

Galeano, D. (2008) 'En nombre de la seguridad. Lecturas sobre policía y formación estatal'. *Cuestiones de Sociología* 4: 102–128.

García, P. (1995) *El drama de la autonomía military: Argentina bajo las juntas militares*. Alianza: Madrid.

García Basalo, J. C. (1979) *Historia de la Penitenciaría de Buenos Aires, 1869–1880*. Servicio Penitenciario Federal: Buenos Aires.

García Peña, A. L. (2006) *El fracaso del amor. Género e individualismo en el siglo XIX mexicano*. El Colegio de México, Universidad Autónoma del Estado México: México.

García-Alejo, R. H. (1991) *El delincuente y su patología: Medicina, crimen y sociedad en el Positivismo argentino*. Consejo Superior de Investigaciones Científicas: Madrid.

Gargarella, R. (1996) *La justicia frente al gobierno: Sobre el carácter contramayoritario del poder judicial*. Ariel: Buenos Aires.

Garland, D. (2001) *The Culture of Control. Crime and Social Order in Contemporary Society*. University of Chicago Press: Chicago.

Garner, P. (2001) *Porfirio Díaz*. Longman: London.

Gat, A. (2006) *War in Human Civilisation*. Oxford University Press: Oxford .

Gaviria, A. and C. Pagés (1999) *Patterns of Crime Victimization in Latin* America. Inter-American Bank Conference on Economic and Social Progress in Latin America: Washington.

Gayol, S. (2000) *Sociabilidad en Buenos Aires: Hombres, honour y cafés 1862–1910*. Ediciones del Signo: Buenos Aires.

Gayol, S. (2004) '"Honor Moderno": The Significance of Honor in fin-de-siécle Argentina'. *Hispanic American Historical Review* **84**(3): 475–498.

Gayol, S. (2008) *Honor y duelo en la Argentina moderna*. Siglo Veintiuno: Buenos Aires.

Gayol, S. and Kessler, G. (eds.) (2002) *Violencias, delitos y justicias en la Argentina*. Manantial/Universidad Nacional de General Belgrano: Buenos Aires.

'Gender and Sexuality in Latin America' (2001) *Hispanic American Historical Review* (special Issue) **81**(3–4).

Geneva Declaration Secretariat (2008) *Global Burden of Armed Violence Report*. Geneva Declaration on Armed Violence and Development: Geneva.

Genovés, S. (1993) *Expedición a la violencia*. Fondo de Cultura Económica: México DF.

Gillingham, J. [1982] (2005a) *The Wars of the Roses*. The Phoenix Press: London.

Gillingham, P. (2005b) *Force and Consent in Mexican Provincial Politics: Guerrero and Veracruz, 1945–53*. Unpublished doctoral dissertation: Oxford University, Oxford.

Gillingham, P. (2010) 'Maximino's Bulls: Popular Protest after the Mexican Revolution'. *Past and Present* **206**.

Ginzburg, E. (1997) 'Ideología, política y la cuestión de las prioridades: Lázaro Cárdenas y Adalberto Tejeda, 1928–34'. *Mexican Studies/Estudios Mexicanos* **13**(1): 55–85.

Gledhill, J. (1990) *Casi Nada: A Study of Agrarian Reform in the Homeland of Cardenismo*. Institute for Mesoamerican Studies: Albany.

Goldstone, J. A. (1991) *Revolution and Rebellion in the Early Modern World*. University of California Press: Berkeley.

Gómez, L. (1970) *Interrogantes sobre el Progreso de Colombia*. Populibro: Bogotá.

Gómez, L. [1933] (1981) 'Victoria, No! Barbarie' in *Obras Selectas* (ed. Alberto Bermúdez), Vol. XV. Cámara de Representantes: Bogotá, 246–248.

Gómez, L. (1981) 'Colección' *Obras Selectas* (ed. Alberto Bermúdez), Vol. XV. Cámara de Representantes: Bogotá.

González, R. (1983) 'Ayacucho: la espera del gaucho. Entrevista a Luis Cisneros Vizquerra'. *Quehacer* **24**: 46–57.

González, F. E., Bolívar, I. J. and Vásquez, T. (2003) *Violencia política en Colombia: De la nación fragmentada a la construcción del estado*. Centro de Investigación y Educación Popular. CINEP: Bogotá.

González, L. (1972) *Pueblo en vilo. Microhistoria de San José de Gracia*. El Colegio de México: México.

González Bombal, I. (1995) 'Nunca Más: El juicio más allá de los estrados' in C. Acuña, A. Vacchieri, C. Smulovitz, E. Jelin, I. González Bombal, L. Alberto Quevedo, O. Landi (eds.) *Juicio, castigos y memorias. Derechos Humanos y justicia en la política Argentina*. Nueva Visión: Buenos Aires, 193–216.

González Bombal, I. and Landi, O. (1995) 'Los derechos en la cultura política' in C. Acuña, A. Vacchieri, C. Smulovitz, E. Jelin, I. González Bombal, L. Alberto

Quevedo, O. Landi (eds.) *Juicio, castigos y memorias. Derechos Humanos y justicia en la política Argentina.* Nueva Visión: Buenos Aires, 147–192.

González Montes, S. (1998) 'La violencia doméstica y sus repercusiones en la salud reproductiva en una zona indígena (Cuetzalan, Puebla)' in *Los silencios de la salud reproductiva: Violencia, sexualidad y derechos reproductivos.* Asociación Mexicana de Población: México, 17–54.

González Montes, S. and Iracheta Cenegorta P. (1987) 'La violencia en la vida de las mujeres campesinas: el Distrito de Tenango, 1880–1910' in C. Ramos et al. (eds.) *Presencia y transparencia de la mujer en la historia de México.* El Colegio de México: México, 111–141.

Goodman, J. (2009) *The Devil and Mr. Casement: One Man's Battle for Human Rights in South America's Heart of Darkness.* New York: Farrar, Strauss and Giroux.

Gootenberg, P. (1991) "North–South: Trade Policy, Regionalism and Caudillismo in Post-Independence Peru". *Journal of Latin American Studies* **23**(2): 273–308.

Gorriti, G. (1982) 'Sendero en El Frontón'. *Caretas* **715**(20–23): 64–65.

Gorriti, G. (1999) *The Shining Path: A History of the Millenarian War in Peru.* University of North Carolina Press: Chapel Hill.

Granados-Shiroma, M. and Madrigal, R. (1998) 'Salud reproductiva y violencia contra la mujer. Un analisis desde la perspectiva de género (El caso de la zona Metropolitana de Monterrey' in S. González Montes (ed.) *Los silencios de la salud reproductiva: violencia, sexualidad y derechos reproductivos.* Asociación Mexicana de Población: México, 107–133.

Grandin, G. (2004) *The Last Colonial Massacre: Latin America in the Cold War.* University of Chicago Press: Chicago.

Grandin, G. (2005) 'The Instruction of Great Catastrophe: Truth commissions, National History, and State Formation in Argentina, Chile and Guatemala'. *American Historical Review* **10**(1): 46–67.

Graziano, F. (1992) *Divine Violence: Spectacle, Psychosexuality, and Radical Christianity in the Argentine 'Dirty War'.* Westview Press: Boulder.

Greenberg, J. (1989) *Blood Ties: Life and Violence in Rural Mexico.* University of Arizona Press: Tucson.

Guatemala Human Rights Commission/USA, Guatemala Peace and Development Network, and New York Office of the Rigoberta Menchu Foundation (2003) *Guatemala: Corrupting State and Society, Foundation for Human Rights in Guatemala.* [WWW document].May. URL http://www.ghrc-usa.org/resources/redporlapaz.pdf [accessed 20 August 2007].

Guerra, F. (2000) *Modernidad e Independencias: Ensayos Sobre Las Revoluciones Hispánicas.* Editorial MAPFRE/Fondo de Cultura Económica: Madrid, Mexico City.

Guerrero, J. [1901] (1996) *La génesis del crimen en México.* Consejo Nacional para la Cultura y las Artes: Mexico.

Gutmann, M. C. (1994) 'Los hijos de Lewis: la sensibilidad antropológica y el caso de los pobres machos'. *Alteridades* **4**(7): 9–19.

Gutmann, M. (1996) *The Meanings of Macho: Being a Man in Mexico City.* University of California Press: Berkeley.

Guy, D. J. (1994) *El sexo peligroso: La prostitución legal en Buenos Aires 1875–1955.* Editorial Sudamericana: Buenos Aires.

Guzmán, A. [1988] (1991) *Interview with Chairman Gonzalo. Interview with the Chairman of the Central Committee of the Communist Party of Peru.* El Diario The Committee to Support the Revolution in Peru: Berkeley.

Guzmán Campos, G. (1986) 'Reflexión crítica sobre el libro 'La Violencia en Colombia' in G. Sánchez Gómez, R. Plänalanda (eds.) *Pasado y Presente de la Violencia en Colombia'.* Fondo Editorial CEREC: Bogotá, 349–3760.

Guzmán Campos, G., Fals Borda, O. and Umaña Luna, E. [1962] (2005) *La violencia en Colombia: Estudio de un proceso social,* Vol. 1. Editora Aguilar: Bogotá.

Habermas, J. (1991) *The Structural Transformation of the Public Sphere: An Inquiry into a Category of Bourgeois Society.* MIT Press: Cambridge.

Hagan, J., Castro, B. and Rodriguez, N. (2008) 'The Effects of US Deportation Policies on Immigrant Families and Communities: Cross-Border Perspectives'. *North Carolina Law Review* **88**: 1800–1824.

Halbwachs, M. [1925] (2004) *Los marcos sociales de la memoria.* Anthropos: Barcelona.

Hamnett, B. (1999) *A Concise History of Mexico.* Cambridge University Press: Cambridge.

Harff, B. (2005) '¿No se aprendieron las lecciones del holocausto? Evaluando los riesgos de genocidio y matanzas políticas desde 1955' in D. Feiernstein (ed.) *Genocidio: La administración de la muerte en la modernidad.* EDUNTREF: Buenos Aires, 171–2100.

Harvey, A., García-Moreno, C. and Butchart, A. (2007) *Primary Prevention of Intimate-Partner Violence and Sexual Violence: Background Paper for WHO Expert Meeting, May 2–3, 2007.* World Health Organisation: Geneva.

Haya de la Torre, A. (1988) *El retorno de la barbarie: La matanza de los penales de Lima en 1986.* 2nd Edition. Bahía Ediciones: Lima.

Hayden, T. (2004) *Street Wars Gangs and the Future of Violence.* The New Press: New York.

Hayner, P. (1994) 'Fifteen Truth Commissions 1974 to 1994: A Comparative Study'. *Human Rights Quarterly* **16**(4): 597–655.

Hayner, P. (2001) *Unspeakable Truth: Confronting State Terror and Atrocity.* Routledge: New York.

Heise, L. L. and García-Moreno, C. (2002) 'Violence by Intimate Partners' in E. G. Krug, L. L. Dahlberg, J. A. Mercy, A. B. Zwi and R. Lozano (eds.) *World Report on Violence and Health.* World Health Organisation: Geneva, 87–113.

Heise, L. L., Ellsberg, M. and Gottemoeller, M. (1999) *Ending Violence Against Women.* Johns Hopkins University School of Public Health-Centre for Communications. Programmes: Baltimore.

Helg, A. (1987) *La Educación en Colombia 1918–1957. Una Historia Social, Económica y Política.* Fondo Editorial Cerec: Bogotá.

Helg, A. (1989) 'Los intelectuales frente a la cuestión racial en el decenio de 1920: Colombia entre México y Argentina'. *Estudios Sociales* **4**: 37–53.

Helú, A. [1946] (1991) *La obligación de asesinar.* Consejo Nacional para la Cultura y las Artes: México DF.

Henderson, J. D. (1988) *Conservative Thought in Twentieth Century Latin America: The Ideas of Laureano Gómez.* Ohio University Press: Athens.

Henderson, T. J. (1998) *The Worm in the Wheat. Rosalie Evans and Agrarian Struggle in the Puebla-Tlaxcala Valley of Mexico, 1906–27.* Duke University Press: Durham.

Henderson, T. (2007) *A Glorious Defeat: Mexico and its War with the United States*. Hill and Wang: New York.

Hewitt, J. D. and Hoover, D. W. (1982) 'Local Modernization and Crime: The Effects of Modernization on Crime in Middletown, 1845–1910'. *Law and Human Behaviour* 6(3–4): 313–325.

Higonnet, E. (ed.) (2009) *Quiet Genocide: Guatemala 1981–1983*. Transaction Publishers: Piscataway.

Hill, C. (1975) *The World Turned Upside Down: Radical Ideas during the English Revolution*. Penguin Books: Harmondsworth.

Hindess, B. (1996) *Discourses of Power: From Hobbes to Foucault*. Blackwell : Oxford.

Hobbes, T. [1651] (1998) *Leviathan*. World's Classics: Oxford.

Hobsbawm, E. J. (1985) *'La Anatomía de "La Violencia en Colombia"'* in. Fondo Editorial Cerec (ed.). Centro Gaitán Fondo Editorial CEREC: Bogotá, 11–24.

Horrobin, D. F. (2001) *The Madness of Adam and Eve: How Schizophrenia Shaped Humanity*. Bantam Books: London.

Houston, S. D. (2001) 'Decorous Bodies and Disordered Passions: Representations of Emotion Among the Classic Maya'. *World Archaeology* 33(2): 206–219.

Howard, G. J., Newman, G. and Pridemore, W. A. (2000) 'Theory, Method, and Data in Comparative Criminology'. *Criminal Justice* 4(July).

Huatay, M. (2002) *Written testimony to the Comisión de la Verdad y Reconciliación. August*. Centro de Información para la Memoria Colectiva y los Derechos Humanos: Lima.

Hu-Dehart, E. (1984) *Yaqui Resistance and Survival: The Struggle for Land and Autonomy, 1821–1910*. University of Wisconsin Press: Madison.

Hudson, W. W. and Mcintosh, S. R. (1981) 'The Assessment of Spouse Abuse: Two Quantifiable Dimensions'. *Journal of Marriage and the Family* 43(November): 873–885.

Huggins, M. K. (ed.) (1991) *Vigilantism and the State in Modern Latin America: Essays in Extralegal Violence*. Praeger: Westport.

Human Rights Watch (2007) *World Report, 2007*. [WWW document]. URL http://www.hrw.org/wr2k7/wr2007master.pdf [accessed 24 August 2007], 206–210.

Hunefeldt, C. (2000) *Liberalism in the Bedroom: Quarreling Spouses in Nineteenth-Century Lima*. Pennsylvania State University Press: University Park.

Hunt, L. (2004) 'The 18th Century Body and the Origins of Human Rights'. *Diogenes* 51: 41–56.

Huyssen, A. (2002) *En busca del futuro pérdido: cultura y memoria en tiempos de globalización*. Fondo de Cultura Económica: Mexico.

Hylton, F. (2006) *Evil Hour in Colombia*. Verso: London.

ICESI (2010) *Encuesta Nacional de Inseguridad*. Instituto Ciudadano de Estudios sobre la Inseguridad, A.C.- Instituto Nacional de Estadística, Geografía e Informática: Mexico City.

INEGI (Instituto Nacional de Estadística Geografía e Informática) (2001) *Violencia intrafamiliar. Encuesta, 1999: Documento metodológico y resultados*. INEGI: Aguascalientes: Mexico City.

INEGI (2005) *Sistema para la consulta del Cuaderno Estadístico Municipal de Nuevo Laredo*. INEGI: Tamaulipas.

INEGI (2006a) *Sistema para la consulta del Anuario Estadístico del Distrito Federal*. INEGI.

INEGI (2006b) *Sistema para la consulta del Cuaderno Estadístico Municipal Juárez.* INEGI: Chihuahua.

InSight Crime (2012) '100 Days into Gang Truce, El Salvador Sizes Up Security Gains'. [WWW document]. InSight Crime, 18 June. URL http:// www.insightcrime.org/news-briefs/100-days-into-gang-truce-el-salvador-sizes-up-security-gains [accessed ?].

InSight Crime (2013) 'El Salvador Sees 45% Drop in Murders: Police'. [WWW document]. InSight Crime, 2 May. URL http://www.insightcrime.org/news-briefs/el-salvador-homicides-gang-truce-2013 [accessed 4 June 2013].

Instituto Nacional de Estadística (2005) *Encuesta nacional sobre condiciones de vida ENCOVI 2000. Guatemala.* Instituto Nacional de Estadística (INE): Guatemala.

Instituto Nacional de Estadística y Geografía (INEGI) (2003) *Encuesta Nacional Sobre la Dinámica de las Relaciones en los Hogares* (ENDIREH). [WWW document]. URL http://www.inegi.org.mx/sistemas/microdatos2/encuestas.aspx?c=26278&s=est [accessed 3 September 2013].

Instituto Nacional de Salud Pública (2003) (Coord. Gral. G. Olaiz, B. Rico, and A. el Rio) *Encuesta Nacional Sobre Violencia Contra las Mujeres,* Mexico.

Inter-American Commission on Human Rights (1980) *Report on the situation of Human Rights in Argentina.* Organisation of American States: Washington.

Isla, A. (2007) 'Delincuencia y militancia en los años setenta' in A. Isla (ed.) *En los márgenes de la ley. Inseguridad y violencia en el Cono Sur.* Ediciones Paidós Ibérica: Buenos Aires, 101–126.

Izaguirre, I. (1997) 'El poder en proceso: la violencia que no se ve'. Unpublished paper delivered at the XXI Congreso de la Asociación Latinoamericana de Sociología. Sao Paulo: Brazil.

Jacobsen, N. and Puhle, H. (1986) *The Economies of Mexico and Peru during the Late Colonial Period.* Colloquim Verlag: Munich.

Jelin, E. (1995) 'La política de la memoria: el movimiento de derechos humanos y la construcción de la democracia en Argentina' in C. Acuña, A. Vacchieri, C. Smulovitz, E. Jelin, I. González Bombal, L. Alberto Quevedo, O. Landi (eds.) *Juicio, castigos y memorias. Derechos humanos y justicia en la política Argentina.* Nueva Visión: Buenos Aires, 101–146.

Johnson, E. A. (1982) 'The Roots of Crime in Imperial Germany'. *Central European History* **15**(4): 351–376.

Johnson, E. A. (1995) *Urbanisation and Crime: Germany 1871–1914.* Cambridge University Press: New York.

Johnson, E. A. (2002) *El terror nazi. La Gestapo, los judíos y el pueblo alemán.* Editorial Paidós: Barcelona.

Johnson, E. A. and Monkkonen, E. H. (eds.) (1996) *The Civilisation of Crime: Violence in Town and Country since the Middle Ages.* University of Illinois Press: Urbana.

Johnson, E. A., Salvatore, R. D. and Spierenburg, P. (2012) 'Murder and Mass Murder in Pre Modern Latin America: From Pre-Colonial Aztec Sacrifices to the End of Colonial Rule, an Introductory Comparison with European Societies'. *Historical Social Research/Historische Sozialforschung* **37**(3): 233–253.

Johnson, L. (ed.) (1990) *The Problem of Order in Changing Societies: Essays on Crime and Policing in Argentina and Uruguay, 1750–1940.* University of New Mexico Press: Albuquerque.

Jonas, S. (2000) *Of Centaurs and Doves: Guatemala's Peace Process.* Westview: Boulder.

References 291

Jones, A. (2005) 'Enfrentando al generocidio' in D. Feiernstein (ed.) *Genocidio: La administración de la muerte en la modernidad*. EDUNTREF: Buenos Aires, 211–238.

Kalifa, D. (1995) *L'encre et le sang: Récits de crimes et société à la Belle Epoque*. Fayard: Paris.

Kalmanovitz, S. (1974) 'Evolución de la estructura agraria colombiana'. *Cuadernos Colombianos* **3**: 353–405.

Kampwirth, K. W. (1996) 'The Mother of the Nicaraguans: Doña Violeta Chamorro and the UNO´s Gender Agenda'. *Latin American Perspectives* **23**(1): 67–86.

Kaplan, M. (1976) *Formación del estado nacional en América Latina*, 2nd edn. Amorrortu: Buenos Aires.

Katz, F. (1980) *The Secret War in Mexico: Europe, the United States and the Mexican Revolution*. University of Chicago Press: Chicago.

Katz, F. (1998) *The Life and Times of Pancho Villa*. Stanford University Press: Stanford.

Keane, J. (1996) *Reflections on Violence*. Verso: London.

Keeley, L. H. (1996) *War Before Civilisation: The Myth of the Peaceful Savage*. Oxford University Press: New York.

Keen, S. (1991) *Faces of the Enemy: Reflections of the Hostile Imagination*. Harper Collins: New York.

Kelley, F. C. (1916) *The Book of Red and Yellow*. Catholic Church Extension Society: Chicago.

Kessler, G. (2009) *El sentimiento de inseguridad: Sociología del temor al delito*. Buenos Aires: Siglo XXI.

Klevens, J. (2001) 'Violencia física contra la mujer en Santa Fé de Bogotá: Prevalencia y factores asociados'. *Revista Panamericana de Salud Pública* **9**(32): 78–83.

Kluckhohn, F. L. (1939) *The Mexican Challenge*. Doubleday and Doran: New York.

Knight, A. (1986a) *The Mexican Revolution*, Vol. **1**. Cambridge University Press: Cambridge and New York.

Knight, A. (1986b) *The Mexican Revolution*, Vol. **2**. Cambridge University Press: Cambridge and New York.

Knight, A. (1990) 'Social Revolution: A Latin American Perspective'. *Bulletin of Latin American Research* **9**(2): 175–202.

Knight, A. (1992) 'Mexico's Elite Settlement: Conjuncture and Consequences' in J. Higley and R. Gunther (eds.) *Elites and Democratic Consolidation in Latin America and Southern Europe*. Cambridge University Press: Cambridge.

Knight, A. (1996) 'México bronco, México manso: una reflexión sobre la cultura cívica mexicana'. *Política y gobierno* **3**(1): 5–30.

Knight, A. (1997) 'Habitus and Homicide: Political Culture in Revolutionary Mexico' in W. Pansters (ed.) *Citizens of the Pyramid: Essays on Mexican Political Culture*. Thela: Amsterdam.

Knight, A. (1999) 'Political Violence in Postrevolutionary Mexico' in K. Koonings and D. Kruijt (eds.) *Societies of Fear: The Legacy of Civil War, Violence and Terror in Latin America*. Zed Books: London.

Knight, A. (2002a) *Mexico: From the Begining to the Spanish Conquest*. Cambridge University Press: Cambridge.

Knight, A. (2002b) 'The Weight of the State in Modern Mexico' in J. Dunkerley (ed.) *Studies in the Formation of the Nation State in Latin America*. Institute of Latin American Studies: London.

Knight, A. (2003) 'The Domestic Dynamics of the Mexican and Bolivian Revolutions' in M. S. Grindle and P. Domingo (eds.) *Proclaiming Revolution: Bolivia in Comparative Perspective*. Harvard Universty Press: Cambridge.

Knight, A. (2006) 'Patterns and Prescriptions in Mexican Historiography'. *Bulletin of Latin American Research* 25(3): 340–66.

Knight, A. (2007a) 'Hegemony, Counterhegemony and the Mexican Revolution' in J. Chalcraft and Y. Noorani (eds.) *Counterhegemony in the Colony and Postcolony*. Palgrave-MacMillan: Basingstoke.

Knight, A. (2007b) 'Las relaciones iglesia-estado en el México revolucionario, 1910-40' in F. J. Lorenzo Piñar (ed.) *Tolerancia y fundamentalismos en la historia*. XVI Jornadas de Estudios Históricos, Universidad de Salamanca: Salamanca.

Knight, A. (2008) 'La cultura política mexicana' in A. Knight et al. (eds.) *La conflictiva y nunca acabada construcción de la democraca deseada*. Porrúa: Mexico.

Krauze, E. (1987) *Vértigo de la victoria: Alvaro Obregón*. Fondo de Cultura Económica: Mexico.

Krauze, E. (1997) *Mexico: Biography of Power*. Harper Collins: New York.

Kritz, N. (ed.) (1995) *Transitional Justice: How Emerging Democracies Reckon with Former Regimes*. Institute of Peace: Washington.

Krupa, C. (2009) 'Histories in Red: Ways of Seeing Lynching in Educador'. *American Ethnologist* 36(1): 20–39.

Kuenzi, M. (2006) 'Crime, Security, and Support for Democracy in Africa'. Unpublished paper delivered at the annual meeting of the Midwest Political Science Association, Palmer House Hotel, , 20–23 April, Chicago, IL.

La Jornada (2004) 'En su propia voz'. *La Jornada*, 28 June, 1–13.

La Prensa (1934) 'El crimen de Tacubaya ha conmovido hondamente a la sociedad'. *La Prensa*, 28 April, 3.

Laclau, E. (1972) *Feudalismo y capitalismo en América Latina. A.* Barcelona: Redondo.

Lahmeyer, J. (n.d.) *Population Statistics*. [WWW document]. URL http://www.populstat.info/ [accessed 1 May 2011].

Lang, M. (2003) 'Políticas públicas, violencia de género y feminismo en México durante los últimos sexenios PRIistas'. Unpublished paper delivered at the II Coloquio Internacional de Historia de Mujeres y de Género en México. September: Guadalajara.

Langel, A. (1942) *Ultimas Noticias*, 22 September, 1.

Langue, F. (2007) *Sensibilidades alternas: Nobles americanos, entre fueros y compadrazgos*. Coloquios: Nuevo Mundo Mundos Nuevos.

Langue, F. (2008) *Bolívar, Mantuano y Héroe: Representaciones y sensibilidades ante el mito republicano*. Coloquios: Nuevo Mundo Mundos Nuevos.

Laqueur, T. (1989) 'Bodies, Details, and the Humanitarian Narrative' in L. Hunt (ed.) *The New Cultural History*. University of California Press: Berkeley and Los Angeles, 176–204.

Lasch, C. (1985) 'Historical Sociology and the Myth of Maturity: Norbert Elias's "Very Simple Formula"'. *Theory and Society* 14(5): 705–720.

Lavrin, A. (1995) *Women, Feminism and Social Change in Argentina, Chile and Uruguay, 1890–1940*. University of Nebraska Press: Lincoln.

Lefebvre, G. [1932] (1973) *The Great Fear of 1789*. Vintage Books: New York.

LeGrand, C. (1997) 'La política y La Violencia en Colombia, 1946–1965: Interpretaciones en la década de los ochenta'. *Memoria y Sociedad* **4**: 79–109.

LeGrand, C. (2008) *'An Exploratory Essay on Legal Narratives on Citizenship and Rights in Colombia during a Period of Political Transition and the Dawning of the Social Question, 1915–1929'*. Unpublished paper delivered at the CALACS. Congress: Vancouver.

LeoGrande, W. M. (1998) *Our Own Backyard: The United States in Central America, 1977–1992*. University of North Carolina Press: Chapel Hill.

León de Leal, M. and Deere, C. D. (2001) *Empowering Women: Land and Property Rights in Latin America*. University of Pittsburgh Press: Pittsburgh.

León de Leal, M. and Rodríguez Sáenz, E. (eds.) (2005) *Ruptura de la inequidad? Propiedad y género en la América Latina del Siglo XIX*. Pontificia Universidad Javeriana: Bogotá.

Lerner, J. (2007) *El Impacto De La Modernidad: Fotografía Criminalística En La Ciudad De México*. Turner, Consejo Nacional para la Cultura y las Artes, Instituto Nacional de Antropología e Historia, Editorial Océano: Mexico City.

Levenson, D. (1989) 'Las "maras": Violencia juvenil de masas'. *Polémica* **7**(2): 2–12.

Levitt, S. and Dubner, S. J. (2005) *Freakonomics*. William Morrow: New York.

Lewis, O. (1961) *The Children of Sánchez. Autobiography of a Mexican Family*. Random House: New York.

Linz, J. (1978) *The Breakdown of Democratic Regimes: Crisis, Breakdown, and Reequilibration*. The Johns Hopkins University Press: Baltimore.

Lomnitz-Adler, C. (2005) *Death and the Idea of Mexico*. Zone Books, distributed by MIT Press: Brooklyn, NY, Cambridge.

López Alves, F. (2000) *State Formation and Democracy in Latin America*. Duke University Press: Durham.

López de Mesa, L. (1920) *Los Problemas de la Raza en Colombia*. Biblioteca de la Cultura: Bogotá.

López de Mesa, L. (1935) *Gestión Administrativa y Perspectiva del Ministerio de Educación – 1935*. Imprenta Nacional: Bogotá.

López Pumarejo, A. [1934] (1979) *López Pumarejo Obras Selectas. Primera Parte (1926–1937)*. Cámara de Representantes. Colección Pensadores Políticos Colombianos: Bogotá.

López Pumarejo, A. [1934] (1986) 'Mensaje Presidencial al Congreso sobre Educación Nacional, el 17 de diciembre de 1934' in A. Tirado Mejía (ed.) *El Pensamiento de Alfonso López Pumarejo*. Biblioteca Banco Popular: Bogotá, 221–226.

López Pumarejo, Alfonso [1936] (2002) 'La Transformación del Temperamento Nacional' quoted in M. Hernández Alvarez, *La Salud Fragmentada en Colombia*. Universidad Nacional de Colombia: Bogotá.

Losada, L. (2009) *Historia de las elites en la Argentina*. Buenos Aires: Editorial Sudamericana.

Luna, A. L. (1993) *La Crónica Policíaca En México: Nota Roja 40s*. Diana: Mexico City.

Lungo, Mario (1996) *El Salvador in the Eighties: Counterinsurgency and Revolution*. (ed. A. Schmidt, trans. A. F. Shogan). Temple University Press: Philadelphia.

Lynch, J. (1998) *Massacre in the Pampas, 1872: Britain and Argentina in the Age of Migration*. University of Oklahoma Press: Norman.

Macera, P. (1986) 'El 18 de Junio'. *Debate* **39**: 39–44.

Macías González, V. M. (2009) 'The Case of the Murdering Beauty: Narrative Construction, Beauty Pageants, and the Postrevolutionary Mexican National Myth, 1921–1931' in R. Buffington and P. Piccato (eds.) *True Stories of Crime in Modern Mexico*. University of New Mexico Press: Albuquerque.

Maestre, J. (1969) *Guatemala: violencia y subdesarrollo*. IEPALA: Madrid.

Mallon, F. E. (2002) 'Decoding the Parchments of the Latin American Nation-State: Peru, Mexio, and Chile in Comparative Perspective' in J. Dunkerley (ed.) *Studies in the Formation of the Nation-State in Latin America*. University of London, Institute of Latin American Studies: London, 13–53.

Mantilla, S. (2013) 'Frente al Pelotón: Prensa y pena de muerte entre 1887 y 1922' in R. Salvatore and O. Barreneche (eds.) *El delito y el orden en perspectiva histórica*. Ediciones Pro-Historia: Santa Fé, 121–138.

Marchesi, A. (2001) *Las lecciones del pasado, memoria y ciudadanía en los informes Nunca Más del Cono Sur*. Facultad de Humanidades y Ciencias de la Educación-Montevideo, unpublished.

Marín Castillo, J. (1964) 'Una antigua teoría'. *Revista de Policía*, September, **23**(283): 28.

Markarian, V. (2006) *Idos y recién llegados. La izquierda uruguaya en el exilio y las redes transnacionales de Derechos Humanos 1967–1984*. Uribe y Ferrari Editores: Mexico.

Márquez Valderrama, J., Casas Orrego, A. and Estrada Orrego, V. E. (2004) *Higienizar, Medicar, Gobernar: Historia, Medicina y Sociedad en Colombia*. Universidad Nacional de Colombia: Medellín.

Marshall, L. L. (1992) 'Development of the Severity of Violence against Women Scales'. *Journal of Family Violence* **7**(2): 103–121.

Marteau, J. F. (2003) *Las plabras del orden: Proyecto republicano y cuestión criminal en Argentina, Buenos Aires: 1880–1930*. Editores del Puerto: Buenos Aires.

Matos Rodríguez, F. V. (1999) *Women and Urban Change in San Juan Puerto Rico, 1820–1868*. University of Florida Press: Gainesville.

McCaa, R. (2000) 'The Peopling of Mexico from Origins to Revolution' in R. Steckel and M. Heines (eds.) *The Population History of North America*. Cambridge University Press: Cambridge, 241–304.

McCaa, R. (2003) 'The Missing Millions: The Demographic Cost of the Mexican Revolution'. *Mexican Studies/Estudios Mexicanos* **19**(2): 367–400.

McCleary, R. (1997) 'Guatemala's Postwar Prospects'. *Journal of Democracy* **8**: 2.

McClintock, C. (1998) *Revolutionary Movements in Latin America: El Salvador's FMLN and Peru's Shining Path*. United States Institute of Peace Press: Washington, DC.

McFarlane, A. (1995) 'Rebellions in Late Colonial Spanish America: A Comparative Perspective'. *Bulletin of Latin American Research* **14**(3): 313–338.

McGee Deutsch, S. (1991) 'Gender and Sociopolitical Change in Twentieth Century Latin America'. *Hispanic American Historical Review* **71**(2): 259–306.

Meade, E. K. (2005) *Anatomies of Justice and Chaos: Capital Punishment and the Public in Mexico, 1917–1945*. University of Chicago Press: Chicago.

Mendoza Vargas, E. (1998) *Gotitas de placer y chubascos de amargura: Memorias de la Revolución Mexicana en las Huastecas*. Universidad Veracruzana: Xalapa.

Menjivar, C. (2008) 'Violence and Women's Lives in Eastern Guatemala: A Conceptual Framework'. *Latin American Research Review* **43**(3): 109–136.

Metinides, E. (2012) in T. Ziff (ed.) *101 tragedias de Enrique Metinides*. Blume: Barcelona.

Mexico (1871) *Código Penal del Estado Libre y Soberano de Guanajhuato* Imprenta de Acona y Peniche: Mexico.

Mexico (1886) *Código Penal del Estado Libre y soberano de Queretaro Arteaga* Impr. de F. Diaz de León: Mexico.

Mexico (1894) *Código Penal del Estado Libre y soberano de Queretaro Arteaga* Imprenta de Luciano Frias y Soto: Queretaro.

Mexico, Poder Ejecutivo (1997) *Secretaria de la Gobernación. Decreto que reforma, adiciona y deroga diversas disposiciones del Código Civil para el Distrito Federal en Materia Común y para toda la República e materia Federal, Diario Oficial, Martes 30 Diciembre*. Primera sección, 2–7.

Meyer, J. A. (1976) *The Cristero Rebellion: The Mexican People between Church and State, 1926–29*. Cambridge University Press: Cambridge.

Middlebrook, K. (1995) *The Paradox of Revolution: Labor, the State and Authoritarianism in Mexico*. The Johns Hopkins Universty Press: Baltimore.

Mignone, E. (1991) *Derechos humanos y sociedad: el caso Argentino*. Ediciones del Pensamiento Nacional and Centro de Estudios Legales y Sociales/CELS: Buenos Aires.

Ministerio del Interior (1986) *Informe No. 01- CMP- FF.PP. Investigaciones realizadas en relación con la participación de los Miembros de la GRP, en los operativos para restablecer el orden en el Penal 'San Pedro', a raíz del amotinamiento de reclusos producidos los días 18 y 19 Jun. 86 4 July 4*. Centro de Información para la Memoria Colectiva y los Derechos Humanos: Lima.

Minutes of the House of Representatives of Argentina, 5 January 1984: 422–424 and National Executive Power Orders 157 and 158, 13 December 1983, *in Boletín Oficial de la República Argentina*, 15 December 1983: 4 and 5.

Minutes of the House of Representatives, 5 January 1984: 422–424, *in Boletín Oficial de la República Argentina*. 15 December 1983: 4 and 5.

Miranda, L., Halpering, D., Limon, F., et al. (1998) 'Las características de la violencia doméstica y las respuestas de las mujeres en una comunidad rural del municipio de Las Margaritas, Chiapas'. *Salud Mental* **21**: 19–26.

Monkkonen, E. H. (2001) *Murder in New York City*. University of California Press: Berkeley.

Monkkonen, E. H. (2006) 'Homicide: Explaining America's Exceptionalism'. *American Historical Review* **111**(1): 76–94.

Monsiváis, C. (1994) *Los Mil Y Un Velorios: Crónica De La Nota Roja*. Alianza Cien/Consejo Nacional para la Cultura y las Artes/Alianza Editorial: Mexico.

Monsiváis, C. (2006) 'In Memoriam Jesús Blancornelas'. *El Universal*, 3 Dec. [WWW document] URL: http://www.eluniversal.com.mx/editoriales/361 26.html [accessed 7 January 2011].

Montgomery, T. S. (1995) *Revolution in El Salvador: From Civil Strife to Civil Peace*. Westview Press: Boulder.

Montufar, V. (1992) 'La violencia como práctica de dominación y transgresión en la mujer del estrato popular urbano, Ecuador: 1860–1920' in A.C. Defossez, D. Fassin, and M. Viveros (eds.) *Mujeres de los Andes. Condiciones de vida y salud*. Instituto Frances de Estudios Andinos, Universidad Externado de Colombia: Bogotá, 377–398.

Mora, T. (2003) *Días de barbarie. La matanza de los penales*. Lima: Asociación Pro Derechos Humanos.

Moreno, R.(h) (1922) *El Código Penal y sus antecedents*. Vol.1. Tomassi Editor: Buenos Aires.

Morrison, A. R. and Orlando, M. B. (1997) *El impacto socioeconómico de la violencia contra la mujer en Chile y Nicaragua*. Washington: Mimeo.

Morrall, P. (2000) *Madness and Murder*. Whurr Publishers: London.

Moscoco, M. (1994) '''Los consejos del Diablo'': Maltrato, adulterio y divorcio en el Ecuador'. *Arenal: Revista de Historia de las Mujeres* **1**(2): 209–222.

Moser, C. and McIlwaine, C. (1999) 'Participatory Urban Appraisal and its Application for Research on Violence'. *Environment and Urbanisation* **11**(2): 203–226.

Moser, C. and Winton, A. (2002) *Violence in the Central American Region: Towards an Integrated Framework for Violence Reduction*. Working Paper 171. Overseas Development Institute: London.

Moser, C., Winton, A. and Moser, A. (2005) 'Violence, Fear, and Insecurity among the Urban Poor in Latin America' in M. Fay (ed.) *The Urban Poor in Latin America*. The World Bank: Washington, 125–178.

Mraz, J. (2002) 'Manuel Alvarez Bravo: Ironizing Mexico'. [WWW document]. *Zone/Zero*, February. URL http://www.zonezero.com/magazine/articles/mraz/alvarezb.html [accessed 2 May 2013].

Munaiz, C. and Mendoza, A. (2007) 'Guatemala: The High Price of Violence'. [WWW document]. *IPS News*, 23 January. URL http://ipsnews.net/news.asp?idnews=36279 [accessed 20 August 2007].

Munck, R. (1987) *Argentina: From Anarchism to Peronism. Workers, Unions, and Politics, 1855–1985*. Zed Books: London and New Jersey.

Muñoz, L. (1935) *La Tragedia Biológica del Pueblo Colombiano*. Editorial Antena: Bogotá.

Muñoz, L. (1940) 'Causas que Imposibilitan el Adelanto en Colombia'. *Revista de Higiene* **5–6**: 4–21.

National Executive Decree No. 187, December 15, 1983. *Boletín Oficial de la República Argentina*, December 19, 1983, 2.

National Executive Decree No. 2772, October 6, 1975. *Boletín Oficial de la República Argentina*, November 4, 1975, 2.

National Executive Power (1975) *Official Bulletin*. Buenos Aires, 5 February, Article 1.

Neier, A. (1995) 'Confining Dissent: The Political Prison' in N. Morris and D. Rothman (eds.) *The Oxford History of the Prison*. Oxford University Press: New York, 350–380.

Newman, G. (ed.) (1999) *Global Report on Crime and Justice*. Oxford University Press: New York.

Newman, G. and Pridemore, W. A. (2000) 'Theory, Method, and Data in Comparative Criminology'. *Criminal Justice* **4**: 139–211.

New York Times, 23 January 1914: 2.

Nino, C. (1992) *Un país al margen de la ley*. Emecé: Buenos Aires.

Nino, C. (1997) *Juicio al mal absoluto: Los fundamentos y la historia del juicio a las juntas del proceso*. Emecé: Buenos Aires.

Nordstrom, C. and Robben, A. (eds.) (1995) *Fieldwork Under Fire: Contemporary Studies of Violence and Survival*. University of California Press: Berkeley.

Novaro, M. and Palermo, V. (2002) *La dictadura militar 1976/1983. Del golpe de Estado a la restauración democratica*. Historia Argentina Collection, Number 9. Paidós: Buenos Aires.

Núñez Becerra, F. (2002) *La prostitución y su represión en la Ciudad de México (siglo XIX). Prácticas y representaciones*. Gedisa: Barcelona.

Ochoa Serrano, A. and Pérez Martínez, H. (1994) *Cancionero Michoacáno, 1830–1940. Canciones, cantos, coplas y corridos*. El Colegio de Michoacán: Zamora.

ODHA (Oficina de Derechos Humanos del Arzobispado de Guatemala) (1998) *Guatemala Nunca Más (4 vols)*. Informe del Proyecto Interdiocesano de Recuperación de la Memoria Histórica: Guatemala.

O'Donnell, G. and Méndez, J. E. (eds.) (1999) *The (Un)Rule of Law and the Underpriviledged in Latin America*. University of Notre Dame Press: Notre Dame.

Official Bulletin, 15 December 1983: 4 and 5. *Boletín Oficial de la República Argentina*.

O'Hea, P. (1966) *Reminiscences of the Mexican Revolution*. Centro Anglo-Mexicano del Libro: Mexico.

Oiga (1986) '¡Horror! . . . Y la violencia cayó sobre ellos'. *Oiga* **285**(23 June): 8–14.

Olaiz, G., Rico, B. and del Rio, A. (eds.) (2003) *Coord. Gral. Encuesta Nacional Sobre Violencia Contra las Mujeres*. Instituto Nacional de Salud Pública: Mexico.

Oquist, P. (1980) *Violence, Conflict, and Politics in Colombia*. Academic Press: New York.

Ordoñez, M., Ochoa, L. H., Ojeda, G. Rojas, G., Gomez, L. C. and Samper, B. (1995) *Colombia: Encuesta nacional de demografía y salud, 1995*. Macro International: Demographic and Health Surveys [DHS]: Bogotá, Calverton.

Organisación Panamericana de la Salud (1996) *Actitudes y normas culturales sobre la violencia en ciudades seleccionadas de la región de las Américas. Proyecto ACTIVA*. World Bank, Division of Health and Human Development: Washington.

Osbaldeston-Mitford, W. B. J. (1945) *Dawn Breaks in Mexico*. Cassel: London.

Oszlak, O. [1982] (1997) *La formación del estado argentino: Orden, progreso y organisación*. Planeta: Buenos Aires.

Palacio, J. M. (2004) *La paz del trigo: Cultura legal y sociedad local en el desarrollo agrario pampeano, 1890–1945*. Edhasa: Buenos Aires.

Palmer, D. S. (ed.) (1992) *The Shining Path of Peru*. St. Martin's Press: New York.

Parker, D. S. (2001) 'Law, Honor, and Impunity in Spanish America: The Debate over Dueling, 1870–1920'. *Law and History Review* **19**(2): 311–341.

Payeras, M. (1981) *Los días de la selva*. Editorial Nuestro Tiempo: Mexico, DF.

Payeras, M. (1987) *El trueno en la ciudad: Episodos de la lucha armada urbana de 1981 en Guatemala*. Juan Pablos Editor: Mexico, DF.

Pécaut, D. (1999) '"Las Violencias y su Interpretación". Entrevista a Alberto Valencia Gutiérrez'. *Ensayo y Error* **4**(6): 153–167.

Pécaut, D. (2001a) *Orden y violencia: Evolución socio-política de Colombia entre 1930–1954*. Editorial Norma: Bogotá.

Pécaut, D. (2001b) *Guerra Contra la Sociedad*. Editorial Planeta: Bogotá.

Pelizzon, V. P. and West, N. M. (2010) *Tabloid, Inc.: Crimes, Newspapers, Narratives*. Ohio State University Press: Columbus.

Pennock, C. D. (2010) 'Mass Murder or Religious Homicide? Rethinking Human Sacrifice and Interpersonal Violence in Aztec Society'. *Historical Social Research/ Historische Sozialforschung* **37**(3): 276–302.

Peñaranda, R. (1992) 'Conclusion: Surveying the Literature on the Violence' in C. Berquist, R. Peñaranda and G. Sánchez (eds.) *Violence in Colombia: The Contemporary Crisis in Historical Perspective*. SR Books: Wilmington, 293–314.

Peñas Felizzola, A. H. (2006) *Génesis del sistema penal colombiano: Utilitarismo y tradicionalismo en el código penal neogranadino de 1837*. Doctrina y Ley: Bogotá.

Pérez, O. J. (2003) 'Democratic Legitimacy and Public Insecurity: Crime and Democracy in El Salvador and Guatemala'. *Political Science Quarterly* **118**(4): 627–644.

Pérez, O. J. (2011) 'Crime, Insecurity and Erosion of Democratic Values in Latin America'. Revista Latinoamericana de Opinión Pública WAPOR-Buenos Aires. *Editorial Teseo* **1**(1): 61–86.

Pérez Contreras, M. de Montserrat (2000) 'Ley de asistencia y prevención de la violencia intrafamiliar para el Distrito Federal: comentarios en torno al contenido de sus reformas'. *Boletin Mexicano de Derecho Comparado (nueva serie)* **33**(98): 909–924.

Pérez Guadalupe, J. L. (1994) *Faites y atorrantes: Una etnografía del penal de Lurigancho*. Centro de investigaciones teológicas: Lima.

Pérez, O. J. (2003) 'Democratic Legitimacy and Public Insecurity: Crime and Democracy in El Salvador and Guatemala'. *Political Science Quarterly* **118**(4): 627–644.

Pesavento, S. J. (2007) *Uma cidade sensível sob o olhar do "outro": Jean-Baptiste Debret e o Rio de Janeiro 1816–1831*. Coloquios: Nuevo Mundo Mundos Nuevos.

Petit, M. (2001) *Lecturas del espacio íntimo al espacio público*. Fondo de Cultura Económica: Mexico.

Piccato, P. (1999) 'Politics and the Technology of Honor: Dueling in Turn-of-the-Century Mexico'. *Journal of Social History* **33**(2): 331–354.

Piccato, P. (2001) *City of Suspects: Crime in Mexico City, 1900–1931*. Duke University Press: Durham.

Piccato, P. (2003) *Estadísticas del crimen en México: Series históricas, 1901–2001*. [WWW document]. URL http://www.columbia.edu/~pp143/estadistica scrimen/EstadisticasSigloXX.htm [accessed 7 January 2011].

Piccato, P. (2005) 'Communities and Crime in Mexico City'. [WWW document]. *Delaware Review of Latin American Studies* **6**(1). URL http://www.udel.edu/LAS/Vol6-1Piccato.html [accessed 8 September 2013].

Piccato, P. (2010a) *The Tyranny of Opinion: Honor in the Construction of the Mexican Public Sphere*. Duke University Press: Durham and London.

Piccato, P. (2010b) 'Altibajos de la esfera pública en México, de la dictadura republicana a la democracia corporativa: La era de la prensa' in G. Leyva, B. Connaughton, R. Diaz, N. Gurcia Canclini, and C. Illades (eds.) *Independencia y Revolución: Pasado, presente y futuro*. Fondo de Cultura Económica-Universidad Autónoma Metropolitana: Mexico City.

Piccato, P. (2012) '"Ya Saben Quién": Journalism, Crime and Impunity in Mexico Today' in S. Berruecos and G. Philip (eds.) *Mexico's Struggle for Public Security: Organized Crime and State Responses*. Palgrave Macmillan: London, 47–70.

Piccato, P. (forthcoming) 'Murders of Nota Roja: Truth and Justice in Mexican Crime News.' *Past and Present*.

Pimentel, S. A. (2003) 'The Nexus of Organized Crime and Politics in Mexico' in J. Bailey and R. Godson (eds.) *Organized Crime and Democratic Governability: Mexico and the US-Mexican Borderlands*. University of Pittsburgh Press: Pittsburgh.

Pinker, S. (2002) *The Blank Slate: The Modern Denial of Human Nature*. Penguin Books: London.

PNUD (Programa de Naciones Unidas Para el Desarrollo) (1999) *Proyecto Regional RLA 97–014. Informes Nacionales Sobre la Situacion de la Violencia de Género contra las Mujeres*. Informe Nacional: Nicaragua.

PNUD (Programa de las Naciones Unidas para el Desarrollo) (2005) *¿Cuánto le cuesta la violencia a El Salvador?* Cuadernos sobre desarrollo humano, no. 4. PNUD: San Salvador.

PNUD (Programa de Naciones Unidas para el Desarrollo) (2006) *Informe nacional de desarrollo humano, Guatemala 2005*. Ciudad de Guatemala: Guatemala.

Poccorpachi Vallejos, A. (2002) *Testimony No. 700065 given to the Comisión de la Verdad y Reconciliación*. Centro de Información para la Memoria Colectiva y los Derechos Humanos: Lima.

Poppa, T. E. (1998) *Drug Lord*. Demand Publications: Seattle.

Pratt, J. (2007) *Penal Populism*. Routledge: London and New York.

Prillaman, W. C. (2003) *Crime, Democracy, and Development in Latin America*. Policy Papers on the Americas, Volume 14, Study 6. Center for Strategic and International Studies (CSIS): Washington.

'Punishment and Death' (2006) *Radical History Review* (special issue) **96**(Fall).

Quann, N. and Hung, K. (2002) 'Victimization Experience and the Fear of Crime: A Cross-National Study' in Paul Nieuwbeerta (ed.) *Crime Victimization in Comparative Perspective: Results from the International Crime Victims Survey, 1989–2000*. Boom Juridische uitgevers: Den Haag.

Quevedo, E., Borda, C. Eslava, J. C., García, C. M. del Pilar Guzmán, M., Mejía, P. and Noguera, C. E. (2004) *Café y Gusanos, Mosquitos y Petróleo*. Universidad Nacional de Colombia: Bogotá.

Quijano, A. (2007) 'Coloniality and Modernity/Rationality'. *Cultural Studies* **21**(2–3): 168–178.

Quirk, R. E. (1967) *An Affair of Honor: Woodrow Wilson and the Occupation of Veracruz*. W. W. Norton: New York.

Quiroz Cuarón, A., Gómez Robleda, J, and Argüelles Modína, B. (1939) *Tendencia y ritmo de la criminalidad en México*. Instituto de Investigaciones Estadísticas: Mexico City.

Raby, D. (1974) *Educación y revolución social en México,1921–40*. Sepsetentas: Mexico, DF.

Rafart, G. (2008) *Tiempo de violencia en la Patagonia: Bandidos, policías y jueces, 1890–1940*. Prometeo Libros: Buenos Aires.

Ramírez, M. (2003) 'El hombre que faltaba. Testigo clave revela por primera vez detalles de la masacre de terroristas de Sendero Luminoso'. *El Comercio*, 1 February, 2–3.

Ramírez-Rodríguez, J. C. (2006) 'La violencia de varones contra sus parejas heterosexuales: Realidades y desafíos. Un recuento de la producción Mexicana'. *Salud Publica de México* **48**(Supplement 2): 315–327.

Ramírez Rodríguez, J. C. and Patiño Guerra, M. C. (1997) 'Algunos aspectos sobre la magnitud y trascendencia de la violencia doméstica contra la mujer: un estudio piloto'. *Salud Mental* 20(2): 5–16.

Ramos, S. R. (1938) *El perfil del hombre y de la cultura en México*. Pedro Robredo: Mexico.

Rancière, J. (1999) *Disagreement: Politics and Philosophy* (trans. Julie Rose). University of Minnesota Press: Minneapolis.

Reed, J.-P. (2004) 'Emotions in Context: Revolutionary Accelerators, Hope, Moral Outrage, and Other Emotions in the Making of Nicaragua's Revolution'. *Theory and Society* 33(6): 653–703.

Reed, N. (1964) *The Caste War of Yucatán*. Stanford University Press: Stanford.

Reguillo Cruz, R. (2005) 'La Mara: Contingencia y Afiliación Con El Exceso'. *Nueva Sociedad* 200: 70–84.

Rénique, J. L. (2004) *La voluntad encarcelada. Las luminosas trincheras de combate de Sendero Luminoso*. Instituto de Estudios Peruanos: Lima.

Riding, A. (1985) *Distant Neighbors*. Vintage Books: New York.

Rivera Reynaldos, L. G (2006) *Crímenes pasionales y relaciones de género en México, 1880–1910*. [WWW document]. Nuevo Mundo Mundos Nuevos: Coloquios. URL http://nuevomundo.revuews.org/index2835.html [accessed 1 September 2013].

Roberts, J. V. and Hough, M. J. (2005) *Understanding Public Attitudes to Crimnal Justice*. Open University Press: Maidenhead.

Robins, N. A. (2005) *Native Insurgencies and the Genocidal Impulse in the Americas*. Indiana University Press: Bloomington.

Rodgers, D. (2003) *Dying for It: Gangs, Violence and Social Change in Urban Nicaragua*. Crisis States Programme Working Papers Series No. 1. London School of Economics Development Research Centre (DESTIN): London.

Rodríguez, J. (2006) *Civilizing Argentina. Science, Medicine, and the Modern State*. University of North Carolina Press: Chapel Hill.

Rodríguez, J. L. (2007) 'Periodismo y narcotráfico en México'. *Reforma* 5 June. [WWW document] URL: http://site.securities.com/doc.html?pc=MX&doc_id=140026767 [accessed 7 January 2011].

Rodríguez Molas, R. (1984) *Historia de la tortura y el orden represivo en la Argentina*. EUDEBA: Buenos Aires.

Rodríguez Munguía, J. (2007) *La Otra Guerra Secreta : Los Archivos Prohibidos De La Prensa Y El Poder*. Random House Mondadori, SA: Mexico City.

Rojas, C. (2002) *Civilization and Violence: Regimes of Representation in Nineteenth Century Colombia*. University of Minnesota Press: Minneapolis.

Rojas, R. (2007) *El miedo a la revolución y los 'deberes del patriotismo': el debate Acosta-Riera Aguinagalde frente a la guerra federal en Venezuela, 1859–1863*. Coloquios: Nuevo Mundo Mundos Nuevos. [WWW document]. URL http://nuevomundo.revues.org/49 [accessed 1 September 2013].

Rojkind, I. (2004) 'La revista controversia: reflexión y polémica entre los argentinos exiliados en México' in P. Yankelevich (ed.) *Represión y destierro. Itinerarios del exilio argentino*. Ediciones Al Margen: La Plata, 223–251.

Roldán, M. (1998) 'Violencia, Colonización y la Geografía de la Diferencia Cultural en Colombia'. *Análisis Político* 35: 3–25.

Roldán, M. (2002) *Blood and Fire: La Violencia in Antioquia, Colombia, 1946–1953*. Duke University Press: Durham.

Romanucci-Ross, L. (1986) *Conflict, Violence and Morality in a Mexican Village*. University of Chicago Press: Chicago.

Rosenberg, T. (1991) *Children of Cain: Violence and the Violent in Latin America*. William Morrow and Co.: New York.

Ross, S. R. (1995) *Francisco I. Madero: Apostle of Mexican Democracy*. Columbia University Press: New York.

Roth, R. (2009) *American Homicide*. Harvard University Press: Cambridge.

Rozo Lesmes, P. (2008) *Mujeres víctimas de homicidio en Bogotá: Una realidad por revelar*. Universidad Nacional de Colombia, Programa Interfacultades Doctorado en Salud Pública. Mimeo: Bogotá.

Ruggiero, K. (1992) 'Wives on 'Deposit': Internment and the Preservation of Husbands. Honor in Late Nineteenth-Century Buenos Aires'. *Journal of Family History* **17**(3): 253–270.

Ruggiero, K. (1994) 'Honor, maternidad y el disciplinamiento de las mujeres: Infanticidio en el Buenos Aires de finales del siglo XIX' in L. Fletcher (ed.) *Mujeres y cultura en la Argentina del siglo XIX*. Feminaria Editora: Buenos Aires.

Ruggiero, K. (2004) *Modernity in the Flesh: Medicine, Law, and Society in Turn-of-the Century Argentina*. Stanford University Press: Stanford.

Ruibal, B. (1990) 'El control social y la policía de Buenos Aires: Buenos Aires 1880–1920'. *Boletín del Instituto de Historia Argentina y Americana* **2**: 75–90.

Rummel, R. J. (1994) *Death by Government*. Transaction Publications: New Brunswick.

Sábato, H. (2008) *Buenos Aires en armas. La revolución de 1880*. Siglo XXI: Buenos Aires.

Sáenz, J., Saldarriaga, Ó. and Ospina, A. (1997) *Mirar la Infancia: Pedagogía, Moral y Modernidad en Colombia, 1903–1946*. Colciencias: Medellín.

Sagot, M. and Carcedo, A. (2000) *Ruta crítica de las mujeres afectadas por la violencia intrafamiliar*. Pan American Health Organisisation: Washington.

Salessi, J. (1995) *Médicos, maleantes y maricas. Higiene, criminología y homosexualidad en la construcción de la nación argentina (Buenos Aires 1871–1914)*. Beatriz Viterbo Editora: Rosario.

Salvatore, R. D. (1992) 'Criminology, Prison Reform, and the Buenos Aires Working Class'. *Journal of Interdisciplinary History* **23**(2): 279–299.

Salvatore, R. D. (2000) 'Repertoires of Coercion and Market Culture in Nineteenth-Century Buenos Aires Province'. *International Review of Social History* **45**: 409–448.

Salvatore, R. D. (2001) 'Sobre el Surgimiento del Estado Médico Legal en la Argentina (1890–1940)'. *Estudios Sociales* **20**(1): 81–114.

Salvatore, R. D. (2003) *Wandering Paysanos: State Order and Subaltern Experience in Buenos Aires during the Rosas Era*. Duke University Press: Durham.

Salvatore, R. D. (2005) 'Positivist Criminology and State Formation in Modern Argentina (1890–1940)' in P. Becker and R. Wetzell (eds.) *Criminals and Their Scientists: Essays on the International History of Criminology*. Cambridge University Press: Cambridge, 252–279.

Salvatore, R. D. (2009) 'Violencia sociopolítica y procesamiento judicial en la Argentina (1890–1920)' in M. Sozzo (ed.) *Historias de la cuestión criminal en la Argentina*. Editores del Puerto: Buenos Aires.

Salvatore, R. D. (2010) *Subalternos, derechos y justicia penal. Ensayos de historia social y cultural Argentina, 1829–1940*. Gedisa: Barcelona.

Salvatore, R. D. and Aguirre, C. (eds.) (1996) *The Birth of the Penitentiary in Latin America: Essays on Criminology, Prison Reform, and Social Control*. University of Texas Press: Austin.

Salvatore, R. D., Aguirre, C. and Jospeh, G. (eds.) (2001) *Crime and Punishment in Latin America. Law and Society since Late Colonial Times*. Duke University Press: Durham.

Salvucci, R. (2006) 'Export-Led Industrialisation' in V. Bulmer-Thomas, J. Coatsworth and R. Cortes Conde (eds.) *The Cambridge Economic History of Latin America: The Long Twentieth Century*, Vol. 2. Cambridge University Press: London, 249–292.

Sánchez, G. (1985) 'La Violencia in Colombia: New Research, New Questions'. *Hispanic American Historical Review* 65(4): 789–807.

Sánchez, G. (1991) *Guerra y política en la sociedad colombiana*. El Ancora Editores: Bogotá.

Sánchez, G. (1992) 'The Violencia: an Interpretative Synthesis' in C. W. Bergquist, R. Peñaranda and G. Sánchez Gómez (eds.) *Violence in Colombia: The Contemporary Crisis in an Historical Perspective*. SR Books: Wilmington, 1–8.

Sánchez, G. and Meertens, D. (2001) *Bandits, Peasants, and Politics: The Case of 'La Violencia' in Colombia*. University of Texas Press: Texas.

Sánchez, G. and Peñaranda, R. (eds.) (1986) *Pasado y Presente de la Violencia en Colombia*. Fondo Editorial CEREC: Bogotá.

Sánchez, G. (1991) *Guerra y Política en la Sociedad Colombiana*. El Ancora Editores: Bogotá.

Sánchez Vázquez, A. (1980) *Filosofía de la Praxis*. Editorial Grijalbo: Mexico, DF.

Sanjuán, A. M. (2003) 'Dinámicas de la violencia en Venezuela: tensiones y desafíos para la consolidación de la democracia' in L. Bobea (ed.) *Entre el crimen y el castigo: Seguridad ciudadana y control democrático en América Latina y el Caribe*. FLACSO/Woodrow Wilson International Centre/Nueva Sociedad: Caracas.

Santos, G. N. (1984) *Memorias*. Grijalbo: Mexico.

Santoyo, A. (1995) *La Mano Negra: Poder regional y Estado en México (Veracruz, 1928–1943)*. Consejo Nacional para la Cultura y las. Artes: Mexico.

Sarlo, B. (2002) *Tiempo presente: Notas sobre los cambios en la cultura*. Siglo XXI: Buenos Aires.

Sarlo, B. (2004) *La pasión y la excepción*. Buenos Aires: Siglo XXI.

Sarmiento, D. F. (1845) [1998]. *Facundo, or, Civilization and Barbarism* (trans. M. Mann). Penguin Books: New York.

Schele, L. and Frieden, D. (1990) *A Forest of Kings*. William Morrow: New York.

Scheper-Hughes, N. (1992) *Death Without Weeping. The Violence of Everyday Life in Brazil*. University of California Press: Berkeley.

Scherer García, J. and Monsiváis, C. (2003) *Tiempo de saber: Prensa y poder en México*. Aguilar: Mexico City.

Schirmer, J. (1998) *The Guatemalan Military Project: A Violence Called Democracy*. University of Pennsylvania Press: Philadelphia.

Scott, J. C. (1990) *Domination and the Arts of Resistance: Hidden Transcripts*. Yale University Press: New Haven.

Scribano, A. and Vergara Mattar, G. (2009) 'Feos, sucios y malos. La regulación de los cuerpos y las emociones en Norbert Elias'. [WWW document]. *Caderno CRH* **22**: 56. URL http://www.cadernocrh.ufba.br [accessed 15 September 2013].

Sedeillán, G. (2009) 'Los delitos sexuales: La ley y la práctica judicial en la provincia de Buenos Aires durante el período de codificación del Derecho Penal argentino (1877–1892'. *Historia Crítica* **37**.

Seibel, B. (1999) *Crónicas de la Semana Trágica. Enero de 1919*. Ediciones Corregidor: Buenos Aires.

Sen, A. (1991) *Wars and Famines: On Divisions and Incentives*. Research paper no. 33. Suntory-Toyota International Centre for Economics and Related Disciplines, LSE: London.

Senate of Argentina Republic, Minutes, February 9, 1984, 318.

SERPAJ (1989) *Uruguay : Nunca Más*. Montevideo: SERPAJ.

Servín, J. M (2010) *DF. Confidencial: Crónicas de delincuentes, vagos y demás gente sin futuro*. Editorial Almadia SC: Oaxaca de Juárez, Oaxaca.

Shelley, L. I. (1981) *Crime and Modernization: The Impact of Industrialization and Urbanization on Crime*. South Illinois University Press: Carbondale.

Sieder, R. (ed.) (1998) *Guatemala after the Peace Accords*. Institute of Latin American Studies, University of London: London.

Sieder, R., Thomas, M., Vickers, G. and Spence, J. (2002) *Who Governs? Guatemala Five Years after the Peace Accords*. Hemisphere Initiatives: Cambridge.

Sikkink, K. (2008) 'From Pariah State to Global Protagonist: Argentina and the Struggle for International Human Rights'. *Latin American Politics and Society* **1**: 1–30.

Silva, R. (2005) *República Liberal: intelectuales y cultura popular*. La Carreta Histórica: Medellín.

Silva, R. (2006) *Sociedades campesinas, transición social y cambio cultural en Colombia*. La Carreta Histórica: Medellín.

Simon, J. (1993) *Poor Discipline: Parole and the Social Control of the Underclass, 1890–1990*. University of Chicago Press: Chicago.

Simpson, E. (1937) *The Ejido: Mexico's Way Out*. Universty of North Carolina Press: Chapel Hill.

Siqueiros, D. A. (1977) *Me llamaban el coronelazo*. Editorial Grijalbo: Mexico.

Sistemas (2006) *Sistema para la consulta del Cuaderno Estadístico Municipal Juárez, Chihuahua, Edición 2006*. [WWW document]. URL http://www.inegi.gob.mx/est/contenidos/espanol/sistemas/cem05/estatal/tam/m027/index.htm [accessed 29 April 2008].

Skocpol, T. (ed.) (1984) *Vision and Method in Historical Sociology*. Cambridge University Press: Cambridge.

Smutt, M. and Miranda, L. (1998) *El fenómeno de las pandillas en El Salvador*. UNICEF/FLACSO: San Salvador.

Snodgrass Godoy, A. (2006) *Popular Injustice: Violence, Community, and Law in Latin America*. University of California Press: Stanford.

Socolow, S. M. (1986) 'Introduction' in L. Schell Hoberman and S. Socolow (eds.) *Cities and Society in Colonial Latin America*. University of New Mexico Press: Albuquerque.

Sofsky, W. (2003) *Violence: Terrorism, Genocide, War*. Granta: London.

Speckman Guerra, E. (1998) 'De matadores de mujeres, amantes despechadas y otros sujetos no menos peligrosos. Crímenes pasionales en la nota roja y la literatura porfirianas'. *Allpanchis: Revista del Instituto de Pastoral Andina* **3052**: 113–139.

Speckman Guerra, E. (2002) *Crimen y Castigo: Legislación penal, interpretaciones de la criminalidad y administración de justicia (Ciudad de México, 1872–1910)*. El Colegio de México/Universidad Nacional Autónoma de México: Mexico.

Speckman Guerra, E. (2006) 'De méritos y reputaciones: El honor en la ley y la justicia (Distrito Federal, 1871–1931)'. *Anuario Mexicano de Historia del Derecho* **18**: 331–361.

Spektorowski, A. (2003) *The Origins of Argentina's Revolution of the Right*. University of Notre Dame Press: Indiana.

Spierenburg, P. (ed.) (1998) *Men and Violence: Gender, Honor, and Rituals in Modern Europe and America*. Ohio University Press: Columbus.

Spierenburg, P. (2008) *A History of Murder: Personal Violence in Europe from the Middle Ages to the Present*. Polity Press: Cambridge.

Stannard, D. E. (1993) *American Holocaust: The Conquest of the New World*. Oxford University Press: New York.

Stavans, I. (1993) *Antihéroes: México Y Su Novela Policial*. Joaquín Mortiz: Mexico City.

Stern, S. (1982) *Peru's Indian Peoples and the Challenge of Spanish Conquest: Huamanga to 1640*. University of Wisconsin Press: Madison.

Stern, S. (1988) 'Feudalism, Capitalism, and the World-System in the Perspective of Latin America and the Caribbean'. *American Historical Review* **93**(4): 829–872.

Stern, S. (1995) *The Secret History of Gender: Women, Men and Power in Late Colonial Mexico*. University of North Carolina Press: Chapel Hill.

Stern, S. (ed.) (1998) *The Shining and Other Paths: War and Society in Peru, 1980–1995*. Duke University Press: Durham.

Stern, S. (2000) 'De la memoria suelta a la memoria emblemática: Hacia el recordar y el olvidar como proceso histórico (Chile, 1973–1998)' in M. Garces, P. Milos, M. Olguín, J. Pinto, M. T. Rojas and M. Urrutia (eds.) *Memoria para un nuevo siglo: Chile, miradas a la segunda mitad del siglo XX*. Sin Norte Collection. LOM: Santiago de Chile, 11–33.

Stevenson, L. S. and Seligson, M. A. (1996) 'Fading Memories of the Revolution: Is Stability Eroding in Mexico?' in Roderic A. Camp (ed.) *Polling for Democracy: Public Opinion and Political Liberalization in Mexico*. SR Books: Wilmington.

Stoller, R. (1995) 'Alfonso Lopez Pumarejo and the Liberal Radicalism in 1930s Colombia'. *Journal of Latin American Studies* **27**(2): 367–397.

Strauss, M. A. (1979) 'Measuring Intrafamily Violence and Conflict: the Conflict Tactics Scales'. *Journal of Marriage and the Family* **41**(February): 75–88.

Strocka, C. (2006) 'Youth Gangs in Latin America'. *SAIS Review of International Affairs* **26**(2): 133–146.

Suárez Findlay, E. J. (1999) *Imposing Decency: The Politics of Sexuality and Race in Puerto Rico, 1870–1920*. Duke University Press: Durham.

Suriano, J. (ed.) (2000) *La cuestión social en Argentina 1870–1943*. Buenos Aires: Editorial La Colmena.

Suriano, J. (2001) *Anarquistas. Cultura y política libertaria en Buenos Aires, 1890–1910*. Manantial: Buenos Aires.

Sutton, S. H. (2007) 'Identificadores de los judaizantes y la resignificación de sus rituales en el contexto novohispánico'. *Fronteras de la Historia* **12**: 79–117.

Tarrow, S. (1994) *Power in Movement: Social Movements, Collective Action and Politics*. Cambridge University Press: Cambridge.

Taussig, M. (2003) 'The Language of Flowers'. *Critical Inquiry* **30**: 98–131.

Taussig, M. (2005) *Law in a Lawless Land: Diary of a Limpieza in Colombia*. University of Chicago Press: Chicago.

Taylor, D. (1997) *Disappearing Acts: Spectacles of Gender and Nationalism in Argentina's 'Dirty War'*. Duke University Press: Durham.

Taylor, L. (2006) *Shining Path: Guerrilla War in Peru's Northern Highlands, 1980–1997*. Liverpool University Press: Liverpool.

Taylor, W. (1979) *Drink, Homicide and Rebellion in Colonial Mexican Villages*. Stanford University Press: Stanford.

Taylor, W. (1996) Magistrates of the Sacred: Priests and Parishioners in Eighteenth-Century Mexico. Stanford University Press: Stanford.

Téllez Vargas, E. , and Garmabella, J. R. (1982) ¡*Reportero De Policía! El Güero Téllez*. Ediciones Océano: Mexico City, DF.

Tenenbaum, B. (1986) *The Politics of Penury: Debts and Taxes in Mexico, 1821–1856*. University of New Mexico Press: Albuquerque.

Terán, O. (1986) *José Ingenieros: Pensar la nación*. Alianza: Buenos Aires.

Terán, O. (1987) *Positivismo y nación en la Argentina*. Puntosur: Buenos Aires and Montevideo.

Tilly, C. (1985) 'Retrieving European Lives' in O. Zunz (ed.) *Reliving the Past. The Worlds of Social History*. The University of North Carolina Press: Chapel Hill, 11–52.

Tilly, C., Tilly, L. and Tilly, R. (1975) *The Rebellious Century, 1830–1930*. Harvard University Press: Cambridge.

Timmons, P. (2007) 'The Meanings and Experience of Violent Deaths in Twentieth-Century Latin America'. *Latin American Research Review* **42**(1): 224–237.

Tirado Mejía, A. (1981) *Aspectos Políticos del Primer Gobierno de Alfonso López Pumarejo 1934–1938*. Instituto Colombiano de Cultura: Bogotá.

Toch, H. (1972) *Violent Men: An Inquiry into the Psychology of Violence*. Pelican Books: Harmondsworth.

Torres, C. (1985) 'La Violencia y los Cambios Socio-Culturales en las Áreas Rurales Colombianas' in Fondo Editorial Cerce (ed.) *Once Ensayos sobre la Violencia*. Fondo Editorial CEREC: Bogotá, 53–115.

Torres Falcón, M. (2004) *Violencia contra las mujeres en contextos urbanos y rurales*. Programa Interdisciplinario de Estudios de la Mujer. El Colegio de México: Mexico.

Torres Rivas, E. (1980) 'Vida y muerte en Guatemala: reflexiones sobre la crisis y la violencia política'. *Revista Alero* **5**(4).

Torres-Rivas, E. (1997) *Negociando el futuro: La paz en una sociedad violenta. La negociación de paz en 1996*. Colección debate No. 36. FLACSO: Guatemala.

Trouillot, M.-R. (1995) *Silencing the Past: Power and the Production of History*. Beacon Press: Boston.

Tulchin, J. S. and Ruthenburg, M. (2006) *Toward a Society Under Law: Citizens and Their Police in Latin America*. Woodrow Wilson International Centre: Washington.

Tutino, J. (1988) 'Agrarian Change and Peasant Rebellion in Nineteenth-Century Mexico: The Example of Chalco' in F. Katz (ed.) *Riot, Rebellion and Revolution: Rural Social Conflict in Mexico*. Princeton University Press: Princeton.

UNFPA (2005) 'Gender-Based Violence: A Price too High' *UNPA, State of World Population, 2005. The Promise of Equality. Gender Equity, Reproductive Health and the Millennium Development Goals*. UNFPA: New York, 64–73.

United Nations (1993) *Declaration on the Elimination of Violence against Women*. General Assembly Resolution: December.

Uribe, M. V. (1990) *Matar, rematar, y contramatar: las masacres de la violencia en el Tolima, 1948–1964*. Centro de Investigación y Educación Popular–CINEP: Bogotá.

Uribe, M. V. (2004) 'Dismembering and Expelling: Semantics of Political Terror in Colombia'. *Political Culture* **16**(1): 79–95.

Uribe-Uran, V. M. (2007) 'Movimientos Indígenas, Constituciones, Justicia Plural y Democracia en América Latina' in J. M. Palacio and M. Candioti (eds.) *Justicia, política y derechos en América Latina*. Prometeo Libros: Buenos Aires, 83–104.

USAID (US Agency for International Development) (2006) *Central America and Mexico Gang Assessment*. USAID bureau for Latin America and Caribbean Affairs. Office of Regional Sustainable Development: April.

US Department of State (2008) *Bureau for International Narcotics and Law Enforcement Affairs, International Narcotics Control Strategy Report*. Washington, February 2008.

Usigli, R. (1944) *Ensayo de un crimen*. Editorial America: Mexico City.

US State Department, Bureau of Democracy, Human Rights, and Labor (2004). *El Salvador, Country Reports on Human Rights Practices*. Released 28 February 2005.

Valdez Santiago, R. (2004) 'Del silencio privado a las agendas públicas. El devenir de la lucha contra la violencia doméstica en México' in T. Falcón (ed.) *Violencia contra las mujeres en contextos urbanos y rurales*. El Colegio de México-PIEM: Mexico, 417–447.

Valencia, A. (1999) 'Las Violencias y su Interpretación: Entrevista a Daniel Pécaut'. *Ensayo y Error* **4**(6): 153–167.

Valerio Jiménez, O. S. (2009) 'New Avenues for Domestic Disputes and Divorce Lawsuits along the U.S. -Mexico Border, 1832–1893'. *Journal of Women's History* **21**(1): 10–33.

Van Young, E. (2001) *The Other Rebellion, Popular Violence, Ideology and the Mexican Struggle for Independence, 1810–21*. Stanford University Press: Stanford.

Vanderwood, P. (1981) *Disorder and Progress. Bandits, Police and Mexican Development*. University of Nebraska Press: Lincoln.

Vanderwood, P. J. (1992) *Disorder and Progress: Bandits, Police, and Mexican Development*. Scholarly Resources: Wilmington.

Vanderwood, P. J. (1998) *The Power of God Against the Guns of Government*. Stanford University Press: Stanford.

Varese, F. (2001) *The Russian Mafia: Private Protection in a New Market Economy*. Oxford University Press: Oxford.

Vaughan, J. M. and Feere, J. D. (2008) *Taking Back the Streets: ICE and Local Law Enforcement Target Immigrant Gangs*. Center for Immigration Studies:

Washington, DC. URL http://www.cis.org/articles/2008/back1208.pdf [accessed 17 April 2011].

Vaughan, M. K. (1997) *Cultural Politics in Revolution: Teachers, Peasants, and Schools in Mexico, 1930–1940*. University of Arizona Press: Tucson.

Vega, R. (2009) *Incidencia de la violencia doméstica en Puerto Rico*. Mimeo, 19 May. Term paper for advanced statistics, MATH 6400.

Velloso, M. P. (2008) *Las Ciudades de los sentidos: Paris, Rio de Janeiro y Buenos Aires*. Coloquios: Nuevo Mundo Mundos Nuevos.

Vezzetti, H. (2002) *Pasado y presente: Guerra, dictadura y sociedad en la Argentina*, Buenos Aires. Siglo Veintiuno Editores: Buenos Aires.

Vezzetti, H. (2012) 'Uses and Limits of the Figure of Genocide'. *African Yearbook of Rhetoric* 3(2): 29–40.

Villadelángel Viñas, G. and Ganado Kim, E. (2008) *El Libro Rojo: Continuación. I*, 1868–1928. Fondo de Cultura Económica: Mexico, DF.

Villagrán de, M. (2004) 'La desaparición forzada. Una aproximación desde la psicosociología'. Tesis de Maestría en Psicología Social y Violencia Política. Escuela de Ciencias Psicológicas, Universidad de San Carlos de Guatemala: Guatemala.

Villegas del Castillo, C. (2006) *Del hogar a los juzgados: reclamos familiares en los juzgados superiores en el tránsito de la colonia a la República, 1800–1850*. Universidad de los Andes Faultad de. Ciencias: Bogotá.

Wacquant, L. (2001) *Parias urbanos. Marginalidad en la ciudad al comienzo del milenio* (trans. J. Auyero). Manantial: Buenos Aires.

Wade, N. (2007) *Before the Dawn: Recovering the History of Our Lost Ancestors*. Duckworth: London.

Walsh, R. J. (1981) *Obra literaria completa*. Mexico, DF: Siglo XXI Editores.

Walzer, M. [1977] (1992) *Just and Unjust Wars: A Moral Argument with Historical Illustrations*. Basic Books: New York.

Warman, A. (1976) *Venimos a contradecir: Los campesinos de Morelos y el estado nacional*. INAH: Mexico.

Warner, M. (2002) *Publics and Counterpublics*. Zone Books, Distributed by MIT Press: New York, Cambridge.

Wasserman, M. (2000) *Everyday Life and Politics in Nineteenth Century Mexico*. University of New Mexico Press: Albuquerque.

Weber, M. (1974) *Economía y Sociedad*. Fondo de Cultura Económica: México DF.

Weems, J. E. (1974) *To Conquer a Peace: The War Between the United States and Mexico*. Doubleday: New York.

Wiarda, H. J. (2001) *The Soul of Latin America*. Yale University Press: New Haven.

Wilkinson, D. O. (1980) *Deadly Quarrels: Lewis F. Richardson and the Statistical Study of War*. University of California Press: Berkeley.

Womack, J. (1970) *Zapata and the Mexican Revolution*. Random House: New York.

Wood, E. J. (2003) *Insurgent Collective Action and Civil War in El Salvador*. Cambridge University Press: New York.

World Bank (n.d.) *Guatemala: Country Brief*. [WWW document]. URL http://www.worldbank.org [accessed 4 April 2008].

Yankelevich, P. (ed.) (2004) *Represión y destierro. Itinerarios del exilio argentino*. La Plata: Al Margen, 239–243.

Yooll, A. G. (1989) *De Perón a Videla*. Editorial Legasa: Buenos Aires.

Young, R. (1991) *White Mythologies: Writing History and the West*. Routledge: London and New York.

Zabludovsky, G. (2007) *Norbert Elias y los problemas actuales de la Sociología*. Fondo De Cultura Economica: Mexico.

Zamora, J. R. (2007) 'Editorial'. [WWW document]. *El Periódico*, 18 March. URL http://www.elperiodico.com.gt/es/20070318/12/37825/ [accessed 13 September 2013].

Zanatta, L. (1996) *Del estado liberal a la nación católica. Iglesia y ejército en los orígenes del Peronismo 1930–1943*. Quilmes: Universidad Nacional de Quilmes.

Zehr, H. (1975) 'The Modelnization of Crime in Germany and France, 1830–1913'. *Journal of Social History* 8(4): 117–141.

Zepeda Lecuona, G. (2004) *Crimen sin castigo: Procuración de justicia penal y ministerio público en México*. Fondo de Cultura Económica-Cidac: Mexico City.

Zimmermann, E. (1992) 'Los intelectuales, las ciencias sociales y el reformismo liberal: Argentina 1880–1916'. *Desarrollo Económico* 31: 124.

Zimmerman, E. (1995) *Los liberales reformistas: La cuestión social en la Argentina 1890–1916*. Editorial Sudamericana/Universidad de San Andrés: Buenos Aires.

Zimmerman, E. (ed.) (1999) *Judicial Institutions in Nineteenth-Century Latin America*. Institute of Latin American Studies: London.

Žižek, S. (2008) *Violence*. Profile Books: London.

Archive Sources

AHPN (Archivo Histórico de la Policía Nacional) (1954–1955) Libro especial para anotar la entrada y salida de individuos filocomunistas consignados al Comité de Defensa Nacional contra el Comunismo. GT PN 24. Fondo del 2° Cuerpo de la Policía Nacional.

Anonymous (1958) Letter to President Ruiz Cortines, August 1958. Fondo Adolfo Ruiz Cortines, 541/1002. Archivo General de la Nación, Mexico City.

Archivo CONADEP (2010) Secretaría de Derechos Humanos de la Nación (data updated as of March 2010).

Carbajal Flores, R. (1961) Letter to President López Mateos, 10 May, Fondo Adolfo López Mateos, 541/606. Archivo General de la Nación: Mexico City.

Consul Burt to State Department, 3 Feb. 1938, US State Dept Records.

Esquivel, Balentina (1940) Letter to Agustin Castro, Mexico City, 22 September. Dirección General de Gobierno, 2/012.2 (29)/5, caja 78 exp. 6. Archivo General de la Nación, Mexico City.

Estrada Aguirre, Macrina (1959), Letter to President López Mateos, Mexico City, 11 June, Archivo General de la Nación-Fondo Adolfo López Mateos, 541/93.

Gómez Pérez, Antonio (1958) Letter to José Aguilar y Maya, Mexico City, 7 August. Fondo Adolfo Ruiz Cortines, 541/1003. Archivo General de la Nación, Mexico City.

González, J. (1959) Letter to President López Mateos, Mexico City, 28 April, Fondo Adolfo López Mateos, 541/79. Archivo General de la Nación: Mexico City.

Lucero, Francisco Macario (1955) Letter to President Ruiz Cortines, 11 August. Fondo Adolfo Ruiz Cortines, 541/254. Archivo General de la Nación, Mexico City.

Rodríguez Cárdenas, Florencio (1959) Letter to President López Mateos, Mexico City, 10 March. Fondo Adolfo López Mateos, 541/64. Archivo General de la Nación, Mexico City.

Romo Castro, Waldo (1942) Letter to Miguel Z Martinez, Mexico City, 12 January. Fondo Manuel Avila Camacho, 541/430. Archivo General de la Nación, Mexico City.

Salgado, Reinalda (1942) Letter to President Avila Camacho, Cuernavaca, 8 September. Fondo Manuel Avila Camacho, 541/630. Archivo General de la Nación, Mexico City.

Torres Pérez, Javier (1958) Letter to President Ruiz Cortines, 28 August. Fondo Adolfo Ruiz Cortines, 541/1003. Archivo General de la Nación, Mexico City.

Trabajadores de Caminos (1936). Letter to President Cárdenas, 11 March. Fondo Lázaro Cárdenas, 444.92/42. Archivo General de la Nación, Mexico City.

Vélez, Jorge (1948). Letter to President Alemán, Port Isabel, 26 September. Fondo Miguel Alemán Valdés, 541/50. Archivo General de la Nación, Mexico City.

Interviews

Aragón, R. (2003) CONADEP Procedures Secretary, 3 December. Buenos Aires.

Barragán, P. (2004) author of Nover Again report. 14 December, Buenos Aires.

Calvo, A. (2005) Former disappeared person, 18 May, Buenos Aires.

Mansur, A. (2004) Legal Affairs Secretary, San Martín, 1 September. Province of Buenos Aires.

Meijide, G. F. (2004) member of the Permanent Assembly for Human Rights, 26 August, Buenos Aires.

Filmography

The People of the Shining Path, 1992. Directed by Yezid Campos, Marc de Beaufort, James Rutenbeck, and James Bellini. London: Channel 4 Television.

Régimen penitenciario, 2002. CVR. Lima: Lima.

Index